Gothic Architecture and Sexuality

IN THE CIRCLE OF

Horace Walpole

Gothic Architecture and Sexuality

IN THE CIRCLE OF

Horace Walpole

MATTHEW M. REEVE

The Pennsylvania State University Press | University Park, Pennsylvania

Supported by a Publications Grant from the
Paul Mellon Centre for Studies in British Art

PAUL MELLON CENTRE
for Studies in British Art

Library of Congress Cataloging-in-Publication Data

Names: Reeve, Matthew M., author.

Title: Gothic architecture and sexuality in the circle of Horace Walpole / Matthew M. Reeve.

Description: University Park, Pennsylvania : The Pennsylvania State University Press, [2020] | Includes bibliographical references and index.

Summary: "Addresses the question of how and why Horace Walpole and the men of his circle promoted the Gothic style in art, architecture, and literature in the latter half of the eighteenth century"—Provided by publisher.

Identifiers: LCCN 2019059653 | ISBN 9780271085883 (cloth)

Subjects: LCSH: Walpole, Horace, 1717–1797—Friends and associates. | Walpole, Horace, 1717–1797—Homes and haunts—England—London. | Walpole, Horace, 1717–1797—Art collections. | Strawberry Hill (Twickenham, London, England) | Gothic revival (Architecture)—England. | Homosexuality and architecture—England—History—18th century.

Classification: LCC NA966.5.G66 R44 2020 | DDC 720.9421—dc23

LC record available at https://lccn.loc.gov/2019059653

Design and typesetting by barb barnett graphic design llc

Printed in Korea

Published by The Pennsylvania State University Press,
University Park, PA 16802–1003

The Pennsylvania State University Press is a member of the Association of University Presses.

It is the policy of The Pennsylvania State University Press to use acid-free paper. Publications on uncoated stock satisfy the minimum requirements of American National Standard for Information Sciences—Permanence of Paper for Printed Library Material, ANSI Z39.48–1992.

Contents

Illustrations

Preface

MEDIEVALISM, MODERNITY, AND THE HISTORY OF SEXUALITY

No doubt men who speak as I do will be charged with being mere medievalists. I dispute the adjective but accept in its fullest sense the substantive part of the charge.

—George Edmund Street, "On the Future of Art in England" (1858)

This book was written by a medievalist, albeit one with broad interests in the history of art and culture. It addresses a question of significance to medieval art history, to historians of eighteenth-century art (and thus to discussions of the Enlightenment and "modernity" in general), and to historians of sexuality. That question is, how and why did Horace Walpole (1717–1797) and the men in his circle actively shape and promote the Gothic as a new style of art and architecture (and, although it is not my subject, literature)? To the eighteenth-century specialist, the justification for posing this question is straightforward: Horace Walpole and his Gothic productions—*The Castle of Otranto: A Gothic Story* (1764/65) and his Gothic villa at Strawberry Hill in Twickenham (1747–97)—are central monuments in most accounts of the period, and the Gothic stands now (as it did in the eighteenth century) as one of the dominant aesthetic movements of English modernity. Along with Chinoiserie and other new styles, the Gothic was considered one of the "modern styles" that challenged the authority of Palladianism as the dominant language of architecture.

To the medievalist, the justification for posing this question is less straightforward, although no less germane to the discipline as it is currently practiced. For me, and for many others working on the history of medieval art, the question delves deeply into the very origins of the discipline through examination of some of its most influential practitioners. Horace Walpole and the men in his circle were among the first students and collectors of medieval art in England, and their commentaries, collections, and houses stand as significant "texts" in the historiography of the discipline. Led by Walpole, these men substantially imagined, invented, and promoted a profoundly influential vision of the Middle Ages that is still very much with us. Walpole's dark, psychologically intense, glamorous, violent, and even "camp" vision of the Gothic established the form of the Gothic novel and its later iterations in art, literature, and cinema. For Walpole, the Gothic was articulated not simply as a temporal period but as an aesthetic, ideological, and social "other." In John Fletcher's useful epitome, the Gothic became "the discourse of modernity about its own pre-history, about the archaic that has been surpassed for modernity to be put in place. . . . [It is a] repository of whatever is felt to have been lost in the advance of civilisation and Enlightenment."[1] Many of our most vibrant medievalist productions, from the *Game of Thrones* television series to Peter Jackson's *Lord of the Rings* films, draw deeply from a medievalist well that Horace Walpole bored centuries earlier.

The question I pose above is hardly new. In this book I look at it afresh, however, and propose that some valuable answers to it can be found within the complex sexual and social bonds Horace Walpole and the men in his circle shared. Recent studies have explored the broadly homoerotic culture of these men and the expression of that culture in letter writing, literature, and, to a far lesser extent, art and architecture. Walpole and his intimate circle belonged to and helped to define the so-called "third sex" of homoerotically inclined men that emerged as a new category of sexual subjectivity in England after ca. 1700. At the core of this book is thus an exploration of interrelationships between two contemporary phenomena: the development of a new mode of sexual subjectivity and the development of "the modern styles" of art and architecture, and in particular the Gothic style that Walpole and his circle adopted as their own. Of course, these men were by no means the first or only practitioners of the style, but they were the most influential, and it is with them—variously "the Strawberry Committee," as Walpole would have it, or the Strawberry Hill Set, to cite the title of Brian Fothergill's study[2]—that Georgian culture has associated the Gothic taste. How and why this was so are questions I explore in the pages that follow.

It must be said that this thesis could be, and in some cases has been, explored across other productions of this circle—historiography, theater, literature (where the most productive discussions of Walpole's sexuality have taken place), the history of collections, the history of fashion, etc.—but my main concern is with the architectural patronage of half a dozen men surrounding Walpole. His famous villa at Strawberry Hill was a vital nexus for Gothic designs, and many of the men who collaboratively designed the building in and beyond the Strawberry Committee disseminated the "Strawberry Hill Gothic" mode in a handful of significant commissions, which are considered here. These houses and their collections amount to one of the most fascinating and compelling sequences of buildings in what would be called the Gothic Revival in the nineteenth century. "Gothic Revival" might better be placed in quotation marks here not only because the concept did not exist in Walpole's period (a point I shall return to) but because the Gothic was a mode of architectural design that was employed consistently from the Middle Ages onward, and recent commentators have, rightly I believe, preferred to call it the Gothic tradition.[3]

For scholars of medieval art, Horace Walpole is well known as an effete eccentric, a "typically British" scholar whose quirky commentaries on medieval art, whose recording and replication of medieval forms, whose collection of medieval objects and its context at Strawberry Hill, are often quoted but seldom explored. He appears as a "father" of medieval art history in many survey texts, in which his architectural and literary Gothic get a few prefatory pages of description, or he is referenced in accounts of the afterlives of medieval objects or in accounts of medieval art collections.[4] Apparently as "whimsical," phony, and affected as the man himself, they are figured as amateur, early, and flawed episodes of medievalism that would be "corrected" by later Victorian practitioners who gave birth to an official, empirical, academic medieval art history. Such superficial treatment of Walpolean Gothic, it might be said, reflects the inability of the discipline to historicize itself. Walpole's dismissal from medieval art history can be understood as arising from what Kathleen Biddick has called "the shock of medievalism." As Biddick has shown, the shaping of medieval studies as a modern discipline emerged from a traumatic splitting of positivist methodologies favored by the academy—philology, archaeology, codicology, diplomatics, etc.—considered then as "scientific" approaches and therefore more intellectually rigorous, from less positivist, or "nonscientific," methods that would then be called "medievalism," a camp into which Walpole's Gothic productions squarely fit.[5]

Walpole had little time for the approach to taxonomy and classification that would shape the history of art and architecture during his own period (methods borrowed from the burgeoning study of natural history) and manifest particularly in the early nineteenth century (one thinks of Thomas Rickman's *Attempt to Discriminate the Styles of English Architecture* [1817]).[6] Unlike later students of the Middle Ages, from the nineteenth through the twenty-first centuries, Walpole did not depersonalize his desire for the past. On the contrary, Walpole's was an erotic, subjective, and emotional Middle Ages, and he approached it not in terms of quantification and careful sequencing of styles and dates but as a broad historical idiom in which political and social modes of being were wed inextricably to architectural form. Biddick rightly shows that medieval studies is impoverished by abandoning these methods—by evacuating a sensory subjectivity from our studies in favor of purely empirical approaches. She also shows that the splitting of methods artificially created two fields: medieval studies, defined by quantifiable approaches, and medievalism, the "less-positivist, 'nonscientific'" approach to the medieval past. This division has been maintained through much of twentieth-century medieval art historiography and has often enough been employed to divide "the *real* Middle Ages," which might be understood to end with the Dissolution of the Monasteries (1536–41) or another imposed chronological marker, from "medievalism," figured as series of postmedieval reimaginings of the Middle Ages, from Renaissance Italy to the present.

Happily, much work has helped to question, if not dissolve, these rather arbitrary ideological and temporal divisions. The field or subfield of medievalism is now thirty years old and seemingly well established in the humanities, even if the lion's share of scholarship is conducted by historians and literary critics.[7] A number of excellent recent studies in the history of art, however, by Kathryn Brush, Michael Camille, William Diebold, Robert Mills, Kevin Murphy, Amy Knight Powell, and others indicate that medievalism—the study of postmedieval replications, appraisals, and re-presentations of the Middle Ages—is becoming increasingly central to the broader intellectual project of medieval art history. (I have elsewhere described this as a "historiographical turn" in medievalist art history.)[8] And honestly, how could it be otherwise? The period I am concerned with here, which stretches from the early eighteenth century to the early nineteenth, substantially developed the very idea of "the Middle Ages" and "the Gothic" employed today. It witnessed the creation of the earliest texts on the history of medieval art (including Walpole's) and the popularization of the Gothic as a dominant style for modern architecture and the decorative arts. Less tangibly, the scholarly apparatus for analyzing and recording medieval art came into being then, in part as a result of the significant destruction or "restoration" of medieval buildings and their components (tombs, choir screens, wall paintings, sculpture, etc.) and the urgent need to study and record them. Nostalgia and necessity were equal drivers in the formation of a medieval art history.[9] As we pressure and question the temporal structure of the Middle Ages and its period labels—Romanesque, Gothic, Byzantine, etc. (none of which, of course, had any meaning in the periods to which they have been assigned)—we are aware of the Middle Ages' status as a dominant historical myth of modernity, and arguably *the* dominant historical myth of modernity. The initial formulations of the mythology of the Middle Ages and of the Gothic by Raphael, Vasari, and others in the humanist art historiography of the sixteenth century necessarily separated a "middle age" from classical antiquity and from what was perceived as its revival in the so-called Renaissance.[10] The invention of the Middle Ages—and the Gothic in particular—was itself an episode of medievalism conceived in the formative moment of the history of art, as Erwin Panofsky pointed out long ago.[11]

These ideas and labels, of course, remain part of the very fabric of art history as a discipline and are not easily divorced or disentangled from it. One useful way forward has been to abandon the academic chauvinism that aims to restrict forms or ideas to singular temporal periods—an agenda advanced, for example, at the Gothic Modernisms conference organized at the Rijksmuseum in Amsterdam in 2017—and to acknowledge that the continuing research into and representation of the Middle Ages is all the work of medievalism. Such a project is buttressed by current thinking on the anachronic or multitemporal nature of art and ideas in the medieval and modern periods.[12] In Leslie Workman's formulation, "the Middle Ages quite simply has no objective correlative. . . . It follows quite simply that medieval historiography, the study of the successive recreation of the Middle Ages by different generations, *is* the Middle Ages. And this of course is medievalism."[13] This perspective has been increasingly central to recent formulations of medievalism and guides my approach here.[14] While this book will, I hope, be of interest to scholars of medieval art (proper), medievalism, the history of architecture, and to specialists of eighteenth-century English culture—including those specifically interested in sexuality—it was conceived as an extension of my research into medieval art and its histories. In this, Horace Walpole and the men in his circle stand as our predecessors, whose quarry, like my own, was the forms of medieval art and their re-representation in their modern present. Although, it must be said, they did it with much greater flair than their academic successors, their project is our project.

If Walpole's construction of the Gothic was influential in shaping one of modernity's dominant discourses, it is significant to acknowledge that reception of his construction was neither linear nor constant. His Gothic productions were appreciated and appropriated by a range of thinkers and movements for various subjective and political ends that are relevant to the concerns of medievalists taking "the long view" of these productions (and, of course, the long view of medievalism itself). Walpole and his Gothic productions have enjoyed a reception history in LGBTQ studies, and he is a significant figure in later twentieth-century accounts of "the history of sexuality." (For example, he received an entry in the recent *Who's Who in Gay and Lesbian History* [2002].)[15] In this context he has often enough been placed within genealogies of queer writers, including his friend Thomas Gray, William Beckford, Oscar Wilde, and Lytton Strachey.[16] Susan Sontag, in her famous 1964 essay "Notes on Camp," was the first to read a modern "camp" sensibility into Walpole's queer affect and into the design of Strawberry Hill, a sensibility she sees starting in Walpole's milieu and developing into the modern present.[17]

Walpole's Gothic products cast an equally long shadow across psychoanalysis in the nineteenth and twentieth centuries. Not only did psychoanalysts engage with Gothic fiction as what some believed was a mode of psychoanalysis in and of itself, but later critics found psychoanalysis to be a fitting tool to excavate the dense sexual and familial trauma that lay at the heart of Gothic fiction. Walpole famously employed the Old Testament concept of "the Sins of the Fathers" as a central trope of the Gothic to articulate the irrepressibility of sin (and, latterly, of trauma) as the dominant narrative of the Gothic.[18] Scholars have variously credited the Gothic with the invention of a systematic discourse on the irrational, an invention that anticipates Freud's discussions about the unconscious, and with the invention of a language of sexological critique for sexual alterity (or "dysfunction") that precedes psychoanalysis's introduction of a "theory" of homosexuality.[19] An extensive bibliography of psychoanalytic readings of Walpole's Gothic fiction can now be cited.[20] Walpole's Gothic also enjoyed a heritage among surrealist writers in the early and middle twentieth century: André Breton, among others, considered Walpole a sort of proto-surrealist, an apt characterization in many respects given the spatial, temporal, and narrative instability of *The Castle of Otranto* and, by extension, of Strawberry Hill, upon which it is based. For Breton, the novel was a forerunner of "the surrealist method," since it emerged from a dream and was composed in a manner akin to the surrealists' "psychic automatism," or "automatic writing."[21] Employing a range of medieval/medievalist sources, surrealists engaged with Walpole's homosociality, theatricality, and dandyism. It is, of course, beyond the current study to address these discourses, but they remain part of the very fabric of Walpole's Gothic, and they suggest a broader historical trajectory for medievalism itself.

The origins of this book stretch back to my days teaching at the University of London about a decade ago, when living through what Umberto Eco called "the New Middle Ages" as an academic medievalist posed some interesting challenges.[22] The school system had not prepared university students for the sheer brilliance of medieval art, its intellectual sophistication, or the extraordinary possibilities of the medieval imagination, much of which was still obfuscated by a post-Renaissance historiographical construct that considered the Middle Ages an ugly precursor to modernity (sorry cliché though it was and is). But one could deal with this through good teaching and some additional (and, for a medievalist, *remedial*) lectures on medieval art and history. What was more challenging and less readily fixed was teaching against the backdrop of the remarkable medievalist productions of the present age, including the aforementioned *Lord of the Rings* films, not to mention major exhibitions in London during those years, such as *Gothic Nightmares: Fuseli, Blake, and the Romantic Imagination* at Tate Britain (2006).[23] While students knew these were not representations of the *real* Middle Ages (something we would struggle to define), they were nevertheless informing an imagination for the Middle Ages, whether academics liked it or not.

So, it was time to go to war with these medievalist productions (and, to some extent, with my students) by teaching them in a new course. Beginning with the early texts by Raphael and Vasari that constructed "the Middle Ages," my students and I marched forward in time to explore the broad morphology of "medieval," and thus of "medieval art" as a historiographical construct, with a particular focus on the Gothic. This was a win-win, since it has been a lifelong fascination of mine, and London and its environs held as much Gothic and Gothic Revival art and architecture as we could hope to study in a lifetime. I took the broadest possible approach, and I, naively as it turned out, opted to work through the seventeenth through nineteenth centuries with classes on the Gothic novel, ending with the construction of the Gothic (or the "American Gothic") in cinema. I could not have imagined how popular this class would be. Students embraced Eco's concept of a perpetual reimagining of the Middle Ages, from its rather unfixed temporal point(s) to the present. This not only made "the Middle Ages" considerably more palatable for them and unpacked the Renaissance construction of a "middle" age, but it also brought into sharp focus our own location within this unfolding mythology. We naturally came across Horace Walpole and Strawberry Hill and, eventually, the series of buildings built by the men and his circle, including parts of the Vyne in Hampshire, Dicky Bateman's Old Windsor, and Donnington Grove in Berkshire, all of which were within a short train ride from central London. Having read *The Castle of Otranto*, we were primed to explore the house, which was then just beginning an extensive restoration. My students *got* Horace Walpole and they *got* Strawberry Hill. These Gothic productions were manifestly familiar to them, since they had viewed many versions of them either directly or through their innumerable iterations in subsequent art, literature, and cinema. Walpole presented to them, and to me, an uncannily familiar face.

Horace Walpole has continued to occupy much of my thought and writing since then. While it could hardly be said that aspects of Strawberry Hill and Walpole's conception of the Gothic style have not been carefully studied, a key part of the story seemed to be missing. As my understanding of Walpole's sexuality came into focus, it offered a crucially important insight, not only into his promotion of the Gothic as a kind of counterstyle to the Palladian, but also into the often suggested but seldom articulated kinship between Walpole and the men in his Strawberry Committee. I published a number of essays on the subject in the *Art Bulletin*, *Architectural History*, the *Burlington Magazine*, and elsewhere, and my work was featured in a piece in the *Financial Times* by Jonathan Foyle.[24] But the topic seemed to exceed even the lengthiest essay word limit, and so this book needed to be written. It is not, I hasten to state, a "queering" of the origins of the Gothic Revival, since the early Gothic Revival might be understood to be in need of a straightening out rather than a queering, to paraphrase a treasured colleague. It is also not an attempt to "out" Horace Walpole or his circle. Readers looking for this can certainly find it in other sources, not only in recent scholarship but in critical accounts published during Walpole's lifetime. It is, instead, a study that aims to locate sexual and aesthetic changes within a shared historical trajectory.

I am pleased to thank the people and institutions who helped make this book possible. Ellie Goodman at Penn State University Press deserves hearty thanks for her early and sustained interest in the project and her careful attention to detail throughout the transformation of my early ideas into this book. I am also grateful to Brian Beer and the staff of Penn State for their careful attention to the text and for compiling the index. As with all scholars of Walpoliana, an enormous debt of gratitude is owed to the remarkable Lewis Walpole Library and the Center for British Art at Yale. I was honored to hold fellowships at both places when working on this material, and I incurred a long series of debts. Susan Walker, Cynthia Roman, and Kristen McDonald at the Lewis Walpole Library tirelessly answered questions, sent images, and looked things up so many times I have lost count. All scholars should be so lucky to have such excellent and supportive archivists (and fellow obsessives) to work with. I can say the same of Bernard Nurse from the Society of Antiquaries of London, who was tremendously helpful in and out of the society's library. A generous three-year grant from the Social Sciences and Humanities Research Council of Canada allowed me to travel to do the work, and a Mid-Career Fellowship from the Paul Mellon Centre in London allowed me a term free of teaching to finish the writing. The Paul Mellon Centre and the Principal's Fund at Queen's University also awarded me generous publication grants, which allowed this book to be more fully illustrated than it might have been. Turning to my academic colleagues, it might be best to begin with the medievalists and specialists in Gothic architecture: William Diebold, Anne Hedeman, Stephen Murray, Stephen Perkinson, and Ittai Weinryb invited me to speak on this topic at a range of venues, from one side of the continent to the other. In Toronto, Matt Kavaler and his work on Renaissance Gothic architecture were an early and vital influence.[25] Others in the field offered support and even venues to publish early musings, including Colum Hourihane, Nina Rowe, and Sherry Lindquist. Laura Ashe, Robert Mills, Linda Neagley, and Maurice Howard each offered expert advice and a rare image or two. My colleagues in the history of sexuality and related disciplines offered me their time and friendship as I came to terms with eighteenth-century sexualities, namely George Haggerty, Randolph Trumbach, and especially Whitney Davis, whose influence and generosity will be manifest in one way or another on many pages of this book. At Queen's, I was lucky to have excellent colleagues who discussed this material with me and read parts of it at various stages, particularly Pierre du Prey and Stephanie Dickey. Ruth Wehlau and Leslie Ritchie invited me to give two packed lectures to the English Department, which were inspiring and a lot of fun. Our wonderful art-history librarian, Lucinda Walls, tracked down countless things for me from far and wide.

In the course of things, I was honored to be welcomed into the field of "British Art" (which generally excludes medievalists), and I want to thank Tim Barringer for inviting me to speak in his seminar at Yale, Timothy Brittain-Catlin for having me present an iconoclastic paper at the Pugin conference at the University of Kent, and Jongwoo Kim, Dominic Janes, and Whitney Davis (again) for taking part in the "Queer Gothic" session that Ayla Lepine and I organized at the College Art Association in Chicago. I was also welcomed into the intimidating world of "Eighteenth-Century Studies," and I enjoyed excellent exchanges with Stephen Calloway, Stephen Clarke, Noah Heringman, Crystal Lake, and Dale Townsend. In the years since, many of these scholars became friends and have offered me their knowledge and humor in London, Chicago, New York, Los Angeles, Yale, and elsewhere. Peter Lindfield invited me to give a keynote lecture at the Gothick Symposium at Oxford and went on to be a friend, collaborator, and fellow student of Walpoliana. We were both writing books on Walpolean Gothic simultaneously and exchanged chapters and shared much during the research and writing. Final talks on the material were given at the Gothic Modernisms conference at the Rijksmuseum in Amsterdam, the Yale Center for British Art, Strawberry Hill, Columbia University, and the Bard Graduate Center in New York.

I conclude by offering thanks to the mentors who taught me a great deal about art history as an undergraduate at the University of Toronto and a graduate student at Cambridge, a genuflection that is surely emblematic of being "early mid-career." None of them were directly instrumental in shaping this project, nor do they work in the field, but their example and wisdom nevertheless permeate what follows: Suzanne Akbari, Paul Binski, Patricia Brückmann, Michael Koortbojian, Elizabeth Legge, Alexander Nagel, and Malcolm Thurlby. Although this is a book about men, it is dedicated to the women with whom I share my life, my wife, Tia, and our daughter, Adelaide, whose arrival into the world coincided with the completion of this book.

Abbreviations

BL	British Library
BRO	Berkshire Record Office
HantsRO	Hampshire Record Office
Hazen	Hazen, Allen T. *A Catalogue of Horace Walpole's Library*. 3 vols. New Haven: Yale University Press, 1969.
HW	Horace Walpole
HW Corr	*The Yale Edition of Horace Walpole's Correspondence*. 48 vols. New Haven: Yale University Press, 1937–83.
HWSH	Snodin, Michael, ed. *Horace Walpole's Strawberry Hill*. New Haven: Yale University Press, 2007.
HRO	Herefordshire Record Office
JBAA	*Journal of the British Archaeological Association*
JSAH	*Journal of the Society of Architectural Historians*
LWL	Lewis Walpole Library, Yale University, Farmington, Connecticut

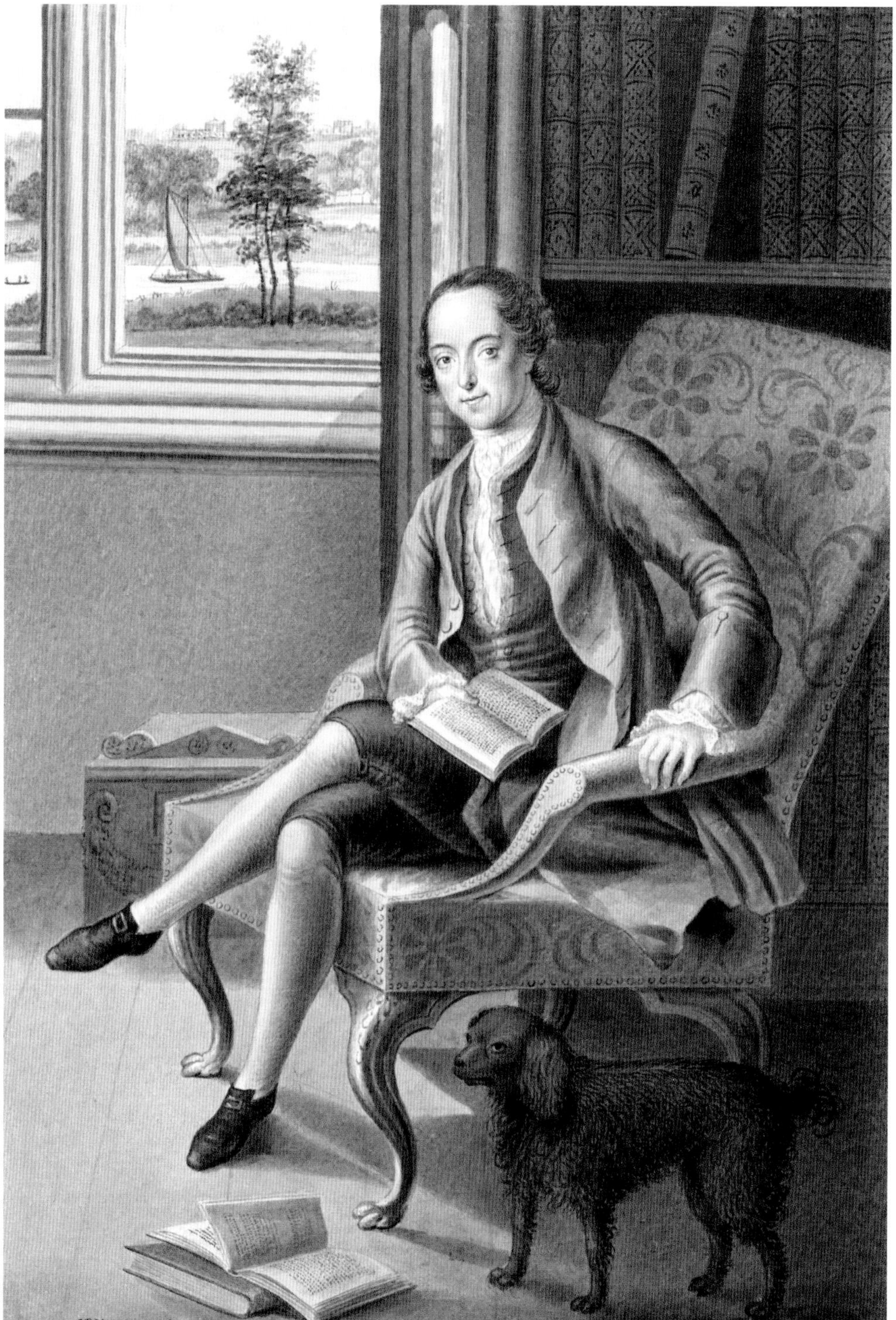

Fig. 1 George Perfect Harding after J. H. Müntz, *Horace Walpole in His Library* [at Strawberry Hill], undated. LWL SH Contents H263 no. 12 Box 105. Courtesy of The Lewis Walpole Library, Yale University.

Introduction

GOTHIC ARCHITECTURE AND SEXUALITY IN THE CIRCLE OF HORACE WALPOLE

This book explores the role that Horace Walpole (fig. 1) and his circle of friends, designers, and associates played in the promotion and mythologization of the Gothic style in eighteenth-century England. Locating Walpole's own Gothic villa at Strawberry Hill at its center (fig. 2; rented 1747, purchased 1748, designed and decorated up to Walpole's death in 1797), the book demonstrates the influence of this important building and its collection on a range of houses and additions built by Walpole's circle. These homes were built in the "Strawberry Hill Gothic" style in the environs of London (often using common architects and designers), at sites such as Grove House in Old Windsor, the Vyne in Hampshire, Donnington Grove in Berkshire, and Lee Priory in Kent. Collectively, they constitute some of the most significant statements of eighteenth-century English medievalism in architecture and interior design. Although focused on architecture, this book also considers the collections that these houses held. Collecting, exchanging, and displaying objects and images was as fundamental to aesthetic and social exchange in Walpole's circle as their Gothic homes.

Since the inception of Strawberry Hill, a critical tradition (shaped to some extent by Walpole himself) has considered him the dominant arbiter of the Gothic taste in the period and awards Strawberry Hill a significant place in the development of the Gothic during the eighteenth century. Walpole ostensibly championed a marginal style that was employed in architecture and the decorative arts in the second quarter of the eighteenth century. If not the style's creator, he was "London's first celebrity medievalizer," in Michael Alexander's apt phrase.[1] Nonetheless, Walpole's originary role was reprised and

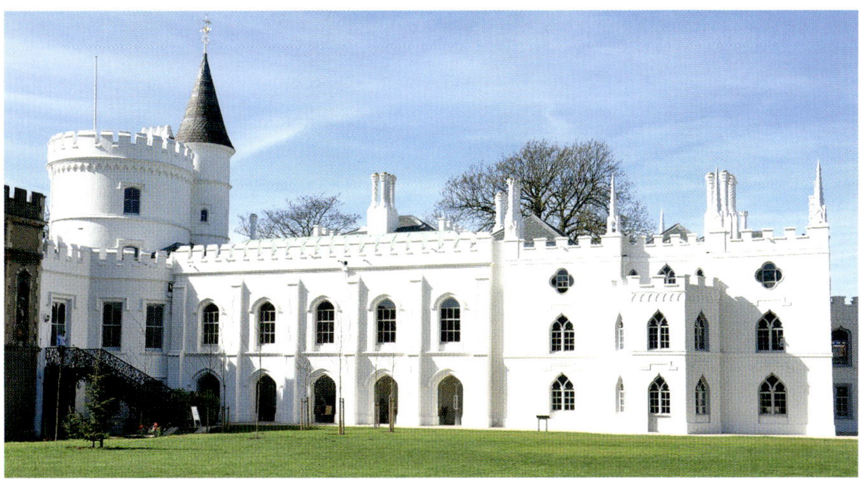

Fig. 2 Horace Walpole's Strawberry Hill, after restoration. Photo: author.

elaborated in nineteenth- and twentieth-century teleologies of what came to be called the Gothic Revival, in which he was framed (or dismissed) as a witty, eccentric, and loquacious medievalist, a ringleader of a group of lesser-known early patrons of the style. Following this line of interpretation, Walpole adapted some of the early Gothic designs of William Kent, Batty Langley, and others employed at houses such as Esher Place, Surrey (1729–33), and transformed them into Strawberry Hill Gothic, a mode that was then disseminated via his close friends and associates.[2] "Strawberry Hill Gothic" was one of a handful of terms used to describe these emulative structures, although it has rightly come under scrutiny in contemporary scholarship because it is "hackneyed and imprecise," at least in terms of its formal cohesiveness as a style label.[3] My use of it here reflects a filial connection between Strawberry Hill and buildings built in its wake. As Richard Griffin Braybrooke said rather sourly of the chapel at Audley End, designed by John Hobcraft in 1768, it "was newly fitted up . . . in the style called after its patron, *Strawberry Hill Gothic*, a mode of decoration sufficiently objectionable under any circumstances."[4] In various modern accounts, a *k* was added to "Gothic" (i.e., "Gothick") to distinguish it from earlier and later manifestations of "Gothic," a term that is occasionally interchangeable with "Georgian Gothic" or "rococo Gothic."[5] More recently, Michael McCarthy, Clive Wainwright, and others have explored the prosopographical issues involving the authorship, design sources, and chronology of many of the buildings built by these men, a corpus of some of the most significant buildings of what McCarthy has called "the origins of the Gothic Revival."[6] While much of value comes out of these excellent accounts, locating Strawberry Hill and related buildings at the beginning of a style that would develop for centuries and would not receive scholarly articulation until 1872, under a very different aesthetic and intellectual regime in Charles Eastlake's *History of the Gothic Revival*, has tended to obscure its radical character and the aesthetic and social contexts in which it was formed. Considered "early," "experimental," or just "not Gothic enough," Strawberry Hill Gothic is often dismissed as a false start to a later movement, a "light-hearted" or "whimsical" style of aesthetic jouissance from the days before more archaeologically correct simulations of medieval design began to be produced in the last decades of the eighteenth century.[7]

In this book I explore an alternate context for the patronage and design of these buildings and, to some extent at least, for the origins of the English Gothic Revival itself. I argue that the patronage and promotion of the Gothic for which Walpole and his circle are principally known were the products of their own broadly homoerotic culture. That is, the Gothic was not simply a coterie taste in an unqualified sense but served as a complex signification of their own alternate aesthetic and sexual subjectivity. Walpole stood at the center of a series of overlapping coteries of largely homoerotically inclined men. These included John Chute (1701–1776), longtime friend to Walpole, skilled designer and draughtsman, who effectively codesigned Strawberry Hill, renovated the Chute ancestral estate at the Vyne in Hampshire, and designed other Gothic buildings such as Donnington Grove; Chute's partner, Francis Whitehead (1720–1751), who did the Grand Tour with him (Walpole would collectively call them "the Chuteheads"); Thomas Gray (1716–1771), friend, poet, and scholar of medieval art and architecture and probably a lover of Horace Walpole in his youth; the draughtsman and collector Richard Bentley (1708–1782), who was also employed at Strawberry Hill; Thomas Pitt (1737–1793), the connoisseur, designer, Grand Tourist, and Twickenham neighbor; George Montagu (1713–1780), a longtime friend from Eton; Dicky Bateman (1705–1773), patron of the remarkable Gothic church at Shobdon in Herefordshire and the Gothic villa at Old Windsor; Horace Mann (1706–1786), diplomat and collector; Thomas Barrett (1744–1803), builder of Lee Priory in Kent; and others. Walpole playfully troped the paired sexual and aesthetic subjectivities of his circle as "the Strawberry Committee," "Quadruple Alliance," "brother monks," and so on. These men form the dramatis personae in this study.

Much recent attention has been paid to the sexualities of Walpole and his circle, with a particular focus on the Strawberry Committee, with whom Walpole designed, bought and collected for, and generally obsessed over Strawberry Hill. This comprised Walpole, Richard Bentley, and John Chute, and occasionally placed within this group are Thomas Gray, Dicky Bateman, George Montagu, and others. Conducted largely by biographers such as Timothy Mowl and specialists in English literature like Raymond Bentman, Jill Campbell, Abby Coykendall, Andrew Elfenbein, George Haggerty, and Anne Williams, these studies have pursued the implications of Horace Walpole's sexuality in accounts of his letters and the language of epistolary exchange he shared with his companions, and the "queer" poetics of his literature, with a particular focus on Walpole's influential Gothic novel, *The Castle of Otranto: A Gothic Story* (1764/65), the setting of which was based in part upon his own villa at Strawberry Hill.[8] Walpole's Gothic literature did not offer a homoerotic vision of the medieval past, something that would be explored by subsequent Gothic writers, but a "queer" one that locates sexual alterity and perversity in its myriad forms within a distant medieval, foreign, and Catholic setting. Transposing illicit sexuality from the polite English present to the "barbarous" medieval past for interrogation and analysis—literally to the "long labyrinth of darkness" of a Gothic castle or a Catholic monastery—validates Haggerty's view of Gothic architecture as a "sexual laboratory" for eighteenth-century culture.[9]

Despite critical attention paid to these issues in literature and other fields, the relationship of sexuality to art and architecture within Walpole's milieu had not been carefully considered before my own research, even if sexuality haunts the reception history of the Gothic style like a ghost in its shell.[10] In modern scholarship, Kenneth Clark, in his *Gothic Revival: An Essay in the History of Taste* (1928), for example, suggests the causal effect of Walpole's sexual subjectivity on his architectural tastes in a thinly veiled code: "Bad art flourishes in every epoch, but art may be healthily or unhealthily bad, and Strawberry Hill was bad in a peculiarly ominous way."[11] In doing so, Clark echoes a lengthy critical tradition on Strawberry Hill, beginning in Walpole's own lifetime, that considered its style to be a product of a distempered, diseased, or "queer" imagination. In John Betjeman's *Ghastly Good Taste* (1933), the author suggests that the queer Gothicists Horace Walpole and William Beckford (1760–1844) were to blame for the decay of English architecture. When Betjeman says that "an incipient Romanticism that was started by Horace Walpole writing scandal from his Gothick palace at Strawberry Hill, furthered by the mysterious doings of William Beckford in his miraculous Fonthill Abbey, no doubt started the trouble," he alludes to sexuality but never directly addresses it.[12] More-recent accounts of eighteenth-century Gothic, or "Rococo Gothic," as Clark preferred it, point to its effeminacy or "queerness,"

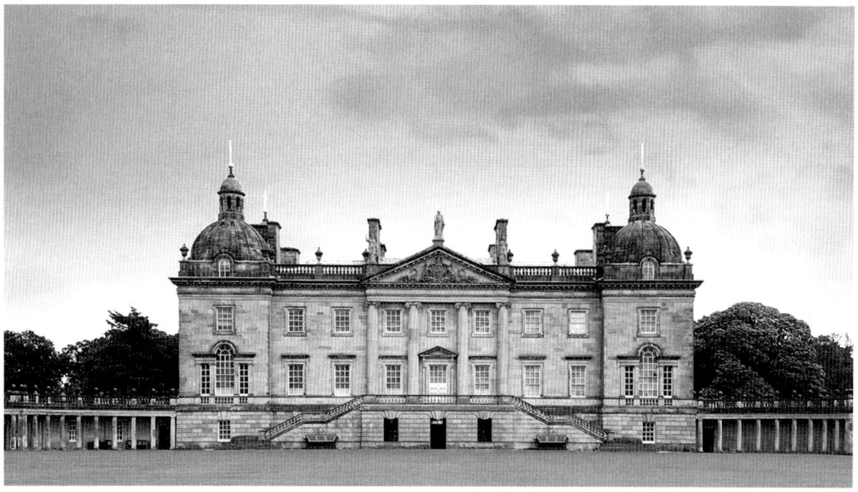

Fig. 3 Houghton Hall, Norfolk. Photo: author.

as in Chris Brooks's view that during the eighteenth century Palladianism was "subverted by the naughty curves of the rococo style" or Michael Hall's account of the "Gothick" idiom as "light, frivolous, witty, and even slightly naughty," all epithets that were certainly applied to Walpole in his lifetime and afterward.[13] Perhaps the most provocative commentary on the aesthetic consequences of Walpole's sexuality for the design of Strawberry Hill and his promotion of the Gothic in general was Timothy Mowl's controversial biography *Horace Walpole: The Great Outsider* (1996). In a few short paragraphs, Mowl comes to the conclusion that Walpole's "homosexuality" is the ever-present but largely overlooked or ignored key to understanding his aesthetics. Walpole's employment of the Gothic becomes a statement of his "high-camp defiance of normal conventions," thus emphasizing his denial of the Palladian idiom, which was employed in no less significant an architectural statement than his father's own Palladian estate at Houghton Hall, Norfolk, designed in 1722 by Colen Campbell, James Gibbs, and William Kent (fig. 3).[14] As the "plaything" of a wayward son, Strawberry Hill becomes "a large Gothick 'closet' to which Horace Walpole could sometimes retire when he wished to express his true persona with intimate friends" and an expression of a "deliberate rebel counterculture."[15] Mowl's thesis has rightly been criticized for its inappropriate application of contemporary sexual categories, terminologies, and politics to the eighteenth century. And yet, aside my own work, few, if any, accounts have attempted a rigorous critique of architecture and sexuality at Strawberry Hill or in Walpole's circle more broadly.[16] The otherwise excellent volume accompanying the exhibition on Strawberry Hill and its collection mounted by the Yale Center for British Art and the Victoria and Albert Museum (2009), for example, devotes only a few pages to the homoerotic cultures of the Committee of Taste, focusing on their letters.[17] In the wake of this volume, a handful of valuable studies have explored the Strawberry Hill press and printing house during Walpole's lifetime, the associative meanings of the house and garden, and the estate's furniture, leaving the relationship between sexuality and art and architecture largely untouched.[18]

Several reasons originating within the very practices of English art and architectural history might account for this. First, because the study of Georgian architecture has been preoccupied with design sources, the formal development of style, and the roles of artists and draughtsmen, it has usefully charted the careers of the men in Walpole's circle, but this preoccupation has left little room for considering why their designs looked like they did or what social apparatus might have facilitated their creation and transfer in the first place. The maintenance of its established preoccupations has allowed Matthew Craske to characterize English architectural history's attitude toward developments in cognate fields, including the history of sexuality, as "sublime indifference." In Craske's words, "The sense of 'the problem' in architectural history of this period [i.e., the eighteenth century] all too frequently begins and ends with the analysis of the dynamics of relationships between patrons and architects," thereby leaving the potentially unpleasant or risqué premise for their relationships and its possible influence on their art unexplored.[19] A second and related reason might be an inherent lack of comfort with sexuality and same-sex erotics in particular in twentieth-century British scholarship, despite the fact Horace Walpole's sexuality and sexual affect (and that of his circle) have been consistently commented on from his lifetime onward.[20] Herein lies an interesting paradox, because the rhetoric of architecture in England during Walpole's period and beyond was, at its core, deeply corporeal. Architecture and the human body shared a common location in art writing, and their ethical and sexual natures were frequently critiqued together or compared in the period as paired manifestations of common social conditions. The very possibility that the forms of architecture could signal sexual alterity for a viewer (or sexual/bodily normativity, for that matter) was premised on this long-standing tradition in English architectural culture, what I call the "body-building analogy." Finally, there is the problem of the inherently interdisciplinary nature of Walpolean Gothic. Walpole's medievalism unfolded across his art criticism, letters, literature, and art and architectural patronage. He felt none of our modern disciplinary chauvinism in which architecture is often studied independent of art writing, literature, poetry, or historiography; rather, Walpole considered his Gothic "texts"—whether built or written—to be mutually informing products of a singular imagination. For this reason, scholars of architecture who marginalize Gothic literature and other sources as only tangentially relevant to the built environment—or, for that matter, historians of literature who aim to provide synthetic accounts of Walpole's Gothic but are insufficiently attentive to the archaeology of the buildings or their design, decoration, and manufacture—do so at their own peril. For the art historian, the architectural culture of Walpole's circle thus poses some significant challenges. In rising to this challenge, I can only say that I have tried to ignore modern disciplinary prejudices and have charted a course through these monuments based as closely as possible upon Walpole's brilliant, if eccentric, lead.[21]

Gothic Architecture, the Modern Styles, and the Third Sex

At the center of this book is the observation that the revival of the Gothic as a "new" mode of architectural design—one of the "modern styles" of early eighteenth-century England (including Chinoiserie and other styles)—paralleled and was informed by new formulations of human sexuality and subjectivity. Even before Thomas Laqueur's foundational *Making Sex* (1990), profound changes in the very structure of gender and sexuality were considered characteristic of the eighteenth century.[22] Historians of sexuality have proposed that a new and definable category of male sexuality emerged in England in the years around 1700, a sexuality that was principally defined by sexual desire for men, in contrast to earlier constructions of sexuality structured by age (intergenerational sexuality) or by a more fluid bisexuality between adult males and male youths and women. The shift from a Renaissance sexual culture, in which men freely had sex with boys and with women, to a culture in which men were broadly expected to have sex exclusively with women or, in the minority case of the third sex, exclusively with men constitutes what Randolph Trumbach has called "the modern sexual system." In the modern sexual system, sexual acts and choice(s) were no longer essentially untethered to gender identity and instead became defining features of human selfhood and subjectivity.[23] Of course, such a broad shift was neither tidy nor finite: some men identified as being of the third sex, including John, Lord Hervey (1696–1743), raised children within marriages while pursuing male lovers outside of them. Located between but separate from males and females, the construction of the third sex was based in part on the perception of a mixture or corruption of genders: the adoption of "female" manners rendered males effeminate, a regular adjective for men of the third sex, their personal affect and tastes. In the eighteenth century, the third sex was a new identity around which a nascent "queer culture" began to form, and art, architecture, and fashion were the vehicles with the potential to express what John Cleland in *Fanny Hill* describes as "that stamp" of modern man.[24] If a shared sexual subjectivity served as the binding feature of Walpole's circle of friends, aesthetes, and designers, their shared tastes in the Gothic were their most profound expression of it.

A significant critical tradition during and after Walpole's lifetime elided his sexual orientation and that of his circle with their affect or style of being. Walpole, Gray, and others in this circle were often feminized and discussed as women: Gray, for example, was called "Miss Gray" while at Cambridge, and Walpole was grouped among the Blue Stockings as "the Right Honourable Lady Horace Walpole, Countess of Orford."[25] In his withering *Reply to the Counter-address* (1764), for example, William Guthrie insinuates (probably correctly) that Horace Walpole had an *affaire du coeur* with his cousin Henry Seymour Conway. Turning to describe Walpole, his critique focuses on Walpole's writing style as a projection of his own sexual subjectivity:

> there is a weakness and an effeminacy in it, which seems to burlesque even calumny itself. The complexion of the malice, the feeble tone of the expression, and the passionate fondness with which the *personal* qualities of the officer in question are continually dwelt on, would almost tempt one to imagine, that this arrow came forth from a female quiver; but as it wants both the true delicacy and lively imagination which characterize a lady's pen, the attack must probably have been made from a neutral quarter, from a being between both, neither totally male or female . . . so halting between the two, that it would very much puzzle a common observer to assign to him his true sex. The description of the hermaphrodite horse which is just brought to town, may, perhaps, not unaptly represent him; "he possesseth all the characters of both sexes, but the odd

> situation and transposition of the parts, appear as it were the sport of nature, and render him the greatest curiosity ever seen."[26]

Guthrie draws particular attention to Walpole's apparent gender indeterminacy and, by extension, the gender indeterminacy of his own productions, the latter apparently an extension of the former. Although he falls just short of calling Walpole a man of the third sex, this is clearly his drift. His account in fact presents a catalogue of some of the developing tropes that would be applied to men of the third sex. These included a physical performativity that was understood to be effeminate or to satirically appropriate or *burlesque* "female" modes of comportment; tastes in conventionally "female" commodities that were either decorative or diminutive or both (fabric, furniture, toys, jewelry, etc.); and patterns of sociability confined to (generally) platonic relationships with females and romantic, fraternal, and sexual relationships with males. Compared to a specimen from natural history—a hermaphrodite horse apparently on display in London—Walpole becomes a sexual freak, a corruption of natural form. "Hermaphrodite" and the cognate terms "fribble," "finger-twirler," "macaroni," and the like were common contemporary metaphors for the third sex: originating in the story of Salmacis and Hermaphroditus in Ovid's *Metamorphoses*, the hermaphrodite was one of a list of Greco-Roman myths and historical figures (including Antinous, the lover of the emperor Hadrian; Ganymede, cupbearer to Zeus; etc.) in use as codes for homoeroticism both in and out of homoerotic cultures. Unsurprisingly, Walpole's circle collected, exchanged, and displayed images of all of these figures in their homes as coded allusions to a shared sexuality (I discuss these collections in chapters 3–5).

A dominant strand of the critical tradition surrounding Walpole and his circle elided their sexuality with their tastes for the Gothic and the modern styles. George Hardinge, who knew Walpole, comments in a posthumous account (1813) of him that Walpole's "effeminacy of manner . . . was lost in his wit, ingenuity and whimsical but entertaining fund of knowledge." He then turns to Walpole's circle, "some of whom," he notes, "were as effeminate in appearance and manner and were as witty [referencing John Chute and George Montagu]. . . . But others had effeminacy alone to recommend them. In his [Walpole's] taste for architecture and *virtu* there was both whim and foppery, but still with fancy and genius."[27] Hardinge thus considers their tastes in art and architecture to be a natural extension of their sexual affect. Thomas Babington Macaulay's caustically homophobic account of Walpole's life (1833), goes further, commenting on his "diseased and disorganized mind," which produced a "grotesque house [decorated] with pie-crust battlements" (thereby presaging Kenneth Clark's account of Walpole's "unhealthy" tastes). Employing "diseased" and "unhealthy" as common euphemisms for same-sex desire in his description of Walpole and his tastes, Macaulay develops an elaborate analogy between the apparent flimsiness of Strawberry Hill (and thus its character as a medievalist simulation) and Walpole's physical and sexual self: in all of Walpole's endeavors, according to Macaulay, Walpole wore "a mask within a mask," but "his real tastes perpetually show themselves through the thin disguise."[28] Macaulay's commentary focuses on the fictive materiality of Strawberry Hill Gothic, in which "real" medieval, stone-built Gothic architecture is simulated in modern materials: stone vaulting is erected in papier-mâché, monumental stone screens are miniaturized and transformed into woodwork

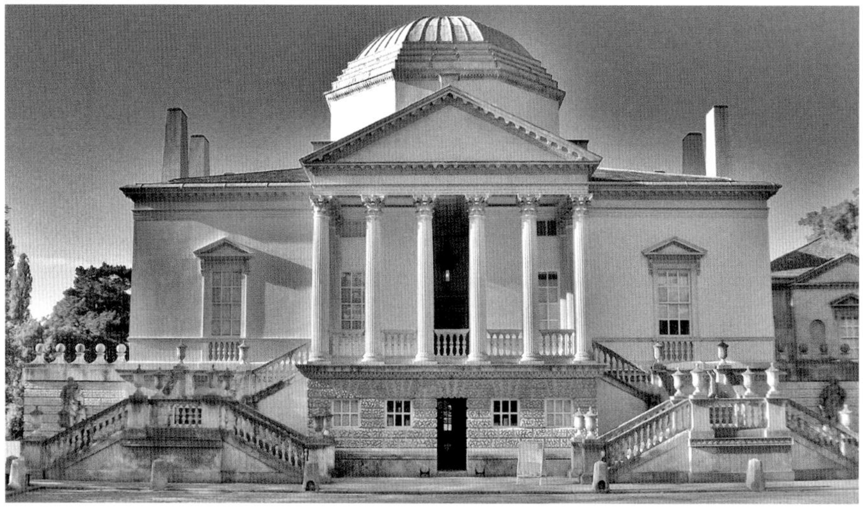

Fig. 4 Lord Burlington's villa at Chiswick. Photo: author.

and painted to simulate stone, and medieval devotional spaces—cloisters, chapels, oratories, etc.—are secularized, transformed, and given domestic functions. Writing within a subsequent and very different architectural culture, Macaulay fails to acknowledge that these departures were fundamental to Walpole's appraisal of the Gothic as a "licentious" style premised on formal divergences from its models. Macaulay also fails to appreciate the rich and fluid paradox of the Gothic's modernity that was central to its appreciation by Horace Walpole and his contemporaries. Focusing on the mobile forms and motifs of medieval architecture rather than on its material or structural character (as their Victorian successors would), Walpole and his circle employed medieval buildings as a point of departure in the creation of modern, associative works of architectural fiction. In the language of modern criticism, we might understand that the ambiguous space between modern representation and its historical referent in Walpole's oeuvre was thematically unstable, a "queer" space (in the broadest sense of the term) that was critical, ironic, parodic, and subversive.

These critiques of Horace Walpole and his circle as effeminate men of taste and fashion feel familiar, since they preface many modern constructions of homosexuality and "camp" performativity and its material manifestations in art, design, theater, and other areas. But they had their roots in some of the earliest formulations of the third sex in the eighteenth century, some of which were developed within or as a response to Walpole's circle and their art and architectural patronage. Men of the third sex were not, of course, the exclusive patrons of the modern styles—women also played a dominant role in designing and patronizing them. The eighteenth century located these aesthetic and social/sexual changes within a broad moral arc of decline that, for conservative critics, defined "modernity" in general.[29] "The god of taste that ruled Georgian aesthetics wore antique clothing" (in Amanda Vickery's words), and embracing the Gothic and the modern styles implied a challenge to the authority of the established neoclassical tastes of the period.[30] Vickery continues, "Rigid Palladians and self-appointed authorities on architecture tended to type pure classicism as masculine, and diversions from uniformity and proportion as feminine and undisciplined or effeminate and corrupt."[31] Unsurprisingly, Samuel Johnson defined "modernism" as "deviation from the ancient and classical manner," signifying a rebuke of the established mores of the classical

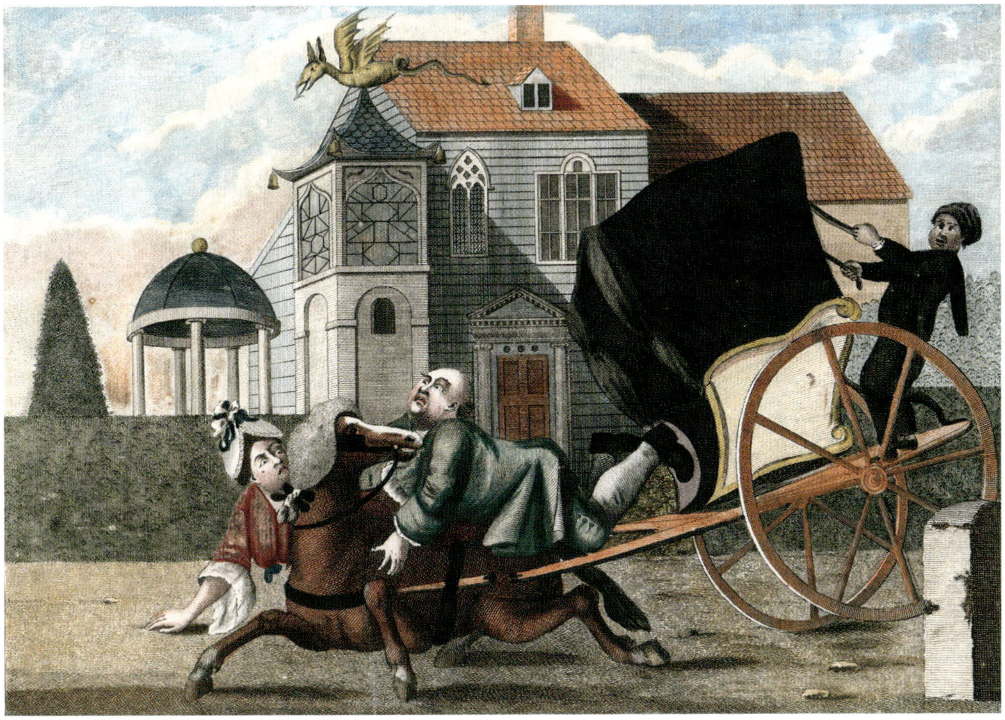

Fig. 5 "A Common Council Man of Candlestick Ward and his Wife on a Visit to Mr Deputy at his Modern Built Villa near Clapham," London, 1771. LWL 771.11.01.02+. Courtesy of The Lewis Walpole Library, Yale University.

canon in eighteenth-century life.[32] Neo-Palladianism had been established a generation earlier and was championed by the political elite, including Horace Walpole's father, Sir Robert Walpole, at Houghton Hall, and Lord Burlington at his nearby villa at Chiswick (fig. 4) (both buildings of significance to Horace Walpole).[33] Although Walpole was by no means the first active proponent of the Gothic over classicism in the eighteenth century, he and his committee "helped to carry the rebellion to polite society."[34] I shall have cause to nuance relationships between the Gothic and classicism in the pages that follow, but it will suffice here to note that, for many, Palladianism served as a vehicle for the establishment of British government, aristocracy, and patriarchy, the hegemonic authority of empire in the "long eighteenth century."[35]

From Walpole's perspective, the preference for the Gothic and modern styles—the freedom to choose alternative modes of design as vehicles of self-expression—was understood in political terms as a new "liberty of taste," a freedom from oppressive aesthetic norms that defined modernity itself.[36] This would have significant connotations for other erotic and sexual expressions of the modern present that were likewise understood to run counter to established conventions. From a critical, conservative perspective, appreciation and acquisition of the modern styles not only could reflect a denial of normative male taste located in neo-Palladianism but could signify a range of ills from effeminacy to an arrested aesthetic development, and potentially homoeroticism itself. John Brown, in his turgid *Estimate of the Manners and Principles of the Times* (1757), considered these phenomena to be signs of the "vain, luxurious, and selfish effeminacy" that characterized the modern present, and his was just one voice of many.[37] Unsurprisingly, perhaps, the modern villas that are the subjects of this book, those built in the new Gothic or Chinese styles (or mixtures of both), were critiqued in the popular press and prints in a new genre of architectural satire (fig. 5).[38] Signifying the "degeneracy of [British] national taste," the modern villa is pictured as a lamentable sign of the times that reflects an aspiring nouveau riche class of patron, his affected and effeminized lifestyle, and the new forms of sexuality to which it was often related. All of these factors were positioned to contrast with the modes and manners of a "true" aristocracy in the generation preceding.[39] Writing in the *World* in 1753, one author sardonically advises, "If one wished to see a coxcomb expose himself in the most effectual manner, one would advise him to build a villa; which is the *chef-d'œuvre* of modern impertinence, and the most conspicuous stage which Folly can possibly mount to display herself to the world."[40] The villa is not only a very public emblem of self-fashioning (or "exposure") but a locus of novelty, an architecture that emblematizes the perceived degeneration and corruption of eighteenth-century life. It is the product of the coxcomb, a new category of narcissistic, effeminized masculinity, which might include the "macaroni," fop, or dandy, all of which could, and often did, serve as synonyms for men of the third sex. In this critical context, the modern villa becomes a product of, or even an analogue for, modern male sexualities.

A range of new stereotypes of the third sex as men of taste and fashion and purveyors of the modern styles developed during the middle years of the eighteenth century. These popular stereotypes—themselves exaggerations of recognizable affects in the Georgian present—had a significant role in critiquing and constructing queer forms of visibility and self-expression, as Dominic Janes has recently shown.[41] Some emerged from within queer cultures. Horace Walpole was the first to record and employ many of these terms. He notes, for example, that "macaroni" (a fashionable and effeminate male urbanite) is "synonymous to beau, fop, coxcomb, *petit maître*, etc." and that at the "Maccaroni club" "old fools will hobble after young ones" (fig. 6).[42] Walpole followed Lady Mary Wortley Montagu's derisive account of John, Lord Hervey, claiming that "there were three sexes: men, women, and Herveys," thus positioning a senior queer man of taste in an intersexual position between males and females.[43] In "A Fairy Tale," of 1743, Walpole feels no hesitation in satirizing Lord Hervey as a "Fairy" whose "whimsical attire made Him doubt of its sex; or rather doubt, if it were of any sex."[44] Using the term "Fairy" for Hervey as a suitably genderless label, and reprising a categorization of the "third sex," "A Fairy

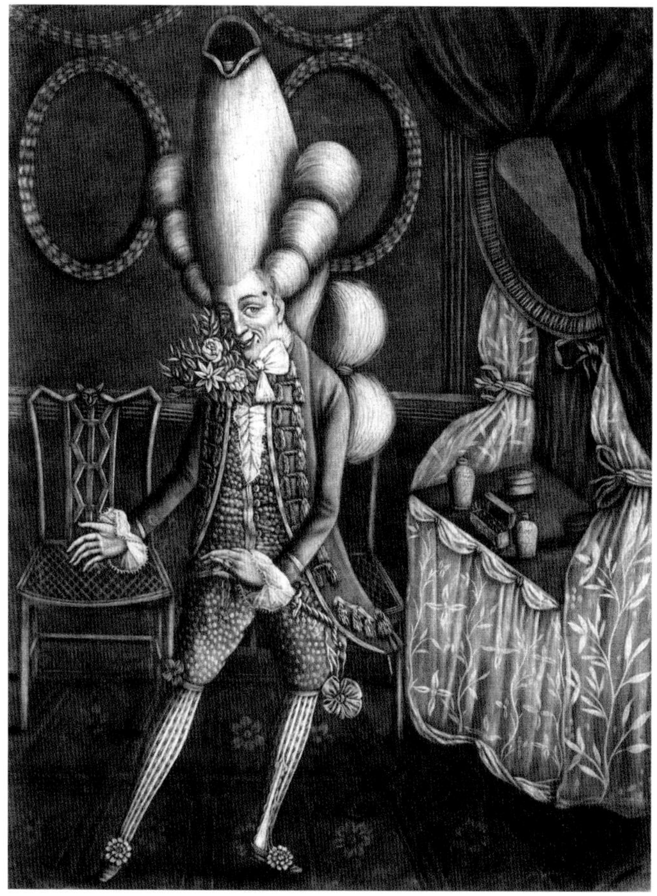

Fig. 6 Philip Dawe, "The Macaroni: A real Character at the late Masquerade," 1773. LWL 773.07.03.01.2+. Courtesy of The Lewis Walpole Library, Yale University.

Tale" articulates Walpole's fascination with Hervey's "queer" sexual persona (as in Hervey's words "I am not a woman; I am my lord *Hervey*!"). In a discussion of heraldry with John Chute, Walpole would inject the same bitchy humor, observing that "the Late Lord Hervey said, his arms should be *a cat*, scratchant, with this motto, *for my friends where they itch, for my enemies where they are sore*," thereby imposing a feline (literally "catty") bitchiness on Hervey.[45] As Lucy Moore has suggested, Walpole's derision might have been due to the fact that he conceived himself in his other, an uncomfortable doubling of sexual persona and physical form.[46] In any case, the solidarity Walpole often expressed for the men within his intimate circle did not necessarily extend to queer men outside of it.

Other stereotypes were imposed upon the third sex: for example, Horace Mann (Horace Walpole's cousin and correspondent) and his friends were called "finger twirler[s] . . . a decent word for Sodomite[s]," to describe their apparently flamboyant gestures.[47] Various new stereotypes were developed on the London stage and in prints, literature, and poetry during the middle quarters of the eighteenth century, such as Sir Novelty, Sir Fopling, (William) Whiffle, and (Mr.) Fribble (among others), as satires of this new category of urban gentleman whose sexuality and affect were seemingly natural extensions of his predilection for the fashionable modern styles.[48] In varying combinations, these characters embodied a pronounced and effeminized domesticity and a vulgar acquisitiveness for fashionable modern commodities that contradicted the aesthetic regime of neo-Palladianism. Horace Walpole and the men in his circle were the very models for some of these caricatures, as the theatergoing public noticed. Contemporaries variously suggested that Mr. Fribble, from David Garrick's 1747 play *Miss in Her Teens*, was modeled either on Dicky Bateman, a famous buyer and purveyor of Chinoiserie and other modern styles (Walpole celebrated Bateman as the "founder of the Sharawadgi [Chinese] taste"), or on Walpole himself. As I note in chapter 4, "fribble" and "fop" were not only nouns developed to describe the third sex but came to be employed, in the first English critiques of what would now be called "queer architecture," as adjectives ("fribble" and "foppish") to describe the houses and interiors that the fribbles and fops built and inhabited. Here a new image of domesticity is promoted by a queer aesthetic subjectivity that actively exploits the new products of modern capitalism and empire (since of course many of these objects were imported or based upon foreign objects) to its own ends.[49]

It is not a coincidence that the main architectural projects of Walpole's circle were domestic rather than civic or religious. On the basis of antique architectural theory, Walpole often commented upon decorum in domestic architecture (and the villa in particular) versus the great church or civic architecture: the Gothic was appropriate for the former because it allowed for irregularity and informality; it was a style of unfixed rules (in architectural terms) that could connote or even *promote* a new mode of being likewise unhemmed by modern convention.[50] Walpole manifestly understood the gendering of architectural form and followed the Vitruvian tradition (employed subsequently in England by Inigo Jones and others) in suggesting that architecture "has . . . two sexes; its masculine dignity can only exert its muscles in public works and at public expense; its softer beauties come better within the compass of private residence and enjoyment."[51] The domus, for Walpole, was gendered feminine and was a site for "softer beauties" unregulated by the social and political conventions of monuments to public dignity. The domestic interior was thus a vital locus of "self-fashioning" in the Georgian period and beyond.

In arguing for the interconnectedness of the third sex and the modern styles as reflecting profound changes in the very structure of modernity, I am seeking to integrate what McCarthy has called "the origins of the Gothic Revival" with broader narratives of eighteenth-century culture. To argue that what Rudolph Wittkower termed the eighteenth century's "chaos of styles" in architecture shaped and was shaped by changes in human sexuality and subjectivity now seems like a short leap indeed, particularly since related studies have explored the effects of the third sex on Georgian fashion and theater.[52] Arguably, both architecture and sexuality form part of a broader Enlightenment project to zealously order the phenomenological universe—both natural and man-made—into discrete categories, typologies, and genealogies. Recent accounts of queerness and architecture in the nineteenth and twentieth centuries, by Michael Hatt, John Potvin, Matt Cook, and others, have shown that architecture and interior decoration were vital arenas in which battles over male identity and sexuality were waged.[53] My study likewise shows that the domestic architectural projects of Walpole's circle created spaces in which new sexual mores were tested, performed, and critiqued. As such, I argue for a much longer history of the nexus between queer sensibilities and the new styles and modes of being in the domestic sphere. Although it is far beyond the bounds of the present study to do so, joining the arc of this study to later periods might provide terrain upon which to construct a longer and fuller history of queerness and the history of art and architecture in modern Britain than previously understood.

Structures of Patronage

I have already suggested that the teleological approaches that have long characterized the Gothic Revival, in which Strawberry Hill and Strawberry Hill Gothic are considered as originary statements in a long history of style, have not served our understanding of either well. Walpole's Gothic productions were conceived within the confines of an elite coterie in Georgian London and were in no sense intended to become the fountainhead of a new style of architecture and the decorative arts. Although Walpole and his circle were only *primus inter pares* of the dominant tastemakers and disseminators of the Gothic in England, they were unique in appropriating and promoting the Gothic as a coterie taste. A rich series of medieval or medievalizing tropes were developed to describe the Gothic as such: Thomas Gray could compliment his friend Thomas Warton on his new Gothic home in London, stating, "I am glad you have entered into the spirit of Strawberry Castle"; Walpole could speak of "the Strawberry annals" in describing the development of the house to Richard Bentley, while he could elsewhere chide his friend's designs because they did not "have the Strawberry imprimatur," a perceived sense of the ideality of the Strawberry Hill Gothic mode.[54]

The Gothic style that Walpole and his circle promoted was a signally important product of their homoerotic and homosocial culture. The structuring of this culture and its related self-generating and self-defining mythology is significant for an understanding not only of how it functioned but also of how art and architecture became an articulation of its myths, many of which were centered around a preexisting construction of the family in Georgian culture. A central thesis of this study is that the art patronage of Walpole's circle structured what has been called a "queer family romance" in art patronage and collecting. Based upon a rereading of Sigmund Freud's 1909 essay "Family Romances" ("Der Familienroman der Neurotiker"), which explores the child's conscious remaking of his or her lineage during adolescence, when the faults of his or her parents become evident, queer family romance charts the creation of alternative "queer," nonbiological, or "chosen" families of homoerotically inclined individuals. Whitney Davis has explored queer family romance in queer art collections (and particularly that of William Beckford at his Gothic "monastery," Fonthill Abbey), where he identifies it as "the witting (or even witty) invention of alternate inheritances by a person who finds himself or herself disoriented in the imprinted norms of the parental matrix."[55] Within queer art collections, queer family romance articulates "family resemblances among forms that allowed queer significances (homosexual or not) to emerge into visibility even when particular artifacts did not inherently possess a queer iconography," and "relays [the] imaginations of a better social order, and possibly a radically different one."[56] Queer family romance thus charts a particular strategy of patronizing, purchasing, sharing, and displaying works of art that, in the minds of their owners and intimate coterie at least, reflect and articulate an alternate social order that is more fitting to the minoritized subjectivities of its patrons/users and often serves to critique the dominant social order.[57] As a strategy for creating and using art to suggest alternative, nonbiological kinship, aspects of which may be fully intelligible to a select few, queer family romance shares some features with the art patronage of other minoritized subjectivities in eighteenth-century England—for example, with the covert visual culture of contemporary Jacobites.[58] The construction of family in queer family romance is in fact far closer to eighteenth-century ideas of the family than those practiced in the twentieth century (i.e., the "nuclear family"). As Martha Vicinus has argued, the "metaphoric language of the family" was commonly employed in eighteenth-century homoerotic unions to articulate romantic bonds. This was based on Georgian constructions of family that typically expanded far beyond the bounds of biological kin to include friends, servants, and other members of a household family or retinue.[59] As such, the development of queer family structures in eighteenth-century England was anticipated by and, arguably, normalized within the already fluid dynamics of the family itself.

I employ the term "queer family romance" as a strategy to explore how and why art and architecture was appreciated as a shared taste between Walpole and his circle. Why was Strawberry Hill and its art collection so influential and what did it mean to replicate aspects of it within Walpole's coterie? Why were there so many direct quotations of it, or "Strawberryisms" (to borrow Nick Groom's term), in subsequent buildings?[60] In thinking about this question, I have expanded Davis's initial approach to collections to also consider the patronage and design of monumental architecture, the development and dissemination of architectural designs, and of course the employment of a common style among a "family" coterie. This approach is not after-the-fact theorizing but is based on the very realities of patronage in Walpole's circle. Suggesting a perceived relationship between Strawberry Hill and other buildings built in its wake by his friends, Walpole spoke of them in familial terms as children, or "offspring," of Strawberry Hill. He rapturously commented upon Thomas Barrett's Lee Priory in Kent (discussed at length in chapter 5), built by James Wyatt (1746–1813), which emulated Strawberry

Hill (even including a "Strawberry room," or "closet"), calling it "a child of Strawberry prettier than the parent, and . . . so flattering to me!"[61] In doing so he articulated the quasi-familial bonds he shared with the men in his circle, between the buildings they built and the objects they owned and shared. These associations were also reinforced by the various picture hangs in their houses: frequently adopting the technologies of family portraiture, these hangs figured overlapping coteries of queer family members. Understood in these terms, Horace Walpole's appeal to the Gothic extended beyond its inherently alternative formal character as an "anticlassical" architecture. The Gothic castle, or great house, complete with its conventional trappings of heraldic blazons and its family portrait genealogies—both features of the Gothic for Georgian audiences—offered an ideal template for the examination and subversion of patriarchy and biological lineage. As in Walpole's Gothic architecture, so in his literature: literary critics (often referring to Freud's 1909 essay) have shown that the Gothic as a new literary form invigorated by Walpole had at its core troubled family dynamics, hubristic patriarchy, incest and sexual violence, and what John Fletcher (following Walpole and the original biblical citation in Exodus 34:7) has valuably described as "the sins of the fathers."[62] Issues of kinship—biological and nonbiological—run through Walpole's Gothic architecture and literature and indicate something of the very nature of Walpole's interpretation of the Gothic idiom.

From my perspective, approaching the Gothic homes of Walpole's circle in these terms provides a useful corrective to some of the positivist methodologies that have framed previous studies. This approach partially replaces the rather sterile concept of artistic "influence," or at least qualifies and contextualizes it. The idea of "influence" has rightly received much attention within the history of art, in which it is still employed as a causal explanation for the development or appropriation of style—a narrative writ large in the largely biomorphic patterns of development still evident in the "Gothic Revival." The term, as Michael Baxandall has said, is "shifty," "the curse of art criticism," because it reverses "the active/passive relation which the historical actor experiences and the inferential beholder will wish to take into account."[63] In Baxandall's terms, rather than award agency to the original work (X) in "influencing" the second, or replicative, work (Y), it is far more useful to award agency to Y in actively appropriating (or not) aspects of X. Y's appropriation of X within Walpole's circle is not fully explicable in terms of "artistic development" or "influence" but is readily comprehensible as an expression of a complex homoerotic network of men, tastes, and ideas in Georgian London, the center of which was Horace Walpole and Strawberry Hill.

Some further clarifications should be offered here. In discussing eighteenth-century sexual coteries, I am uncomfortable with the unqualified imposition of the labels "gay" or "homosexual" onto Horace Walpole, his circle, or their conception of the Gothic (what David Halperin has called "a kind of anti-historicist backlash" in gender studies).[64] Walpole's world was unencumbered by the conventions of "homosexuality" and "heterosexuality," which of course would not be invented for almost a century after Walpole's death, even if some anticipatory concepts like the "third sex" were developed in his time. Although this book focuses on a circle of male patrons of architecture, it would be remiss not to note that Walpole maintained many close correspondences with aristocratic women.[65] Later in his life he cultivated and promoted female artists and authors such as Diana

Beauclerk, Mary Berry, and Anne Damer, daughter to his intimate cousin Henry Seymour Conway, through whom she would inherit Strawberry Hill at Walpole's death. Damer and Berry were understood to have maintained a "Sapphic" relationship toward the end of Walpole's life (Damer in particular was known for "liking her own sex in a criminal Way").[66] Walpole's promotion of these and other amateur female artists to the level of great artists in his art writing was as controversial with respect to the canon of the fine arts as it was a reflection of his personal allegiances. While it is unlikely that Walpole ever considered their sexuality to be akin to his own (as might be understood at present), the apparent transgressions of social and sexual decorum for which these women were known "apparently fascinated Walpole or at least did not disturb him."[67] Walpole would also befriend and entertain the Chevalier d'Eon at Strawberry Hill and collect and extra-illustrate the *Lettres, mémoires et négociations particulières du Chevalier d'Éon*. Although we would now describe the chevalier as transsexual, Walpole had no such language to describe d'Eon, preferring (in French) "M. ou Mlle d'Éon."[68] Here, as elsewhere in studies of eighteenth-century sexualities, present-day scholars struggle against language to articulate that which was manifest in culture but sometimes never clearly articulated on the written page. While I insist on the profound differences between Georgian constructions of homosexuality and contemporary constructions, Walpole and his Gothic productions enjoy an important place within the genealogy of ideas that ultimately constructed contemporary ideas of "homosexuality," and as such we cannot absolutely separate his world from our own; it is useful, as H. G. Cocks suggests, to acknowledge that modern constructions of homosexuality "testify to traces of the traces of its past."[69]

This aside, it bears stating that we know rather less about the actual sexual practices of these men than we would like (or than we could really expect to know). Although their homoerotic inclinations are clear, the evidence is often insufficient to locate them concisely within any of the four "pre-homosexual" (i.e., pre-1869) categories or models famously proposed by Halperin (effeminacy; pederasty, or "active" sodomy; friendship, or male love; and passivity, or inversion), although it seems that some of these roles were played by the men in Walpole's circle in combination.[70] As Haggerty has suggested, while these models might usefully interrogate classical and medieval sexual structures, they are not as easily applied to the eighteenth century.[71]

Little is known of Walpole's sexual life in particular, since he appears to have censored parts of it. He loved lewd jokes about the male anatomy and relished salacious gossip about the homoerotic activities of fellow antiquaries and connoisseurs on the Grand Tour. And although Walpole composed phallic writings, such as his poem "Little Peggy" (1742–44), which literally focuses upon Lord Lincoln's penis, or "The Judgment of Solomon" (1753), which transforms the story of two women appealing to Solomon over their parental claims to a baby into one about two women appealing for a man's giant phallus, these were intended for a private audience who were manifestly "in the know."[72] And yet, for their occasionally libidinal humor and effeminate and "camp" affect, Walpole and others in his circle were not libertines. As elite gentlemen, they stood to one side of London's "molly" subculture, which took place in established bawdy houses patronized principally by working-class men. The performative aspects of the molly house—the elaborate rituals of cross-dressing, faux "marriages," and other burlesques—have been central to recent writings on the history of homosexuality but have little to do with Walpole's milieu.[73]

Indeed, Walpole and his circle could be rather prudish about sexuality and largely disapproved of excessive sexual display, a stance that surely has as much to do with their class, education, and social position as with their sexuality. Fortunately, the specifics of their sex lives are not strictly relevant to the present study, even if I have occasion to comment upon them below. Rather than make assumptions about these men's sex lives or impose contemporary stereotypes upon them, I allow their productions to speak for themselves.[74] Here I follow George Haggerty and others in characterizing Walpole's elite circle as broadly homoerotic and in considering their shared sexual subjectivity as the fundamental premise of their unions. But I also follow Richter and Haggerty (again) in noting that romantic friendship provides the most useful model with which to explore these unions.[75] Walpole's circle was, of course, only one of a number of overlapping homosocial and/or homoerotic networks that characterized eighteenth-century artistic culture (what Samuel Johnson called "the clubbable" world of Enlightenment London). The Society of Dilettanti, the Monks of Medmenham Abbey, the Society of Antiquaries of London, and others were homosocial cultures that formed around new orientations and agendas separate from the confines of family or profession and that met within specially designed settings.

Although focused on art and particularly architecture within a homoerotic coterie, my account broadly agrees with Simon Richter's view of the eighteenth century as the "age of homosocial friendship and cultural production."[76] In arguing across both the history of art and the history of sexuality, I hope largely to sidestep what has been called "a longstanding (and, some would argue, sterile) ideological dispute within social science between 'essentialists' and 'constructionists,'" in which essentialists argue that homosexuality is biologically determined, whereas constructionists assume that sexual desires are learned.[77] Biologically determined or not, sexual and aesthetic subjectivities are, in my view, interconnected, and even indissoluble, components of human selfhood, even if one cannot be readily reduced (or explained) by the other.[78] This study straddles both camps. I take the eighteenth century to have witnessed the creation of a new queer subjectivity, itself a fundamental change in the structuring of modernity. I also follow recent work that has emphasized that the social, cultural, and even sexual practices of homosexuality were *learned* within queer cultures.[79] In discussing the influence of one man's home on others, I do so in the belief that his own mode never signified an objective and sterile stylisticality (as though such a thing could exist).[80] On the contrary, the development and dissemination of forms followed and were facilitated by a homoerotic coterie that employed them as a fundamental form of self-expression.

This study opens by considering the construction of the Gothic idiom by Walpole and his circle in their art historiography, letters, and literature. Walpole's circle developed a complex range of ideas around the Gothic, implicating religion, history, and aesthetics. Walpole's Gothic amounted to a reversal of some of the emotional and sensory values of early Georgian aesthetics advocated by Joseph Addison, Lord Shaftesbury, and others. Countering the essentially masculine and paternalistic mode of disinterested contemplation, Walpole's Gothic suggested a new emotional engagement with art and architecture and an inherently subjective interpretation of it. This subjectivity opened one venue for the homoerotic interpretation of art and architecture. The second chapter considers Walpole's villa at Strawberry Hill itself and its idiomatic style of Strawberry Hill Gothic. Walpole and his friends understood the house to represent "a court of Gothic taste": it was the physical manifestation of decades of shared endeavor between these men and the architectural signification of their union. Its style had a premise no less radical: theorized by Walpole as a style of licentiousness, Strawberry Hill Gothic positioned itself at an ironic distance from the medieval models it emulated. Strawberry Hill not only established a significant template for the Gothic house in the eighteenth century but also proposed a new mode of queer living and being (a theme developed in subsequent chapters). The third chapter explores the famous collections at Strawberry Hill and their strategies for display. I focus in particular on images and objects that articulated the familial bonds that Walpole and his circle shared. The villa's interiors offered new strategies in articulating alternate families, through, for example, the juxtaposition of portraiture of biological and queer families and the display of gifts and collaborations between these men. The final chapters explore the emulation of Strawberry Hill in the art and architectural patronage of Walpole's circle, beginning with an extended account of the little-known villa at Old Windsor owned by Dicky Bateman. Old Windsor was expanded in the Strawberry Hill Gothic mode in the later 1750s and 1760s by Walpole's own designers, and like Strawberry Hill, it became a cause célèbre for many aristocratic Londoners. The final chapter discusses emulations of Strawberry Hill at the Vyne in Hampshire, under the patronage of John Chute; at Donnington Grove (designed by Chute), for James Pettit Andrews; and at Lee Priory in Kent, for Thomas Barrett. I conclude by considering the relationship of architecture and sexuality around 1800 and the demise of the Strawberry Hill Gothic style.

1 The New Medievalism

CONSTRUCTING THE GOTHIC IN THE CIRCLE OF HORACE WALPOLE

The Path that leads to yonder shattr'd Pile
Is now perplex'd with many a sordid Brier:
No Crowd is seen within the Sacred Isle,
The Sabbath mourns its long-deserted Quire.

—Edward Jerningham, "An Elegy Written Among the Ruins of an Abbey," 1765

Nostalgia is simply not capacious enough a word to name the source of this sensation, this homesickness for things. What we momentarily encounter there is the living, pulsating afterlife of the past.

—Michael Ann Holly, *The Melancholy Art*

Although Strawberry Hill and the other buildings considered in this study are the most tangible manifestations of the medievalism of Horace Walpole's circle, these men were also actively involved in the promotion and mythologization of the Gothic in their letters, literature, poetry, and art criticism contemporary with their construction and decoration. Around 1747, when Walpole began work at Strawberry Hill, there were no significant published accounts that praised the Gothic in architectural writing, much less a coherent theory of the Gothic as an architectural style, and no established tradition of "Gothic" fiction. These would be key productions of Walpole's oeuvre, and collectively they would constitute a profoundly new conception of the Gothic during the second half of the eighteenth century. Walpole's writings on the Gothic spanned multiple genres, from literature to art writing to letters. His medievalist fantasy *The Castle of Otranto: A Gothic Story* (1764/65), originally published as a translation of a medieval text (before Walpole, in its second edition, of 1765, 'fessed up to writing it), is set in a fictive structure based loosely upon Strawberry Hill. His *Mysterious Mother* (1768) would stage another medievalist fantasy in late medieval Narbonne. Walpole's remarkable chapter "State of Architecture to the End of the Reign of Henry VIII" in his *Anecdotes on Painting* (1762) provides his fullest historical-theoretical account of the Gothic as an architectural style, albeit one located within a monumental account of the history of painting. He did entertain writing a separate history of Gothic architecture, but this was never realized.[1] Finally, Walpole's many letters (and occasionally his poetry) provide penetrating, funny, and deeply emotive accounts of Gothic architecture and its owners, patrons, and designers, both medieval and modern. Spread across literary genres, Walpole's writings on the Gothic—and those of his contemporaries—demand synthetic treatment. Walpole felt no conflict in exploring and mythologizing a broad historical idiom across these different literary genres—none of which had formalized into our present academic disciplines—and we should guide our studies accordingly.

Horace Walpole was the most prolific commentator on the Gothic within his circle (what has been called "the antiquarian School of Walpole"),[2] but his was only the loudest and most loquacious voice. The medievalists in his circle approached the Gothic in their writings (when they approached it at all) in various ways and from various perspectives, not all of which were consistent with Walpole's, even if they shared common features. Thomas Gray's scholarship advanced some of the earliest style-based taxonomies of medieval architecture that differentiated styles (i.e., Norman, Gothic, etc.) on the basis of a chronological sequence of ornament. Gray's biographer confirms that "he did not so much depend upon written accounts, as that internal evidence which the buildings themselves give of their respective antiquity" (1775).[3] In this, he stood with some contemporaneous antiquaries who attempted to create a chronological stylistic sequence of medieval architecture (Gray's "Architectura Gothica," which, despite its title, was an early formal description of the Norman, or "Romanesque," style in England, was published posthumously in 1814 by Thomas Mathias).[4] Gray anticipated the increasingly formalist approaches to the study of medieval architecture typical of the late years of the century, including Francis Grose's 1772 essay on Gothic architecture, which provided a critical review of the "Saracenic Theory" of the Gothic.[5]

Sophisticated and rigorous though Gray's approach was, Walpole had little time for what he took to be a form of academic and formalist pedantry. In his *Anecdotes* he could quip, "It was difficult to ascertain the period when one ungracious form jostled out another," a jab that Gray understood was directed toward him and his methods.[6] But Thomas Gray was an antiquary and academic, not a patron or a man of fashion. John Chute and Dicky Bateman were connoisseurs and fashionable men of taste who wrote nothing scholarly on the Gothic or on art and architecture, as far as we now know, but their aesthetic preferences can nevertheless be ascertained from their drawings, letters, patronage, and collecting practices. James Pettit Andrews and Thomas Barrett were both antiquaries and authors, although neither wrote extensively on the Gothic. Andrews nonetheless followed Walpole's lead in commissioning John Chute to design and build Donnington Grove and in patronizing poems set in Donnington, a creative rethinking of the paradigm established by *The Castle of Otranto*, in which real architecture served as the mythical setting of medievalist literature (discussed in chapter 5). Walpole's circle also included medievalists such as Rev. William Cole (1714–1782), from Eton, a leading antiquary and collector (in an unusually deferent episode, Walpole would claim to be Cole's "disciple in antiquities").[7] Cole advised Walpole on his designs for Strawberry Hill (e.g., on the garden gates, built by James Essex and designed by Cole after the model of the tomb of Bishop William de Luda [d. 1298] at Ely Cathedral),[8] and he created his own elegant Gothic garden pavilion at his home in Bletchley and a small but significant Gothic home in Milton, Cambridgeshire, which included paneling from local buildings and, in the newly formed Gothic windows, stained glass taken from various Cambridge colleges.[9] Thomas Warton (1728–1790), a friend and correspondent of Walpole's, was professor of poetry at the University of Oxford and made significant contributions to the scholarship on medieval art and literature, including a separate history of Gothic architecture.[10] Warton was also a patron of the new Gothic style in his London home, based upon Walpole's influential model.[11]

As proponents, and on certain occasions theorists, of Gothic architecture, Walpole and his circle inherited little more on the subject than a handful of denigrating references in neoclassical texts based ultimately in the wisdom of Vitruvius and Giorgio Vasari. In England, John Evelyn (1620–1706) and Ephraim Chambers (1680–1740) followed the Renaissance myth that the Gothic was the style of barbarian invaders who destroyed the architecture of antiquity and replaced it with a debased style of building, while Christopher Wren (1632–1723) was the first Englishman to argue for the "Saracenic" origins of the Gothic during the Crusades (in *Parentalia*, published posthumously in 1750, to which Walpole subscribed).[12] To the writings by these worthies could be added a new popular discourse on architecture in the press, such as James Ralph's *Critical Review of the Publick Buildings* (1733–34), which pitted the Gothic against Burlingtonian classicism, the author's preferred mode.[13] The medievalist scholarship of Walpole and his circle engaged in the Georgian period's debate between classicists and medievalists, in which discourses on architecture as much as literature were couched in oppositional terms.[14] Inverting a long-standing tradition that vilified the aesthetic values of the Gothic in comparison to the dominant classical, Walpole's circle positioned themselves as aesthetic others, fashionable contrarians in a rapidly developing Georgian culture.

Although a handful of pattern-book authors, such as William Halfpenny, Charles Over, and Batty Langley, had popularized Gothic designs for English audiences in the years leading up to and including Walpole's work (fig. 7), none offered anything like a theory for, much less a history of, the style.[15] Their designs were employed

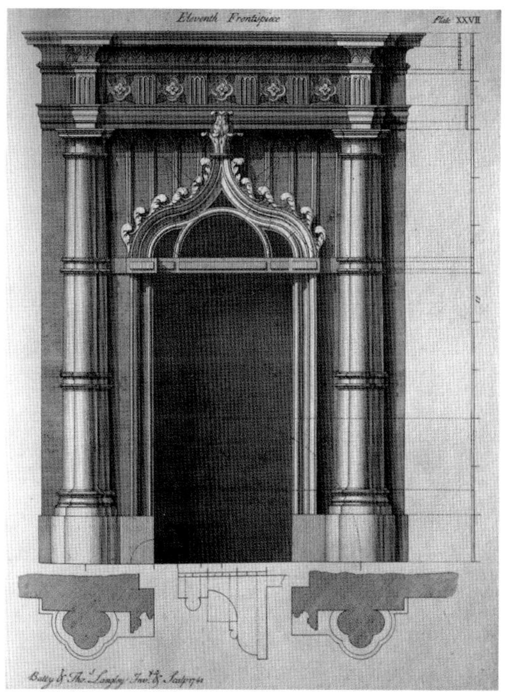

Fig. 7 Batty Langley, "Eleventh Frontispiece." From *Ancient Architecture* (1741–42), plate 27. Photo: author.

in a long list of contemporary buildings.[16] Around 1750 Walpole, Chute, and others within Walpole's circle employed aspects of Langley's designs at Strawberry Hill and probably also at Old Windsor, but by the mid to late 1750s they would be denigrating these sources and other related pattern books.[17] In 1755 Walpole lamented to Richard Bentley that Latimers, Buckinghamshire, had "undergone Batty Langley-discipline: half the ornaments are of his bastard Gothic, and half of Hallet's mongrel Chinese." Anticipating the critiques of A. W. N. Pugin (1812–1852) on the commodification and tasteless mixing of architectural ornament of various historical periods, he states, "I want to write over the doors of most modern edifices, *Repaired and beautified, Langley and Hallet, churchwardens*."[18] Elsewhere, in expressing his fondness for "the true Gothic *un-Gibbs'd*" (italics Walpole's), Walpole cattily laments what he considers the destructive nature of James Gibbs's Gothic work.[19] It is emblematic of Walpole's acerbic and frequently obfuscatory commentary on his rivals that he neither acknowledges his own competition with Langley nor his connection to Latimers as the former home of his much-loved cousin Henry Seymour Conway. Self-contradiction, revision, and simple contrariness are evident in many of Walpole's writings on art. He understood this to be his purview as an elite man of taste, an approach that decisively separated him from the increasingly positivist methods of gentlemen antiquaries and jobbing draughtsmen and designers in the period. As Lawrence Lipking has cogently stated, Walpole's "devotion to facts is always at the mercy of his fascination with style. . . . Walpole mixes a unique blend of high fashion and history. Nowhere is this blend more characteristic or more peculiar than in his discussion of Gothic style."[20]

Walpole's Gothic productions were not, of course, created in a vacuum: around the same time that his *Anecdotes of Painting* (1762) appeared, significant accounts of medieval style and form—for example, Richard Hurd's *Letters on Chivalry and Romance* (1762) and Warton's *Observations on the Faerie Queene* (1762), which included an extended discussion of Gothic architecture—appeared as part of a broader movement to reform British antiquarian research, a movement that also counted among its exemplars works by Richard Gough, the Society of Dilettanti, and others.[21] Warton's own observations followed earlier—albeit visual—meditations on the medievalism of Spenser's poem, namely, William Kent's posthumous drawings for the edition published in 1751, which betray their execution a decade or more previously (fig. 8).[22] But unlike Hurd and Warton, and unlike many Gothicists who would follow him, such as John Carter, A. W. N. Pugin, and the Cambridge Camden Society, Walpole did not have an abiding interest in the specifically English nature of Gothic architecture, and he never attempted literally to revive the medieval practice of chivalry.[23] Walpole's approach to the Middle Ages in his Gothic works was double-edged. On the one hand, he often expressed a deep longing for the aesthetic and religious environments of the Middle Ages (particularly in his letters), while on the other, his medievalisms suggest a critical, parodic, and subversive detachment by which he employed the Middle Ages as a space to critique contemporary culture (notably in *The Castle of Otranto*). This is one of the internal contradictions in Walpole's medievalism, and it is arguably a contradiction that stands at the core of all Gothic revivals: the inability to live in and with the past.

Of course, Walpole's construction of the Gothic was not focused on sexuality, even if this is one of its imbrications of meaning and one of the contexts in which it was imagined and explored. Walpole and his

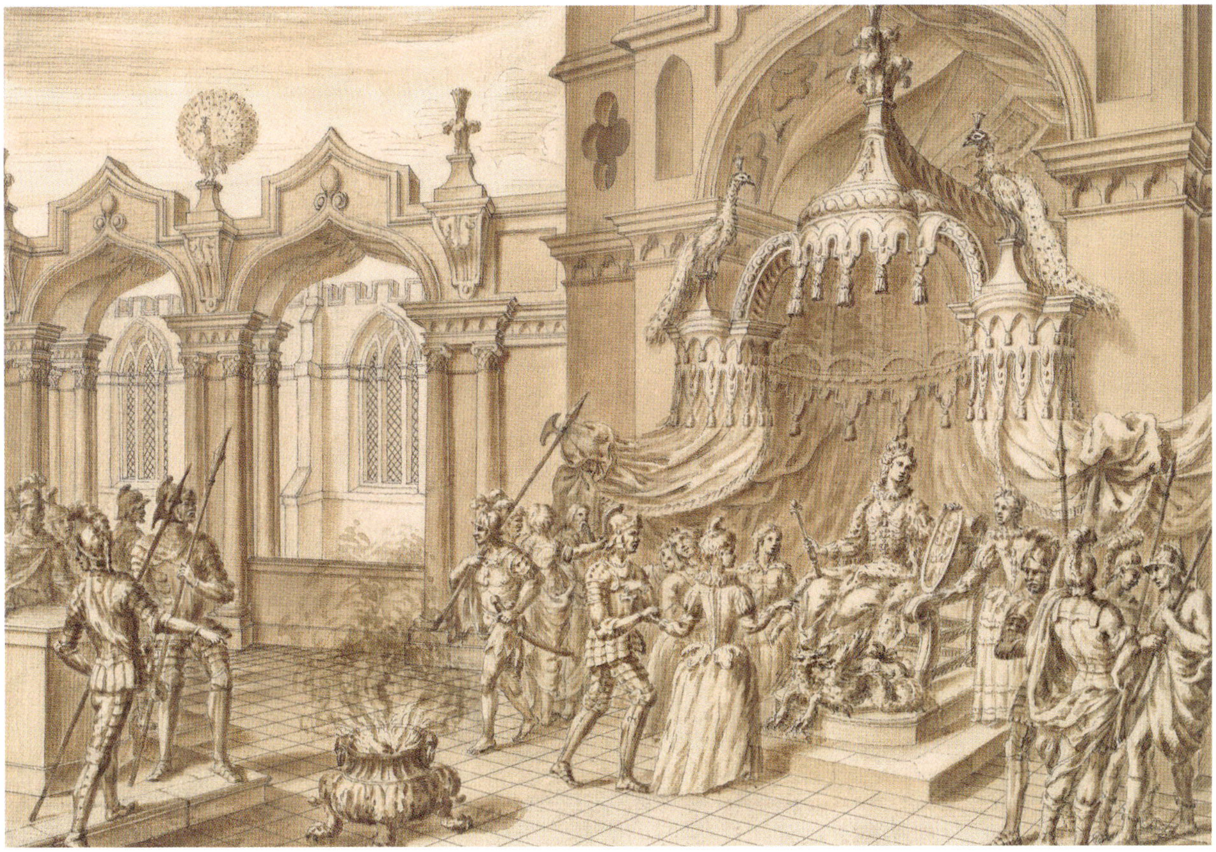

Fig. 8 William Kent, "The Redcross Knight Introduced by Duessa to the House of Pride." Illustration for Edmund Spenser's *Faerie Queene*, 1729–48. Museum no. E.876-1928. Photo © Victoria and Albert Museum, London.

circle manifestly understood the multiple possible "sexualities" of architecture and the gendering of ornament as masculine, feminine, or other genders, but they never articulated a specific relationship between architecture or the decorative arts and the new third sex (although others did). What does emerge strongly is the status of the Gothic as an idiom shared among these men, an elite coterie bound by common sexual and aesthetic orientations. Emblematically, Walpole could applaud Dicky Bateman for transforming his villa at Old Windsor (using Walpole's friends and designers from the Strawberry Committee) from the flippantly fashionable hybrid Chinese-Gothic mode of the 1730s and 1740s to the Strawberry Hill Gothic mode of the 1750s through 1770s, "the style of the elect," and elsewhere state that the Gothic was "our taste."[24] Here, as elsewhere, Walpole's architectural judgment was patently slanted in favor of the Gothic works of his circle, and he could write with equal lack of objectivity against commissions outside of his circle that rivaled his own. Thomas Barrett's rebuilding of Lee Priory, for example, was "the quintessence of Gothic taste," while Sanderson Miller's extraordinary Belhus was "in Gothic, and very true, though not up to the perfection of the committee."[25] From Walpole's partisan perspective at least, his own Gothic architecture and that of his friends in and beyond the Strawberry Committee were the productions of a gilded coterie who embraced a "perfect" and stylistically "chaste" Gothic that trumped the "imperfect" Gothic works of architects such as Sanderson Miller or William Kent.

It was, of course, inconceivable within the historiographical traditions and social/sexual climate of the eighteenth century to discuss the relationship of Gothic architecture and alternative sexuality from a noncritical perspective, and frankly, the language to do so barely existed. Yet in discussing the promotion of the Gothic by Walpole and his circle, we might follow Whitney Davis in arguing that, from its origins, art history was written from the closet, or even *as* a closet.[26] That is, while written often by homoerotically inclined authors, including Joachim Winckelmann, Baron von Stosch, Richard Payne Knight, Horace Walpole, and others, the specifically homoerotic judgments of the authors were erased from their writings or sterilized, or they were obscured behind multifaceted euphemisms. Therefore, rather than unproductively discuss the Gothic's "queerness," as has been done often enough, I prefer to shift perspective here and consider how the Gothic as an alternative mode may have appealed to the new homoerotic subjectivities of the eighteenth century. It would require another study altogether to explore all of the writings of these men on the Gothic, so I will focus instead on the common tropes of aesthetic attachment, political liberty, and religion that run through them.

Gothic Aesthetics

Walpole's circle's construction of the Gothic took place within the flourishing of writing on art and aesthetics in England characterized by the works of Joseph Addison, Lord Shaftesbury, Lord Burlington, Joshua Reynolds, and others who articulated the values of classicism for the British public. Pursuing a radically different trajectory, Walpole's circle consistently advanced the concept that the Gothic not only was formally divergent from classicism but was wed to a different mode of aesthetic perception. This placed it at odds with the dominant discourse in England, which aimed to establish normative conventions for art and architecture through discourses on proper "taste," a defining feature of eighteenth-century art and aesthetics.[27] In these texts, proper taste is broadly consonant with the aesthetics of neoclassicism. This discourse advocated a removal of individual subjectivity—of one's desire and libidinal or sensory attraction for objects or images—from aesthetic judgment to create a form of disinterestedness in which beauty is judged according to universal and objective rules. In Elizabeth Bohls's words, the rise of disinterested contemplation "constructs the aesthetic subject through a process of exclusion: disinterested contemplation, or the aesthetic attitude, is a special mode of attention defined as excluding any practical stake in the existence of the object."[28] Focusing on formal purity over material particularity, advancing harmony and symmetry of form over "disorder," disinterestedness denies self-interest in favor of a broader aesthetic order. Taste for correct, classically inspired art leads to the advancement of morality, proper comportment, and ultimately the establishment of the British Empire. The forging of this paradigm of perception—with its cognates in political philosophy and the discourse on civic humanism—becomes a "cultural means toward the ultimately political end of homogeneity and solidarity among England's governing classes."[29]

The responses to Gothic art and architecture within Walpole's circle were couched within a nascent eighteenth-century cult of sensibility defined by the "man of feeling."[30] Overturning the established view of disinterestedness, Walpole's theory on the Gothic advocated something close to the opposite: for Walpole, the Gothic was an art that, inherently perhaps, drew deeply emotional aesthetic responses from the viewer. From his *Anecdotes on Painting*, consider two antitheses between the Gothic and classicism that polarize the values of the two styles:

> It is difficult for the noblest Grecian temple to convey half so many impressions to the mind, as a cathedral does of the best Gothic taste. . . . The latter exhausted . . . knowledge of the passions in composing edifices whose pomp, mechanism, vaults, tombs, painted windows, gloom and perspectives infused such sensations of romantic devotion. . . . One must have taste to be sensible of the beauties of Grecian architecture; one only wants passions to feel Gothic. In St. Peter's one is convinced that it was built by great princes—in Westminster-abbey, one thinks not of the builder; the religion of the place makes the first impression—and though stripped of [its] altars and shrines, it is nearer converting one to popery than all the regular pageantry of Roman domes. Gothic churches infuse superstition; Grecian, admiration.[31]

Passages like this do an enormous amount of cultural work. Walpole's Gothic is positioned to appeal to the viewer's emotional, rather than intellectual, faculties. Walpole asserts that "passion" of an undefined nature, rather than the socially constructed notion of "taste" ("superstition" rather than "admiration"), is the requisite condition to appreciate the Gothic. Its appeal is framed in terms of ecstatic religious response; it is mystical, irrational, somatic. Apparently capable of converting the viewer to Catholicism, or "popery," the Gothic appeals to what was understood in the period as an alternate, illicit, and eroticized religious subjectivity. Walpole's source in this passage is Joseph Addison's *Spectator* essays and his *Remarks on Several Parts of Italy*.[32] Countering and parodying Addison's treasured formulations of aesthetic judgment, which denied the particular, the subjective, and, by extension, the erotic, Walpole's Gothic has a prescriptive force, aiming to rebut established tenets of contemporary culture. In architecture and in literature, Walpole considered the Gothic to be an antidote to the constraints of modern life—to "a strict adherence to common life," as he calls it—thus suggesting a reattachment of a viewer's aesthetic subjectivity to his emotive and erotic subjectivity.[33] Glossing these ideas elsewhere in his writing, Walpole could compare the Gothic and classicism to modes of written expression: "A Gothic cathedral strikes one like the enthusiasm of poetry; St. Paul's, like the good sense of prose."[34] "Enthusiasm," or subjectivity, is consistently positioned above the socially constructed and inherently objective "good sense" in Walpole's aesthetics.

Within the aesthetic tradition in which the Gothic was revived, not only were the Gothic and the modern styles understood to be in "bad taste," but they were frequently elided with a range of social ills consonant with or the products of modernity: effeminacy, luxury, the dissolution of conventional social and sexual categories, the rise of a mercantile nouveau riche middle class and the decline of an established aristocratic order, and the vulgar new commodities in the modern styles flooding (or polluting) the metropolis, which appealed to "the crude gratification of the appetites," to the body rather than the mind.[35] Focusing on tastes for the Gothic as an ornamental architecture, Alexander Gerard's *Essay on Taste* of 1759 typifies a dominant strand of this critique: "The profusion of ornament bestowed on the *parts*, in *Gothic* structures, may please one who has not acquired enlargement of the mind sufficient for conceiving at one view their relation to the *whole*; but no sooner is this acquired, than he perceives superior elegance in the more *simple* symmetry and proportion of *Grecian* architecture. . . . Where refinement is wanting, taste must be coarse and vulgar."[36] For Gerard and others, tastes for the modern styles, and for the Gothic in particular, are products of an arrested development, a juvenile aesthetic imagination defined by its fascination for the glossy, the ornamental, and the disordered. The modern villas that are the subjects of this study were regular targets of this critique: John Gilbert Cooper, for example, lamented "the splendid Impertinence, the unmeaning Glitter, the tasteless Profusion and monstrous Enormities" of London's suburban villas, a critique that elides a perceived aesthetic degeneracy with social degeneracy (or "corruption").[37] For critics such as Gerard and Cooper, these tastes were associated with femininity or effeminacy, since both women and effeminate males (the argument follows) possessed juvenile imaginations incapable of transcending the particular for the abstract in the tradition of disinterestedness and as such were attracted to the richly ornamented surfaces of the modern styles. Antiquarianism was likewise understood to be an "odd" practice that potentially signified an underdeveloped or deviant sexual and aesthetic subjectivity beneath a veneer of disinterested contemplation.[38] This argument was grounded in current physiology according to which all humans were born into one effeminized sex, which only at puberty became fully differentiated, or not, in the case of effeminate males.[39] This appraisal of sexual-aesthetic *aisthesis* would be most forcefully stated in Sigmund Freud's account of "homosexuality," which was likewise premised on same-sex eroticism resulting from arrested psychological development, but it had its roots in Georgian England, and in the debates about the modern styles in particular.

Ever the contrarian, Walpole turned this critical tradition on its head. In his *Anecdotes* he describes the Gothic as a new "species of modern elegance"—characterized as "genteel," and with "grace" and "refinement"—thus associating the style with the mores of urban modernity.[40] Walpole could grandly describe the Gothic and Chinoiserie in a letter of 1750 to Horace Mann as emblems of the new "liberty of taste" of modern England in opposition to the restrained (and *con*strained) classical tastes of Italy. Here the ability to choose something that is inherently preferable to an individual's sensibilities or tastes, to assert one's alterity through object choice outside of established convention, becomes a key feature of modernity itself. Modernity creates the appropriate social and aesthetic contexts for the Gothic to be revived and relived, thus uncannily bending the arc of time and joining two phases of history. Most troubling to its critics, the revival of the Gothic confronted the Enlightenment idea of historical progress, and it signaled something deeply disruptive to the conception of an "enlightened" present.[41] Creating a "liberty of taste," modernity offers the possibility of new, alternative modes of architecture and of aesthetic experience, with imbrications of meaning that extend to other modes of being, including sexuality. In Walpole's aesthetics, the Gothic becomes a medium or signifier of social change in itself.

Although the emotive and transcendental ends of their aesthetics were different, Walpole, Addison, and many of their contemporaries interpreted art within the context of contemporary associationism. In this paradigm, a work of art unfolded a range of associations in a viewer's mind to enable him or her to "be" in the historical context of a historicist work of art, whether the edificatory and philosophical context of Athens or the gloomy, superstitious space of the Gothic church or castle. Consider Walpole's sensual response to Hampton Court, partly remodeled in the Gothic style by William Kent:[42] "It was moonlight and late, and very hot, and the lofty façade of the palace, and the trimmed yews and canal, made me fancy myself of a party in Grammont's time—so you don't wonder that by the help of imagination I never passed an evening more deliciously. When by the aid of some historic vision and local circumstance I can romance myself into pleasure, I know nothing transports me so much."[43] Walpole alludes to the Gothic's apparent power to convert and persuade, quite literally to seduce the viewer. Eroticism of a sort is seldom far from the surface of Walpole's responses to Gothic architecture, and it would also inform his other "architectural" writings (including his *Castle of Otranto*). Writing to the Cambridge antiquary William Cole in 1777, Walpole offers a visceral response to King's College Chapel, Cambridge: "the beauty of King's College Chapel, now it is restored, penetrated me with a visionary longing to be a monk in it," a fantasy that distorts King's into a monastic, rather than collegiate, foundation (fig. 9).[44] Associationism thus offered the possibility of deeply subjective responses to works of art—of employing the work as a catalyst of wish fulfillment—based upon an individual's personal orientations. Walpole's appreciation of the medieval past cannot be readily understood outside of his broader erotic and emotive subjectivity: on the contrary, Walpole's construction of the Gothic was an extension of it.

It is neither accurate nor valuable to reduce modes of aesthetic response to modes of sexual attraction or vice versa, particularly during the eighteenth century, which witnessed the development of complex discourses around masculinity and aesthetic judgment that could be, but were not necessarily, homoerotic in orientation. The emotional reactions to art and architecture recorded by Walpole and his circle nevertheless suggest an alternate "aesthetic attitude," or "sensibility," that opposed the dominant mode of masculine perception embraced by the ruling classes, itself a form of political unconscious within England's elite culture. Shared forms of aesthetic judgment became a defining feature of communities in Georgian England. If, as Bohls demonstrates, women were excluded from what became an established, elite mode of aesthetic judgment for English males, there is good reason to extend this critique to men of the third sex.[45] Walpole's letters richly describe his and his friends' emotional and frequently "camp" responses to Gothic art and architecture. George Montagu, for example, when Walpole took him to Strawberry Hill in 1754, "was in raptures, and screamed, and whooped, and hollaed, and danced, and crossed himself a thousand times over," thereby blending his own approbation with a mock religious sanctity.[46] Timothy Mowl may use contemporary terminology anachronistically to describe such responses as those of a "screaming queen," but this does not mean that, terminology aside, he is far from the mark.[47] Walpole's emotional reactions certainly could and did register as "feminine" and were subsumed or rationalized within a larger critique of the effeminization of English males in the period. A long list of satiric characters was

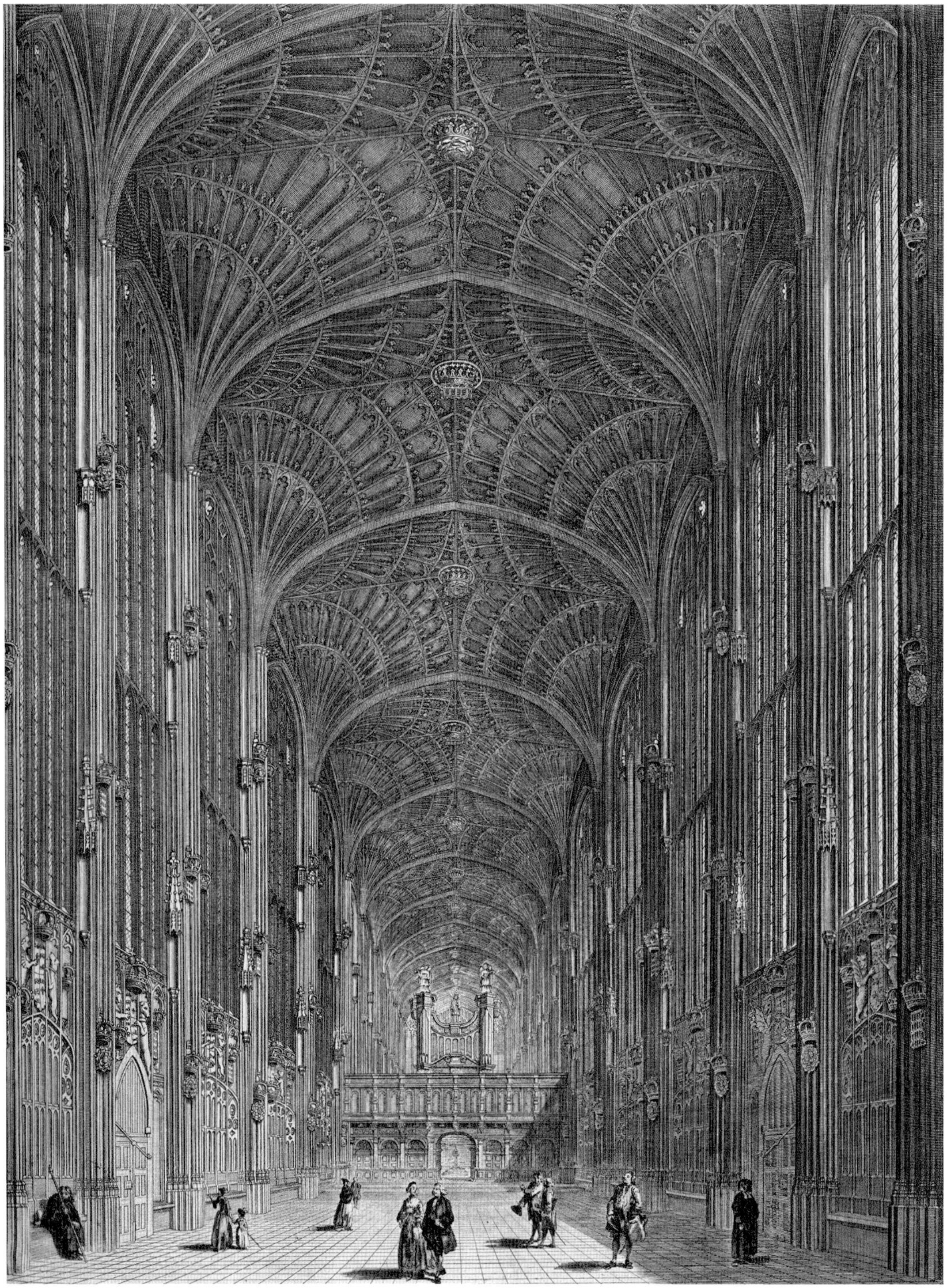

Fig. 9 Canaletto, *Interior of King's College Chapel, Cambridge*, 1746–55. This image hung in the Blue Bedchamber. LWL 30 30 Copy 4 Folio, p. 24. Courtesy of The Lewis Walpole Library, Yale University.

developed in the eighteenth century to articulate an association between homosexuality, effeminacy, and emotional engagement with art and architecture. Tropes such as these—exaggerations though they were—point to the possibility that Walpole's *interestedness* formed part of what was understood by many as a queer approach to art and architecture.

It is not a coincidence that the disinterested contemplation advocated by Addison, Shaftesbury, and others emerged contemporaneously with the onset of the modern styles and the third sex. As such, it became "an alternative site for a harmony perceived to be slipping away in other areas of life."[48] I favor the view that the third sex and the Gothic are manifestations of a fundamental change in the aesthetic-sexual formation of eighteenth-century culture consonant with what is now called "modernity." Although it has rarely been acknowledged, the exclusion of women, femininity, and effeminacy from the dominant construction of aesthetic-sexual norms also extended to the third sex (or they were *configured* to exclude the third sex). By extension, it is also not a coincidence that an oppositional queer sensibility developed alongside but in opposition to a masculine mode of aesthetic perception in these very years.

Gothic Liberty

Central to Walpole's construction of the Gothic was his conception of it as a style of aesthetic liberty and creative freedom and that its revival was made possible by the new "liberty of taste" in the Georgian present. Walpole's celebration of the apparent "lawlessness" of the Gothic and its exemplification of artistic and social freedom invigorated a central trope in the historiography of Gothic architecture that would be explored by A. W. N. Pugin, John Ruskin, William Morris, Walter Crane, and others and would eventually feature in twentieth-century scholarship on medieval art, which framed the Gothic period as a time of social and artistic freedom in which the artist was unencumbered by either political or social control.[49] His chapter "State of Architecture to the End of the Reign of Henry VIII" provides an outline of this theory, much of which is qualified and expanded in his letters, poetry, and art patronage. While most of *Anecdotes* was based upon George Vertue's original notebooks, which Walpole acquired, this chapter was his own invention. He drew his evidence from extant antiquarian publications and from his friends, such as Thomas Gray, to provide the first integrated political-aesthetic history of the Gothic in English.[50] In writing it, Walpole denigrated what he took to be a pedantic obsession with origins and taxonomies of form and their related nationalist discourses (e.g., the question whether the pointed arch originated in England, France, Spain, or elsewhere).[51] He nevertheless understood a chronological system in which "Saxon" (i.e., Romanesque) architecture, which descended from the architecture of Roman antiquity, was a clumsy and inelegant prequel to the Gothic, its forms and ornamentation "all evidences of barbarous and ignorant times."[52] As Walpole would explain in a letter to Cole, his system of architectural development began "with the round Roman arch" and went on to show "how they plastered and zig-zagged it, and then how better ornaments crept in, till the beautiful Gothic arrived at its perfection; then how it deceased in Henry the Eighth's reign."[53]

Walpole's vision of the Gothic style has little in common with that employed in later art history, which may justify a lack of serious attention paid to it by medievalists. For Walpole, Gray, and others, the Gothic properly began in the reign of Henry III (1216–72), due both to Henry's establishment of a royal center at Westminster and his father's signing of Magna Carta (1215). Walpole's dismissal of what would subsequently be understood as "Early English Gothic" architecture circa 1170–1250 may have had as much to do with his political appraisal of the period as it did with the blending of antique and Gothic prevalent forms in it.[54] The Gothic reached its "perfection" in the interval from the reign of Henry IV (1367–1413) through 1507, the date of the tomb of Archbishop Warham at Canterbury (what Walpole called "the last example of unbastardized Gothic").[55] Its perfection was achieved by the creation of "singular" essays in aesthetic freedom; King's College Chapel, Cambridge (1446–1515), in particular was praised as "a bird of paradise," which was "above all rules," a "bold and unique [essay] that resemble[s] nothing else" (fig. 9).[56] During the reign of Henry VIII (1509–47) the style began to decline, and it eventually terminated in the reign of James I (1603–25).[57] As such, Gothic architecture, as he understood it, was consistent with what Thomas Rickman in 1817 would call the Decorated and Perpendicular styles of the later thirteenth through sixteenth centuries.[58] Walpole not only understood the Gothic as an "improvement" upon the classical (and cited the pointed arch as an improvement on the round-headed arch), but he implicitly argued for a development of Gothic form culminating in the great Perpendicular buildings of royal authority, notably King's College Chapel at Cambridge and Henry VII's chapel, Westminster. The Gothic declines toward the end of the reign of Henry VIII due to two related developments: the importation of Italian artists into England during Henry's reign and their importation of "Grecian," or antique-derived, forms in architecture. Thereafter, the two architectural systems became corrupted and produced a "mongrel species" of architecture blending antique and Gothic forms.

Typical of the political contours of Walpole's historiography, artistic style is a reflection of the political character of its period, leading to an integrated, moral reading of the history of art.[59] Walpole broadly understood the Glorious Revolution of 1688 and the rise of the Whig party to signal a return to political and artistic freedom that allowed for the revival of Gothic architecture and other arts, such as landscape gardening. Art followed parliamentary principle: for Walpole, creative freedom (and thus the free play of subjectivities) was possible only when "a good government . . . indulges its subjects in the exercise of their own thoughts . . . refinements will follow and much pleasure and satisfaction will be produced."[60] Walpole's understanding of Gothic freedom, or "liberty," was rooted in an established tradition that located the freedom of Britons from monarchical absolutism in the "ancient Gothic constitution" of the Saxons, which was confirmed in the signing of Magna Carta.[61] The Gothic constitution was central to seventeenth- and eighteenth-century political debate: at its core was the myth of the Goths, who sacked Rome and populated England as the hearty, free people of the North (based on a reading of Tacitus).[62] Their constitution, as much as their Northern climate, endowed the Goths with mental vigor, physical hardiness, political liberty, and freedom from oppression, all of which contrasted with the politics and climate of the South (i.e., the Romans), whose supine laziness made them susceptible to overlordship by despots. Walpole was to emphasize this association through display of a copy of Magna Carta and the death warrant of Charles

I (1649) on either side of his bed at Strawberry Hill; he would be followed by Dicky Bateman, who painted the shields of the baronial signatories of Magna Carta on his staircase at Old Windsor, and also by William Beckford, who likewise referenced Magna Carta in his Gothic interiors at Fonthill Abbey, in a planned "Baronial Hall" that bore all the shields of the barons.[63] Son of the Whig prime minister, Walpole considered the current Whig administration (of which he was a peripheral member) to be the inheritors and champions of a medieval tradition of "Gothic liberty," and he famously called himself the "only unadulterated Whig left in England."[64]

As Walpole knew well, these ideas flourished in the 1730s and 1740s. Gilbert West's poem *The Institution of the Order of the Garter*, for example, makes the connection between architecture and politics explicit: "Complete the noble Gothick pile / That on the rock of Justice rear'd shall stand / In symmetry, and strength, and fame."[65] Lord Lyttelton's 1735 *Letters from a Persian in England, to His Friend in Ispahan* describes the government of England through the eyes of an outsider, providing an apparently "objective" account of contemporary politics.[66] These letters trace the development of Whig ideals from Saxon times up to a breaking point with the Stuart dynasty. Following the reign of the Stuart kings, the ideals and principles of government were restored in accordance with "ancient Saxon principles."[67] The association of Gothic architecture in the built environment with political freedom had been established in building projects in the years immediately preceding Walpole's acquisition of Strawberry Hill, including William Kent's Merlin's Cave at Richmond (1736) and James Gibbs's Gothic Temple of Liberty at Stowe (1741; fig. 10), which bore the inscription "Je rends grace aux Dieux de nestre pas Romain" (I thank the Gods I am not a Roman).[68] Walpole was well apprised of the political significance of these structures. Recounting a visit to Stowe in a letter to John Chute of 4 August 1753, he exclaims, "The Grecian Temple is glorious: this I openly worship: [but] in the heretical corner of my heart I adore the Gothic building"; and in his unpublished notes he discusses the overt political bent of its imagery.[69]

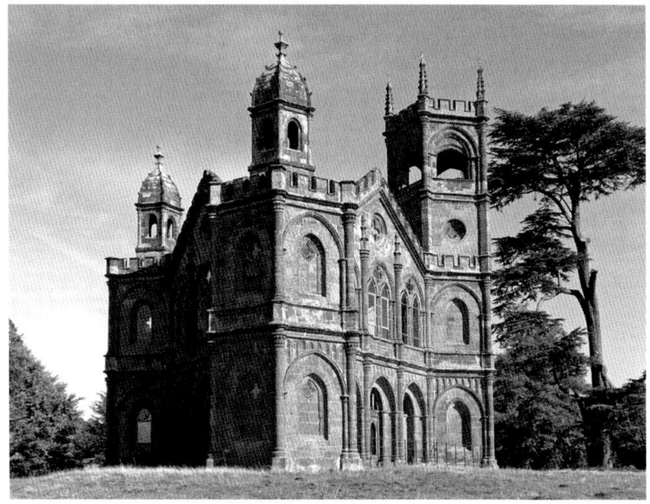

Fig. 10 Temple of Liberty, Stowe. Photo: author.

While this is manifestly the context of Walpole's thought, it is vital to understand that his conception of Gothic liberty was not restricted to, or even centrally about, politics.[70] For Walpole, Gothic liberty signified a broader cognitive condition of creative, aesthetic, and libidinal freedom in the Middle Ages that was revived in the modern present. Transforming this political narrative into Enlightenment art history, Walpole considered the Gothic a period of freedom, elegance, artistic refinement, and ornamental extravagance between two periods of repressive, ascetic classicism: the "Saxon," or Romanesque, and the "Grecian," or neoclassical.[71] This is emphasized in his *Anecdotes*, in what is perhaps the most telling polarization of classicism and the Gothic, when he compares "the rational beauties of regular architecture [i.e., classicism], and the unrestrained licentiousness" of the Gothic (a critique I explore in the next chapter).[72]

Walpole had already developed these ideas in his early writing: his 1738 schoolboy poem "Verses in Memory of King Henry VI, Founder of King's College" explores the idea of classicism as a nullification or destruction of the aesthetic and creative freedom of the Gothic:

> When Henry bad this pompous Temple rise,
> Nor with presumption emulate the skies,
> Art and Palladio had not reached the land,
> Nor methodiz'd the Vandal Builder's hand:
> Wonders, unknown to rule, these piles
> disclose;
> The Walls, as if by inspiration, rose.
> The Edifice, continued by his care,
> With equal pride had form'd the sumptuous
> square.[73]

Walpole frames the advent of classicism in sixteenth-century English architecture as a "reform" of Gothic; Henrician classicism is elided with broader social "reforms," notably the Dissolution of the Monasteries, and the resulting destruction of much of England's Gothic art. "Reform" in Walpole's *Anecdotes* is figured as an oppressive force of traditional morality, which he compares to the physical frigidity of Siberia and the political tyranny of Nero.[74] Walpole employs a similar critique of architectural styles in a 1742 letter to Horace Mann, in which he compares his father's Palladian estate (and Horace's ancestral home) to the frigidity of Siberia.[75] Signaling the end of "true Gothic," a style that he implies is only possible in an environment of religious and social freedom, these reforms gave way to a mixed, or "mongrel," Gothic, which continued until the final death of the style with the Puritan revolution, or English Civil War, of the seventeenth century. These replaced an "Arbiter elegantiarum" with a "Censor morum."[76] Free of moral censorship and the confines of aesthetic regulation, the Gothic becomes the product of a mind free to express its aesthetic and libidinal desires.

Walpole's reference here is significant. His "arbiter elegantiarum" is a well-known Latinism from Tacitus's *Annals* (16.18), in which the author describes the fashionable life of Petronius at the court of Nero:

> He spent his days in sleep, his nights in attending to his official duties or in amusement, that by his dissolute life he had become as famous as other men by a life of energy, and that he was regarded as no ordinary profligate, but as an accomplished voluptuary. His reckless freedom of speech, being regarded as frankness, procured him popularity. . . . Afterwards returning to his life of vicious indulgence, he became one of the chosen circle of Nero's intimates, and was looked upon as an absolute authority on questions of taste (*elegantiae arbiter*) in connection with the science of luxurious living.[77]

Tacitus's portrait of Petronius could hardly better describe Horace Walpole and his own aspirations to be London's *arbiter elegantiarum* of the Gothic. In his letters Walpole's regular references to Petronius as a tastemaker leave little doubt that he considered Petronius a literary ancestor. Here, as elsewhere in Walpole's literary allusions, sexuality is not far from the surface. Petronius penned the outrageous *Satyricon*, a bawdy homoerotic tale that Walpole not only owned but often enough referred to.[78]

What is significant here, however, is that Walpole sees the Gothic period as a period of social and artistic freedom with various imbrications of meaning that extend to morals, manners, and sexuality. Following Walpole's line of thought, the present age of "enlightenment" (or "reform")—signified in architectural terms by the classical or neoclassical—becomes an agent of social control and a model of aesthetic and corporeal repression. Walpole's preference for the "unreformed," libertarian character of the Gothic is decisively manifest in the style of his house and in its notation in his motto (borrowed ultimately from his namesake, the Roman poet Horace, although more recently from his father, Sir Robert Walpole), *Fari quae sentiat* (Say what one feels), which was painted on the library ceiling of Strawberry Hill and featured in his graphic works (fig. 11). Personal liberty of a complex sort was central to Walpole's descriptions of Strawberry Hill. With comic effect and not, perhaps, without double entendre, Walpole writes to Henry Conway in 1755 of his "Gothic spirit" and of "Strawberry Castle, where you know how I love to enjoy my liberty. I give myself the airs, in my nutshell, of an old baron," while also being "Whig to the backbone."[79] Walpole transforms his Gothic mansion into a nutshell and his own liberty into something that is not purely or even principally political. Writing in this context to his much-loved cousin, Walpole does not define precisely what "liberty" means, but he hints at an aesthetic and possibly erotic subtext. The very doubleness of Walpole's perspective on Gothic liberty was sensed by his critics. In his account of Walpole, Thomas Babington Macaulay opines that Walpole's "Whiggism . . . was of a very harmless kind," which he kept "as he kept the old spears and helmets at Strawberry Hill, merely for show."[80] While Macaulay's overtly homophobic critique surely overstates the point to his own rhetorical ends, it does point to an alternate understanding of the trope of the Gothic's "freedom" that extends beyond politics to embrace a wider range of aesthetic, erotic, and emotive states of being.

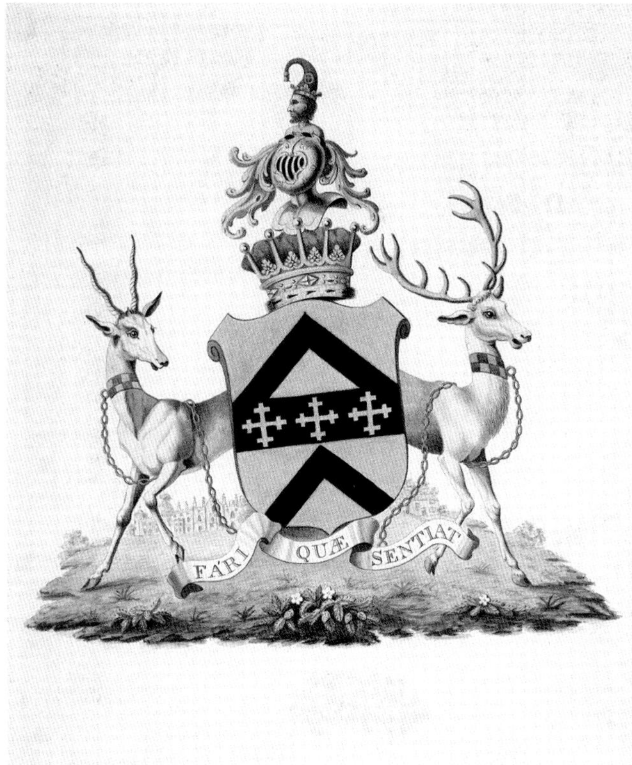

Fig. 11 Walpole arms with stags and the family motto, *Fari quae sentiat*. From Walpole, *Description* (1784; extra-illustrated copy owned by William Bawtree). LWL 30 30 Copy 4 Folio, p. 3. Courtesy of The Lewis Walpole Library, Yale University.

These ideas would be explored by others within Walpole's circle. Thomas Warton developed a division of styles with parallel erotic states of being in his 1782 poem *Verses on Sir Joshua Reynolds's Painted Window at New-College Oxford*. Warton's poem, seemingly praise for Joshua Reynolds's Oxford glazing designs, in fact offers a complex account of the erotic and emotional significations of the Gothic and classicism. Beginning with his love of the Gothic as the "fond illusions of a wayward mind," Warton presents the Gothic as a lover offering "ravished pleasures" from a "treacherous hand," a lover from whom he is forced to part, a projection of an unacceptable and seemingly illicit erotic subjectivity onto the built environment:

> From bliss long felt unwillingly we part:
> Ah, spare the weakness of a lover's heart!
> Chase not the phantoms of my fairy dream,
> Phantoms that shrink at Reason's painful
> gleam!
> That softer touch, insidious artist, stay,
> Nor to new joys my struggling breast betray![81]

Brought back to the "truth" of classicism, whose "powerful hand has broke the Gothic chain, / And brought my bosom back to truth again," Warton, like Walpole, elides the Gothic with an unrestrained sexuality, and classicism with the perceived values of civilization, which are presented here as antitheses. He is enticed from his acceptable, "chaste" love of classicism by the Gothic's "treacherous hand," which does not "spare the weakness of a lover's heart" for "ravished pleasures." Eroticism, and alternative sexuality in particular, was a dominant motif of the Gothic and one that Walpole was instrumental in shaping.[82]

Walpole's elision of political and social or sexual freedom with artistic style has important parallels in contemporary art historiography.[83] In this sense—and in this sense only, perhaps—*Anecdotes* can be compared to Winckelmann's contemporary *History of Ancient Art* (1764), in which "freedom" operates as an elaborate and multifaceted euphemism to describe the values of artistic cultures of Greek antiquity. Alex Potts and Whitney Davis have shown that Winckelmann's *History* coded his own homoerotic *aisthesis* behind or within the history of Greek art, in which freedom served as a perceived model of "social-sexual organization."[84] As Richard Sha has so forcefully argued in his account of romantic aesthetics, political liberty and sexual liberty were closely intertwined concepts for eighteenth-century authors, including Richard Payne Knight, Winckelmann, and, I suggest, Walpole. Sha shows that Georgian authors considered nonreproductive sexuality not only to be a site for exploring freedom from regulation or convention but also, potentially, to have become an allegory for political power itself.[85]

Gothic Catholicism

The construction of the Gothic by Walpole's circle as a historical and modern mode confronted a significant historiographical issue, namely, the Gothic's signification of Catholicism. In England the official end of Catholicism with the Dissolution of the Monasteries (1536–41) established a fundamental break in religious structures, which by many accounts (including Walpole's) extended to its heritage in Gothic architecture. Catholicism and the Gothic shared a temporal location in Walpole's historiography, and both were associated with a form of sensory and libidinal freedom (what he called "visionary enjoyments"), a state of being he felt was diminished by the "extinction" of Catholicism, chivalry, and the Gothic style.[86] For Walpole, a revival of the Gothic meant a return not simply to the forms of later medieval architecture but also to its spiritual and perfomative modes, or at least to a specific conception of them. While Walpole and most in his circle never formally converted to Catholicism, a love of "Popery" and an aesthetic fascination with the glamour and sensory enrichments of the Catholic rite formed part of a broader shared enthusiasm for the Gothic. Typical of this is Walpole's description of the lavish funeral of George II at Westminster Abbey in 1760:

> But the charm was the entrance of the Abbey, where we were received by the Dean and chapter in rich copes, the choir and almsmen all bearing torches; the whole Abbey so illuminated, that one saw it to greater advantage than by the day; the tombs, long aisles, and fretted roof all appearing distinctly, and with the happiest chiaroscuro. There wanted nothing but incense, and little chapels here and there with priests saying mass for the repose of the defunct—yet one could not complain of its not being Catholic enough.[87]

Walpole and his circle actively and playfully explored the Catholic and quasi-religious nature of their Gothic homes. The Strawberry Hill "Oratory" (fig. 12), for example, was a functionless exterior prayer niche with basins for holy water, iron-railed window openings, and a fifteenth-century cast-latten angel.[88] In a letter of 1753 to Horace Mann, Walpole describes his plans for his new "monastery" at Strawberry Hill:

> You say, "you suppose my garden is to be Gothic too." That can't be; Gothic is merely architecture; and as one has a satisfaction in imprinting the gloomth of abbeys and cathedrals on one's house, so one's garden on the contrary is to be nothing but *riant*, and the gaiety of nature. I am greatly impatient for my altar, and so far from mistrusting its goodness, I only fear it will be too good to expose to the weather, as I intend it to be, in a recess in the garden. I was going to tell you that my house is so monastic that I have a little hall decked with long saints in lean arched windows and with taper columns, which we call the Paraclete, in memory of Eloisa's cloister.[89]

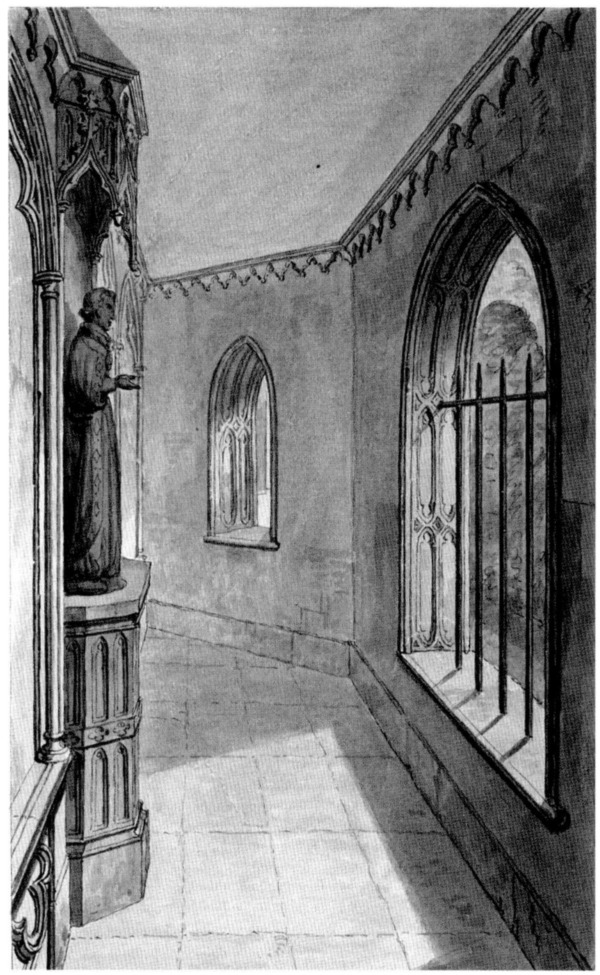

Fig. 12 John Carter, view in the Oratory at Strawberry Hill. LWL 33 30 Copy 11 Folio, p. 29. Courtesy of The Lewis Walpole Library, Yale University.

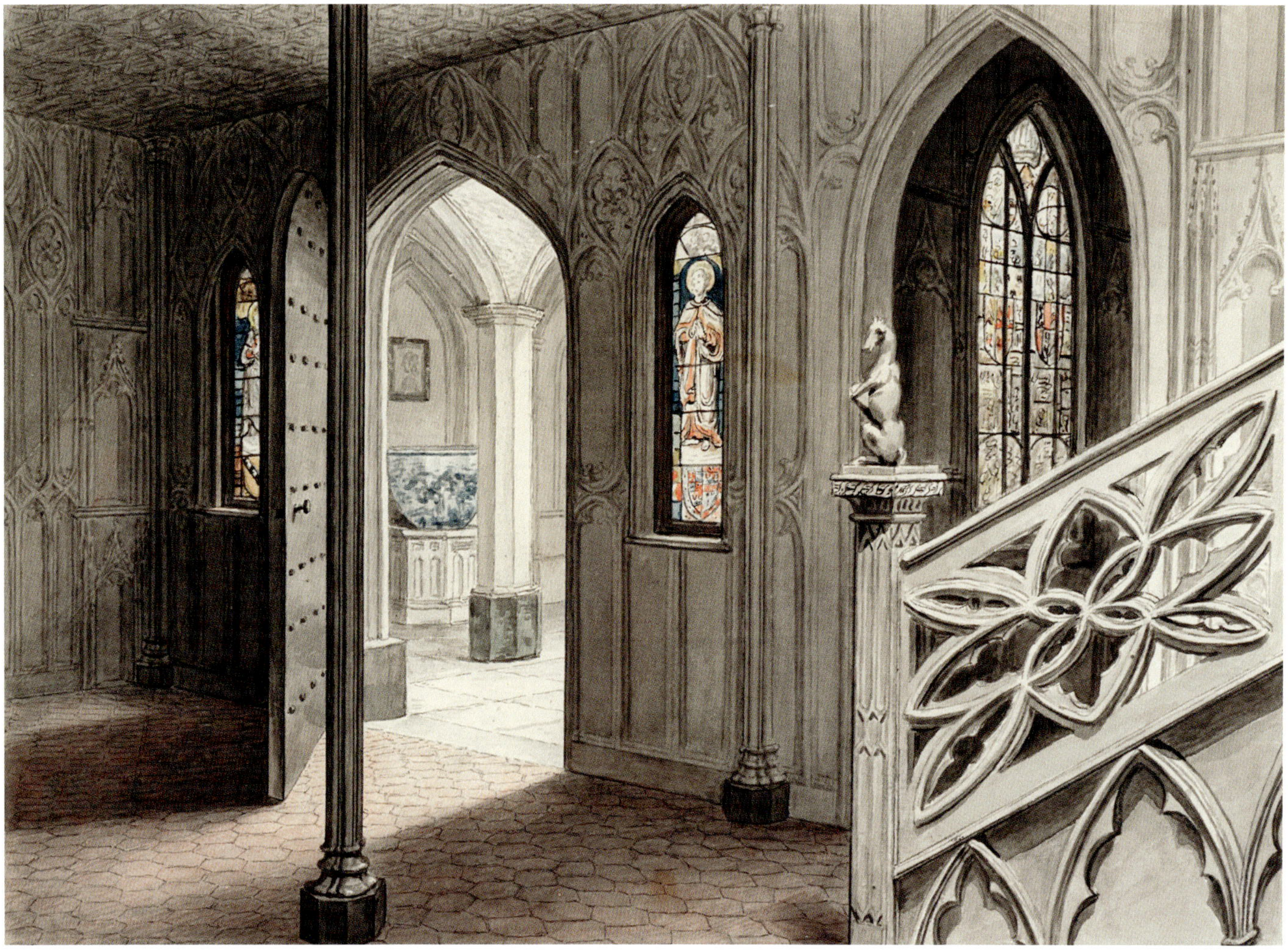

Fig. 13 John Carter, view from the Hall at Strawberry Hill, 1788. LWL Folio 49 3582, p. 24. Courtesy of The Lewis Walpole Library, Yale University.

This letter is typical of the range of religious significations and in-jokes that he and his circle shared, in which Catholicism and its rites, settings, and rituals were subjects of a highly nuanced coterie taste. He concludes with a reference to the Paraclete, or Entrance Hall (fig. 13), the name of which was borrowed from Alexander Pope's *Eloisa to Abelard* of 1717, a canonical medievalizing text that locates an illicit love affair within a medieval monastery, offering what Paul Baines has called the "infiltration of the divine by the sexual."[90] Elsewhere, in describing the rebuilding of Dicky Bateman's hybrid rococo villa in 1758 by the Strawberry Hill designers Richard Bentley and Johann Heinrich Müntz, Walpole claims that Bateman's villa "has changed its religion . . . from Chinese to Gothic," thereby adopting the aesthetic and apparently spiritual mode of Strawberry Hill.[91] Signaling a return to the aesthetic modes, if not the doctrinal cultures, of the Middle Ages, the appeal of Catholicism would constitute part of the contested core of Walpole's revival of Gothic forms.

This appeal extended to the Gothic religious art collected by Walpole and his circle, much of which was either medieval Catholic art or modern Continental

Catholic art. Numerous critics of these men's homes were shocked by the collection and display of Catholic liturgical *ornamenta*, including altars and altarpieces, crucifixes, stained glass, reliquaries, rosaries, etc. When Mrs. Delany visited Dicky Bateman's newly Gothicized villa in Old Windsor, she disdained his "popish" chapel: "What must offend every serious observer must be the intent of this chapel, for if he does *not* make use of it in *good earnest*, his making a joke of it is *shocking*; and at least he should have omitted the *sacred figure*, which ought to strike us with awe and reverence, besides nobody can justify turning any religion into ridicule, though some ceremonies may be trifling and absurd, but I don't suppose he desires to be thought a papist, and perhaps he would rather be thought a heathen!"[92] I return to this passage later in this study, but for the moment, it is clear that, for Mrs. Delany, Catholic religious art smacked of the superstitious tenets of contemporary Continental or medieval English religious culture. The appearance of Catholic religious art in a private home was enough for some critics to assume that, while these men presented themselves publicly as Protestants, their private lives were oriented toward alternate allegiances—what would now be called "alternative lifestyles." Clare Haynes has recently shown that English appreciation of Catholic art—encountered by many on the Grand Tour—was colored by anti-Catholic rhetoric. Authors expressed an anxiety that Catholic art incited excessive religious enthusiasm that was unpalatable in an English-Protestant context. Catholic art raised fears of idolatry, of an unhealthy *interestedness* in the image.[93] And yet it was this very *interestedness*—the romantic, melancholic, and sensual nature of Catholic art—that appealed to Walpole and his circle. Typical of the contrarian stance of many of Walpole's writings on the Gothic, his perspectives overturned conservative critiques of Catholic art as superstitious and therefore dangerous to reason. Good Gothic art, after all, was able to convert viewers to "popery."

A romantic sympathy for pre-Dissolution Catholicism was an established feature of English antiquarianism (John Carter could describe preservationists of medieval buildings as the "Gothic," "Catholic," or "Popish Party" rather than as "Presbyterian" or classicist destroyers).[94] For Walpole and for many medievalists in the eighteenth century, the roots of these Catholic sentiments (or nostalgia *for* Catholicism as a lost devotional structure) were located in the legacy of antiquarian literature they inherited from the Elizabethan and Stuart periods, and in particular the works of William Camden (1551–1623), John Stow (1525–1605), Henry Spelman (1562–1641), and William Dugdale (1605–1686).[95] Writing in the wake of the Dissolution, Dugdale and his contemporary antiquaries were, as Walpole and many of the Gothicists in his circle were to be, sympathetic to the aesthetic and sensory character of medieval Catholicism, even if few publicly confessed to be "papists."[96] Considering the Dissolution to be an "unparalleled catastrophe" that "arrested the stream of English life" through the destruction of much of the nation's heritage in religious art,[97] they elided the Gothic with Catholicism as aesthetic/religious emblems of a glorious phase of English art and spirituality that terminated (for the most part) with a pivotal moment in British history.

Typical of the medievalists that preceded him (and many that followed), Walpole, in his construction of the Gothic, placed particular emphasis on the Dissolution of the Monasteries as an event that ended both Catholicism and the aesthetics of the Gothic to which it was related, even if his own political leanings meant that he expressed some ambivalence about the Dissolution.[98] Dugdale was a particular source of inspiration for Walpole and his circle for his texts (*The Antiquities of Warwickshire* [1656], *Monasticon Anglicanum* [1655–73], and *The History of St. Paul's Cathedral in London* [1658]) as much as the extraordinary plates engraved by Wenceslaus Hollar, which offered reproductions of Gothic architecture. Walpole not only read and absorbed the wisdom of Dugdale's texts but used Hollar's accompanying engravings as models for a number of Gothic installations (fireplaces, cabinetry, etc.) at Strawberry Hill, thereby "imprinting" (to use his verb) this nostalgic vision of the Gothic on the interior of his home. Going further still, he actively promoted Hollar's drawings as important models for subsequent designs, an idea quickly adopted by patrons within his circle and derided by critics outside of it. Thomas Warton, offering something like a gloss on Walpole's promotion of Dugdale, wrote his mournful "Sonnet Written in a Blank Leaf of Dugdale's Monasticon," which laments the Dissolution and concludes, "Nor rough nor barren are the winding ways / Of hoar Antiquity, but strewn with flowers."[99] These texts offered Walpole and subsequent Gothicists the structure of medieval Catholicism *as* a structure of desire: a yearning for an idealized past that itself became a place for the projection of subjectivity. In Susan Stewart's account of eighteenth-century revivals of anachronistic forms, she usefully suggests that such forms expose the "gap between past and present as a structure of desire. . . . We see this structure of desire as the structure of nostalgia; that is, the desire for desire in which objects are the means of generation and not the ends."[100]

Sexuality was central to this structure of desire. As a subversive "other" mode of spiritual and political allegiance within Protestant England that was anachronistic and/or decisively foreign, Catholicism and alternative sexuality was "marked by a history of tropological substitution and interimplication" for contemporary audiences.[101] Although historians of Victorian art and literature have established a trajectory for "the Gothic, both literary and architectural, [as] a privileged rhetoric for . . . the coupling of Catholicism and sexual deviance," this "coupling" was already manifest in the eighteenth century.[102] As alternative and illicit identities in England, Catholicism and "homosexuality" not only shared common tropes of introspective investment, homosocial brotherhood, the sensory pleasure derived from the unveiled male form, and "the elaborate stagecraft of ritualism [in which] they celebrated the effeminate effusions of the dandy," but also shared common aesthetic and performative strategies akin in some respect to what would later be termed "camp."[103] Accounts of the eighteenth-century Gothic novel have shown that its emphasis on deviant or alternative forms of sexuality was normalized by its displacement to a distant Catholic and frequently conventual setting. The Gothic novel represented the structures of Catholic monasticism—and especially its monosexuality—as inherently conducive to illicit sexual desire, whether involving partners of the same sex or opposite sexes.[104] Forming an analogue to this literary tradition, a rich tradition of satiric prints in the eighteenth century puts lascivious monks and wayward nuns engaging in sexual acts within Gothic monasteries and castles (fig. 14). "Nun" had a derogatory second meaning as "prostitute," and "nunnery," as "brothel," in the period.[105] But the nexus of Catholicism and homoeroticism was not only located in a historical fantasy of conventual life. Catholic Italy, considered "the Mother and Nurse of sodomy," was widely understood to have transformed

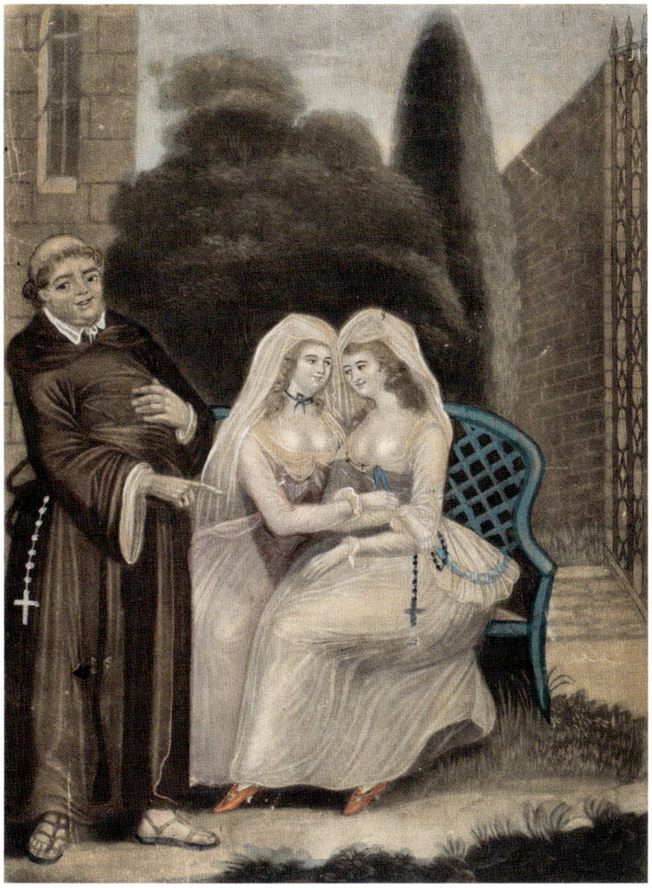

Fig. 14 "A Scene in a Nunnery Garden," printed for Robert Sayer, London, 5 April 1787. "The Scene delightful, Beauty here, what then! / 'Ah, Benedicite! Men are but Men.' / [The women speak:] 'We live recluse and are believed religious, / We but dissemble for our Lusts prodigious.'" LWL 787.04.05.01+. Courtesy of The Lewis Walpole Library, Yale University.

the sexualities of aristocratic travelers during the Grand Tour (of whom Walpole and his friends were examples), thereby enabling homosexuality to be "imported" into England.[106] As Eve Kosofsky Sedgwick has suggested, the artistic connoisseurship acquired by many gentlemen on the Grand Tour, tastes for foreign theatrical performance (particularly the "Barbarous and Gothick" Italian opera), effeminacy, and an inclination toward Catholicism were features that clustered around an emerging concept of "homosexuality" for aristocratic men.[107]

While Walpole and most of the men in his circle were not officially Catholic, they practiced what might be understood as a form of "crypto-Catholicism." Walpole described himself as a "Protestant Goth," and a strain of anti-Catholicism runs through his writing as it does through the period itself,[108] although he felt no tension in claiming to the Reverend William Cole, "I like Popery, as well as you, and have shown I do. I like it as I like chivalry and romance. They all furnish one with ideas and visions, which Presbyterianism does not. A Gothic church or convent fill one with romantic dreams."[109] Walpole playfully allegorized Strawberry Hill as a Catholic shrine ("A Gothic Vatican of Greece and Rome," borrowing his wisdom from Alexander Pope's *Dunciad*), and he was clear that aspects of its interiors were intentional approximations of the splendor and "gaudiness" of medieval Catholic art, with "all the glory of popery."[110] Here Walpole references the Tribune, or "Chapel," a quasi-liturgical space featuring a collection of Catholic liturgical *ornamenta*, including an altar, an altarpiece, a thirteenth-century Limoges reliquary to Thomas Becket (fig. 15), candlesticks, and so on, which stood beside a range of homoerotic objects such as a sculpture of Antinous (fig. 56), the lover of the emperor Hadrian, a "sleeping hermaphrodite between satyrs" (fig. 59), and a miniature representing Ovid's Salmacis and Hermaphroditus—a central myth of homosexuality—given to Walpole by his friend John Chute.[111] Writing to Horace Mann, Walpole was clear about the quasi-sacred nature of the Tribune, which was to have "all the air of a Catholic chapel—bar consecration!"[112] Others manifestly understood and lampooned the conventual nature of Walpole's home: the Catholic duc de Nivernais mistakenly removed his hat upon entry, believing the room to *be* a chapel, while the Englishman Thomas Rowlandson's brilliant satire of

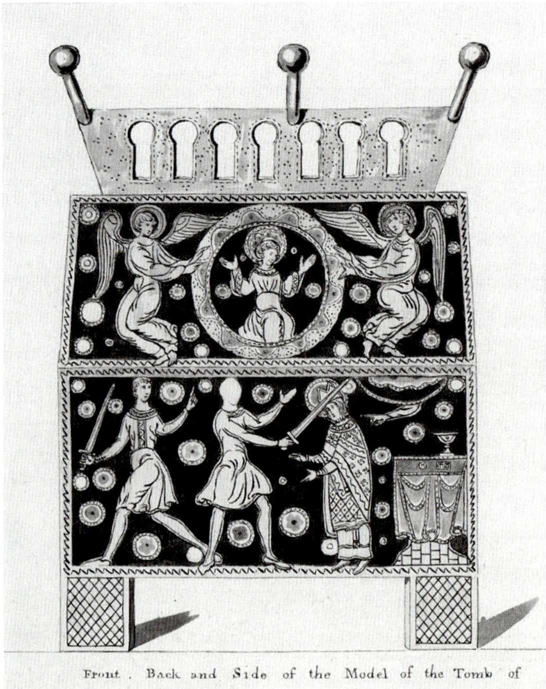

Fig. 15 John Carter, model of the tomb of Thomas Becket [Becket reliquary]. LWL 33 30 Copy 11 Folio, p. 177. Courtesy of The Lewis Walpole Library, Yale University.

Fig. 16 Thomas Rowlandson, *Nuns at Prayer in the Tribune at Strawberry Hill*, ca. 1805. Photo © The Strawberry Hill Collection Trust.

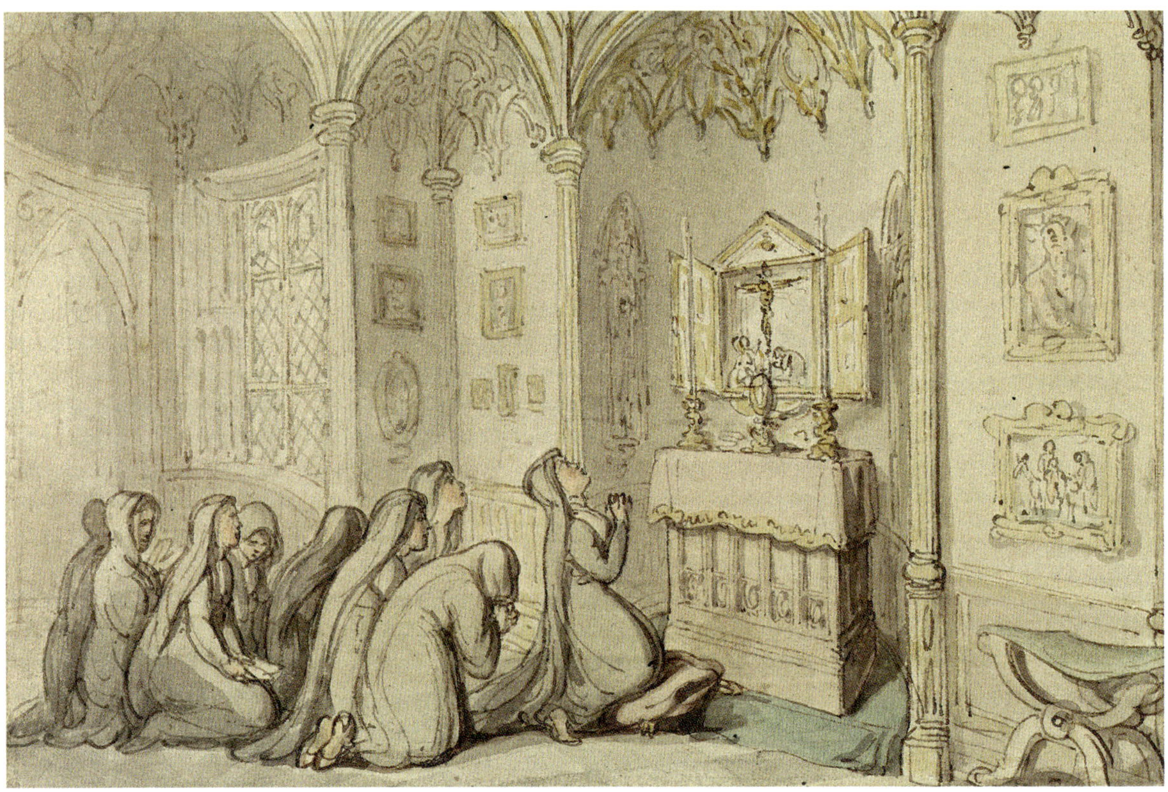

1805, *Nuns at Prayer in the Tribune at Strawberry Hill* (fig. 16), positions kneeling nuns worshipping Walpole's cabinet of miniatures, which is opened to reveal not miniatures but a crucifix, thereby riffing on the inherent religiosity of Walpole's Chapel interior.[113]

Crypto-Catholicism was explored through performance and impersonation in Walpole's circle. Walpole, for example, called himself a "brother monk" and "Abbot of Strawberry," and Strawberry Hill "the Abbey" or a "convent," and Bateman described his own home as a "monastery" or "nunnery," a trope that William Beckford would employ at Fonthill Abbey around 1800.[114] Walpole, Chute, and Montagu conducted a faux Mass at the Vyne, Hampshire, with ancient Mass books and incense, and had a "most Catholic enjoyment of the chapel" there (fig. 118).[115] Walpole could allegorize a visit to Strawberry by his friend George Montagu as "the festival of Saint George Montagu" and speak of the "gorgeous Saints" in stained glass he acquired.[116] Elsewhere Walpole describes dressing his cousin Henry Conway in an old helmet found in a parish church in Hertfordshire, thereby relocating his erotic desire into the Catholic or Gothic past: "how antique and handsome he looked, you would have taken him for Rinaldo [from Torquato Tasso's *Gerusalemme liberata* (1581)]."[117] This would seem like wish fulfillment on Walpole's part, since he considered that "Nature always designed [Conway] for a hero of a romance."[118] I will have occasion to reference further examples elsewhere in this study, but I follow Ellis Hanson in arguing that beneath the cowl of Catholic monasticism was a cult of homoerotic community within Walpole's circle.[119]

But it is significant for our understanding of the mobility of the Gothic's Catholic monastic associations that they were not exclusively employed by homoerotic cultures. Dominantly (if not exclusively) heterosexual cultures also exploited the Gothic's Catholic and particularly conventual associations as a pretext for the performance of illicit sexuality. In the middle years of the eighteenth century, these associations were explored at the former Cistercian abbey at Medmenham and the estate at nearby West Wycombe (Buckinghamshire) owned by Sir Francis Dashwood. Dashwood's "Hellfire Club," which included members from the Society of Dilettanti (including Dashwood), indulged in their illicit, orgiastic exploits in Gothic guise as the "Medmenham monks" or the "Order of St. Francis" under the cloak (literally) of a comic and anticlerical medievalism.[120] The "mock celebration of the more ridiculous rites of the foreign religious orders among the Roman Catholics," to cite one member's description, extended to the accompaniment of "nuns" (prostitutes) to entertain the monks at Dashwood's "convent."[121] Their sexual exploits took place in Gothic architectural settings, including the Cistercian monastery itself and the so-called Hellfire Caves, which were entered via a fictive Gothic church façade erected in knapped flint in 1752 (fig. 17).[122] Sir Francis Dashwood

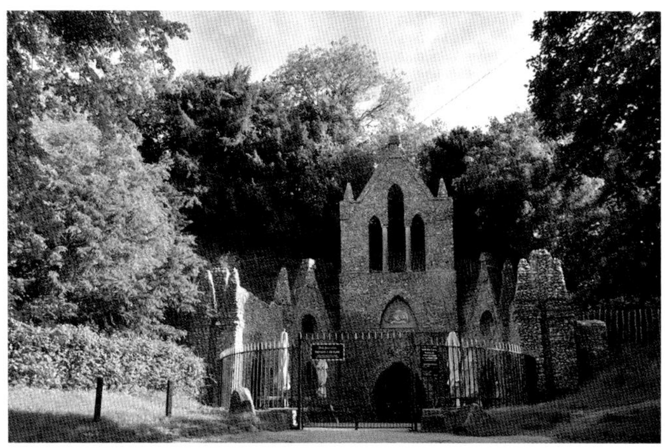

Fig. 17 John Donowell, entrance to the Hellfire Caves, West Wycombe, Buckinghamshire, 1752. Photo: author.

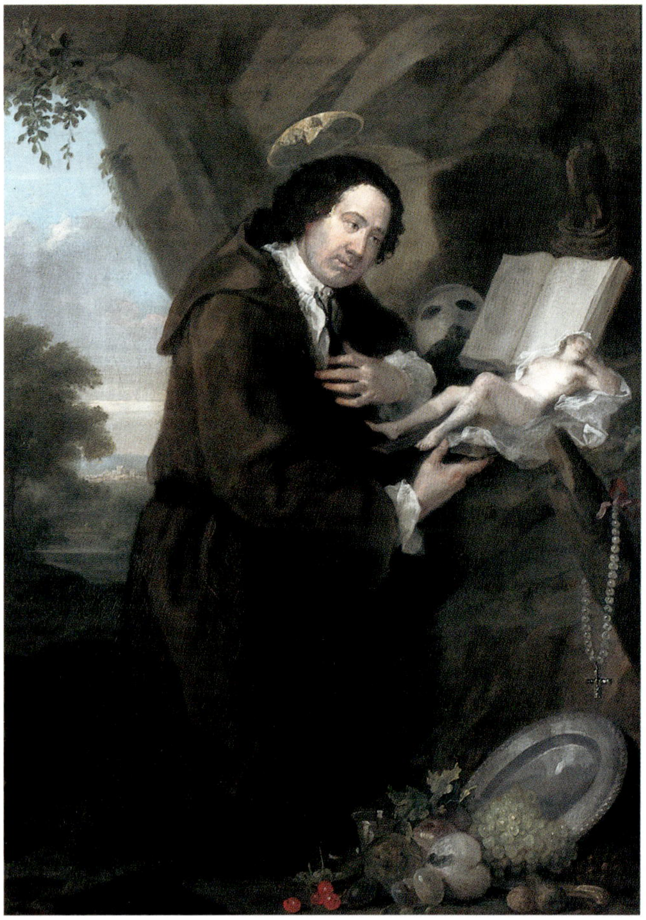

Fig. 18 William Hogarth, *Sir Francis Dashwood at His Devotions*. Private collection. Photo courtesy of Robin Simon.

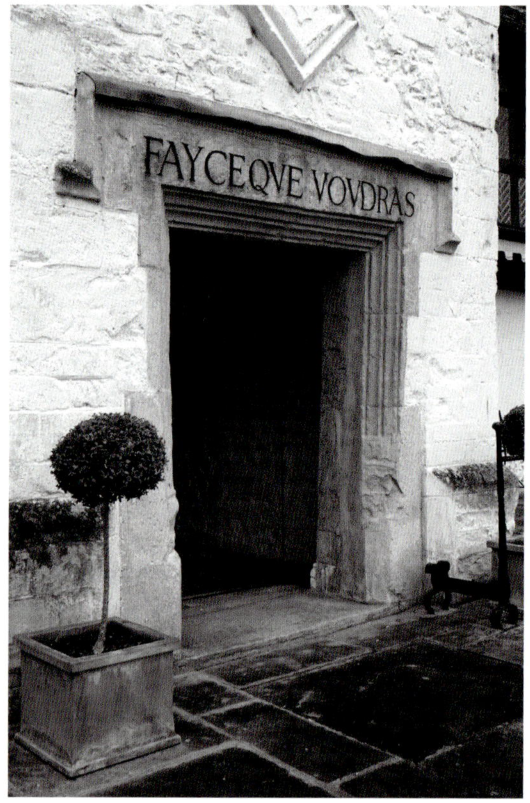

Fig. 19 *Fay ce que voudras*, carved above the main entrance to Medmenham Abbey during the ownership of Francis Dashwood. Photo: author.

was famously represented by Adrien Carpentiers and William Hogarth as *Saint* Francis: Hogarth's painting is a subversive rethinking of Saint Francis's iconography in which Francis gazes not at the conventional skull and crucifix but into the open legs of a voluptuous antique statue of Venus, and the Bible is replaced by Nicolas Chorier's erotic *Elegantiae Latini Sermonis* (1660), an allusion not only to the Dilettanti's antiquarianism but also to its famed sexual exploits (fig. 18).[123]

The Medmenham monks demonstrate that the historiographical construction of the Gothic up to the reign of Henry VIII as a period of freedom—sexual and/or political and religious—was not unique to Horace Walpole. Upon visiting Medmenham, Walpole noted that the chapter house there featured a genealogy of the kings and queens of England, but the image of Henry VIII, who dissolved the monasteries, was deliberately erased, implying the continuation of a sexual tradition of "monastic" life.[124] The comparisons with Strawberry Hill extend to the satiric, tongue-in-cheek motto carved over the entrance to Medmenham, *Fay ce que voudras*, or "Do what you will," an echo of Walpole's own *Fari quae sentiat* (fig. 19). Here the Medmenham monks' reference is to Rabelais's Abbey of Thélème in his sixteenth-century satire *Gargantua and Pantagruel*, in which the monks of the abbey spend their time "not in laws, statutes, or rules, but according to their own free will and pleasure" (chap. 57). Walpole's circle's employment of these monastic-Gothic-sexual tropes was thus not without an important context, even if, as far as we are aware, their "flaunting of sex, sacrilege, and antiquarianism" seems positively benign compared to that of the Dilettanti.[125] The Dilettanti and Walpole's circle nevertheless offer significant polarizations of the new, elite sexual cultures of the eighteenth century, suggesting that they can be usefully understood as different sides of the same coin. George Haggerty is surely correct to note that during the eighteenth century "the monastery is a precursor of the sexual laboratory, and in a sense it functions as the controlled environment in which the habits of an unfamiliar species can be studied."[126]

But it would be a mistake to suggest that the crypto-Catholicism of Walpole's circle was purely sexual and satiric in the sense that it was for the Medmenham monks. Insisting on a "clear division between religious and secular motives" may misleadingly diminish a valid spiritual connection sensed by Walpole's circle.[127] The Catholic tropes of the Gothic served to code the emotional and occasionally sexual bonds of these men within a hallowed (if illicit) monosexual structure. Not only did they reflect an established association between homoeroticism and the aesthetic and social structures of Catholicism, but they offered an elevated and aestheticized space in which homoerotic confraternity could be performed. In this, Catholicism may also have an important place in the development of modern British sexualities. Focusing on the nineteenth century in Britain, Patrick O'Malley has suggested that the development of Catholicism as an interiorized and minoritized subjectivity may have provided a model for the very discourses that constructed a modern "queer" subjectivity epitomized by the "closet" (thus his title "Epistemology of the Cloister," punning on Sedgwick's *Epistemology of the Closet*). The crypto-Catholicism of Walpole's circle suggests the need to extend this critique into the eighteenth century. Conveniently, the very term "closet" shares a Latin root with the term "cloister."

Narrating Gothic: *The Castle of Otranto*

The Gothic novel as a new genre of medievalist literature was one of the main productions of Walpole's circle, and its originary text, *The Castle of Otranto: A Gothic Story* (the title of the 1765 edition), was deservedly labeled, since it shared many of the features of Walpole's appraisal of the Gothic. *Otranto* was the only Gothic novel written within his circle, although its influence can be found in these men's poetry and art patronage. Using the historical and architectural term "Gothic" to describe a literary style, Walpole invites cross-disciplinary study of his Gothic texts, and particularly comparison with Strawberry Hill, upon which its architectural settings were partially based.[128] Set in a castle and monastery in Italy during the twelfth or thirteenth century, the story begins after an ancient regicide, when Manfred, the imposter "prince" of Otranto, attempts to marry his effeminate and sickly son Conrad to Isabella to continue his family's hold on the principality. The plot unravels with the return of the rightful heir, Theodore, but not before Conrad, in what must be one of literature's great narrative non sequiturs, is crushed to death by a gigantic helmet that suddenly falls from the sky into the courtyard. Conrad's death signals the eventual fulfillment of the prophecy that "the castle and lordship of Otranto should pass from the present family, whenever the real owner should be grown too large to inhabit it."[129] Fearing this, Manfred then seeks to divorce his wife, Hippolita, who never provided him an appropriate heir, and marry his son's fiancée, while promising his own unwilling daughter, Matilda, to Isabella's leering father, Frederick. As Theodore returns to the castle and becomes a rival for Isabella's hand, Manfred mistakenly murders his own daughter, believing her to be Isabella. Realizing the tragedy and the depths of his own sadistic urges for sex and power, Manfred nevertheless refrains from suicide, and he and Hippolita repent by retiring to a monastery and a nunnery, respectively. As soon as they exit the castle, its walls crumble and fall, thus fulfilling the prophecy. It is revealed that Manfred's grandfather killed the former prince during the Crusades and usurped the lordship of Otranto by forging his will. At the core of Manfred's downfall, and undercutting Hippolita's somewhat superficial moral gloss on the events as "the vanity of human greatness,"[130] is the Old Testament dictum that the "sins of the fathers" shall be visited upon their children, thus alluding to the irrepressibility of sin as a central theme of the Gothic. Both of Walpole's Gothic "texts," *The Castle of Otranto* and Strawberry Hill, are structured as family romances (a point I explore in subsequent chapters on the house).

Walpole initially published the story as a translation of a medieval text found "in the library of an ancient Catholic family in the North of England,"[131] hinting that it was the product of Catholic recusants. Following the positive reception of the novel in 1765, he admitted to the forgery, having substituting "Humphrey Muralto" for "Horace Walpole." His 1765 edition includes a famous second prologue in which he theorizes his medievalist narrative as "an attempt to blend the two kinds of Romance, the ancient and the modern. In the former, all was imagination and improbability: in the latter, nature is always intended to be, and sometimes has been, copied with success."[132] A hybrid of medieval literature (which for Walpole included Shakespeare) and modern fiction, Walpole's Gothic novel shares a related temporal location with his historiography of Gothic architecture.[133] Like his Gothic architecture, his literature is pitched as social criticism, since, in modernity, "invention has not been wanting; but the great resources of fancy have been dammed up, by a strict adherence to common life."[134]

The Castle of Otranto and some of its successors in the Gothic genre can be usefully understood as a form of architectural writing. This is justified principally by the fact that Walpole based the literary castle upon Strawberry Hill: he claims to have conceived the story in a dream while sleeping in Strawberry: "I had thought myself in an ancient castle (a very natural dream for a head filled like mine with Gothic story) and that on the uppermost bannister of a great staircase I saw a gigantic hand in armour," a reference to his Armory.[135] Walpole goes on to develop Strawberry Hill's dual identity by calling his house "my own little Otranto," himself "Master of Otranto," and his housekeeper "Seneschal of Otranto." He staged various objects within Strawberry Hill to reinforce this association for the viewer—for example, John Carter's drawing *The Entry of Frederick into the Castle of Otranto* (fig. 20), which was hung in the Little Parlour and included both a portrait of Walpole and his heraldry,[136] and of course the suit of armor on the staircase landing that apparently inspired the novel in the first place. Walpole thus created a fictive double for his newly built Gothic mansion, a literary avatar that

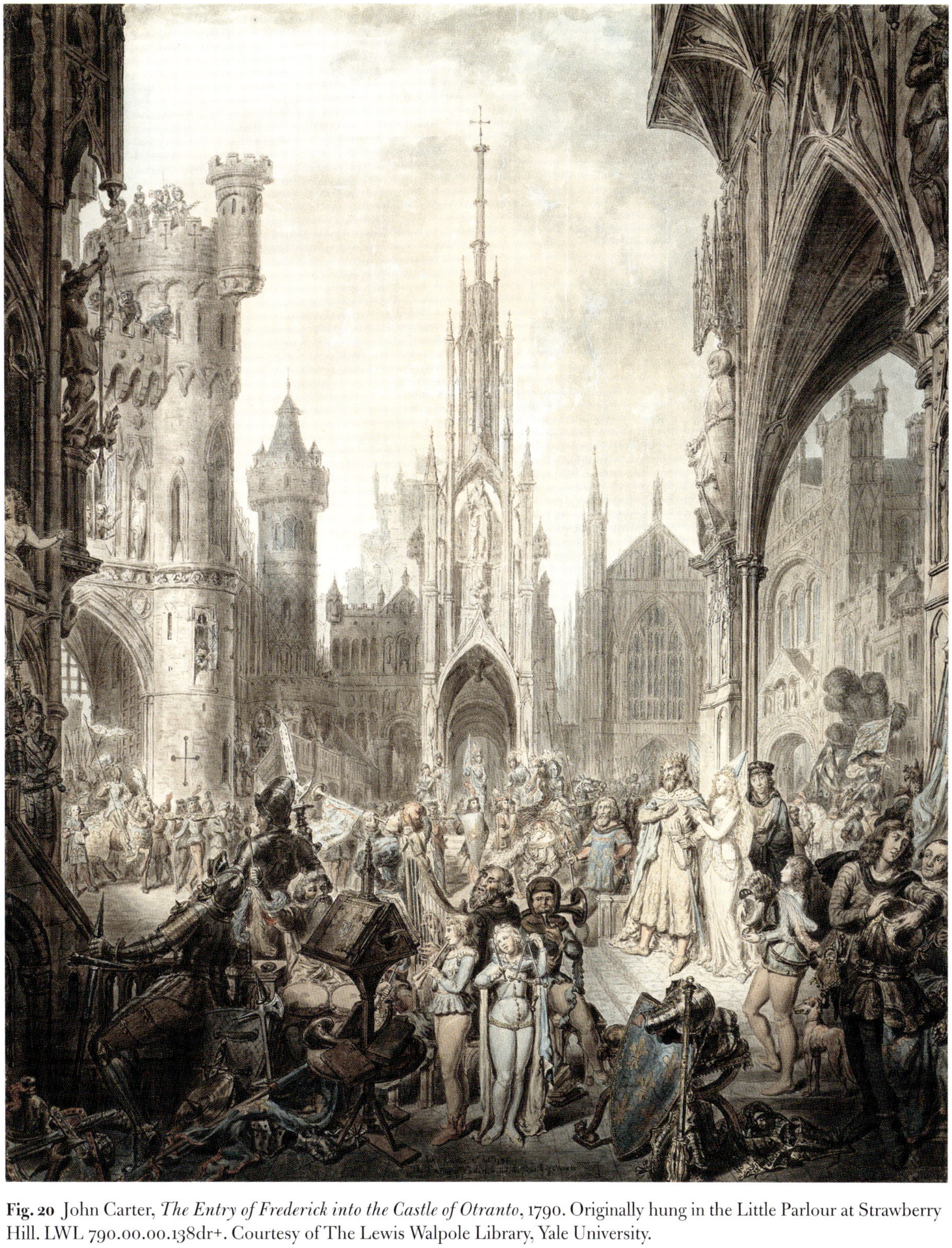

Fig. 20 John Carter, *The Entry of Frederick into the Castle of Otranto*, 1790. Originally hung in the Little Parlour at Strawberry Hill. LWL 790.00.00.138dr+. Courtesy of The Lewis Walpole Library, Yale University.

advertised and mythologized the house for viewers. This was not lost on contemporaries: upon visiting, Francis Burney was surprised by "the unusually shaped apartments" in which "striking recollections were brought to [mind] of his Gothic story of the Castle of Otranto."[137] As such, the novel provides a kind of exegesis on the house, an imaginative and deeply subjective response to the narratives running through it. With the mechanics of Walpole's associationism, the story provides a useful guide to the kinds of things he imagined as taking place within a Gothic building, the kinds of acts and emotions normalized by Gothic architecture. In this sense, *The Castle of Otranto* may serve as Strawberry Hill's imagined historical praxis, or even as a "psychoanalysis" of it, as Anne Williams suggests.[138]

I have noted already that recent accounts of Walpole's sexuality have centered around *The Castle of Otranto*. Unlike later exemplars of the Gothic genre (notably Matthew Lewis's novel *The Monk* [1796]), Walpole's text is not focused on homoeroticism. For Walpole, the medievalist setting imagined in *Otranto* allowed for the relocation of the unsanctioned eroticisms of the present to a Catholic, medieval, and frequently foreign past in which alternative sexual and social practices are normalized by a Gothic setting. For this reason, lust, incest, sexual violence, and same-sex desire feature centrally as "queer" reversals of established sexual decorum in the medievalizing narratives of the Gothic novel.[139] Reading the novel as a subjective response to Walpole's own sexual and emotional life, Max Fincher argues that the narrative of Otranto may chart the dynamics of internalized "homophobia." Walpole's affections for his cousin Henry Seymour Conway had been exposed in a highly public (and vicious) exchange of pamphlets just before the writing of the novel.[140] With its focus on Conrad's effeminacy and its potential nullification of patterns of paternal succession, *Otranto* has been understood not only in terms of Walpole's own paternity but also as "a cipher for how the dynamics of contemporary homophobia operated in its movement towards denigrating both the feminine and the effete."[141] Walpole's Gothic, in an apparent aim to deconstruct the patriarchal family and explore nonnormative genders and sexualities, emerges as a discourse counter to polite fiction, conduct books, and other tracts that focus on sexuality and the family and promote the organization of sexuality along heteronormative lines. Haggerty argues that the rise of Gothic fiction paralleled the codifications of sexuality during the eighteenth century, a thesis that, in some respects, prefaces my own thesis about architecture. For Haggerty, the Gothic novel offers a space to explore alternative sexual realities, "a historical model of queer theory and politics" long before the official codifications of "homosexuality": "Gothic fiction gave sexuality a history in the first place."[142]

Within Walpole's circle, the Gothic was a multifaceted myth explored across a range of media, from art writing to politics, literature, art, and architecture. As I have argued above, the Gothic cannot be reduced to sexuality any more than sexuality can be divorced from it. A coterie taste, the most remarkable aspect of it may have been that it was appropriated within a homoerotic milieu at all. It was the antique world—then at the height of its cultural significance during English neo-Palladianism—and not the Middle Ages that offered a ready model of queer historicism via the established classical iconographies of Antinous, Narcissus, Ganymede, and others. These ideas were known and explored by many Englishmen on the Grand Tour, including Walpole and his circle, who collected, shared, and displayed various antique works of art representing these narratives as aspects of their own homoerotic culture.[143] In the same years, Joachim Winckelmann codified his homoerotic teleologies of antique art in his foundational *History of Ancient Art* (1764). Walpole knew Winckelmann's writing and was connected with him via Horace Mann and his circle of collectors and antiquaries in Rome. But in eighteenth-century England, classicism had a different social and historical trajectory. Walpole positioned the Middle Ages in opposition to the hegemonic authority of neoclassicism and to what he took to be its "establishment" values.

The broader, interdisciplinary perspective I have sketched out here illuminates the ethical and aesthetic agenda behind Walpole's "revival" of the Gothic as an architectural style, and its sexual/libidinal significations. For Walpole, the Gothic represented a lost past, characterized by freedom from sexual "norms" and freedom from artistic and sociopolitical stricture, two features that form part of his aesthetics. Walpole's Gothic becomes a discourse on modernity's prehistory, and particularly on the aspects of human culture that have been lost or erased for modernity to be put into place. Although he would be hesitant to admit it, Walpole's Gothic was very much an Enlightenment construct: his eroticized historiography of the Gothic was consistent with the contours of contemporary art historiography in general, in which aesthetic judgment and (homo)erotic desire, or artistic *aisthesis* and sexual *aisthesis*, were part of the same approach to the phenomenological world and could be paralleled in contemporary writings of Joachim and others.[144] But the most coherent statement of Walpole's own vision of the Gothic was, without doubt, manifest in the sinuous forms of his own villa at Strawberry Hill.

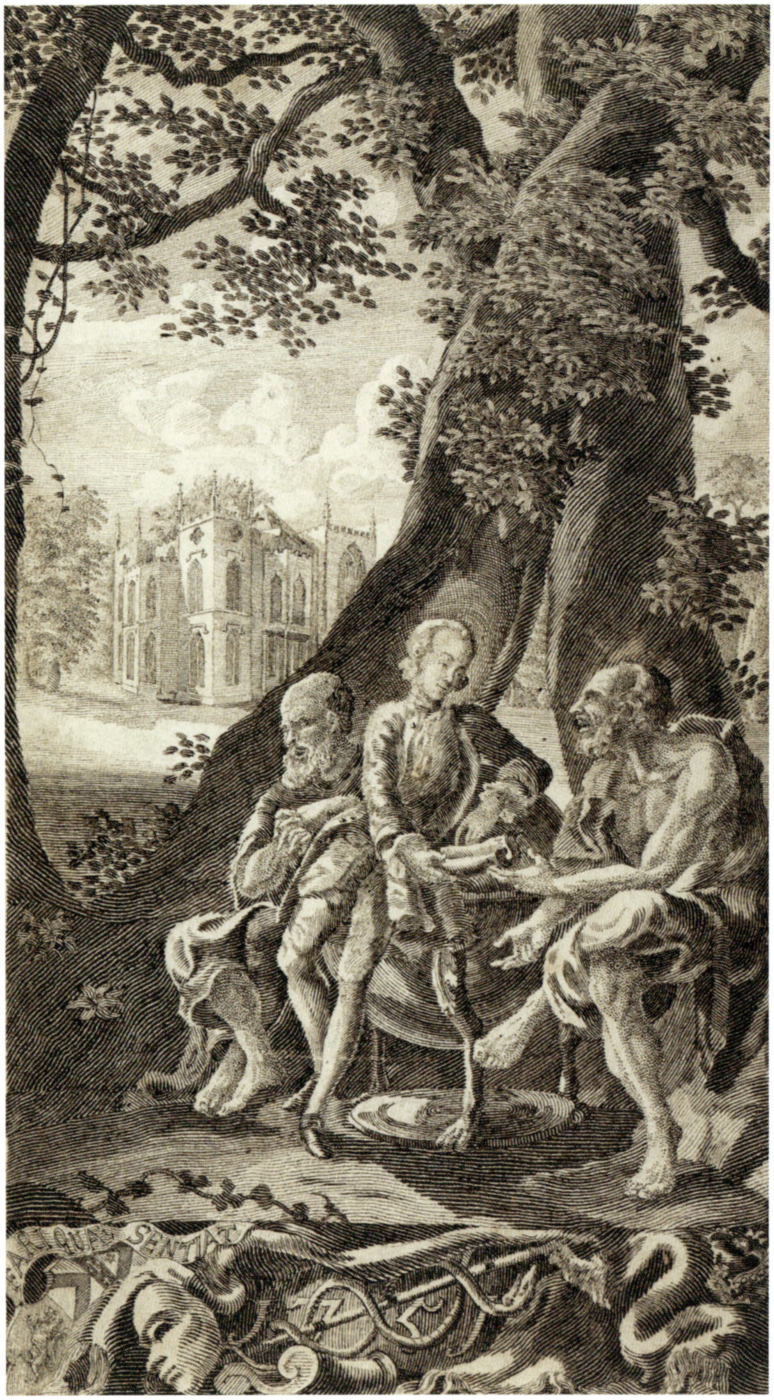

Fig. 21 Richard Bentley, dedicatory frontispiece to Horace Walpole's *Memoires of George II*, undated. Walpole sits between Democritus and Heraclitus on the grounds of Strawberry Hill. LWL MS 152, frontispiece. Courtesy of The Lewis Walpole Library, Yale University.

2 Horace Walpole's Strawberry Hill

You will express yourself in your house, whether you want to or not, so you must make up your mind to a long preparatory discipline.

—Elsie de Wolfe, *The House in Good Taste*, 1913

Richard Bentley's 1753 frontispiece to Walpole's *Memoires of George II* shows Horace Walpole dedicating his unpublished work to the philosophers Democritus and Heraclitus on the grounds of Strawberry Hill. Walpole's preference for the laughing or mocking philosopher (Democritus) over the pitiful and compassionate philosopher (Heraclitus) is clear as he turns from the latter to the former: leaning upon a globe, Walpole's diminutive, elfin form is juxtaposed with the gnarled muscularity of their massive bodies (fig. 21). Bentley's drawing is based upon Walpole's appropriation of Democritus as one of his alter egos: he signed letters "Your old friend, Democritus" and coined a famous aphorism, "*This world is a comedy to those that think, a tragedy to those that feel*—a solution of why Democritus laughed and Heraclitus wept."[1] This image is completed by Walpole's Gothic house in the background left. Its miniaturized form, bright lighting, and polished contours contrast with the ruddier textures and darker coloring of the philosophers and their natural setting, thus depicting the house not simply as an accomplishment of a man of letters but also as a simulation of him. Created by Bentley, a member of the Strawberry Committee, this image is informed by a series of tropes that ran through Strawberry Hill, where, for example, Walpole's sardonic and witty motto *Fari quae sentiat*, or "Say what one feels," would be found. It was, in other words, an intimate and deeply self-referential "portrait" of Horace Walpole and Strawberry Hill composed within the very culture of the place.

In the long historiography of Strawberry Hill, the style of Walpole's influential Gothic villa has, deservedly perhaps, dominated art-historical investigation, leaving the culture of the house largely unexplored. In Charles Saumarez Smith's useful epitome, Strawberry Hill functioned as an "experimental laboratory" for Gothic design, even if it was only "design by transcription," according to Joseph Mordaunt Crook.[2] A casual read through Walpole's voluminous correspondence over the house with Horace Mann or members of the Strawberry Committee, with whom Walpole lovingly obsessed over its minute details, or with fellow medievalists such as Thomas Warton or designers and draughtsmen such as John Carter, leaves no room to question such an assessment. But formalist assessments of the development and dissemination of the Gothic via letters and architectural drawings and the careers of architects or designers have emphasized style and its plastic and graphic articulations at the expense of the underlying social configurations that facilitated their selection, development, and dissemination in the first place.[3] Understood from the dual perspectives of the history of art and the history of sexuality, Walpole's remarkable Gothic villa and collection emerged as a collaboration with the men in his circle, literally the material precipitate of a series of overlapping homosocial and homoerotic relationships.

In this chapter I pursue Saumarez Smith's metaphor by arguing that Strawberry Hill was the site for the development not only of new forms of Gothic design but also of a new formulation of a sexual-aesthetic mode of being. As many commentators remarked in the eighteenth century and afterward, Strawberry Hill and its collections asserted a range of values opposed to the reigning style of political and patriarchal authority in English neo-Palladianism. For some, Strawberry Hill and the Strawberry Hill Gothic mode were understood to mirror or express the tastes and mores of its third-sex, or "queer," culture. But rather than simply "reflect" or signify alternative sexuality, Strawberry Hill and related buildings helped to develop some of the aesthetic conventions that are now associated with queerness itself. Such a statement is less revelatory than it might once have been, since, as I noted above, much recent work has shown that architecture and interior design were a significant testing ground or "laboratory" for new sexual aesthetics in English culture. The forms developed at Strawberry Hill would be referenced and replicated in the subsequent domestic commissions of Walpole's circle; these buildings not only paid homage to Walpole's originary home, but in doing so they extended Strawberry's homoerotic habitus.

Symbiosis: Architecture as Self

In both of its capacities as the residence of a man of letters and taste and as a house designed to be toured and visited, Strawberry Hill served as a complex projection of Horace Walpole himself, a simulation or even avatar of a famous man.[4] This rich mythology was developed in Walpole's literary output (notably his *Castle of Otranto*, which was inspired by Strawberry), in the tourist trade focused upon the house (including Walpole's own *Description of the Villa of Mr. Horace Walpole*, 1774/84),[5] and in its lengthy critical reception in the popular press. Walpole's manipulation of the image of Strawberry Hill is illustrated in a series of pictures that he commissioned of himself and his circle in or in front of his home, including Richard Bentley's 1753 frontispiece (fig. 21).

Bentley's image descends from an established convention of architectural or "estate" portraiture, including an image Walpole commissioned to hang in Strawberry Hill: John Giles Eccardt and John Wootton's *Portrait of Sir Robert Walpole and Catherine Shorter, His First Wife* (1746; fig. 22).[6] Seated among attributes of political and artistic prowess, Lord and Lady Walpole are positioned in front of their Palladian mansion at Houghton, itself the ultimate symbol of Sir Robert's paternal and political authority. In light of such images, Bentley's portrait of Horace Walpole seems playfully subversive, if not iconoclastically so. Representing Walpole as a miniature sprite between two gargantuan male philosophers with the Gothic villa in the background, Bentley's picture suggests a deliberate rethinking of this heterosexual and patriarchal convention in its insistence on the alterity and homosociality of Strawberry Hill. Loftus Jestin is surely

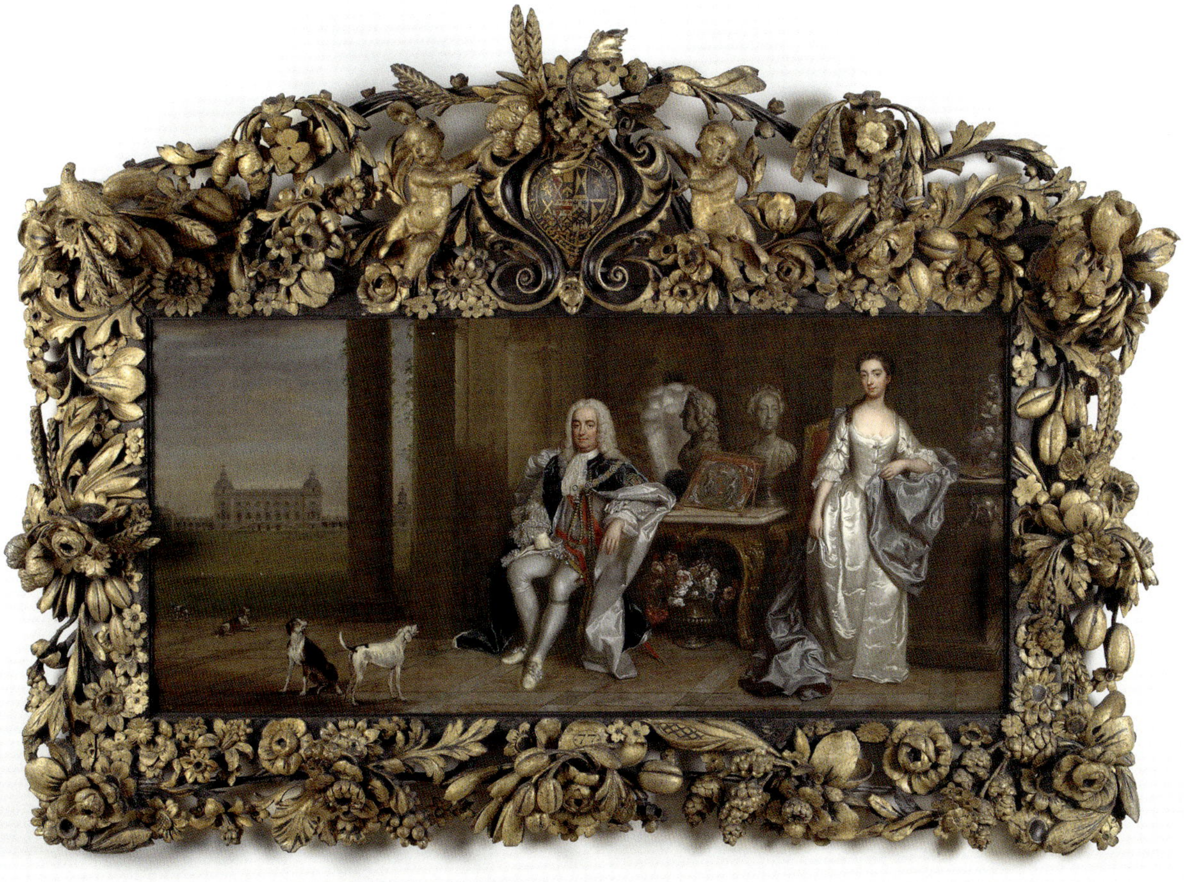

Fig. 22 John Giles Eccardt and John Wootton, *Portrait of Sir Robert Walpole and Catherine Shorter, His First Wife*, 1746. Frame in the style of Grinling Gibbons, ca. 1680. Courtesy of The Lewis Walpole Library, Yale University.

correct to suggest that Strawberry Hill was "a response to Houghton" and that Walpole and Bentley saw in its construction an overturning of the ambitious, even ruthless, figures cut by their own fathers.[7]

The relationship between patron and building was explored in a number of contexts. Walpole could, for example, describe Strawberry Hill—his architectural self—as a lover to whom he was singly faithful. His erotic attachment to the house is suggested by an unpublished poem in his own copy of his *Description*, in which he allegorizes his relationship with his home as that between mankind's first lovers:

> In Eden's lovely garden our grandmother
> Dame Eve
> With an apple of the forest, Old Adam did
> deceive,
> But had I been her husband, the
> Pippin then had fail'd
> And Strawberry, sweet Strawberry alone
> Shou'd have prevailed![8]

In this flippant bit of verse, Walpole rejects Eve's advances in preference for his true love, Strawberry Hill, which becomes a narcissistic projection of himself. But Walpole could also express anxiety about the paired posterity of himself and his home, lamenting: "I am no poet, and my castle is of paper, and my castle and my attachment and I, shall soon vanish and be forgotten together!"[9]

Such associations between architecture and the self had important implications for understanding the house's style and its idiomatic Strawberry Hill Gothic mode. As I have noted, commentators from Walpole's lifetime onward have sensed the "queerness" of its style and explored relationships between the style of the house and Walpole's sexual subjectivity and affect. A posthumous critique simply entitled "Strawberry Hill" interrogates the psychosexual origins of Walpole's taste in art and architecture and compares them with his father's tastes for the Palladian at his own newly built home at Houghton Hall:

> The place may be considered as a picture of the master's mind who formed it, in which there was nothing great, at the same time that it was plentifully stored with elegant knowledge, and gifted with the power of communicating it in a manner of superior polish and amusement. . . . His father distinguished himself as a lover of the arts, by the Houghton collection. . . . [Horace] Walpole may, therefore, be supposed to have inherited a portion of that taste which he cultivated, though in a less elevated course. Nor shall we pretend to determine whether it proceeded from the structure of his mind, the consequent habits of his life, or his physical constitution, which was naturally weak, that his pursuits, though not without taste and elegance, had little of masculine energy or mental capaciousness. If the catalogue of the Houghton pictures were compared with that of the Strawberry Hill curiosities, the minds of the two noble collectors would be distinctly determined.[10]

The author here reads Horace Walpole and his tastes in the Gothic as weak, effeminized versions of Sir Robert Walpole and his neoclassical tastes at Houghton. Lacking "masculine energy" and "mental capaciousness" and possessing a body that was "naturally weak," Walpole is the subject of a common trope of mental and physical degeneracy or weakness as a code for homosexuality, the "consequent habits of his life."[11] In this reading, the apple had fallen too far from the tree: Sir Robert's Palladianism at Houghton was consonant with aristocracy, patriarchy, and the political and moral authority of the empire, while his son's taste for the Gothic was the product of his queerness, an aesthetic and corporeal degeneration of his father's muscular neoclassical example.

In Thomas Babington Macaulay's account, Walpole is "the most eccentric, the most artificial, the most fastidious, the most capricious of men," and his creation of "a grotesque house with piecrust battlements" becomes part of an elaborate analogy between Walpole's queer affect and the materiality of Strawberry Hill.[12] His apparently flimsy fabrication of a literary, connoisseurial, and social persona is elided with the fictive forms of his home, in which modern materials replicate medieval stone construction. For Macaulay, Strawberry Hill is "trifling" and "quaint," a mirror of Walpole's own affectation: "affectation is the very essence of the man. It pervades all his thought and all his expressions. If it were taken away, nothing would be left."[13] As this suggests, George Haggerty's view that "[Walpole] understood that the effect of the house was indistinguishable, even in his own mind at times, from his own personal affect," enjoyed a genealogy in eighteenth- and nineteenth-century writings.[14] In light of psychoanalytic criticism, the relationship between patron and building can be understood as a doubling of Walpole's self: a projection of Walpole's ego that was a subject of his narcissistic desire, while also ensuring his immortality after his death, two features that run through Walpole's own accounts of his home.

The Strawberry Committee

From its inception, the Strawberry Committee was unusual in Georgian architectural culture. Formed of an amateur architect, John Chute, Walpole's closest friend, cohabitant, and "oracle in taste, the standard to whom [he] submitted [his] trifles, and the genius that presided over poor Strawberry";[15] the draughtsman Richard Bentley; the poet and scholar Thomas Gray, who occasionally connected Walpole with Gothic *spolia* as buildings were being dismantled;[16] and the amateur architect Thomas Pitt ("one of the very few that I reckon quite worthy of being at home at Strawberry"),[17] the Committee was a shifting group of men who understood Strawberry Hill to be the focus of their homosocial *convivium*. A number of literary and epistolary portraits of Walpole's circle exist that focus as much on the bonds of a shared aesthetic sexual subjectivity as on a shared queer affect.[18] Significantly, Walpole used the term "Strawberry Committee" only between 1754 and 1759, and he never gave a specific list of members.[19] He intended it to articulate a changing circle of friends and associates working on and around Strawberry Hill, a circle that existed in one form or another from the 1750s through the 1770s. As such, it has sometimes been understood to include figures such as Dicky Bateman, Richard Edgecumbe, and Walpole's cousin Horace Mann, who never actually saw the house but received countless letters narrating its development and helped Walpole secure art for it from Italy.

There is of course something schoolboyish about the Strawberry Committee, or simply "the committee." It was rooted in earlier homosocial constructions in Walpole's life, such as the "triumvirate" and the later "quadruple alliance" at Eton, the latter formed of Walpole, Gray, Richard West, and Thomas Ashton, and Walpole's "out of town party," which comprised George James "Gilly" Williams, George Augustus Selwyn, Richard Edgecumbe, and Walpole, who yearly met at Strawberry Hill and were commemorated in a portrait by Joshua Reynolds that hung there (fig. 77). In many respects, the Strawberry Committee—and Strawberry Hill itself—originated in Walpole's experiences on the Grand Tour. His Grand Tour companions were Chute, twenty years senior to Walpole; Gray, with whom Walpole had a youthful liaison while on the tour; and Mann, also two decades older, who would provide a "symbolic father" to Walpole and others in his circle and a model of sorts for queer sociality.[20] Mann was what might now be called a maven:[21] a well-connected diplomat and man of taste who acquainted Walpole with a homoerotic circle of antiquarians and collectors that notably included Joachim Winckelmann and Baron Philipp von Stosch. Mann's residence in Florence, the quattrocento Casa Manetti, was "the nerve centre of the homoerotic Englishman's Italy" and a hub for Walpole and his friends while abroad.[22] Although radically different in style and orientation, the Casa Manetti offered the young Horace Walpole an archetype of a home as a setting for queer family that Walpole would reimagine at Strawberry Hill.[23] It is no coincidence that the return of "the Chuteheads" from the Grand Tour in September 1746 and the resulting synergy between Walpole and Chute coincided with Walpole's plans to begin works at Strawberry Hill, and it may not be a coincidence that Francis Whitehead's untimely death in 1751, which devastated Chute, resulted in the consolidation of the bond with Walpole and the expansion of Strawberry Hill the following year, where Chute would have his own bedroom.[24]

Walpole inscribed the bonds with these men and their role in the production and design of his home in a variety of contexts. His *Description* (1774/84) ascribes authorship of various pieces of Gothic architecture to these men—that is, chimneypieces and other installations, "designed by Mr. Bentley" or "designed by Mr. Chute"—or connects his friends with objects given by them, such as the stained glass in the Little Parlour, "given by Mr. George Selwyn." The men in Walpole's circle described the Gothic mode of Strawberry Hill as their collective style, a court style of the Committee. Thomas Gray, for example, could state in a letter to Thomas Warton, who was renovating his London home, that he was delighted that Warton had "entered into the spirit of Strawberry Castle," while Walpole happily wrote to Richard Bentley of the tombs at Herstmonceux (Sussex), which were "varied into a thousand little canopies and patterns" in what is now called the Perpendicular style, or what he called "*our* trefoil taste."[25] Elsewhere Walpole could chide Bentley for his designs of the Library bookcases, which could not "have the Strawberry imprimatur," opting instead for designs by John Chute (his "oracle of taste"), whose designs had a more "conventual look," and so forth.[26]

But the Committee's approach to representing Gothic form was neither unified nor static. Bentley's decisively hybrid, or "rococo," manner of Gothic, which dismantled and recombined Gothic forms, contrasted with Chute's more draughtsmanly and scholarly approach, as commentators have often noted. The Committee's conception of Gothic architecture—and particularly that of Walpole and Chute—developed quickly during the 1750s through 1770s.[27] Emerging from an early reliance on the mode of William Kent and Batty Langley, the Committee's awareness of the forms and taxonomy of Gothic architecture was enhanced by various country tours in the early 1750s (some of which would be published in Walpole's "Journals of Visits to Country Seats"), including the aforementioned visit to Herstmonceux.[28] Walpole's own patronage indicates an increasing concern with archaeological accuracy and stylistic homogeneity in the 1760s and 1770s, which found considerable agreement with Chute's draughtsmanly approach to architecture but contrasted with Bentley's blending of forms. Bentley's work with the Committee ended in 1759 due to a quarrel with J. H. Müntz, after which John Chute became the dominant draughtsman. I will have occasion to comment on the transformation of the Gothic within Walpole's circle elsewhere in this study, but for the time being, it is significant to note that Walpole, with humor and ease, carefully managed the developing and inherently different approaches to the Gothic employed by his friends.

Consider an often-cited letter from Walpole to Chute discussing Chute's design of 1759 for the elevation of the Cloister and Long Gallery (fig. 23):

> Well, how delightful! how the deuce did you contrive to get such proportion? you will certainly have all the women with short legs come to you to design high-heeled shoes for them. The cloister, instead of a wine-cellar,

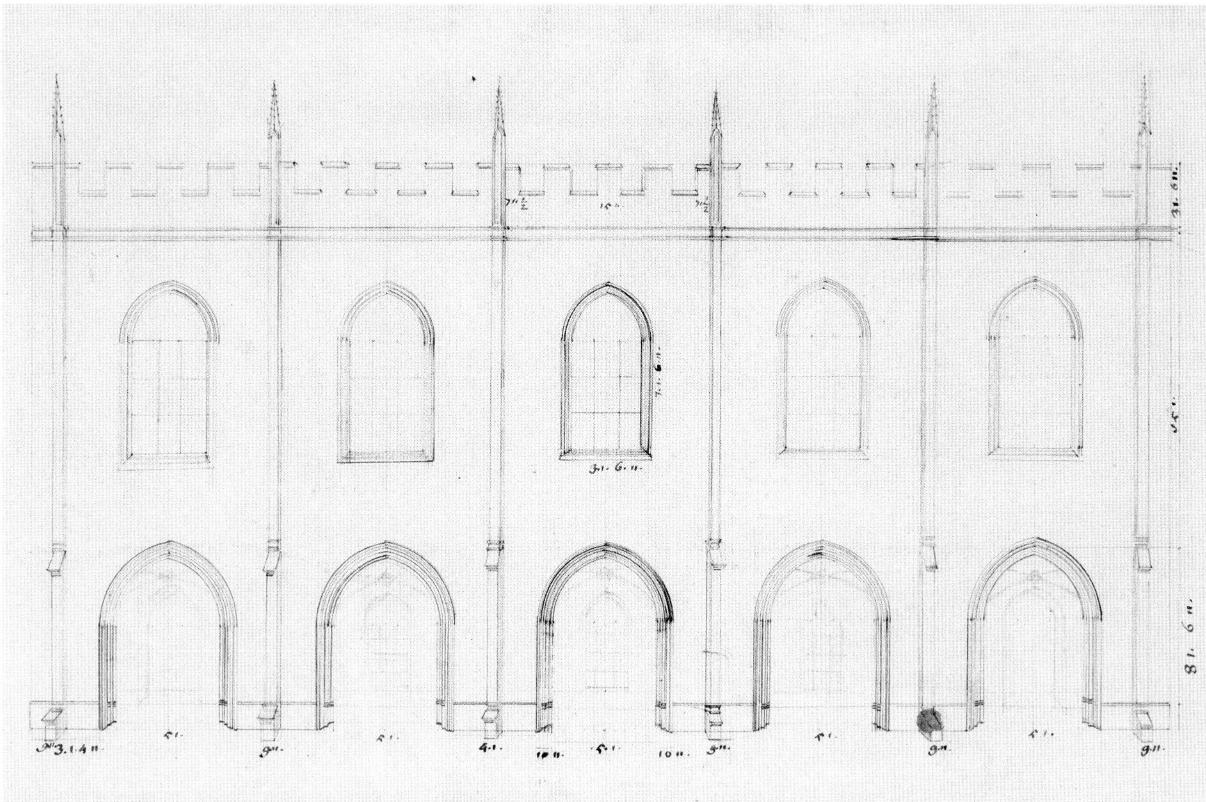

Fig. 23 John Chute, design for the Cloister and Long Gallery at Strawberry Hill, 1759. LWL 49 3582, fol. 103r. Courtesy of The Lewis Walpole Library, Yale University.

> has the air of a college. It has already passed the Seals. Mr Müntz has commended it in a piece of every language, and Mr Bentley is at this moment turning it outside inwards.—I assure you, Mr Chute, you shall always have my custom. You shall design every scrap of the ornaments; and if ever I build a palace or found a city, I will employ nobody but you. In short, you have found a proportion and given a simplicity and lightness to it, that I never expected. I have but one fault to find, and that is no bigger than my little finger; I think the buttresses too slight; and yet I fear, widening them would destroy the beauty of the space round the windows. There is another thing which is more than a fear, for it seems an impossibility, that is, of getting pictures over the windows within; and if I can't, what shall I do with the spaces?[29]

The play on the scale and materiality of architectural design, and the shifting from architecture as a fine art to fashion as a minor or decorative art, by which Chute's design for the cloister could translate as readily to the design of fashionable women's footwear, continue throughout Walpole's description and in the architecture of Strawberry Hill itself. Walpole and Chute shared a deep bond (Walpole joked that he was like a wife to Chute or that Chute was his "other self")[30] that was based in part on a shared appreciation of art and architecture. Writing as he often would to his friend and "spouse" over the design of the new Cloister for Strawberry Hill, Walpole here begins by flattering Chute before suggesting a correction to the design, which is itself diminutive ("no bigger than my little finger"). Walpole understands Chute and knows how to flatter him and how to subtly revise his designs to achieve a particular effect. While there is much humorous bluster in these comments, letters of this sort articulate the subtleties of design of which Walpole's circle were capable and their sincere engagement in the collaborative project that was the building of Strawberry Hill.

Building Strawberry Hill

The desire and finances to build Strawberry Hill came after 1741, during the tumultuous years following Walpole's return from the Grand Tour. Sir Robert Walpole resigned as prime minister in a disastrous vote of no confidence in 1742 and would die in 1745. The following year Walpole reconciled with Thomas Gray, long after their spat on the Grand Tour, and "the Chuteheads" returned from Europe. Although Walpole in 1746 briefly rented a residence outside of London, in the lower ward of Windsor Castle, in 1747 he acquired the property called "chopp'd Straw Hall" from Mrs. (Elizabeth) Chenevix, a Charing Cross toy seller, a three-story cottage built in 1698 on a five-acre plot. The otherwise unassuming original house had the distinct advantages of facing the Thames and having significant recently rebuilt neighboring properties, which were to provide inspiration to the young Horace Walpole. These included essays in Gothic or historicist design, such as Lord Radnor's Thames villa built from 1745 in the form of an Elizabethan prodigy house; Esher Place (fig. 24), expanded for Henry Pelham by William Kent in the 1730s, when Kent added lateral wings to Bishop Waynflete's fifteenth-century gatehouse; Alexander Pope's Twickenham villa and grotto; and the early phases of Dicky Bateman's Old Windsor. Like many of these building projects and much of the work conceived within his milieu, Walpole's work was to be a highly creative synthesis of old and new fabric, a series of brilliant compromises to expand and rethink an original structure. This alone justifies the Ovidian tropes derived from the *Metamorphoses* used to describe these buildings by Walpole and his contemporaries.[31]

The architectural history of Strawberry Hill has been established elsewhere and requires only a brief summary here.[32] For my purposes, the development of the house can be divided into two main phases: the first, from 1747 up to 1759, saw the house transformed into a centrally planned villa, and the second, from 1760 to 1776, witnessed the westward extension involving the Gallery and Round Tower (see figs. 25a and 25b). Walpole's earliest work, the "little improvements" of 1747–48, were to the east-facing room later called the Breakfast Room. These amounted to renovation of an original first-floor bedroom, to which was added an east-facing polygonal bay with Gothic windows and a fireplace. Designed by William Robinson, clerk of works at Greenwich hospital, these works reflect an early and hesitant approach to the Gothic and nothing of the comprehensive employment of the Gothic that would follow, as Walpole would later admit.[33] Manifestly derived from current Gothic taste in and around Twickenham and informed by the designs of Batty Langley and William Kent, these were minor renovations "before there was any design of farther improvements to the house."[34] Although Robinson was maintained as surveyor of Walpole's works, the

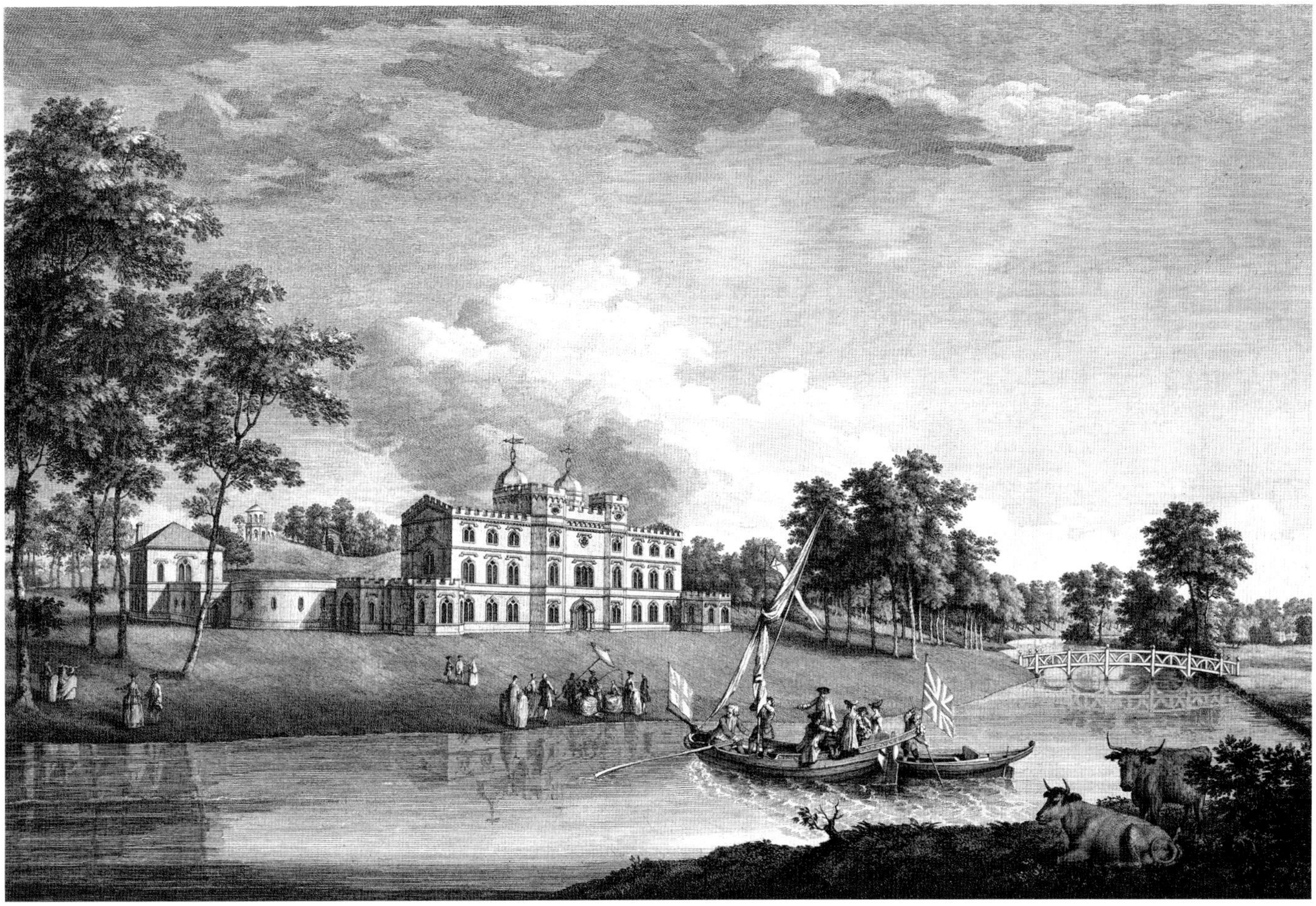

Fig. 24 Luke Sullivan, "A View of Esher in Surry [*sic*], the Seat of the Late Rt. Honble. Henry Pelham Esqr." LWL Topos Su962 no. 15++. Courtesy of The Lewis Walpole Library, Yale University.

years around 1750 saw the consolidation of Walpole's Committee, including Chute and Bentley (first appearing at Strawberry Hill in that year), who would collectively design much of the later building.

In a postscript to a letter to Horace Mann of 10 January 1750, Walpole declares, "I am going to build a little Gothic castle at Strawberry Hill," and asks Mann to acquire any stained glass or arms that he can in Italy.[35] The first major building project to Gothicize Strawberry Hill occurred during 1752–53, when the north, east, and south fronts were given their current Gothic façades, with the addition of a projecting two-story canted bay to the south. Maintaining the floor levels of the original building, Walpole created the central stair that gives access to all levels, and the Armory on the staircase landing, following the designs of Chute and Bentley (fig. 26). Chute's approach to the designs of the façades was essentially symmetrical, reflecting an indebtedness to recent work at Esher (fig. 24). Work continued in 1754, when the two-level extension was added to the north of the original block, creating the Refectory on the lower level and the Library on the upper. These were the only grand rooms in the villa as it was originally envisioned, balancing the additions to the south of the original block.

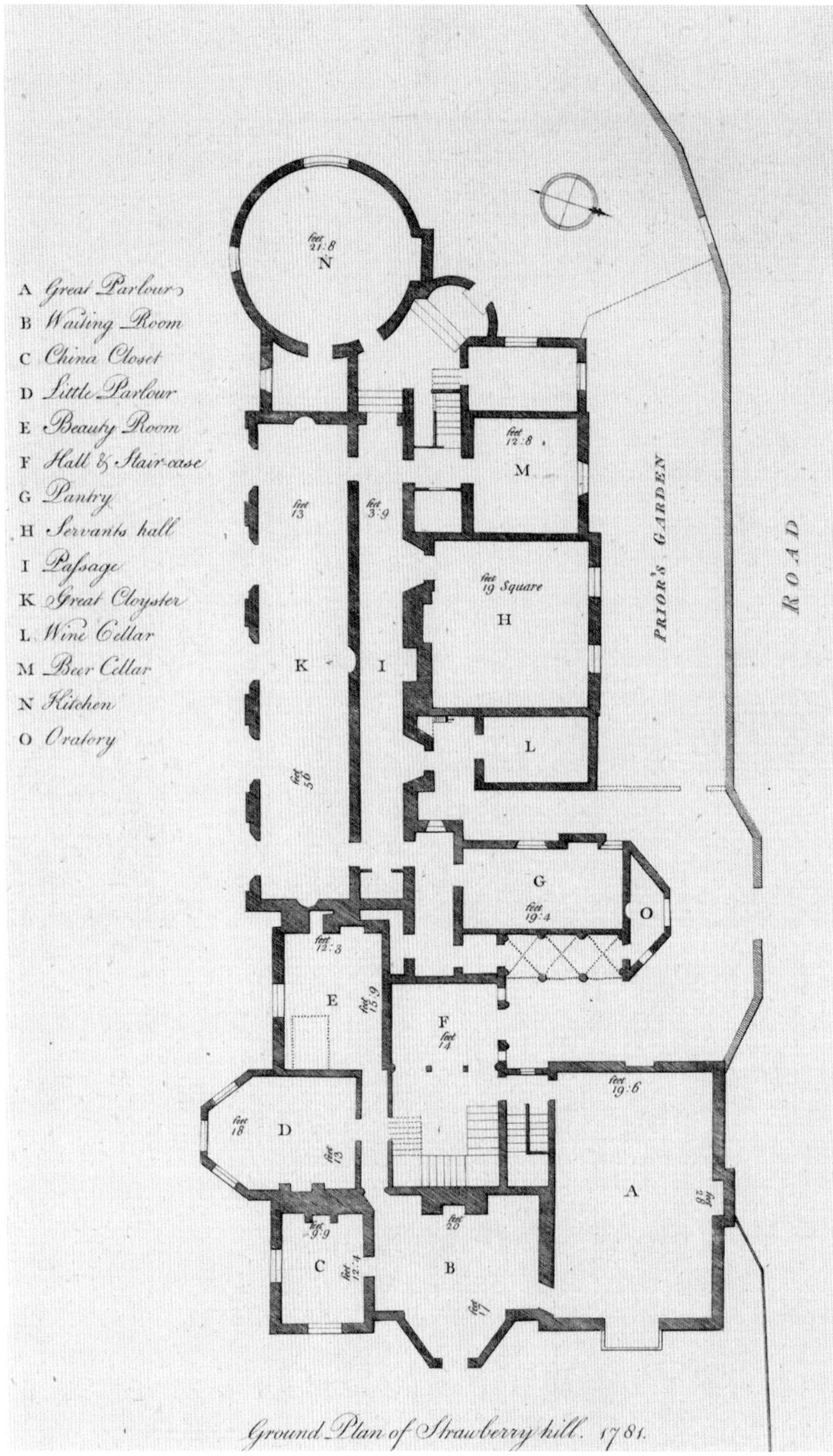

Fig. 25a Ground plan of Strawberry Hill, 1781. From Walpole, *Description* (1784). Courtesy of The Lewis Walpole Library, Yale University.

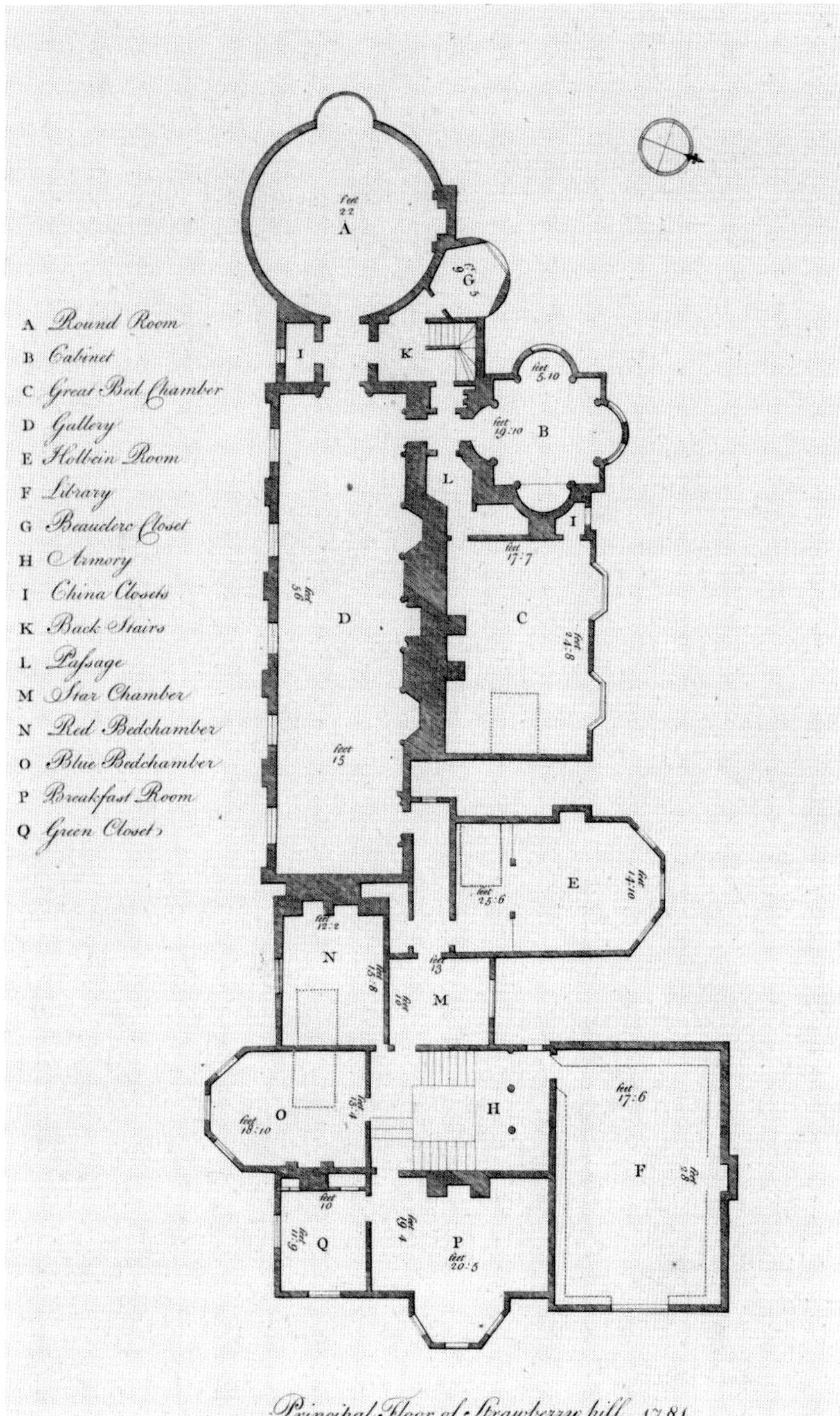

Fig. 25b Floor plan of Strawberry Hill, 1781. From Walpole, *Description* (1784). Courtesy of The Lewis Walpole Library, Yale University.

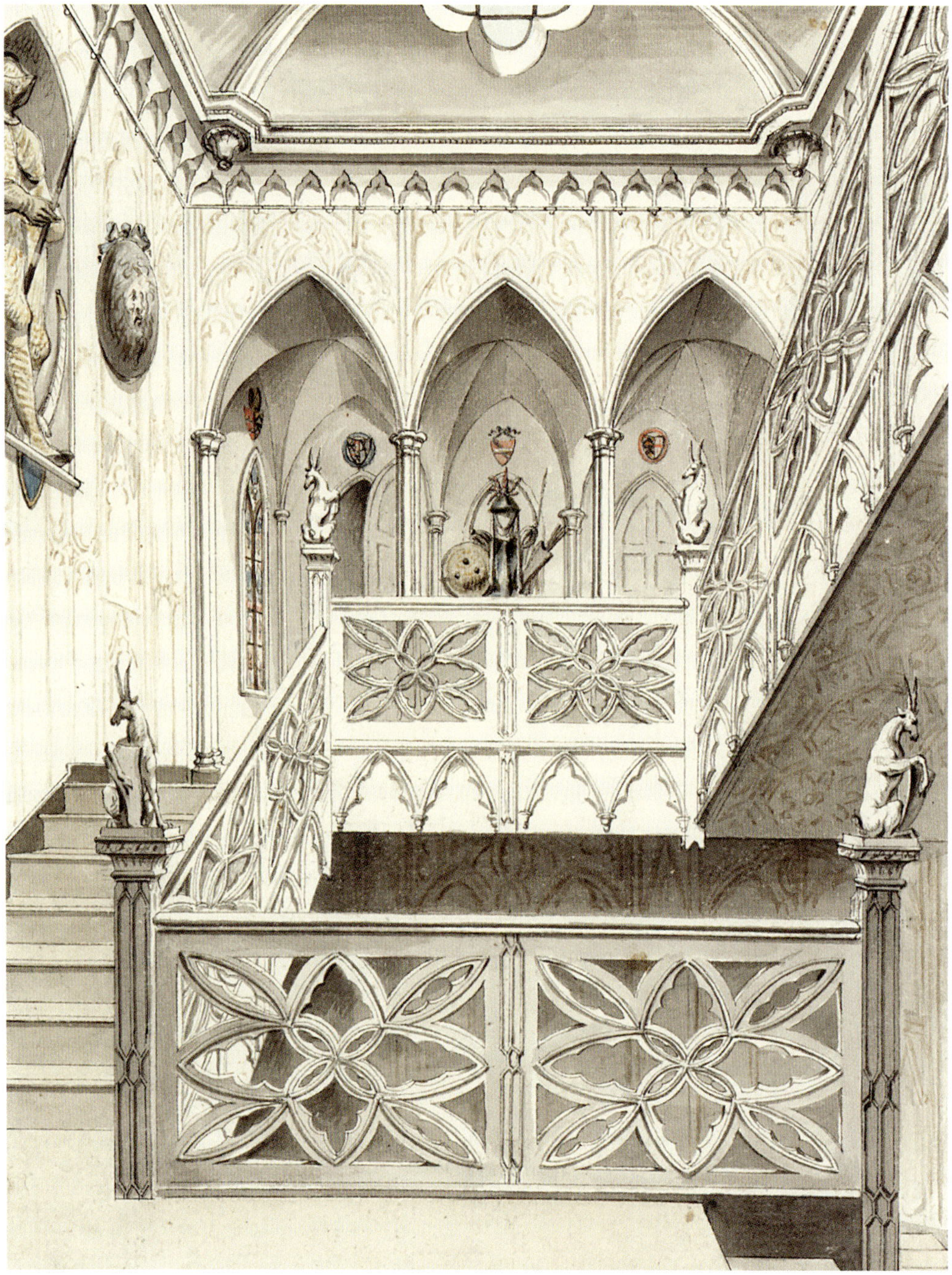

Fig. 26 Edward Edwards, staircase at Strawberry Hill, 1784. LWL 49 3582, p. 70. Courtesy of The Lewis Walpole Library, Yale University.

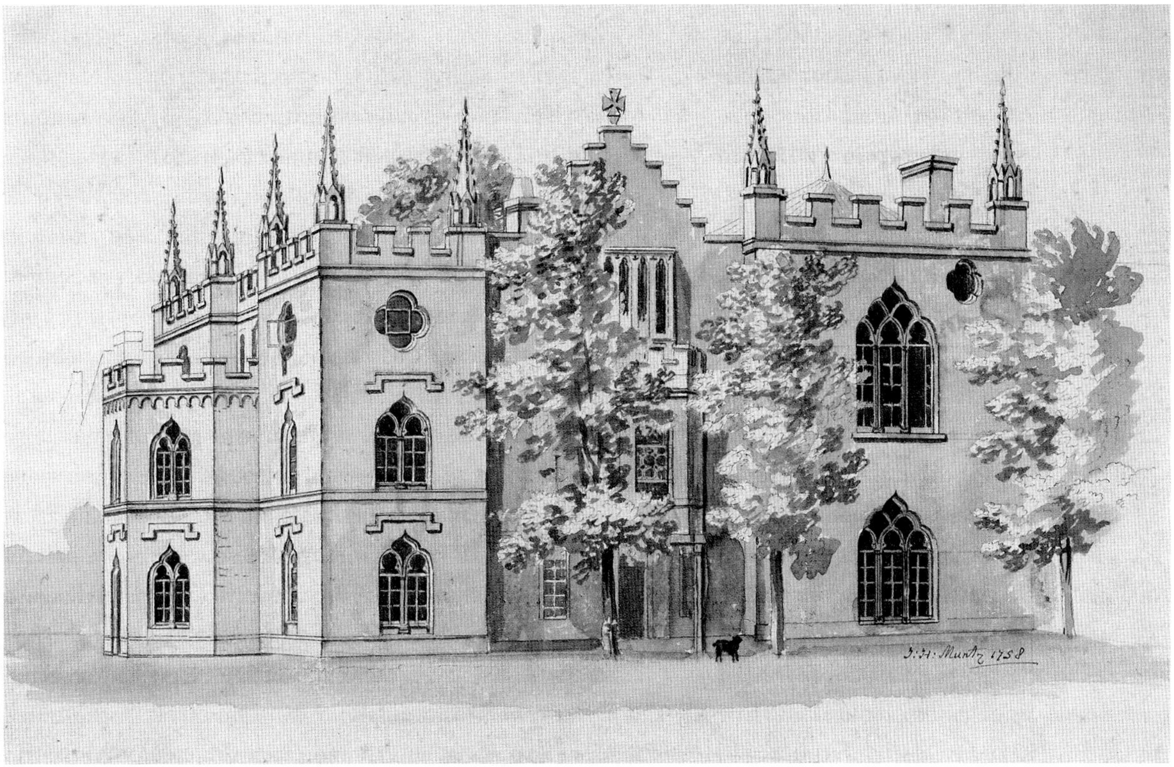

Fig. 27 J. H. Müntz, "East view of Strawberry-hill near Twickenham in Middlesex," 1758. LWL SH Views M92 no. 5 Box 110. Courtesy of The Lewis Walpole Library, Yale University.

To the west, between 1758 and 1759, Walpole built the Little Cloister (following Chute's designs), which led into the dimly lit entrance, or Paraclete. Abutting the cloister he added a two-level Pantry on the lower floor and the Holbein Chamber on the upper. The villa of 1759 was a compact, centrally planned structure, with incursions into the original fabric at each of its cardinal points, as evidenced in J. H. Müntz's contemporary view (fig. 27). Understanding the original form and small scale of the villa in this period, as Walpole and the Committee first imagined it, illuminates the appropriateness of his famous passage comparing his home to Lord Burlington's small centrally planned villa at Chiswick (fig. 4): "As my castle is so diminutive, I give myself a Burlington-air, and say, that as Chiswick is a model of Grecian architecture, Strawberry Hill is to be so of Gothic."[36] It also illuminates other centrally planned houses that followed in the wake of the first major phase of Strawberry Hill, including Chute's emulative work at Donnington Grove, for James Pettit Andrews, circa 1765 (discussed in chapter 5).

The second phase of construction to the house was largely contained in the west-wing extension of the Long Gallery and Round Tower, which was imagined in the late 1750s but only begun in 1760.[37] While Walpole claimed to have lacked the financial means for expansion, it was physically impossible to do so until 1759,

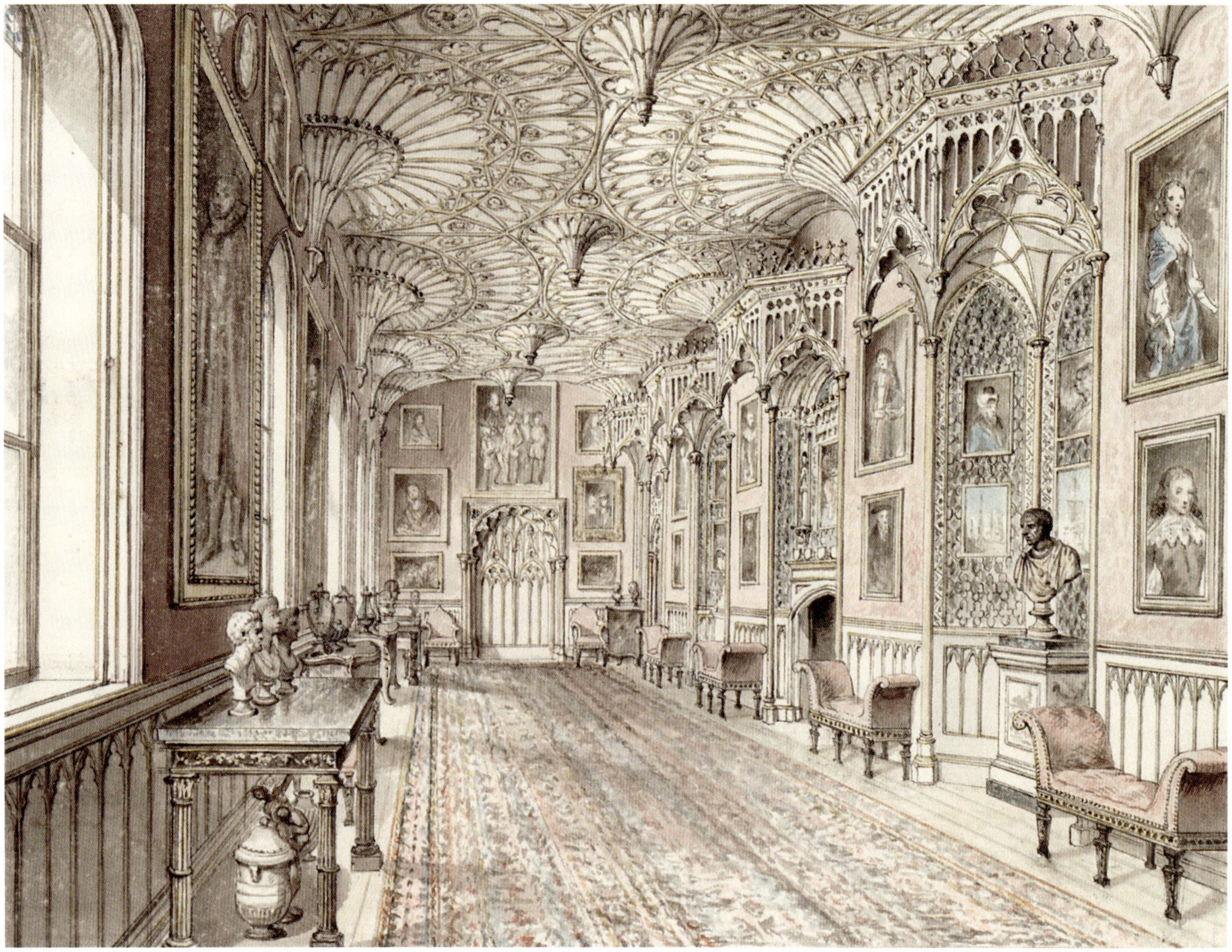

when he acquired the lands to the west of the existing house and diverted to the north the road that ran through the future site of the west wing.[38] Walpole's work of 1760 onward dramatically changed the scale and character of what was a small suburban villa. This addition—comprising the Long Gallery (fig. 28), the Tower and Round Drawing Room (fig. 29) (the latter designed by Robert Adam), and the Tribune (fig. 36)—doubled the footprint of the house and substantially changed it from a quasi-monastic building to a Gothic castle. From 1771 to 1772, the Great North Bedchamber was added in the angle formed by the Tribune and the Long Gallery. By 1776 the architecture of the house was substantially completed with the addition of the Beauclerc Tower, a three-level addition in the angle between the Round Tower and the back stairs. Although the house was complete as a structure, Walpole restlessly decorated it for another decade.

Strawberry Hill was stylistically and formally unique, and its final form owes as much to the existing fabric of "chopp'd Straw Hall" as it does to the organic nature of its development and to the tastes of the men

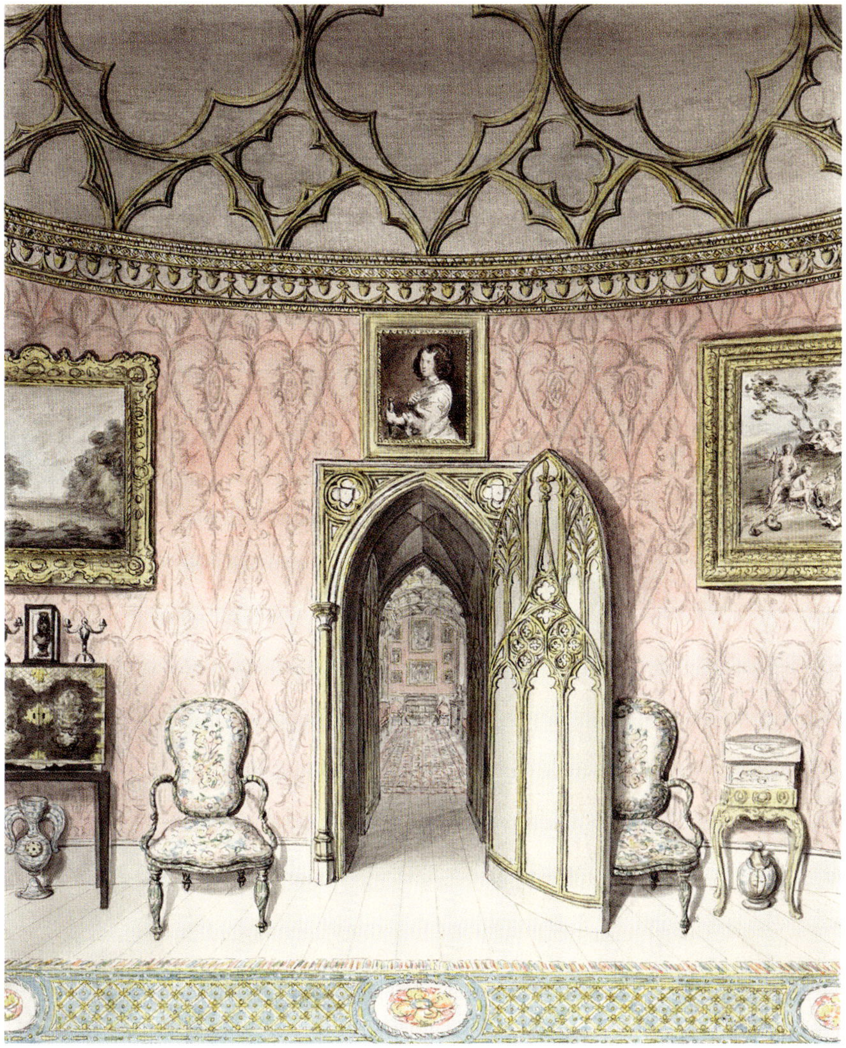

Fig. 28 Edward Edwards, the Gallery at Strawberry Hill, ca. 1781. Photo © Victoria and Albert Museum, London.

Fig. 29 John Carter, the Round Drawing Room at Strawberry Hill, undated. LWL 33 30 Copy 11 Folio, p. 153. Courtesy of The Lewis Walpole Library, Yale University.

who designed it. Unlike previous experiments in the style that employed the Gothic as an ornamental vocabulary to adorn what were Palladian plans and volumes, such as William Kent's Esher Place (which has been called "Palladian Gothic")[39] and John Chute's initial designs for the Vyne (Hampshire) Strawberry Hill mirrors the additive building patterns of medieval architecture, with ornament of different periods and dates, seemingly disconnected spatial volumes, and varying floor levels, all suggesting an ancient architectural history for Walpole's modern home. If not the first Gothic mansion in England, Walpole's villa was the first domestic building to use Gothic ornament to create an overall fictive environment: the villa as an elaborate medieval stage set. Its theatricality is reinforced by the quotation-like nature of its forms, which exist logically within the broader spatial and stylistic ontology of the building but often uncomfortably within the individual rooms of the house, in which they stand as decontextualized citations from historic buildings.

Strawberry Hill Gothic: Form, Materiality, Scale

I have already emphasized that scholarly considerations of Strawberry Hill have tended to impose nineteenth- and twentieth-century conceptions of architectural form and simulation on it, by which the house becomes a kind of amateur attempt at Gothic form, an unstudied pastiche that could only preface the later development of the style in the nineteenth century. The extensive evidence for the house leaves no doubt that Strawberry Hill was a painstakingly rendered exercise in Gothic form, however discordant it might be with nineteenth- and twentieth-century aesthetics. In exploring the Gothic forms of Strawberry Hill, I follow Walpole's own lead in suggesting that "*every true Goth* must perceive that they [the rooms of his house] are more the works of fancy than of imitation."[40] What Walpole describes as "fancy"—a deeply subjective appraisal of form unconstrained by current rules of decorum or absolute fidelity to a historical source—usefully defines his approach to the style. Although Walpole's own tastes and those of the Committee did shift toward more precisely executed Gothic replications in the 1760s and 1770s, Walpole's appraisal of the Gothic as a style of creative and even libidinal freedom remained, and he placed particular value on radical departures from medieval Gothic architecture in his designs.

Uniquely for the period, the relationship of Strawberry Hill's Gothic architecture to its historical sources was glossed by a text, Walpole's *Description*. This provides a brief account of many of Strawberry's Gothic installations, often indicating the original sources for the works in medieval architecture or in antiquarian reproductions and generally attributing authorship of designs to members of the Committee. The Holbein Chamber (from 1758) is a useful starting point (fig. 30): "The ceiling is taken from the queen's dressing-room at Windsor [Castle]. The chimney-piece [fig. 31], designed by Mr. [Richard] Bentley, is chiefly taken from the tomb of archbishop Warham at Canterbury [1450–1532]," a monument Walpole knew from an engraving in John Dart's *History and Antiquities of the Cathedral Church of Canterbury* (1726; fig. 32).[41] Walpole deliberately fractures the "originality" of the fireplace by positioning it within a chain of replications, from the medieval monument to the recording and publication of the monument, the reproduction of specific formal aspects of the monument at Strawberry Hill (note Walpole states it is only "*chiefly*" taken from Warham's tomb), and finally the engraving of the monument for the *Description*. Warham's tomb provided the source for the two tiers of richly adorned Perpendicular niches executed in wood that flank the fireplace, but little else. Bentley used the single columns of niches on either side of the tomb, multiplied them by three, and set them within two semicircular turrets. The canopywork above the tomb is edited and miniaturized into a repetitious frieze of Gothic arches to make space for a main image above the mantel, and the tomb itself is replaced by the fireplace. The design for the ceiling is an elaboration upon the original ceiling on the first floor of Henry VII's Tower at Windsor, built 1497–98, which was used in Walpole's period as the Queen's dressing room.[42]

Turning to the other major Gothic design in the room, the screen, Walpole describes it in shorthand: "The pierced arches of the screen from the gates of the choir of Rouen; the rest of the screen was designed by Mr. Bentley" (fig. 33).[43] The source for the "pierced arches" is in fact the former choir screen of St. Ouen in

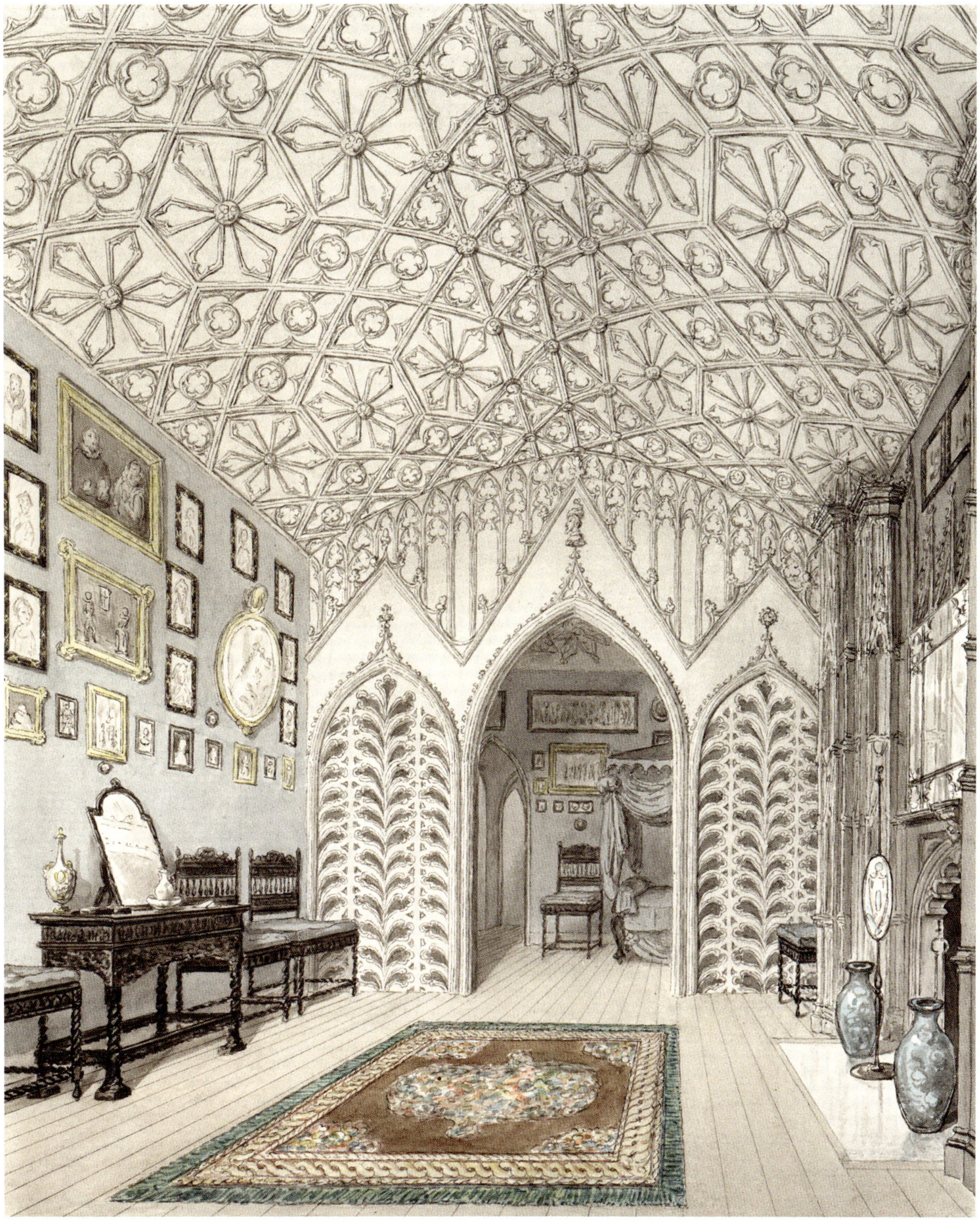

Fig. 30 John Carter, the Holbein Chamber at Strawberry Hill, undated. LWL 33 30 Copy 11 Folio, p. 117. Courtesy of The Lewis Walpole Library, Yale University.

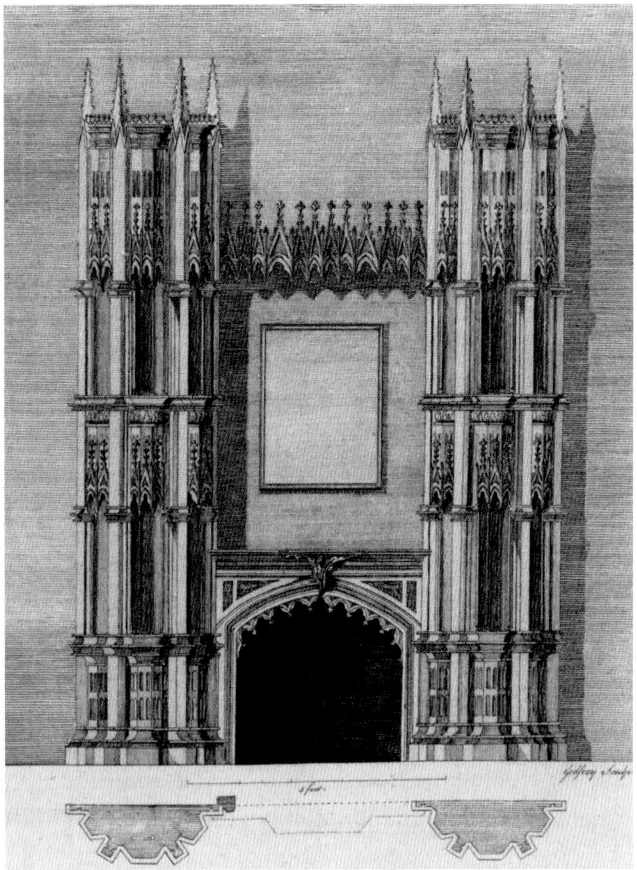

Fig. 31 Chimneypiece of the Holbein Chamber. From Walpole, *Description* (1784). Courtesy of The Lewis Walpole Library, Yale University.

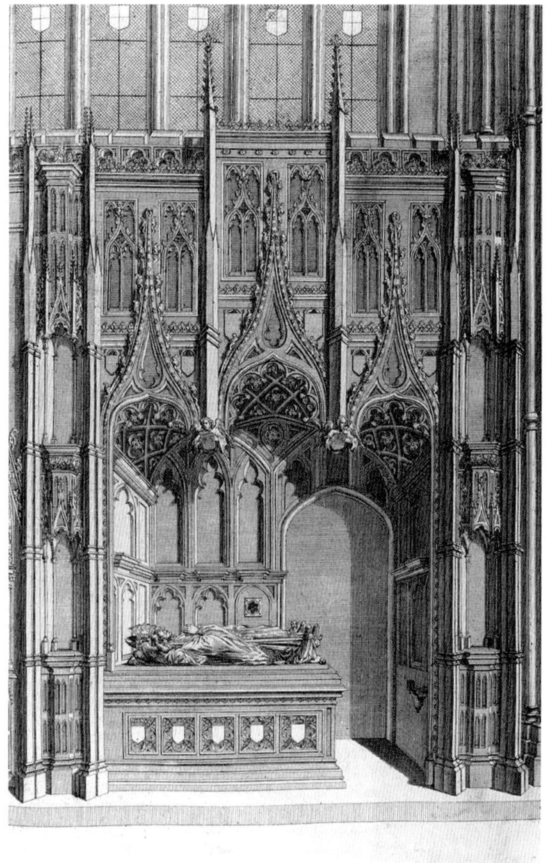

Fig. 32 Tomb of Archbishop Warham. From John Dart, *The History and Antiquities of the Cathedral Church of Canterbury* (1726). Courtesy of W. D. Jordan Rare Books and Special Collections, Queen's University, Kingston, Ontario.

Rouen rather than Rouen Cathedral, a slip on Walpole's part. He does not list a specific source for the design in an antiquarian text, although the most available text was Jean-François Pommeraye's *Histoire de l'abbaye royale de S. Ouen de Rouen* (1662), which shows the door upon which the tracery in the screen is based (fig. 34). Walpole did not own a copy of Pommeraye, although it could have come from another member of the Committee or via the medievalist and scholar of Norman architecture Andrew Coltée Ducarel (1713–1785), with whom Walpole was in contact from 1758, when the Holbein Chamber was begun.[44] A hint that Pommeraye's engraving informed the design is offered by Bentley's earlier drawing for the choir screen, which shows richly encrusted ogee-headed arches terminating in finials that ascend through a frieze of open Gothic arches (fig. 35).[45] The form of the

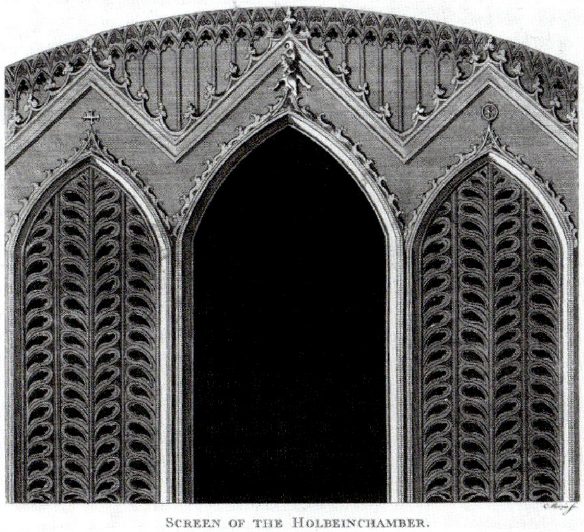

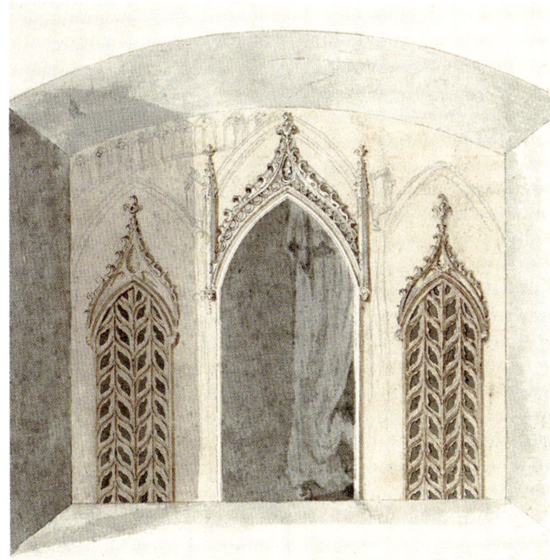

Counterclockwise from top left:

Fig. 33 Screen of the Holbein Chamber. From Walpole, *Description* (1784). Courtesy of The Lewis Walpole Library, Yale University.

Fig. 34 "Jubé de Leglise de St Ouen." From Pommeraye, *S. Ouen de Rouen* (1662), plate 54. Photo: author.

Fig. 35 Richard Bentley, screen in the Holbein Chamber. Preparatory drawing. LWL 49 3585, fol. 55v. Courtesy of The Lewis Walpole Library, Yale University.

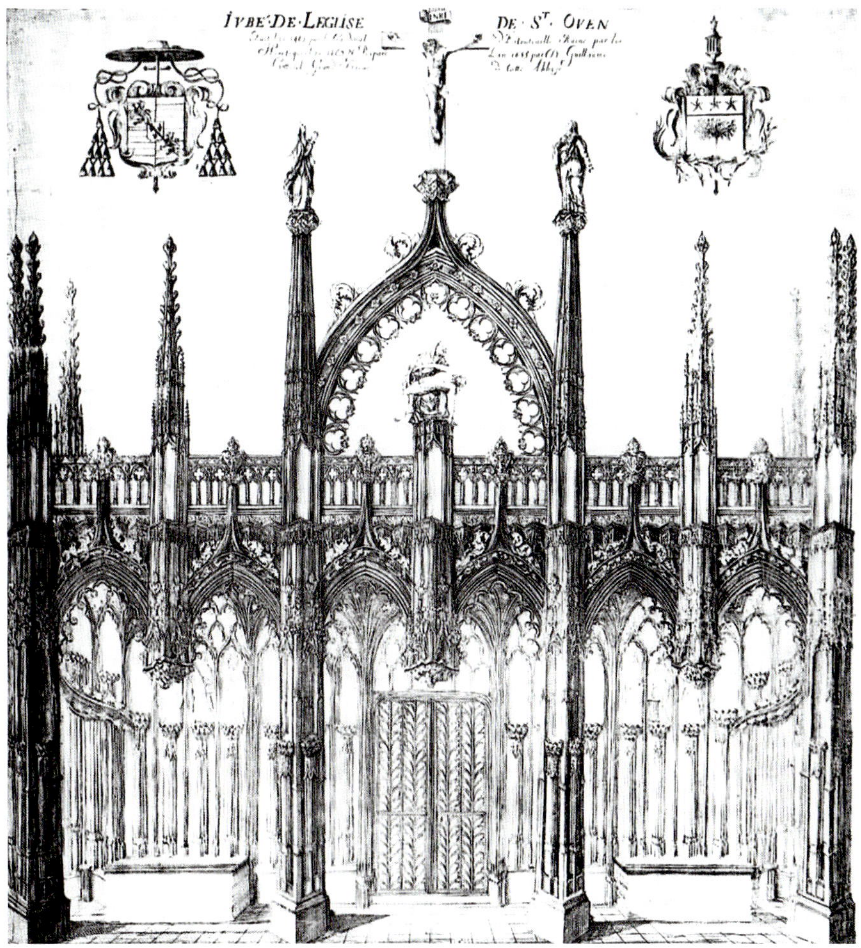

main arches, and perhaps the arches above, appear to be ready translations from the Rouen engraving. Given the Committee's intention to cordon off the room by a screen, employing a medieval screen as a model—however different though it clearly is—was appropriate. Bentley's versions of the Holbein screen, including the final one, each employ motifs from the St. Ouen screen that are assimilated into Bentley's own very different design. Bentley approaches the Rouen screen as a model to adopt and surpass: based upon a triumphal-arch motif, he orders the Rouen arches underneath triple crocketed gables and pushes the frieze of openwork arches upward and transforms them into blind wooden arches, and he employs the tracery from the central door within the lateral portals. Both the late medieval screen, with its *flamboyant* motifs, and Archbishop Warham's tomb were appropriate choices for the Holbein Chamber, which was intended to be an early "period room" featuring objects that celebrated the sixteenth-century history of England (even if some of the sources were not English). The room was conceived as the setting for the display of thirty-three tracings by George Vertue (1684–1756)—themselves modern simulations—of the Royal Collection portrait drawings by Hans Holbein (1497–1543) of members of Henry VIII's court. Walpole acquired the drawings in 1757 and added further aristocratic and royal portraits by or after Holbein and other objects with a related Henrician provenance, including the hat of Cardinal Wolsey (1473–1530).[46]

Throughout the interior of the house, the approach to Gothic form employed by Walpole and the Committee entailed extracting specific motifs from Gothic architecture or its representations in antiquarian publications and adapting them to an altogether different syntax of ornament. Describing what was surely one of the most striking spaces of the villa, the Tribune (or Chapel) of 1760–62, Walpole claims: "It is a square with a semicircular recess in the middle of each side, painted stone-colour with gilt ornaments, and with windows and niches, the latter taken from those on the sides of the north door of the great church at Saint Alban's: the roof, which is taken from the chapter-house at York, is terminated by a star of yellow glass that throws a golden gloom all over the room, and with the painted windows gives it the solemn air of a rich chapel."[47] I have already commented on the quasi-sacred space of the Tribune (fig. 36), centered as it was around an "altar" set within a niche (itself based upon the tomb to the children of Edward III at Westminster Abbey as represented in Dart's *Westmonasterium* [1742]), but its sources warrant further exploration.[48] Walpole is correct to suggest that the niches in the room are derived from St. Alban's, which was drawn by J. H. Müntz in 1759 (fig. 37) and was employed elsewhere in the house, including the door into the Round Room and in the Long Gallery. (He does not note that the dado of cusped shield-bearing quatrefoils with mouchettes in its corners is borrowed from the aforementioned tombs at Herstmonceux, which Walpole and Chute viewed on a sketching tour in 1752.) His suggestion that the "roof" was based on the late thirteenth-century chapter house at York, however, is only partially true. Walpole's source for the chapter house was quite certainly Francis Drake's *Eboracum* (1736), a copy of which he owned (fig. 38).[49] The Tribune ceiling derives its general organization from the York Minster chapter house, with its tierceron vault pattern (created in wood without a central columnar support that is otherwise conventional in English chapter-house design).[50] The "heart-shaped" tracery that decorates the springing of the vault, however, is not derived from the chapter house but from York Minster's great west window (of ca.

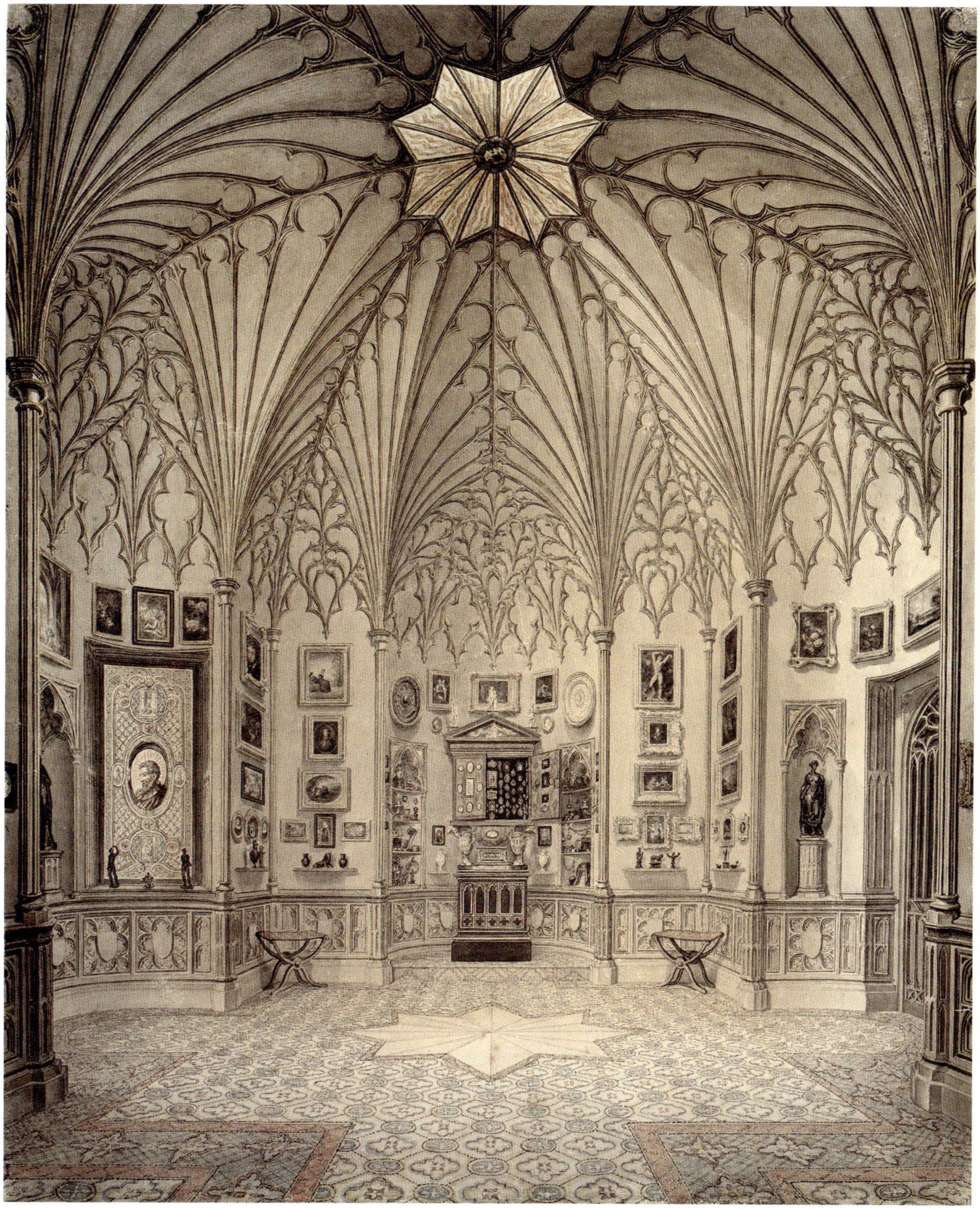

Fig. 36 John Carter, the Tribune at Strawberry Hill, ca. 1789. LWL 789.00.00.73dr++. Courtesy of The Lewis Walpole Library, Yale University.

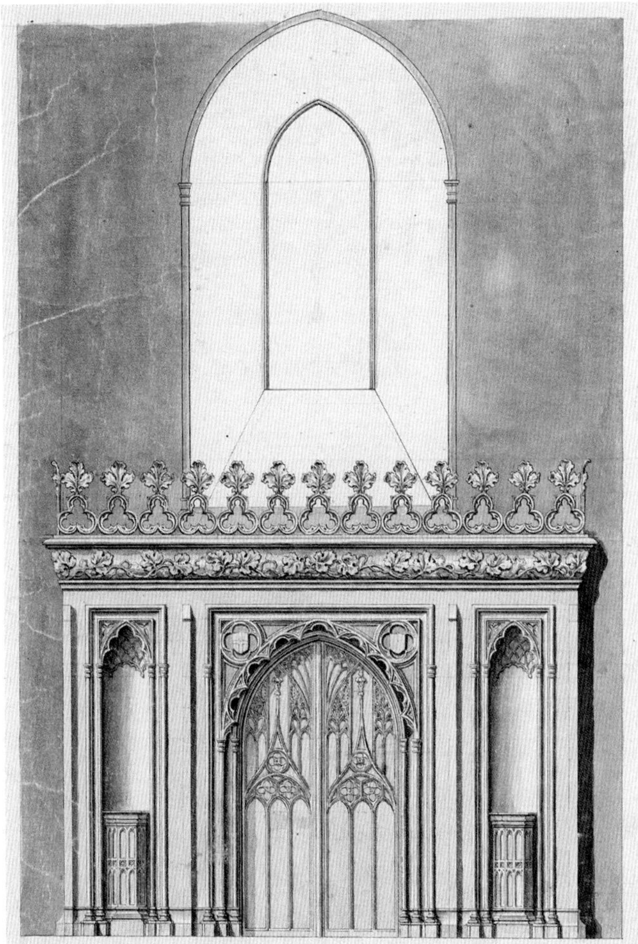

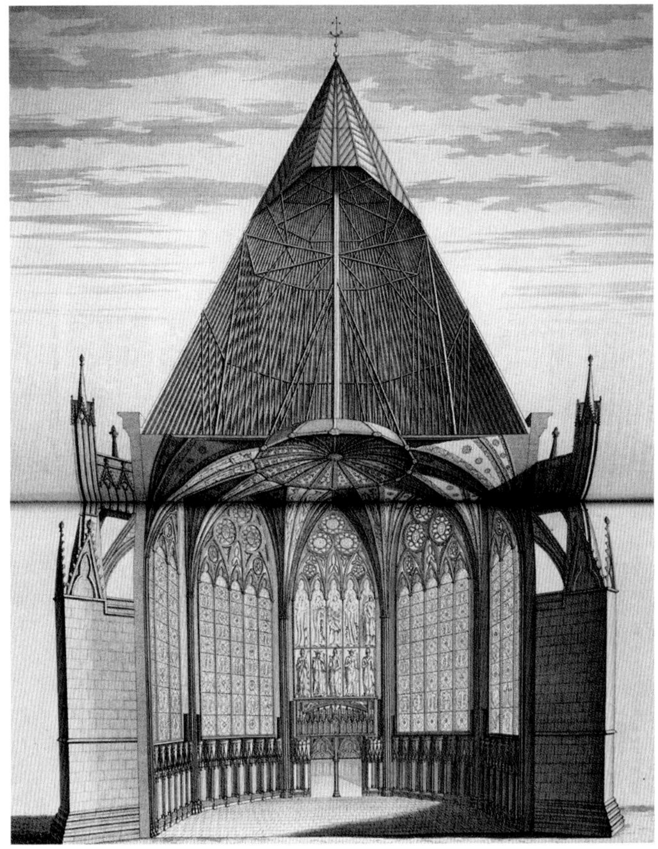

Fig. 37 J. H. Müntz, "From the Inside of the Great Church at St Albans," 1759. LWL 49 3582. Courtesy of The Lewis Walpole Library, Yale University.

Fig. 38 "An internal perspective view of the Chapter house at York." From Francis Drake, *Eboracum: Or, The Antiquities of the City of York* (1736), 476. Courtesy of W. D. Jordan Rare Books and Special Collections, Queen's University, Kingston, Ontario.

1338).[51] Walpole's source for the window tracery was also Drake's *Eboracum*, which features a detailed representation of the west window (fig. 39). As such, Walpole's Tribune at Strawberry Hill is a remarkable synthesis of two parts of the same building, albeit of different dates, assembled from graphic representations from the same antiquarian text spaced just fifty pages apart.[52]

The status of the room as a "tribune," however, suggests that Walpole's underlying reference for the structure of the room (if not its ornamentation) was the late sixteenth-century octagonal Uffizi Tribuna in Florence, which Walpole had seen and admired on the Grand Tour and even owned drawings of (fig. 40).[53] This was an appropriate allusion, since it held the greatest items of the Medici collection in a private apartment that became increasingly open to public in the course of the century. Understood in these terms, the Tribune—one of the house's main spaces for Walpole's collection—becomes a Gothic Uffizi, a place for the display of art within a quasi-sacred context. This association is underscored

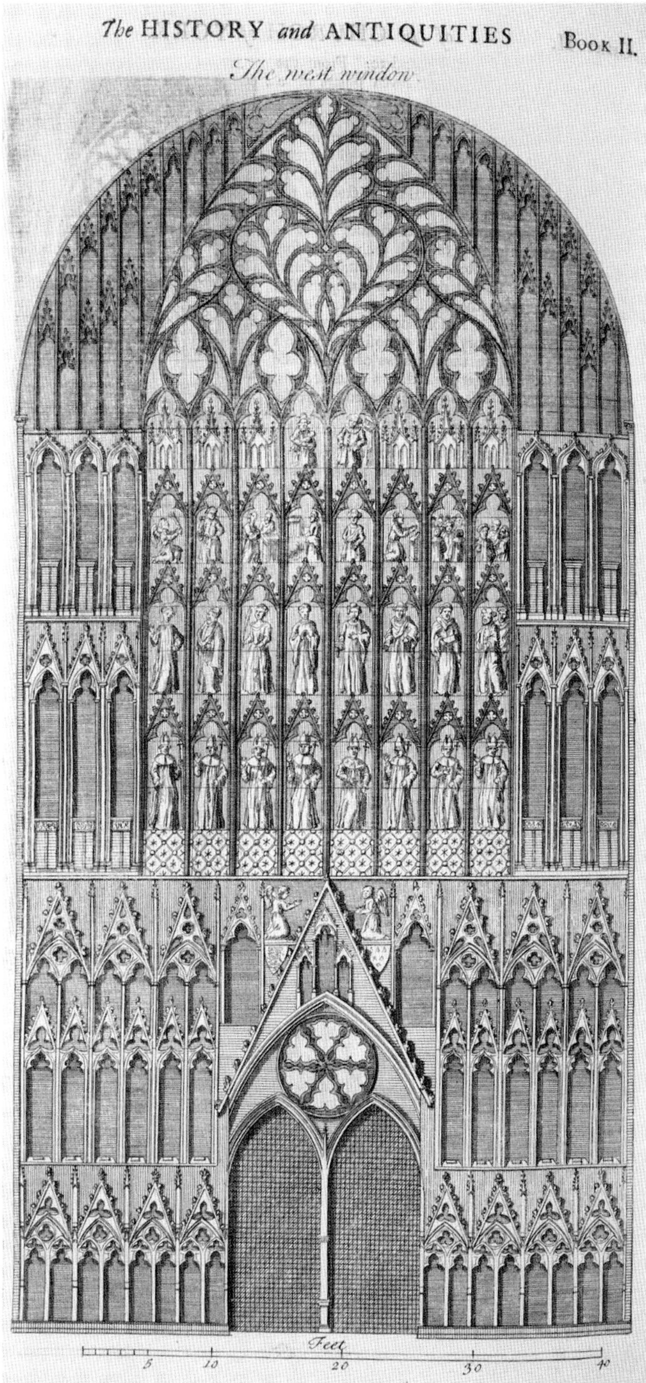

Fig. 39 West window at York Minster. From Francis Drake, *Eboracum: Or, The Antiquities of the City of York* (1736), 526. Courtesy of W. D. Jordan Rare Books and Special Collections, Queen's University, Kingston, Ontario.

by the room's central planning and star-shaped glass in the ceiling, which shed a "golden gloom" over the interior and whose form is repeated on the inlaid floor.[54] The relationship between Strawberry Hill's Gothic ornament and its medieval sources is consistent with Walpole's own understanding of architectural simulation, according to which "all Gothic designs should be made to imitate something that was of that time, a part of a church, a castle, a convent, or a mansion," rather than serve as eye-catchers or garden pavilions, which had no place in medieval building.[55] Although this approach to medieval style has been called "motif-mongering" by recent commentators, it was within Walpole's milieu, a carefully theorized approach to the design of Gothic interiors vis-à-vis their medieval sources.[56]

But the Gothic forms employed at Strawberry Hill were not all based upon existing medieval sources. Many of the designs from the 1750s (and some afterward) were either based upon Georgian Gothic architecture or were original. A useful case study is Bentley's designs for the Refectory—the dining room of Strawberry Hill—built and decorated in the mid 1750s (fig. 41). As Walpole intimates in a letter to John Chute, the cornice of pendants in the Refectory—which would become a common motif of Walpolean Gothic—was modeled upon that in the recent Gothic chapel at Wroxton Abbey, executed "in a pretty Gothic taste" (Walpole saw the house in 1753).[57] The chimneypiece, which eventually appeared in one of the full-page engravings in Walpole's *Description* (fig. 42), was designed by Bentley as the room's focal point. It is an extraordinary combination of Decorated Gothic motifs: the finials turned forty-five degrees that terminate in foliate crockets, the lateral niches with ogee-headed arches and foliate crockets, the sharply pointed open crosses, and the cusped

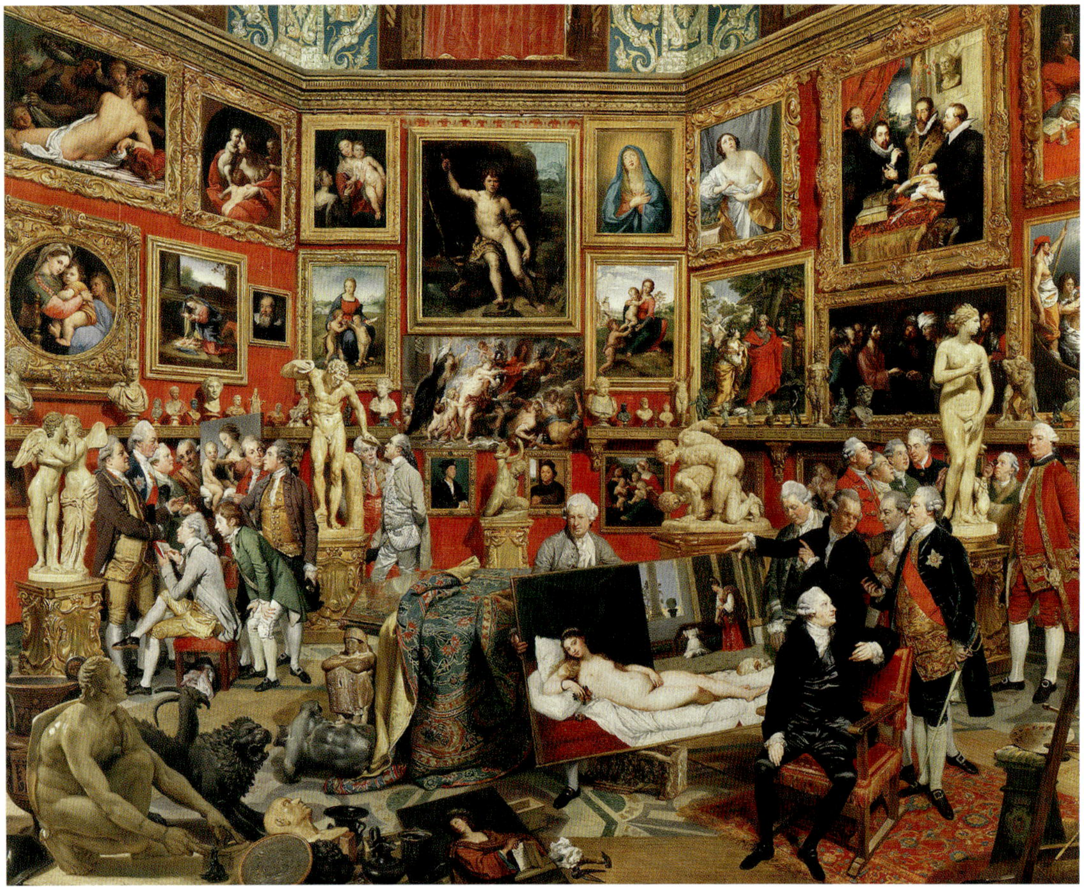

Fig. 40 Johann Zoffany, *Tribuna of the Uffizi*, 1772–79. Royal Collection, Windsor Castle. Royal Collection Trust / © Her Majesty Queen Elizabeth II 2019.

trefoils that undulate along the bottom of the "lintel" all derive from late thirteenth- and early fourteenth-century English architecture. Indeed, typical of other installations at Strawberry Hill and in Walpole's circle generally, Bentley's design here may have been inspired by the canopied court-circle tombs at Westminster Abbey, which provide precedents for some of the forms employed. Bentley uses a similar approach in the room's furniture: in 1755 he and Walpole collaboratively designed eight Gothic chairs (fig. 43) in beech wood that would be painted black to simulate ebony (they were executed by the London furniture maker William Hallett [1717–1781]). The chairs are not based upon medieval furniture but upon medieval architecture: the structure of the openwork tracery on the chair backs is based ultimately upon Decorated window tracery. Picking up the sharply pointed open crosses from the chimneypiece for the tops of the chair backs, the openwork tracery of the chairs adds to these trefoil-headed arches and cusped ovals.[58]

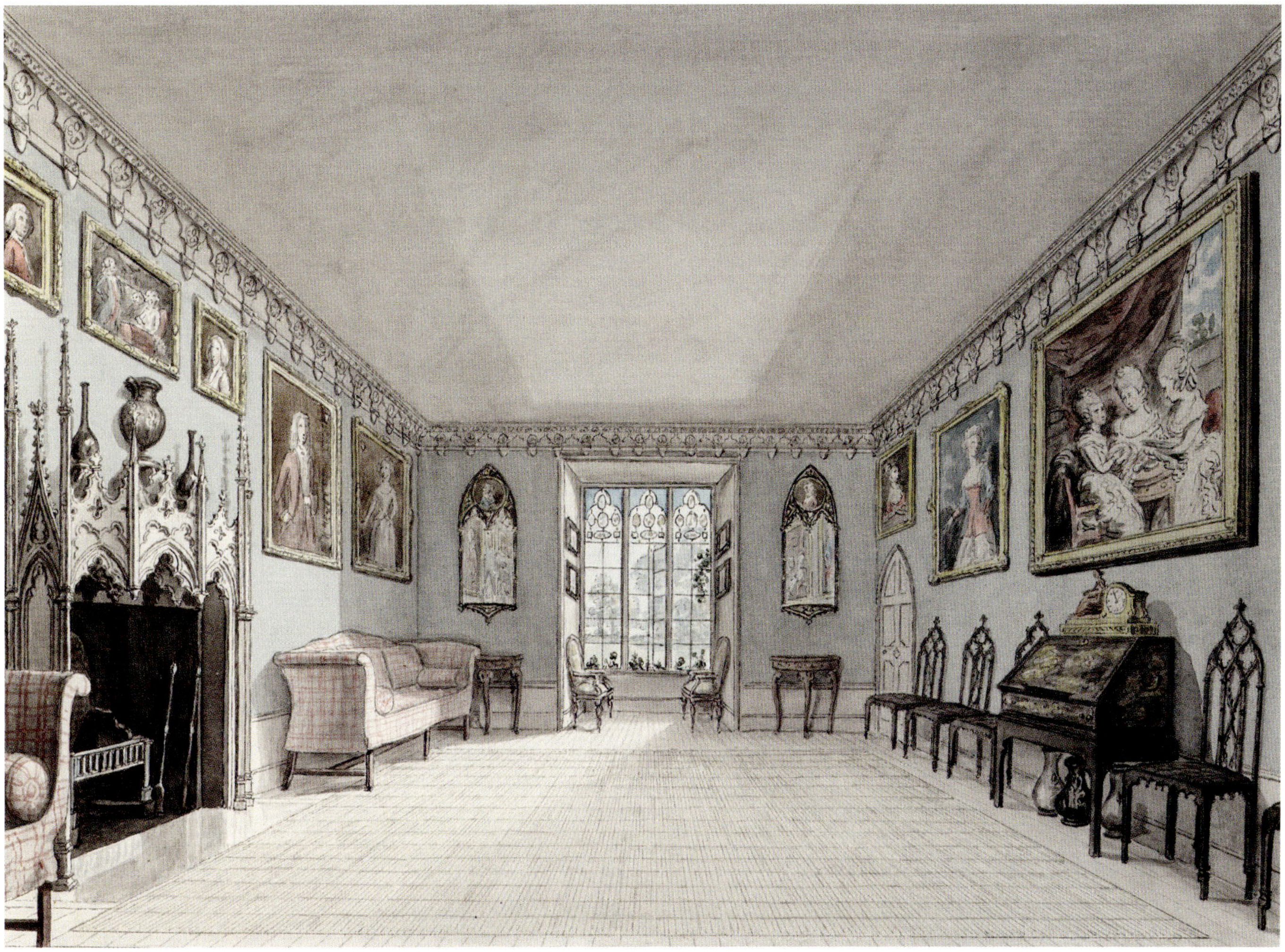

Fig. 41 John Carter, the Refectory at Strawberry Hill. LWL 33 30 Copy 11 Folio, p. 35. Courtesy of The Lewis Walpole Library, Yale University.

For the Refectory, Bentley was also responsible for designing a Gothic table that featured four repeating ogee-headed arches upon spiral legs (fig. 44). The "free-hanging" ogee arches across the apron of the table do have precedents in medieval architecture, but here the most likely source is the Gothic designs of William Kent (a useful comparison is with Kent's designs employed at Dicky Bateman's church at Shobdon, Herefordshire). Bentley's designs are Gothic assemblages rather than replications; transforming existing Gothic motifs into an entirely new syntactical structure, these assemblages *allude* to medieval architecture but deliberately deny any single source or point of origin. Critiques of Strawberry Hill's Gothic installations by Victorian critics such as Charles Eastlake have disparaged them as parodies of medieval Gothic, "with utter disregard for the original purpose of the design."[59] However biased, Eastlake's assessment was at least partially correct. Walpole left plenty of evidence to indicate that parody was a significant aspect of Strawberry

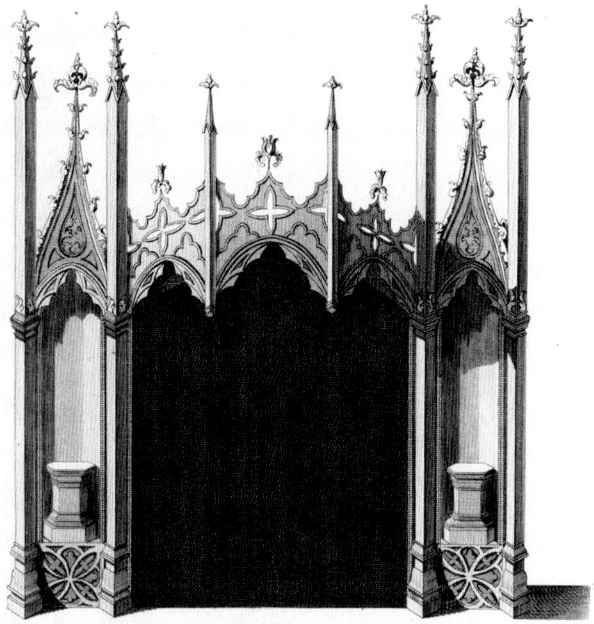

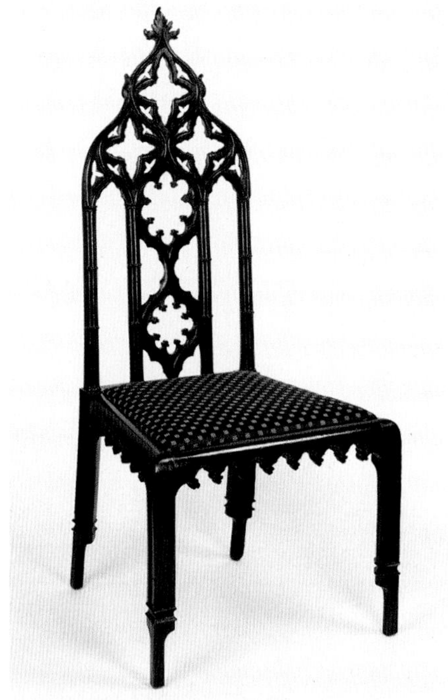

Fig. 42 Chimneypiece in the Refectory, Strawberry Hill. From Walpole, *Description* (1784). Courtesy of The Lewis Walpole Library, Yale University.

Fig. 43 William Hallett Sr., one of eight Gothic chairs for the Strawberry Hill Refectory, after the designs of Richard Bentley and Horace Walpole. Beech painted black, with modern upholstery. Now Lewis Walpole Library. Courtesy of The Lewis Walpole Library, Yale University.

Fig. 44 George Perfect Harding, Gothic table. LWL 30 30 Copy 6, fol. 46r. Courtesy of The Lewis Walpole Library, Yale University.

Hill. Historians of architecture have not, since Eastlake, been sufficiently attentive to the subversive humor of Walpole's famous home, its "wit, visual puns, satire, and vital irreverence."[60] Parody was central to Walpole's medievalism in general, as historians of his literature have recently shown[61] (a point to which I return to below).

Understood in relation to their medieval sources (where they exist), the Gothic installations at Strawberry Hill each performed thematic and material transgressions. Walpole's villa borrowed Gothic forms from sacred contexts derived from the Catholic/Gothic past, as he understood it, and reemployed them in a secular, domestic setting. So transposed, these installations also transgressed the material properties of their original sources, as stone-built medieval Gothic was replicated in modern materials. Most famous, perhaps, is the Long

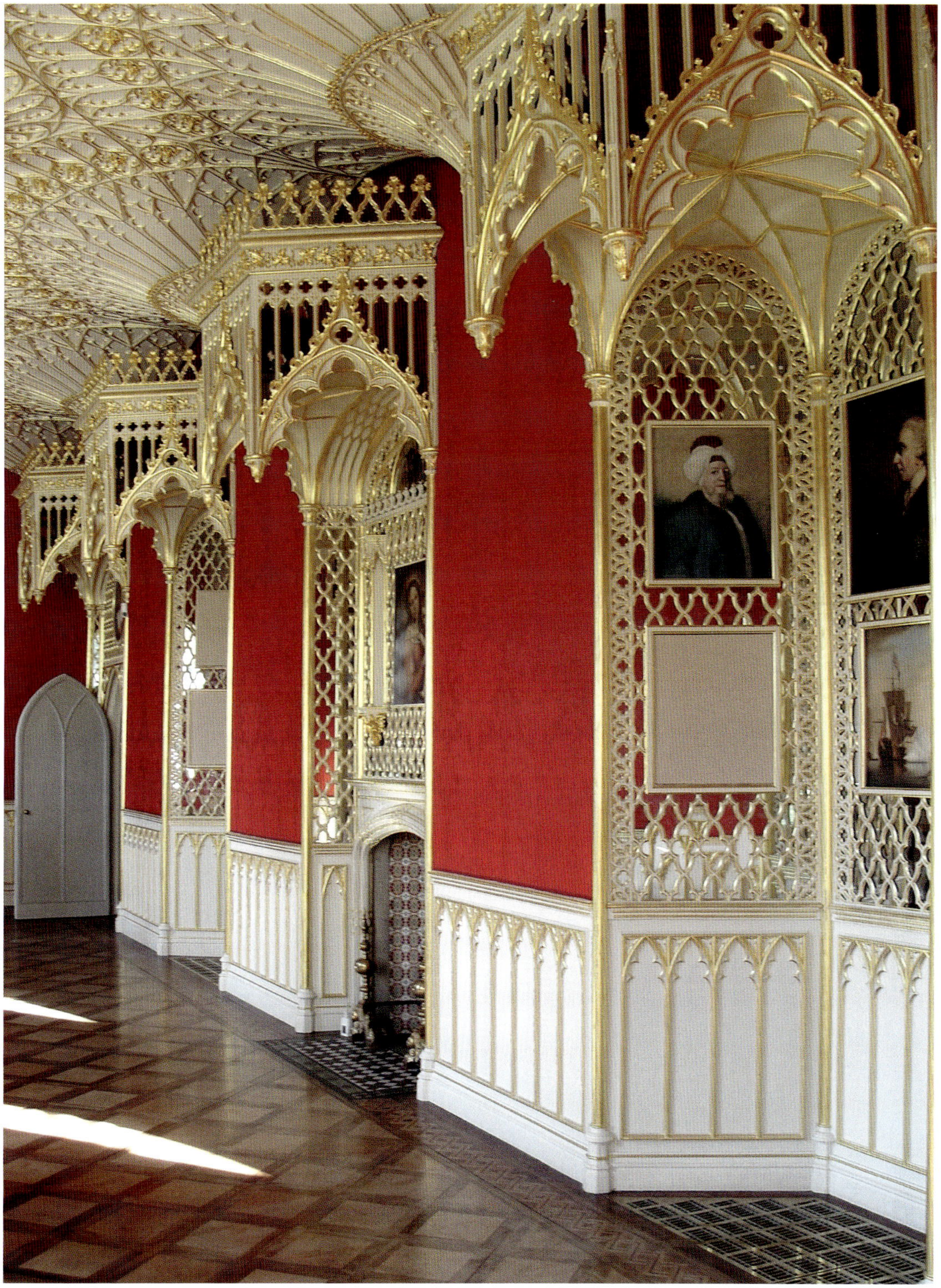

Fig. 45 Gothic canopies in the Long Gallery at Strawberry Hill. Photo: author.

Gallery (figs. 28, 45), vaulted with a stunning gilded fan vault in papier-mâché that followed the model of Henry VII's Lady Chapel at Westminster Abbey (the vault in the Holbein Chamber is likewise executed in papier-mâché).[62] The Long Gallery has a lengthy history in English great houses, notably including the Vyne, Hampshire; and Apethorpe, Northamptonshire.[63] Walpole's Long Gallery was a complex simulation of medieval form, involving not only its papier-mâché vault but also the projecting polygonal Gothic canopies with ogee arches and trefoil cusping in the heads, each in front of a screen of blind trefoil-headed arches in wood simulating stone. Containing historical portraits, the recessed polygonal spaces below are composed of mirrored glass overlaid with complex quatrefoil tracery within which stacked portraits are set. The *Description* ascribes the fireplace to John Chute and Thomas Pitt and suggests that the Gothic "network"—that is, the vaulting beneath the canopies—is based on the late medieval tomb of Archbishop Bourchier at Canterbury. The forms of the canopies themselves derive from a common repertoire of Decorated forms that hearken back to the monuments of Westminster Abbey and St. Stephen's Chapel, Westminster (the canopywork closely resembles that atop the tomb of Edmund Crouchback at Westminster, while the trefoil-headed arcading is common to monuments such as St. Stephen's Chapel and the Coronation Chair). As noted, these forms, or versions of them, had already been known and used by Walpole's circle at Strawberry Hill in the fireplace in the Library, for example, which Walpole correctly attributes to the tomb of John of Eltham at Westminster.[64]

A similar distance between model and copy in form and in material can be charted throughout the ornament in Strawberry Hill. In the Round Room (constructed by 1762; fig. 29), Walpole employed the architect Robert Adam to create on its ceiling one of the house's most dramatic Gothic installations.[65] As Walpole notes in his *Description*, the ceiling was "taken from a round window in old Saint Paul's."[66] His source here was Dugdale's *History of St. Paul's*, from which he derived the forms of the original thir-teenth-century rose window in the north transept (fig.

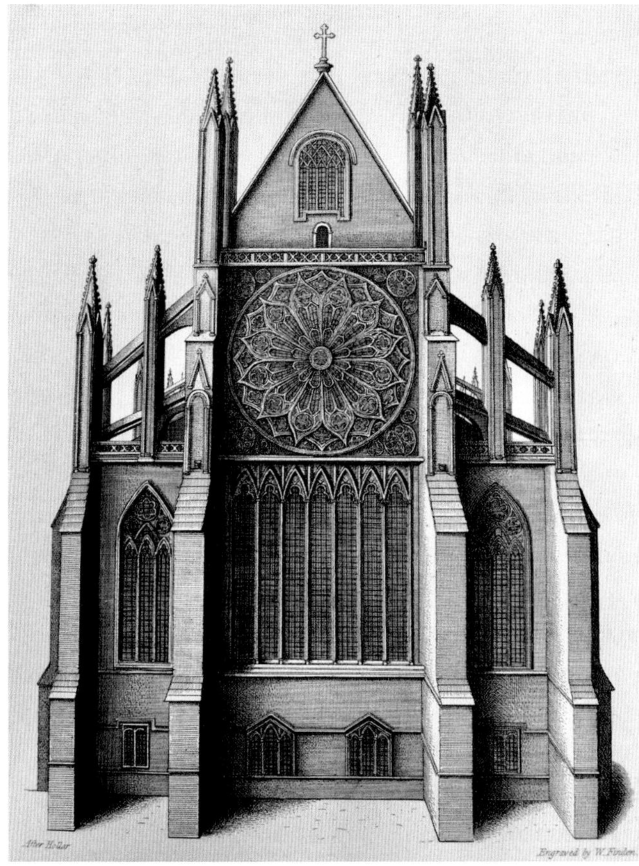

Fig. 46 Wenceslaus Hollar, "Ecclesiae Cathedralis Sti. Pauli Orientalis facies." From William Dugdale, *The History of St. Paul's Cathedral in London* (1658), 166, showing the east transept terminal wall of Old St. Paul's Cathedral, London, with the original rose window. Courtesy of W. D. Jordan Rare Books and Special Collections, Queen's University, Kingston, Ontario.

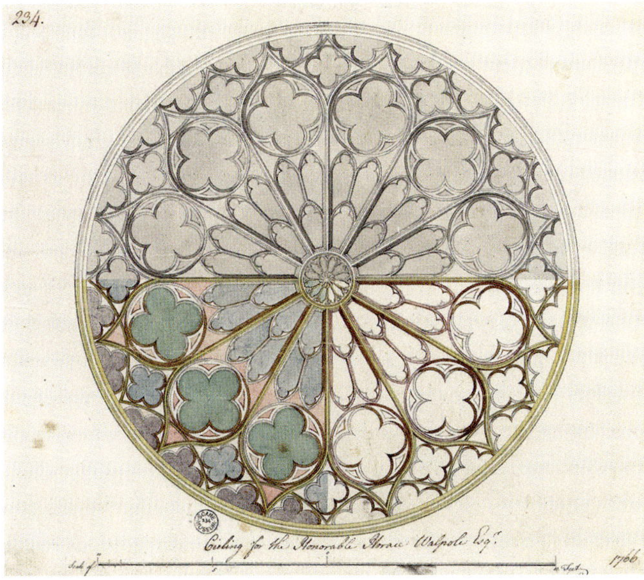

Fig. 47 Robert Adam, design for the ceiling of the Round Room at Strawberry Hill, 1766. Sir John Soane's Museum, London, 11:324. Photo © John Soane's Museum, London.

46). Some sense of Walpole's controlling hand over the design is suggested by a letter of 1766 in which he indicates he has sent copies of both Dugdale's *History of St. Paul's* and Dart's *Westmonasterium* (including page numbers) to direct Adam's designs of the ceiling and of the fireplace (the latter was based very loosely upon the shrine of Edward the Confessor at Westminster).[67] Employing the forms of the engraving, Walpole transposed the linear outlines of the rose window onto the ceiling in paint and plaster. Referencing neither a vault pattern nor a real rose window, Walpole used Wenceslaus Hollar's engraving to endow the Round Room with an elegant Gothic ornament that becomes completely reimagined and decontextualized.[68] Adam's 1766 drawing (fig. 47) shows yellow and brown were proposed for the main tracery, white for the minor tracery, and light blue for the inner lancets and quatrefoils. The greater lancets were pink, the large quatrefoils were green, and the half-quatrefoils around the circumference were purple, thus simulating the coloristic effects (if not the materials) of medieval stained glass.

Similar material transpositions are evident in Strawberry Hill's Entrance Hall, where imitation blind Perpendicular tracery, based on the circa 1502 chantry chapel of Prince Arthur at Worcester Cathedral, was painted onto wallpaper after designs by Richard Bentley (fig. 48). Walpole and his circle appear to have employed Thomas Bromwich of Ludgate Hill, the celebrated wallpaper manufacturer, for their wallpaper and papier-mâché.[69] Walpole's immediate source for the tracery was Francis Sandford's *Genealogical History of the Kings and Queens of England* (1707; fig. 49). The employment of a modern mode of mural decoration as a base for trompe l'oeil representations of medieval stone tracery was surely what Walpole had in mind when he mentioned the "satisfaction of *imprinting* the gloomth of abbeys and cathedrals on one's house" in a famous letter to Horace Mann, cleverly merging "gloom" and "depth."[70] If the allusion to a specific medieval referent was at all significant in creating the staircase, wrapping the fictive tracery around the staircase walls created the effect of Prince Arthur's chapel turned inside out. As Barrett Kalter has shown, Gothic patterned wallpaper during the eighteenth century participated in a "commodification of nostalgia" for the medieval past in its popularization of Gothic ornament in a contemporary, even nouveau riche, mode of interior decoration. It also indicates something of the multiple historicisms at play in Strawberry Hill, since wallpaper was a new object in an ancient style without an original.[71]

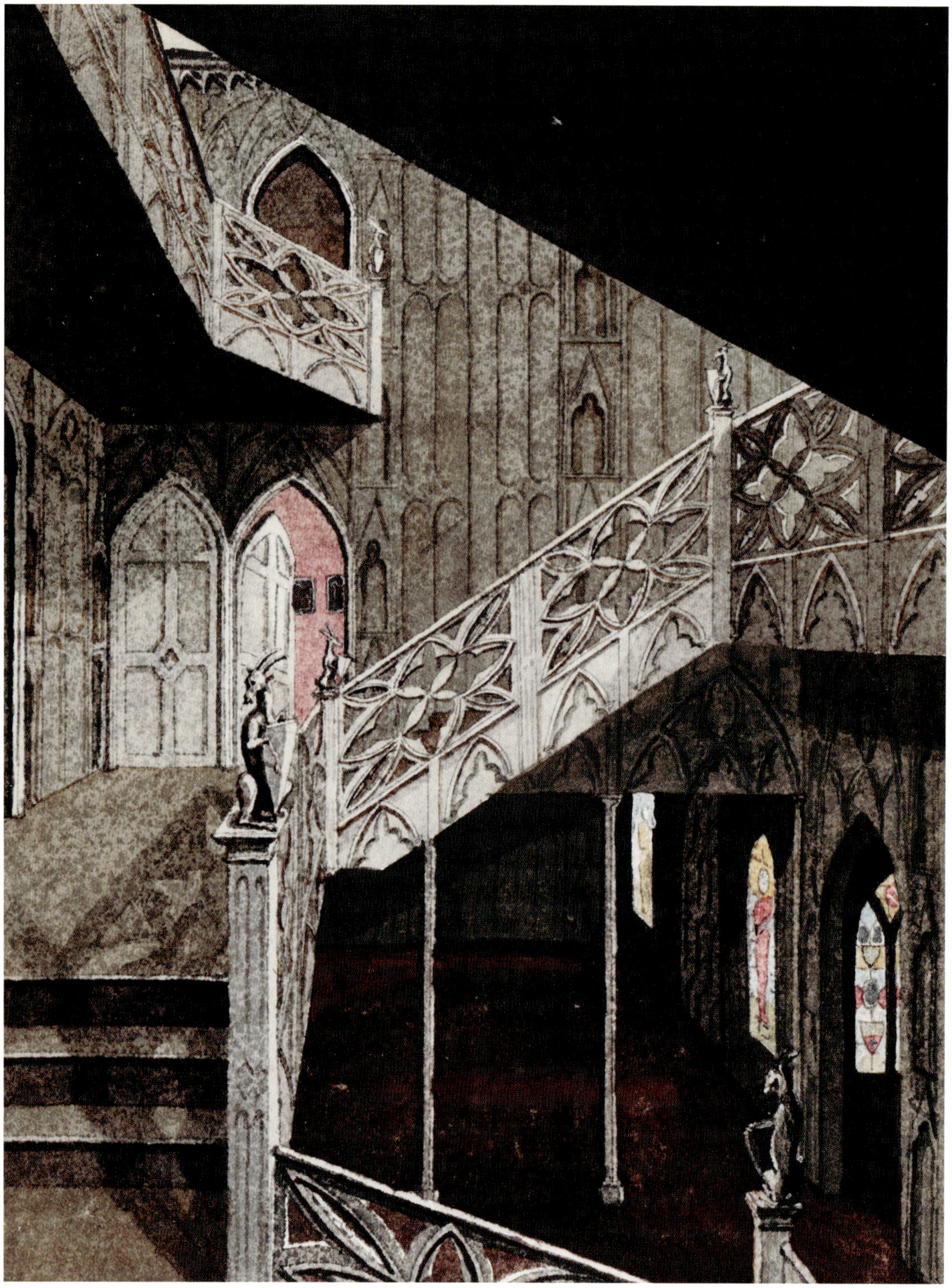

Fig. 48 Richard Bentley, perspective of the Hall and staircase at Strawberry Hill, ca. 1753. LWL 49 3585, fol. 30r. Courtesy of The Lewis Walpole Library, Yale University.

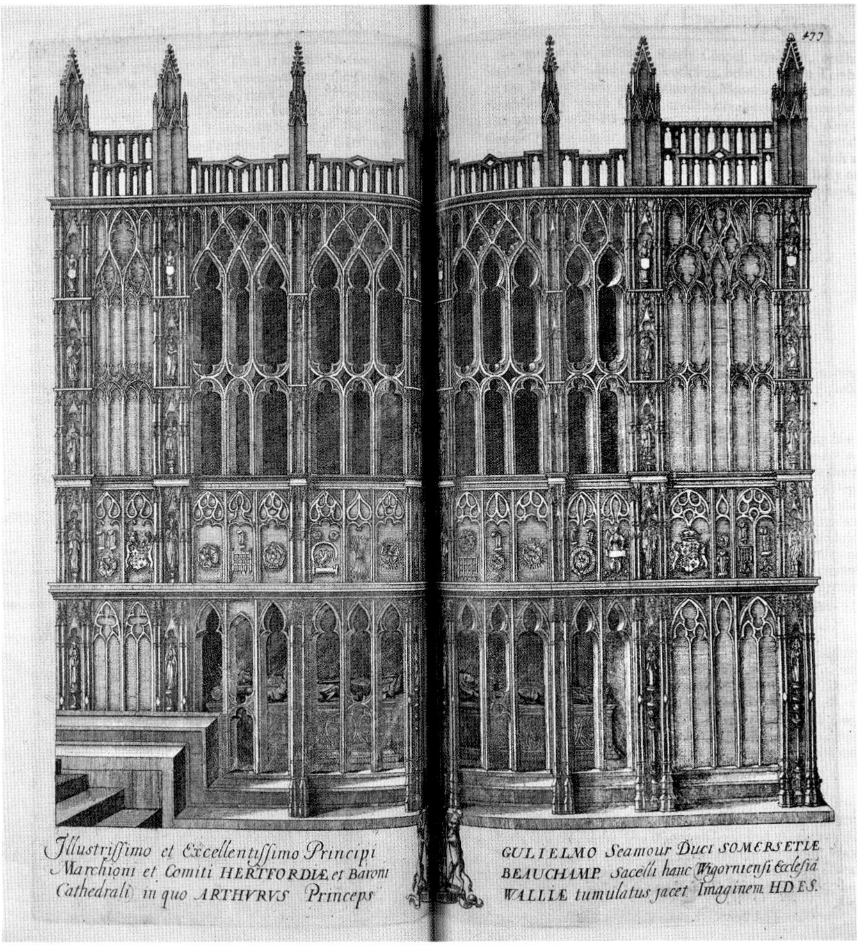

Fig. 49 Chantry chapel of Prince Arthur at Worcester Cathedral. From Francis Sandford, *A Genealogical History of the Kings and Queens of England* (1707), pp. 476–77. Courtesy of W. D. Jordan Rare Books and Special Collections, Queen's University, Kingston, Ontario.

The wallpaper in the staircase was one of a number of illusionistic paintings used to perforate and dissolve the rectilinear volumes of Strawberry Hill. Before the building of the Great North Bedchamber in 1771, the exterior of the Gallery's north wall was painted with tall transomed windows, which endowed it with the air of a late medieval castle or college (fig. 50).[72] In his writings Walpole often enough drew attention to the illusionist and material transgressions in the design of Strawberry Hill. Upon finally seeing the chapel of Prince Arthur, long after he commissioned the wallpaper, Walpole was amazed that the tracery in the wallpaper was larger than the original and that the chapel was not of brass, as he had imagined, but whitewashed stonework![73] He plays upon the fictive materiality of his "paper house" (a double entendre, since it was made partly from papier-mâché and sourced from engravings on paper) when he jokes that a painted Mannerist shield with the face of Medusa that hung in his "armoury" (fig. 26) was "almost in too good taste . . . put[ting] my Gothic house to shame—I wish the Medusa could turn it to stone!"[74]

Strawberry Hill's Gothic designs also indicate deliberate departures from the scale of medieval Gothic architecture. Throughout the house, Gothic ornament is not only taken out of context and reconstructed in new materials but also re-created in an entirely different and

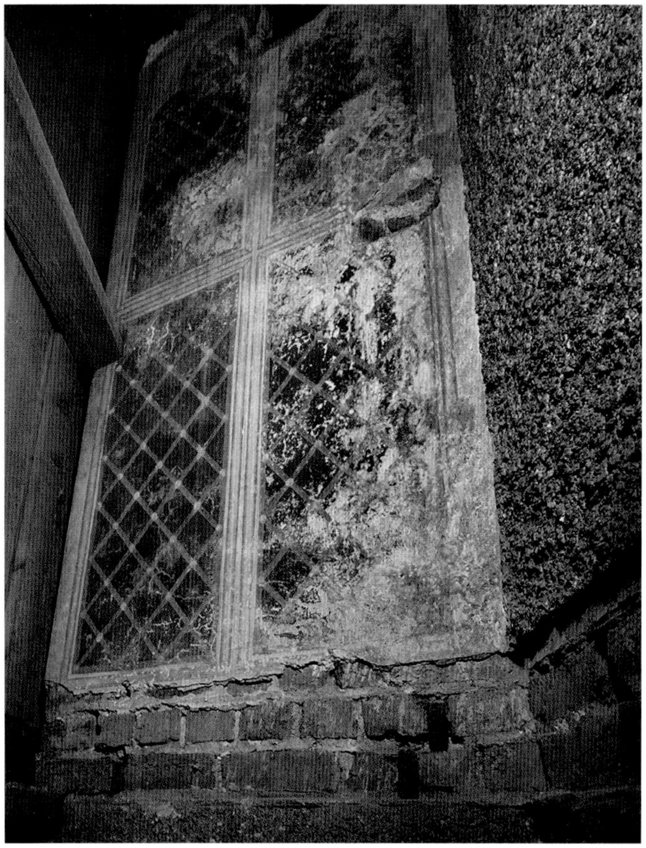

Fig. 50 A painted window formerly employed as fictive tracery on the north front of the Gallery, now hidden beneath paneling in the Great North Bedchamber. Photo: RCHME BB94/5745 © Historic England.

typically diminutive scale. This is evident in a long list of objects I have already noted, from fireplaces using medieval tombs as models for furniture, such as Bentley and Walpole's 1755 Refectory chairs that employ miniaturizations of Decorated window tracery on their backs (fig. 43). The Strawberry Hill Library affords a final example (fig. 51). Wenceslaus Hollar's engraving of the thirteenth-century stone choir screen in Dugdale's *History of St. Paul's* (fig. 52) is Walpole's acknowledged source for the Library bookcases. Typical of the Committee's approach, the entire screen is not replicated; rather, the two flanking doorways are copied in wooden simulations of stone that are repeated in miniature throughout the room's bookcases, described by Timothy Mowl as "compressions of the choir screen at Old St Paul's."[75] As Jill Campbell has shown, the miniaturization and transformation of monumental forms such as this were central to Walpole's design aesthetic and to the language of description he shared with his friends and members of the Committee: "In much of Walpole's correspondence, an aesthetics of 'the miniature' . . . offers a highly developed medium of connection among [the members of the Committee], in the sociable tonalities of epistolary exchange and in the collaborative creation of a 'castlet.'"[76]

Walpole regularly speaks of Strawberry Hill in diminutive terms as "a nutshell" or "a baby-house [dollhouse] full of playthings."[77] Shortly after acquiring the house from the toyshop owner Mrs. Chenevix, he compared it to an *object d'art*: "It is a little play-thing-house that I got out of Mrs Chenevix's shop, and is the prettiest bauble you ever saw." The metaphors of the house as jewelry and therefore as a collectible, precious commodity of the upper classes (and particularly of women) can be traced through his letters, where, for example, Strawberry is

> set in enamelled meadows, with filigree
>   hedges:
> A small Euphrates through the piece is roll'd,
> And little finches wave their wings in gold.[78]

When Walpole invited Thomas Warton to Strawberry Hill, he mentioned "some miniatures of scenes which I am pleased to find you love—cloisters, screens, round towers, and a printing house, all indeed of baby dimensions, would put you a little in mind of the age of [William] Caxton [1422–1491] and Wynken [de Worde, d. 1534]."[79] It was seemingly impossible to resist

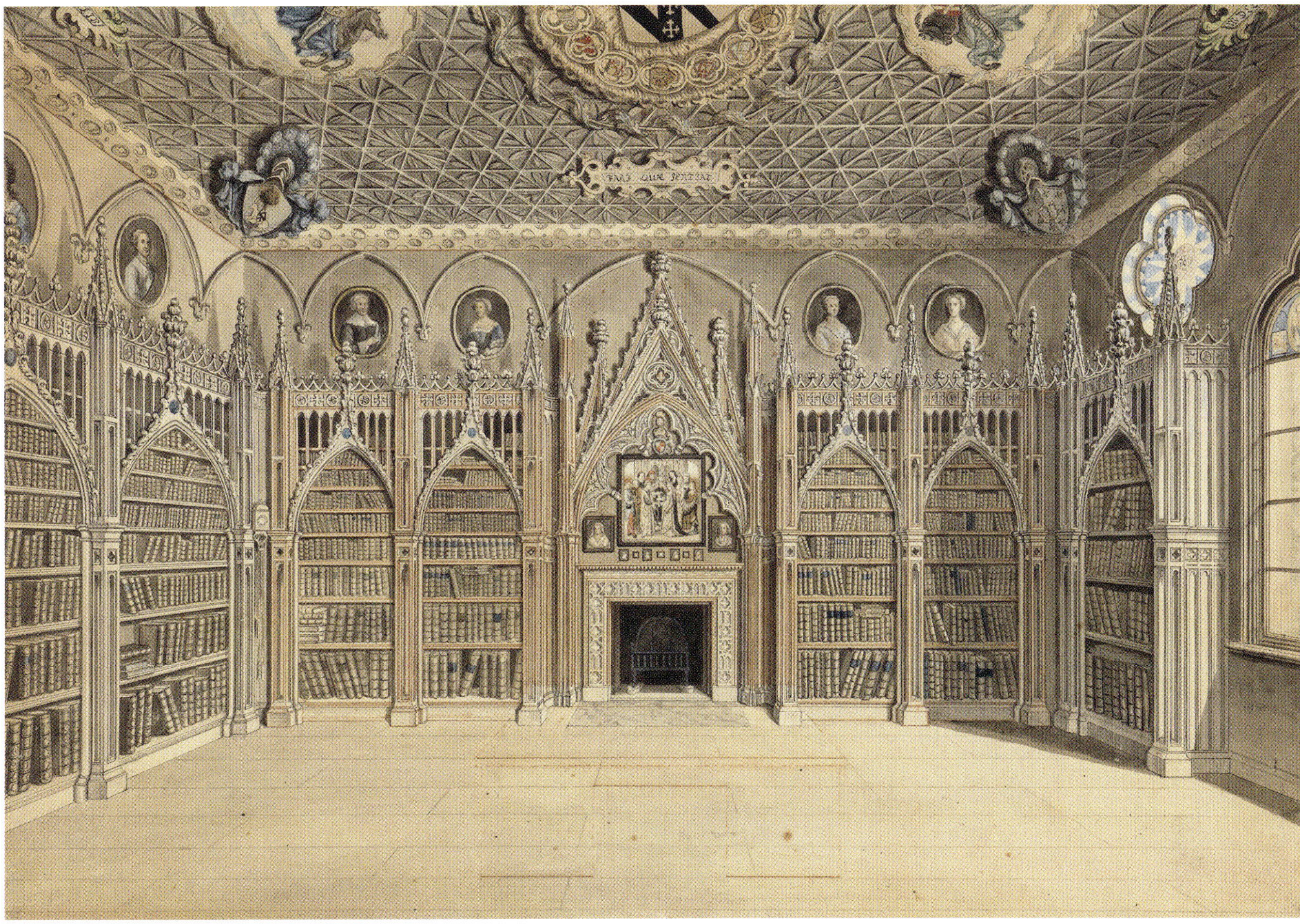

Fig. 51 Edward Edwards, the Library at Strawberry Hill, ca. 1781. LWL SH Views Ed25 no. 7. Courtesy of The Lewis Walpole Library, Yale University.

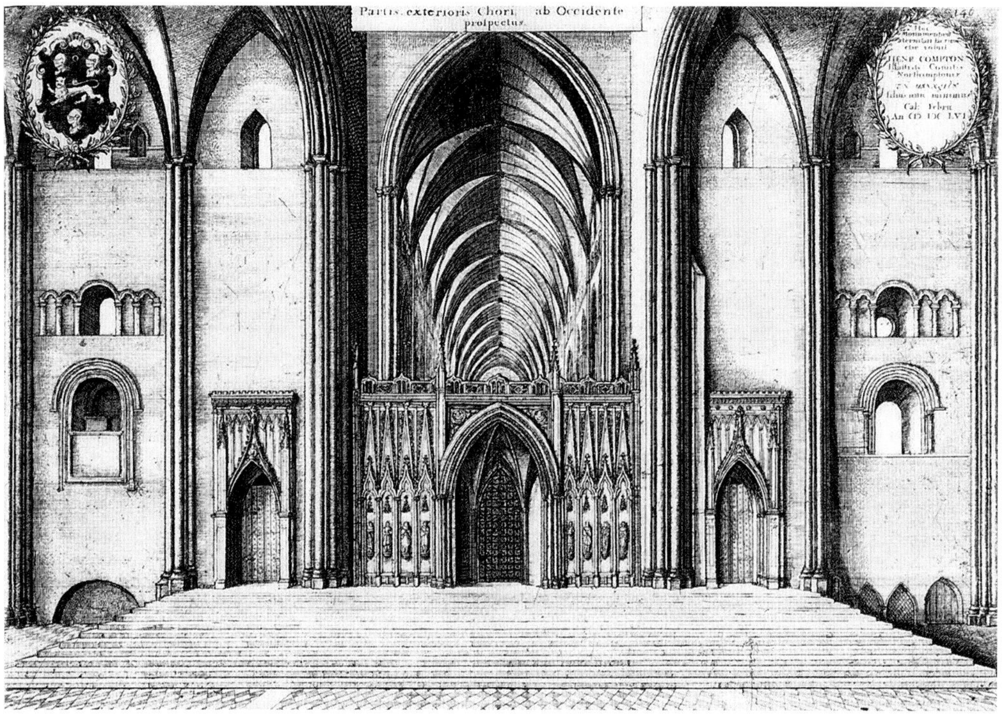

Fig. 52 Wenceslaus Hollar, "Partis exterioris Chori ab Occidente prospectus." From William Dugdale, *The History of St. Paul's Cathedral in London* (1658), 168, showing the Gothic choir screen of Old St. Paul's Cathedral, London. Courtesy of W. D. Jordan Rare Books and Special Collections, Queen's University, Kingston, Ontario.

comparison between his own home and the diminutive settings of Jonathan Swift's *Gulliver's Travels*: in a letter to Bentley of 1754, Walpole commented that his "Lilliputian castle" might be small enough to stand upon one of Bentley's new granite shelves designed for it.[80] Walpole's own miniaturizations of the house and of its ornament—his allegories of the house as collectible object or bauble—suggests not only a language of description shared between writer and reader but a language based on effeminized reversals of normative male taste.

Diminutiveness, or "the little manner"—art as personal commodity or ornament rather than as monumental form—was regularly coded as female in eighteenth-century aesthetics, in contrast to "the grand/great manner" of neoclassicism. Alexander Pope, for example, critiqued these tastes as "those Bawbles most Ladies affect," while Lord Shaftesbury's *Second Characters, or The Language of Forms* states the epitome: "Reason for this little manner, viz. cabinet-furniture, *pieces-de-cabinet* for ladies and the court. Ladies hate the great manner, love baby-sizes, toys, miniature." The homophobic satire *The Pretty Gentleman* (1747) goes further still in comparing the tastes of the third sex to those of women, both of whom are disposed to "softer and more refined Studies; Furniture, Equipage, Dress, the Tiring Room, and the Toy-shop."[81] William Hogarth satirizes "the little manner" in his *Taste in High Life* of 1746 (fig. 53), in which a woman and a fashionable fop obsess over a miniature china cup and saucer too small to actually drink from. The entire scene is set in a trendy parlor with various objects in the modern styles, while the monkey in the foreground reads aloud the menu, which features

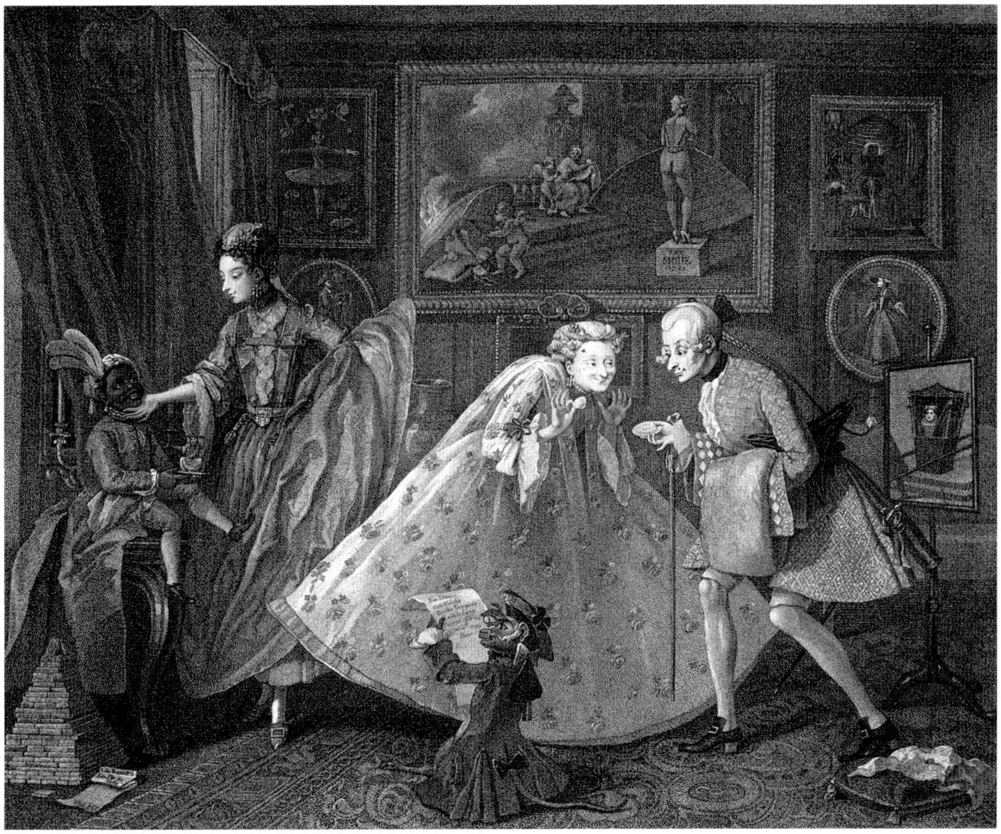

Fig. 53 William Hogarth, *Taste in High Life*, 1746. Etching. The Metropolitan Museum of Art, New York. Harris Brisbane Dick Fund, 1932. Photo: The Metropolitan Museum of Art, www.metmuseum.org.

"coxcombs"—a current name for effeminate gentlemen. These gendered readings of scale and form indicate that in the miniaturized forms of Strawberry Hill and in the developed language of ekphrasis used to describe them, Walpole's Gothic manifests some of the artistic and literary tropes of effeminacy and queerness.

The "Licentiousness" of Gothic

Even if Walpole's "theory" of the Gothic provided a less cohesive model than students of Gothic architecture might wish, he nevertheless left significant clues to how he understood the formal properties of the Gothic and how he approached the problem of replicating it in the present. For Walpole, the Gothic was in his time "considered but as a species of modern elegance" that was characterized as "genteel," and with "grace" and "refinement."[82] He was hardly alone in articulating stylistic and aesthetic differences between medieval and modern Gothic architecture, although most contemporaries did so in negative terms.[83] In an important passage contrasting the corporeality of the classical with the Gothic, Walpole compares "the rational beauties of regular architecture [classical], and the unrestrained *licentiousness* of that which is called Gothic" (my emphasis).[84] Walpole employs the term "licentiousness" here, as elsewhere in *Anecdotes*, to describe physical and aesthetic freedom from moral censorship,[85] but his reference is to an established topos of architectural theory in which the terms "licentiousness" and "license" formed part of an ethical critique of deviations from "proper" antique form.[86] Creative freedom outside social and aesthetic strictures was endemic to the very nature of the Gothic.

Walpole was an attentive student of architectural history, and he knew that in the historiography of the Gothic, "licentiousness" was the most common pejorative employed in commentaries on the style by Henry Wotton, John Evelyn, Christopher Wren, and others.[87] They derided the Gothic as a "fantastical and licentious Manner of Building," focusing in particular on its ornamental character, defined by "crinkle-crankle," not "altogether naked of gaudy sculpture, trite and busy carvings," "not Worthy the Name of Architecture."[88] The deviations articulated by license were gendered as feminine or effeminate elaborations of "proper" antique form. They also potentially nullified the structural character and function of architecture, obscuring its body behind a veil of ornament, or "fancy dress." Similar critiques were advanced by Englishmen about the foreign and equally deviant forms of the architecture of the Continental (and Catholic) Baroque. In the *Vitruvius Britannicus* of 1717, Colen Campbell raged against the effeminate ornamental excessiveness of the Continental Baroque compared to the restraint of English classicism, calling it "affected and licentious," an art that "has endeavoured to debauch Mankind with his odd and chimerical beauties."[89] For Campbell and for Walpole, the ornamental additions of the indigenous Gothic and the Italian Baroque were not only deviations from "ideal" form but a kind of effeminate drag: an ornamental perversion of the architectural body itself. Always the contrarian, Walpole appropriated license as a positive critique of the Gothic, thus turning this critical tradition on its head.

But Walpole's appraisal of the Gothic as a "licentious" style was more than simply a revision of neoclassical aesthetics: it was, I suggest, the very premise of the language of ornament at Strawberry Hill. Strawberry Hill's modernity was manifest in its "licentious" appraisal of medieval buildings—the radical deviations from the form, material, and scale of medieval Gothic. The Strawberry Hill Gothic mode was premised on a critical distance between "model" and "copy," in which the latter both followed and subverted the former through formal deviations. Walpole enjoyed the rich paradox of Gothic modernity (and of Strawberry's "ancient" architectural history) and mentioned it often in his writings.[90] He and his circle developed a complex language to articulate their modern deviations from medieval form. Thomas Gray, for example, coined the term "gothicism" (rather than "Gothic") in describing the Long Gallery (figs. 28, 45), thereby accentuating the replicative and referential nature of his work.[91] Writing to Thomas Barrett in 1783, George Chamberlayne described Lee Priory in theatrical terms as "a *persona*"—a theatrical dramatization—of the ancient Catholic architecture it emulated.[92]

It would be a mistake, however, to restrict the meanings of Walpole's "licentious" to architectural form: it alluded to a broader change of taste and decorum that extended beyond the sphere of architecture. It is not a coincidence that "licentious" and "licentiousness" were also used contemporaneously to characterize effeminate deviations from heteronormative male conduct and homoeroticism in particular in a range of cultural productions. The author of the homophobic satire *A View of the Town* (1735), for example, described homosexuality in traditional terms as "inverting nature to a foul design" and lamented it as the product of a "licentious age," while John Tinney warned that if England were not to fall as Rome had done, it needed to abandon "feeble, sumptuous, and licentious effeminacy" characteristic of the Eastern emperors. Lord Shaftesbury applied this term to the effeminate elaborations in contemporary theater, hoping that men of his class could "restrain the licentiousness of the theatre and make it contribute its assistance to the advancement of morality, and to the reformation of the age."[93] In theater, as in art and architecture, theatricality and ornamental excessiveness threatened established conceptions of decorum, raising the specter of sexual nonnormativity.[94] Posing a fundamental challenge to Augustan aesthetics and its gendered paradigms, Walpole's "licentious"/"licentiousness" registered as a double entendre—a comment on bodies and buildings.

In understanding the corporeal valences of Walpole's Gothic, it is significant that his appraisals of the Gothic, and those of his critics, were informed by a lengthy and multivalent discourse on the propriety and gender of architectural form initiated by the Roman author Vitruvius, much of which was based on direct analogy between architecture and the human body.[95] Within this essentially ethical tradition, the architectural orders were figured as human "types," and their deviations from canons of design registered as analogues for bodily deviations from established modes of conduct. The Elizabethan theorist John Shute (d. 1563), for example, compared the Doric order, in its muscularity, with Hercules (fig. 54), since both possessed the virtue of fortitude, while Henry Wotton (1568–1639) thought the elaborate Corinthian order was "lasciviously decked like a Curtezane," interpreting the plastic enrichments of the capital as an expression of the wantonness of the Corinthians.[96] Within this context, classicism served as a model of the ideal aristocratic body, based on the tenets of symmetry, proportion, harmony, and decorum. For Inigo Jones, classicism was to be "masculine and unaffected" in its external propriety, a sentiment echoed

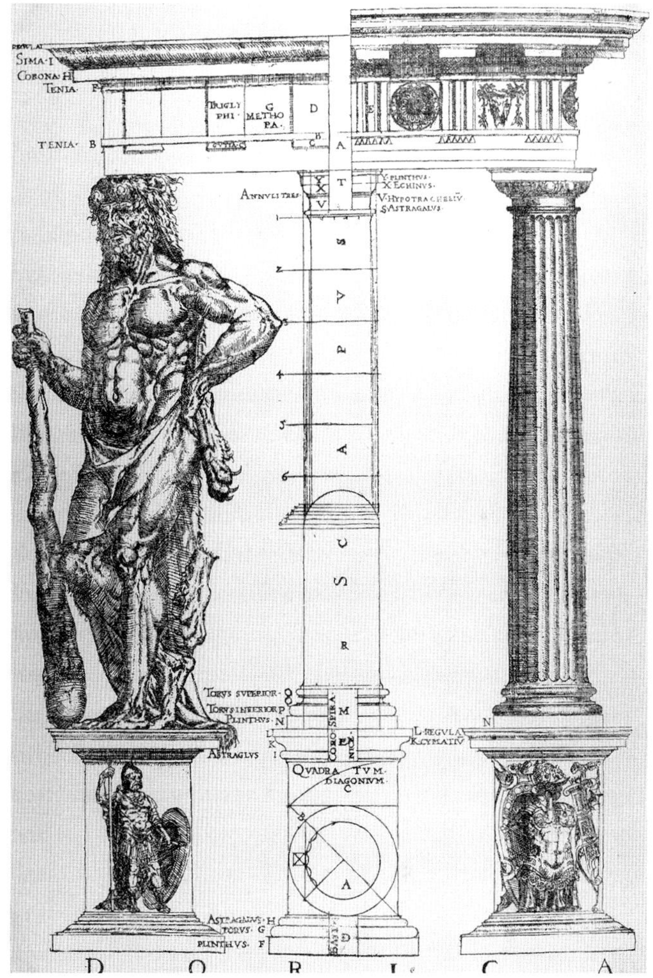

Fig. 54 John Shute, "Dorica." From *The First and Chief Grounds of Architecture* (1563). Photo: author.

throughout eighteenth-century architectural theory.[97] John Evelyn went further, paralleling the asymmetry of architecture—something Walpole advocated in his Gothic compositions—with the present debased state of English taste: "It is from the *Asymmetry* of our *Buildings*, want of *decorum* and proportion in our *Houses*, that the irregularity of our *humours* and *affections* may be shrewdly discerned: But it is from His *Majesties* great *Genius* . . . that we may hope to see it all reform'd."[98] For Evelyn, deviant architecture was the product of deviant subjectivities and could only produce a deviant nation.

Maintaining ancient fabric in building—by which he meant Gothic—was a threat to the social benefits of "good" architecture, to the individual, and to the state.[99] In this tradition, bodies and buildings in the classical mode were characterized by a decorous simplicity in exterior ornamentation, by the privileging of structure over ornament, and by corporeal control and architectonic stability. Eliding morality with physical or decorative restraint, the body-building analogy in the classical mode may be understood as a factor in the formation of the English "stiff upper lip."[100]

It is not a coincidence that the years around 1700 that witnessed the beginnings of the "modern styles" and the changes in human sexuality and subjectivity discussed in this book also witnessed important changes to the body-building analogy by which architecture came to express not simply human forms and genders but wider emotive and subjective states of being. In 1734, for example, James Forrester argued that "Behavior is like Architecture, the Symmetry of the whole pleases us so much, that we examine not into its Parts, which if we did, we should find much Nicety required in forming such a Structure." Forrester goes on to develop an elaborate comparison between the "polite" human body and classicism, in particular Inigo Jones's Palladian Banqueting House, Whitehall, a formal antithesis to Walpolean Gothic.[101] Lawrence Lipking may have been correct in suggesting that Strawberry Hill represents the first expression of the "country house as the physical manifestation of a psychological state."[102] Strawberry Hill's suggestive doubling of its patron's physical and sexual self, the ability of the building and its ornament to signify a queer affect, embodies what Anthony Vidler has called the eighteenth century's "more extended form of bodily projection in architecture."[103] Modernist aesthetics have distanced us from the corporeally resonant nature of architecture for eighteenth-century audiences, even if the body-building analogy was central to English writing on architecture before, during, and after Walpole's period. David Porter and Stacey Sloboda have recently shown that the overtly decorative and distinctly foreign mode of Chinoiserie—and femininity itself, whether expressed by males or females—were "reciprocally constituting categories" in Georgian culture.[104] Conceived of as an "other" to classicism, the Gothic likewise assumed a range of opposite associations related to femininity or sexual alterity.[105] Walpole, of course, was fully aware of these nuances. He suggested that architecture "has . . . two sexes; its masculine dignity can only exert its muscles in public works and at public expense; its softer beauties come better within the compass of private residence and enjoyment."[106] These comments echo his own opinion that "the Grecian is only proper for magnificent and public buildings," and the modern styles of the Gothic (but in his earlier years also Chinoiserie) preferable for the domestic sphere, since they allow "charming irregularities."[107] As this suggests, Strawberry Hill Gothic offered Walpole and his circle a vehicle to unwrite the architectural and corporeal aesthetics of the preceding generations and explore new modes of corporeality, flamboyance, and theatricality that were understood to mirror their own physical affect. In following Jill Campbell's characterization of Strawberry Hill as Walpole's "extended body,"[108] describing it as a supremely defiant statement of architectural self-fashioning, we do not risk imposing contemporary sexual categories on it.

Recent commentators have sensed a familiar rhetoric in Walpole's approach to the revival and replication of the Gothic at Strawberry Hill and have described the house as "camp." A camp affect has likewise been sensed in the medievalizing narrative of Walpole's *Castle of Otranto*, with its frequently over-the-top emotional tenor, theatrical settings, and schlocky horror effects, thus suggesting a common appraisal of the Gothic in different media.[109] In recognizing camp, these commentaries position Walpole's Gothic productions within a queer aesthetic of architecture, decorative arts, performance, and cinema (albeit one imagined in the twentieth century rather than the eighteenth).[110] In Susan Sontag's famous definition from her "Notes on 'Camp'" (1964), "Camp is a certain mode of aestheticism. . . . the way of Camp . . . is not in terms of beauty, but in terms of the degree of artifice, of stylization. . . . Camp is a vision of the world in terms of style. . . . It is the love of the exaggerated, the 'off,' of things-being-what-they-are-not." This definition would, superficially at least, seem well suited to the Gothic installations at Strawberry Hill.[111] Sontag notably located the origins of camp in the eighteenth-century milieu of Alexander Pope, Horace Walpole, and others, in the products of the "modern style," including Chinoiserie and the Gothic Revival (Strawberry Hill is mentioned parenthetically), and in the Gothic novel. Seemingly unaware of Sontag's essay and a rich critical tradition that has followed it, some scholarship continues uncritically to label Strawberry Hill "camp." If such critiques fail because of their anachronistic use of a twentieth-century term to describe the Georgian past, this does not mean that the discourse of camp—itself inextricably bound with the origins of modern aesthetics and sexuality—is not useful for understanding Walpole's modish Gothic interiors.

Considering Strawberry Hill and the Strawberry Hill Gothic mode "camp," or at least locating it within a genealogy of camp, raises two related problems: whether the development of the third sex as a new category of sexual subjectivity after 1700 resulted in the formation of a particular mode of subversive and ironic self-expression in art and architectural patronage consistent with, or anticipatory of, what is now called camp, and, if so, whether this aesthetic subjectivity is inherent in sexual subjectivity or is something learned and taught within queer cultures, as David Halperin has recently proposed.[112] Although it is beyond the bounds of this book to address these problems fully, I want to suggest a tentative yes to the first question and a qualification for the second. A leading thesis of this study has been that the development of the third sex as one of the profound changes in the modern configuration of sexuality had significant effects on the formation of the modern styles and the Gothic in particular. The modern styles developed out of a need for fundamentally different representations that suited and reflected new alternative subjectivities.

Understood in these terms, the modern term "camp" and the ideas that surround it may provide a useful way to explore Strawberry Hill's queer valences. Walpole's complex appropriation of the Gothic—both as a style for replication and as an ancient commodity for collection and assimilation within the modern Gothic fabric of Strawberry Hill—reflects what Andrew Ross has called "a rediscovery of history's waste," a revaluing of broadly discarded styles and objects that were classed as beneath or beyond contemporary standards of polite taste.[113] Something of this is implicit in the many critiques of Walpole's house and collection: "with the sublime and beautiful Walpole had nothing to do, but . . . the third province, the Odd, was his particular domain"; his collection included "cheapening fragments of tapestry, and handles of old lances . . . [and] bits of painted glass";

etc.[114] Continuing the analogy with camp, Walpole's Gothic enjoyed a rhetorical dimension in its self-conscious attempt "to deconstruct the cult of seriousness and 'values'" that characterized architectural and sexual cultures in eighteenth-century England.[115] Here, as elsewhere, camp emerges as a strategy employed at moments of cultural transition to challenge established hegemonies of taste.[116] It is a form of "cultural resistance" based on "a shared consciousness of being inescapably situated within a powerful system of social and sexual meanings. Camp resists the power of that system from within by means of parody, exaggeration, amplification, theatricalization, and literalization of normally tacit modes."[117] While accounts like these must be applied to Walpole's milieu with great care, doing so may pry open some of the rhetorical and political dimensions at play in the forms of Strawberry Hill. My reading of the forms employed in the house and of the language used to describe them suggests that the modern term "camp" and the Georgian term "licentious," as Walpole used it, occupy some common ground with reference to his aesthetics. Like camp, the licentiousness of Strawberry Hill emerges as a complex language of form premised on deviations from normative modes, a language that was understood to be mirrored in the queer body and Walpole's own physicality in particular.

I began this chapter by noting that during the pivotal years of its construction, Strawberry Hill functioned as an experimental laboratory in which new Gothic forms were studied and elaborated by Walpole and the men in the Strawberry Committee. I went on to show that the creation of the idiomatic Strawberry Hill Gothic mode was very much a collaborative project that initially became manifest in Strawberry Hill. As a projection of Horace Walpole, and to a lesser extent the men in his circle, Strawberry Hill and its architectural language signified an alternative subjectivity. In the eighteenth century Walpole's home was, arguably, a rare case in which a famous man and his modes of being came to be elided, in the minds of contemporaries, with his home—a cult of personality in which architecture and architectural style became inseparable from a projected self. The development and elaboration of these forms were themselves developments of a queer culture that would be emulated, revised, and rethought in subsequent architectural productions that paid homage to Strawberry Hill as an originary project of their circle. But the house and its architectural style were only the most obvious statements by Walpole and his circle at Strawberry Hill. The building was designed and expanded to a large extent to house a burgeoning collection of art, objects, and furniture that were as much a collaboration of Walpole's circle as the house itself. Walpole's collection likewise has a place within the social and sexual formation of his circle, since it too served to articulate not only aspects of Walpole's sexual subjectivity but also the quasi-familial bonds he shared with the men in his circle.

3 Queer Family Romance in the Strawberry Hill Collection

> I am deeper than ever in Gothic antiquities; I have bought a monk of Glastonbury's chair full of scraps of the psalms, and some seals of most reverend illegibility. I pass all my mornings in the thirteenth century, and my evenings with the century that is coming on. Adieu!
>
> —Walpole to John Chute, 1 February 1759

During Walpole's lifetime, and up until the dispersal of the contents of the house in a highly public sale in 1842, Strawberry Hill housed a burgeoning collection of artwork, objects, and curiosities that were catalogued in his own *Description of the Villa of Mr. Horace Walpole* (1774/84). As members of his social network were responsible for the design of Strawberry Hill, so were they collaborators in the making of its collection. A wealth of correspondence between Walpole, John Chute, Thomas Gray, Horace Mann, and others in his circle chronicles years of hunting, in England and abroad, for objects, images, paintings, books, and furniture for Strawberry Hill. Works of art functioned as a fundamental currency between these men: they were the focus of broader discussions on aesthetic judgment and the subjects of competition and rivalry, or they were gifts that, when displayed, catalogued, and provenanced in Walpole's letters and *Description*, reinscribed the bonds of these men within the house and articulated their shared codes.

As a totality, Walpole's collection was an extraordinarily heterogeneous and unique assemblage of images, objects, and furnishings that cannot easily be understood in terms of conventional Enlightenment categories (the curiosity cabinet, the Grand Tour collection, the natural history collection, etc.). Containing objects from prehistory to the present, Walpole's collection simultaneously denied and reinforced the fictive historicity of his Gothic house. Although some of the objects considered here were neither from the Middle Ages nor medievalizing in their style or content, their centrality to the development of the house—and vice versa—is not in doubt. Strawberry Hill and its collection offer a formal and thematic synthesis of architecture and objects that has been understood to anticipate the modern museum.[1]

As noted above, contemporaries compared Strawberry Hill's collection to that at Houghton Hall, Sir Robert Walpole's Palladian home, much of whose extraordinary collection of Continental Old Masters would famously be sold to Catherine the Great (Robert Walpole died in 1745, two years before the acquisition of Strawberry Hill).[2] Set within the fashionable confines of Houghton, itself as straightforward a display of political ambition and paternal authority as one could imagine, Robert Walpole's collection has been seen as magnificent but impersonal, a nouveau riche testament to objective—rather than discerning, subjective—taste. It was inspired by the new tastes developed from the Grand Tour (including those of Horace Walpole, who acquired paintings for Houghton), although its patron never did the tour; it rivaled other collections that had been built over generations despite the fact that it was mostly acquired within a quarter of a century.[3] In their content and organization, "the Houghton Hall pictures" and "the Strawberry Hill curiosities" were rightly understood in the period as indices of the aesthetic and sexual subjectivities of their patrons. Strawberry Hill's collection sprang from an "unhealthy and disorganized mind" in which "there was nothing great"; the son inherited "a portion of that taste [i.e., his father's] which he cultivated, although in a less elevated course."[4] Although Horace Walpole prepared an important catalogue of his father's collection (his influential *Aedes Walpolianae* of 1747) and celebrated it (before its dismantling), critics were surely correct to note that the son's collection, like the house itself, was conceived in opposition to the father's illustrious example.

"Unhealthy and disorganized" though Horace's collection seemed to some, Alicia Weisberg-Roberts has usefully shown that a number of deliberate narrative and thematic trajectories, or "discursive trails," were constructed through the display of "singular" objects (to use Walpole's own term) at Strawberry Hill:[5] specifically, literary objects that reminded the viewer of the house's fictive "other," the setting of *The Castle of Otranto*, such as the armor in the Armory (fig. 26) or John Carter's 1790 *Entry of Frederick into the Castle of Otranto* (fig. 20);[6] antiquarian and nationalistic, as in the collection of objects connected with famous figures from British history, including objects such as his copy of Magna Carta and the hat of Cardinal Wolsey; and familial or genealogical, manifest in the construction of royal and family genealogies through the display of portraits and heraldry throughout the house. This chapter focuses on a related "discursive trail" that runs through Walpole's collection, namely its articulation of social and even familial bonds between Walpole and his homosocial circle. Although Walpole's collection has often been studied, little attention has been paid to its homoerotic intelligibility, either in its individual objects, their origins and iconographies, or in the broader logic of its display and ordering, despite the fact that a growing scholarly literature has explored the now-familiar nexus of homosexuality and collecting in the modern period.[7]

Fortunately some attention has been paid to the role of homoerotic relationships in shaping the forms, patterns of exchange, and display of eighteenth-century English portraits such as William Hogarth's *Hervey Conversation Piece* of 1738, which represents Hervey amid his "all-male pseudo-family,"[8] or Edmé Bouchardon's early classicizing marble bust of Henry Fox's lover, Lord Hervey, which was displayed by Fox at Redlynch House, Somerset, and was probably commissioned by Hervey as a gift while both men were together on the Grand Tour. As it happens, Walpole was familiar with both pieces from his own visit to Redlynch in 1762.[9]

These and other recent accounts have explicitly or implicitly argued against Werner Muensterberger's somewhat reductive view of collecting as an "unruly passion" in which the collections become substitutions for unrealized human relationships that are themselves impossible due to trauma caused to the ego during infancy. As such, they become defense mechanisms, substitutions, and fetishes.[10] Framing the collector as pervert or outcast, art collections are understood as sublimations of the self rather than extensions of it (a radical version of this model is provided by John Fowles's novel *The Collector*, of 1963, in which a young man entraps and collects women as "specimens"). Contrary to this view, Walpole's collection, its arrangement, and his interpretation of it would seem to have been a profound assertion of his own aesthetic vision of the world—coded though it sometimes was—and of the intimate bonds he shared with the men in his circle. In this sense, these objects became carefully constructed articulations—some readily apparent, others operating in code—of social and familial bonds, rather than substitutes for them.

This chapter charts a range of potential essays in queer family romance in the Strawberry Hill collection. Although I discuss Walpole's homoerotica, there were few, if any, explicit representations of same-sex lovemaking and only a handful of pieces that represented established queer iconographies. In understanding the queer valences of the collection, I heed the advice of Michael Camille in focusing on "the very structure of relations through which images have been inherited, bought, sold, exchanged, and enjoyed."[11] This structure was articulated not only through hangs of portraits at Strawberry Hill but also through the exegesis on the collection itself in the textual record—namely Walpole's *Description* and his letters—which connects objects with Walpole's range of associates, determines their origins within famous queer collections, and reinforces their status as gifts, purchases, or souvenirs of travels such as the Grand Tour.[12]

It is significant that the originary statement of queer family romance in art historiography was centered on a closely related home: William Beckford's Fonthill Abbey in Wiltshire (1797–1813). Built after Beckford's self-imposed exile, due to scandal over his affair with the youthful Kitty Courtenay, Fonthill was an extraordinary Gothic fantasy in which Beckford articulated and presented multiple queer families through his patronage of art and architecture, both actual and imagined. For example, Beckford's imagery at Fonthill implicated the former owner of the estate, the Elizabethan Mervyn, Lord Audley—himself the subject of England's greatest sodomy trial (1631) before Oscar Wilde—in his own heraldic imagery and adopted Mervyn's motto, *De Dieu tout*, thereby structuring a queer family romance between the very owners and inhabitants of Fonthill.[13] Beckford also destroyed his father's residence onsite (the Palladian mansion Fonthill Splendens) and oriented the sightlines of the Gothic Fonthill to view the site of Mervyn's original home, thereby *reattaching* his home to a homoerotic genealogy. Strawberry Hill was an important touchstone for Beckford, even if he was bitchy about it. Beckford was keenly interested in the patronage of Walpole's circle: he decisively acquired aspects of the Strawberry Hill collection after Walpole's death (including his famous bust of Caligula), employed common tropes of Gothic liberty developed in the patronage of Walpole and his circle (including an expanded display of Magna Carta in a projected "Baronial Hall" featuring the baronial heraldry of 1215, as at Strawberry Hill and particularly at Dicky Bateman's Old Windsor), and even employed common architectural models at Fonthill, including the octagon based on the late medieval Dominican monastery of Batalha, Portugal, which was first imagined at Thomas Barrett's Lee Priory.[14] Beckford's kinship with Walpole veered between admiration and denigration, but one aspect of that kinship, I suggest, was that Strawberry Hill and other buildings built and decorated in Walpole's milieu were, for Beckford, fertile and originary sites in which an alternative sexual subjectivity was explored and articulated in the forms of the houses as much as in their objects and images.

Homoerotica at Strawberry Hill

I have noted already that Walpole's collection was not principally homoerotic in the iconographic formulations of its individual objects. Although it did contain a number of antique or antique-inspired items featuring established queer iconographies, these were balanced by erotica based on antique sources (gems, medals, and cameos) that had a broadly heterosexual bent.[15] In 1757 Walpole did, with the assistance of Horace Mann, attempt to acquire from the infamous homoerotic collection of Baron Philipp von Stosch (1691–1757) "a fine collection of drawings after nudities and prints" and a handful of "bawdy" medals that were very possibly homoerotic in nature, but the attempt was unsuccessful.[16] Even Walpole's most straightforwardly erotic imagery—his copy of *A Collection of the Spintrian Medals of Tiberius* (acquired in 1764)—contained principally heterosexual content (fig. 55).[17] Insofar as any art collection during the period can be used as a straightforward index to an owner's sexual tastes, Walpole's collection of homoerotic imagery was not only small but also carefully and unobtrusively subsumed into the collection as a whole. It is a convenient paradox that while Walpole could be flamboyant in his home and his physical affect, the absence of overt homoerotica at Strawberry Hill seemingly mirrors the carefully obfuscated or concealed details of his sexual life.

As a collector and connoisseur, Walpole owned some of the canonical volumes containing early commentaries on homoeroticism in antique art or homoerotically inflected interpretations of antique art, from Joachim Winckelmann's *Reflections on the Painting and Sculpture of the Greeks* (the 1765 English edition translated by Henry Fuseli) and his *Description des pierres gravées du feu Baron de Stosch* (1760) to Sir William Hamilton and Baron d'Hancarville's *Collection of Etruscan, Greek, and Roman Antiquities* (1766–67), the comte de Caylus's *Recueil d'antiquités Egyptiennes, Etrusques, Grecques, et Romaines* (1752), and Richard Payne Knight's *Account of the Remains of the Worship of Priapus* (1786), which notably included an image of Walpole's own bronze statue of Ceres, the goddess of fertility.[18] While Walpole knew these volumes and many of their authors either

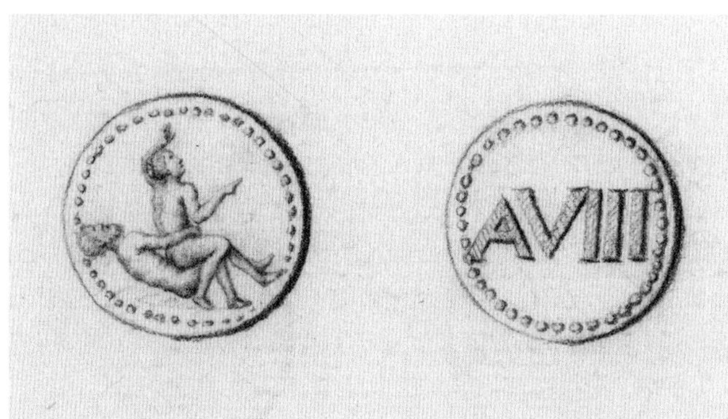

Fig. 55 Detail from *A Collection of the Spintrian Medals of Tiberius*. LWL MS 49 2599, fol. 31r. Courtesy of The Lewis Walpole Library, Yale University.

personally or via correspondence, his collection reflects little of the Winckelmannian tradition of eroticizing the youthful male form in antique art, or of the more aggressively phallic conceptualizations of Richard Payne Knight and others. It also stood to one side of the predominantly heterosexual eroticism of other homosocial fraternities, most notably the Dilettanti, even if his patronage of art was informed by some shared tropes. Walpole's collection bears the unmistakable stamp of his experiences on the Grand Tour—in the display of objects that were acquired there, that commemorate the experience of Italy especially, or that were acquired through connections established there.[19] The tension between an inner homoerotic identity and exterior displays of that identity runs through this study, as it does through Walpole's life and its critical reception. And despite Walpole's vigorous self-fashioning through architecture, his own self was consciously formulated between the poles of his own homoerotic culture and the aristocratic culture in which he was born and raised. George Rousseau is not far off the mark when he notes, with reference to Walpole's disdain for Payne Knight's phallicism, "Walpole learned to conform to the rank and file of aristocratic mores and aesthetic taste, no matter how isolated and solitary he may have been at Strawberry Hill."[20]

With this in mind, it is not, perhaps, a surprise that many of the homoerotic images were located in the Tribune—a space accessible only to particular visitors—which was blocked by a Gothic screen (fig. 36). Among them was a statue of Antinous (fig. 56), the youthful lover of the emperor Hadrian (one of two in Walpole's collection), which was one in a series of niche figures, including representations of his mother, Lady Walpole, the Venus de' Medici, and the *Apollo Belvedere*.[21] Walpole's most overt homoerotica was hidden from view within the

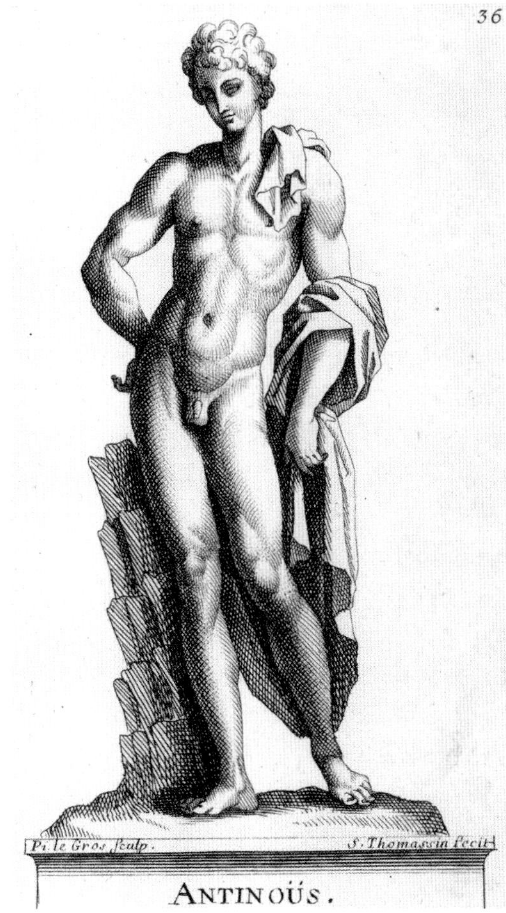

Fig. 56 Simon Thomassin, "Antinoüs." From Thomassin, *Recueil des figures* (1695). This image was added to Richard Bull's extra-illustrated copy of Walpole's 1784 *Description*, now LWL 33 30 Copy 11 Folio, p. 150. Courtesy of The Lewis Walpole Library, Yale University.

doors of his famous cabinet of miniatures, created in 1743 (fig. 57, 58).[22] Moved from his London townhouse, the cabinet became the centerpiece of the Tribune, since it was located atop an altar ("taken from Westminster Abbey") in the fashion of a winged Gothic altarpiece, as Thomas Rowlandson clearly understood in his satire of the room (fig. 16).[23] The cabinet contained, for example, "Two phalli . . . of bronze," a representation of a "sleeping hermaphrodite between two satyrs" (fig. 59),

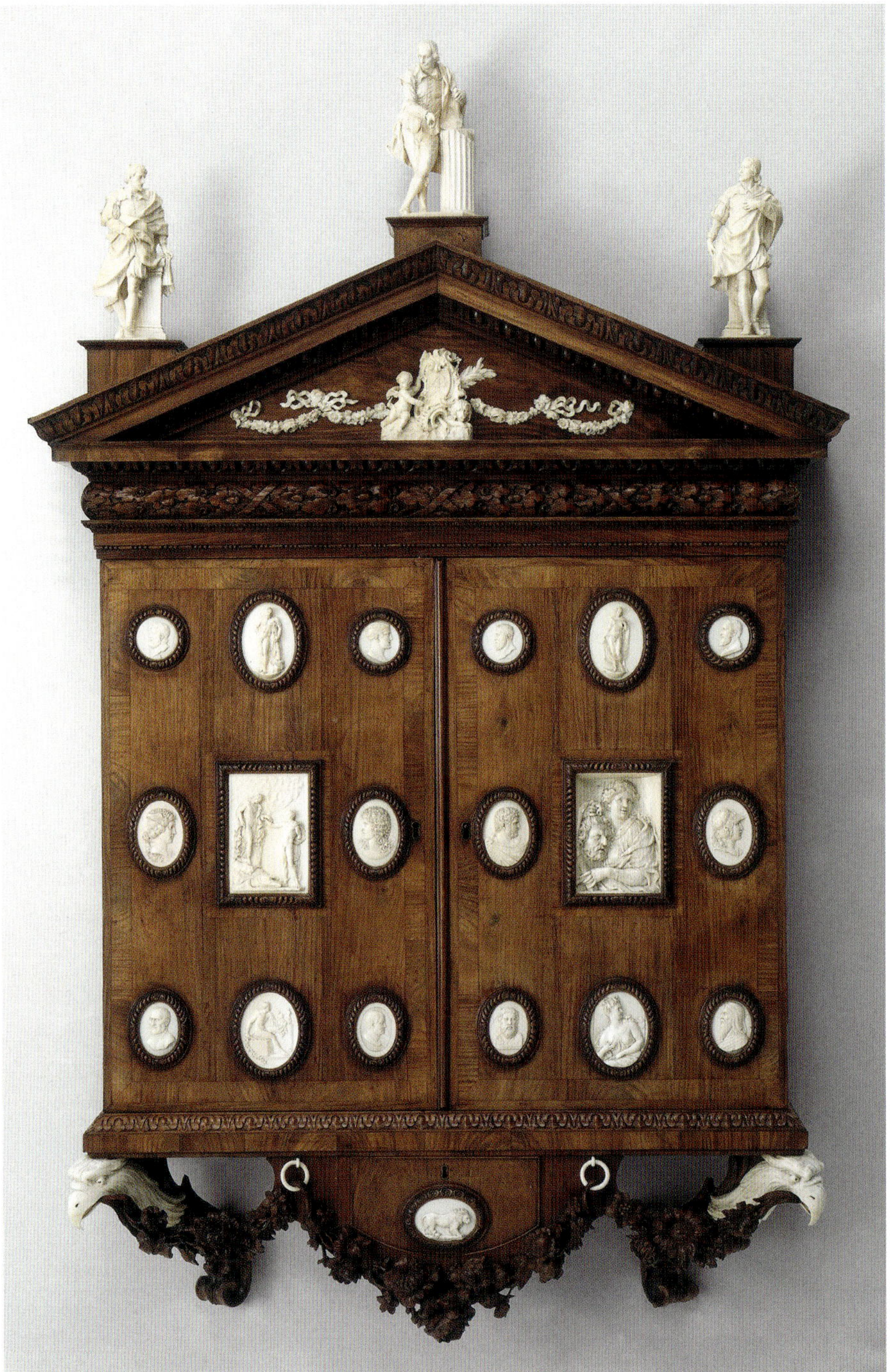

Fig. 57 William Hallett Sr., the Walpole Cabinet (Walpole's cabinet of miniatures), 1743. Rosewood and ivory. Victoria and Albert Museum W.52-1925. Photo © Victoria and Albert Museum, London.

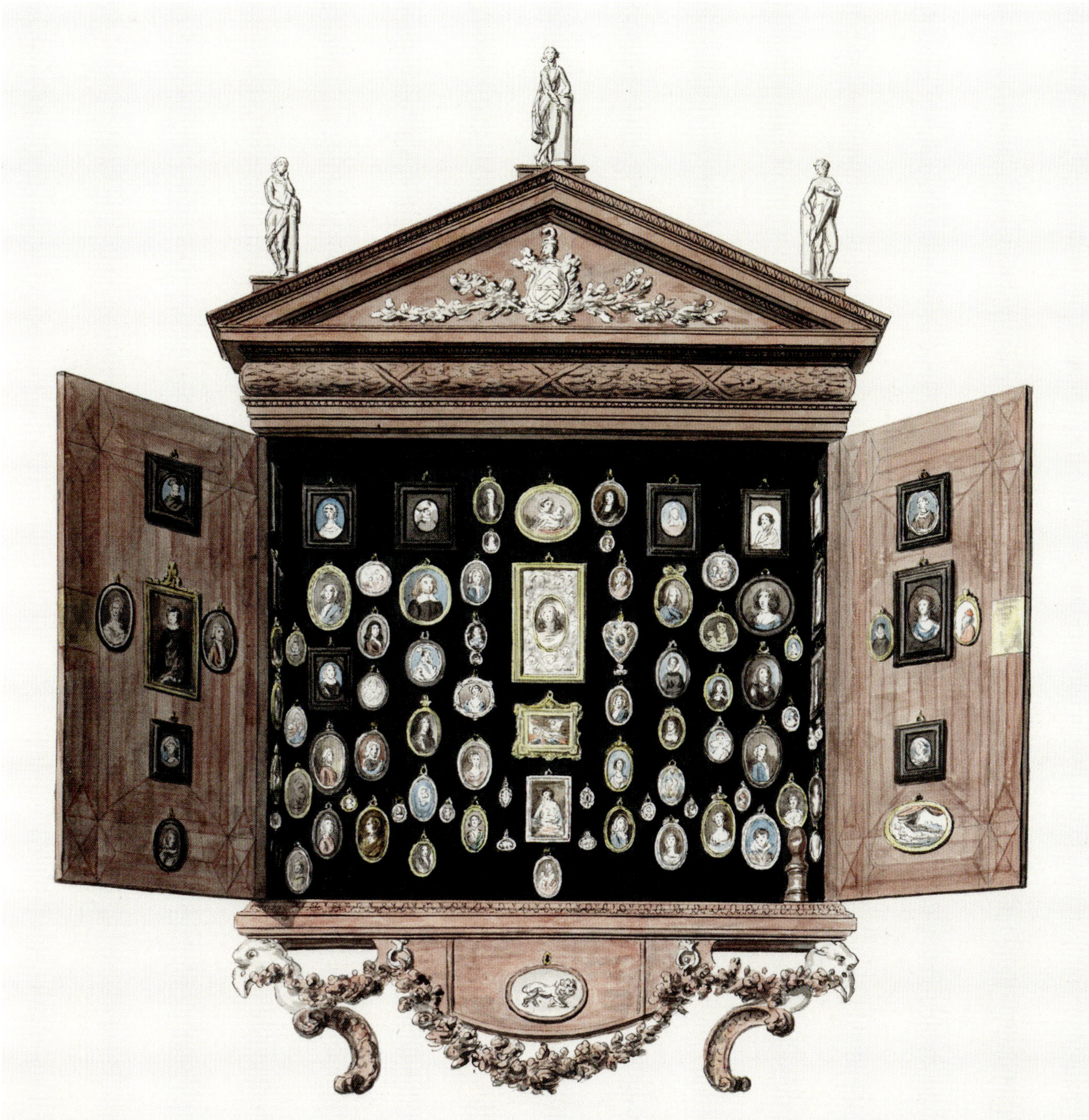

Fig. 58 John Carter, "The Cabinet of Miniatures and Enamels." LWL 33 30 Copy 11 Folio, p. 161. Courtesy of The Lewis Walpole Library, Yale University.

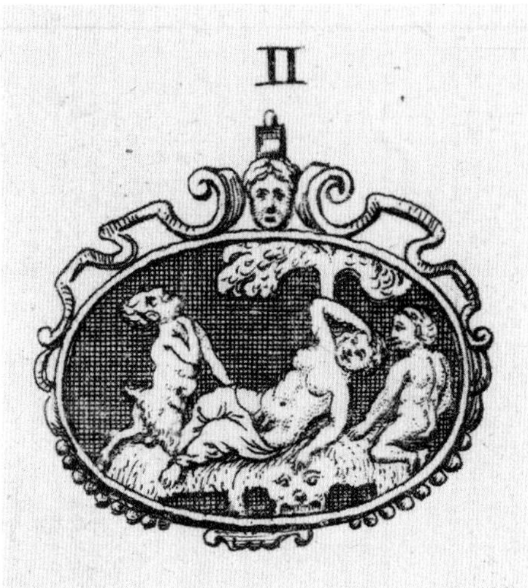

Fig. 59 A miniature from Walpole's cabinet, described as "a sleeping hermaphrodite between satyrs." LWL 49 3582, XXI, detail. Courtesy of The Lewis Walpole Library, Yale University.

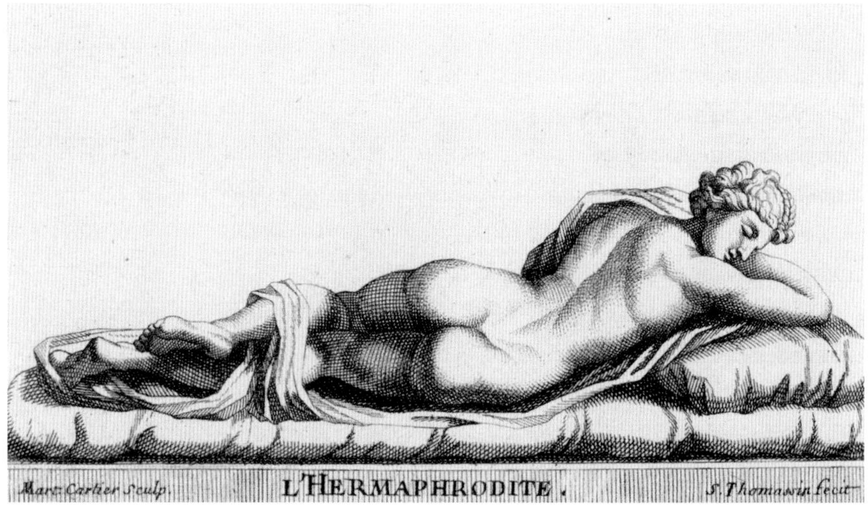

Fig. 60 Simon Thomassin, "L'Hermaphrodite." From Thomassin, *Recueil des figures* (1695). The "Sleeping Hermaphrodite" was based on the copy at Versailles. This image was added to Richard Bull's extra-illustrated copy of Walpole's 1784 *Description*, now LWL 33 30 Copy 11 Folio, p. 167, and reflected another copy in Walpole's collection. Courtesy of The Lewis Walpole Library, Yale University.

and a "Salmacis and Hermaphroditus, a most beautiful miniature by Clinksted [Karl Gustav Klingstedt, 1657–1743]; given to Mr. Walpole by Mr. Chute." The present location of the "Salmacis and Hermaphroditus" from Chute is not known, but it was one of a number of images of the hermaphrodite Walpole owned (fig. 60).[24] Deriving ultimately from Ovid's *Metamorphoses* and retold often in the poetry of the early modern period, the story of Hermaphroditus recounts how the child of Hermes and Aphrodite flees from the advances of a woman and transforms into a male-female hybrid. The story became the canonical text of intersexuality and had a lengthy history in queer discourses from antiquity to the present. I have noted already that "hermaphrodite" was used commonly to describe men of the third sex, including Walpole. Enjoying hallowed antique pedigrees, Walpole's erotic images were of course not uncommon in Enlightenment art collections, whether queer or otherwise: Sir Francis Dashwood's house at West Wycombe, for example, had a life-sized copy of the Borghese Hermaphroditus as garden statuary to articulate what Wendy Frith has called a sense of "contested sexuality."[25]

But the homoerotic significance of the Klingstedt miniature and other homoerotica at Strawberry Hill lies less in the objects themselves and their iconographies than in Walpole's deliberate connection of the objects with men in his circle. As a gift from John Chute, Walpole's intimate, senior friend, and occasional resident of Strawberry Hill, the miniature gains significance beyond its iconographic meaning. Also in the cabinet was Pompeo Batoni's 1745–46 portrait miniature of Chute (fig. 61), made during their Grand Tour (a copy of which was made for Walpole's bedchamber

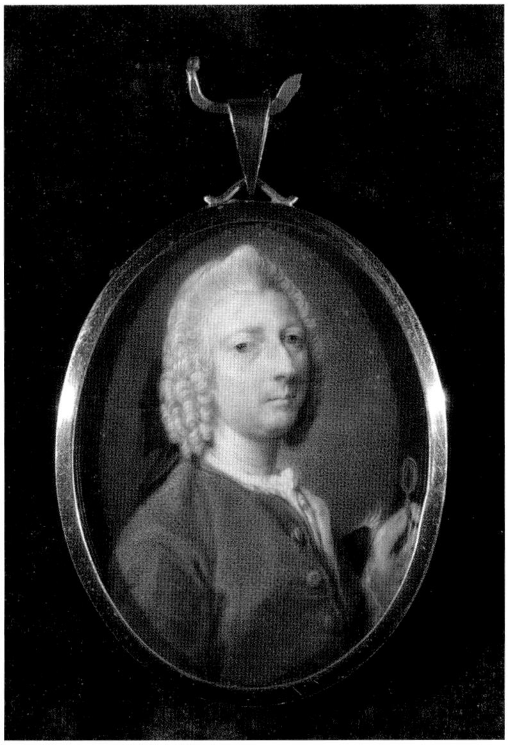

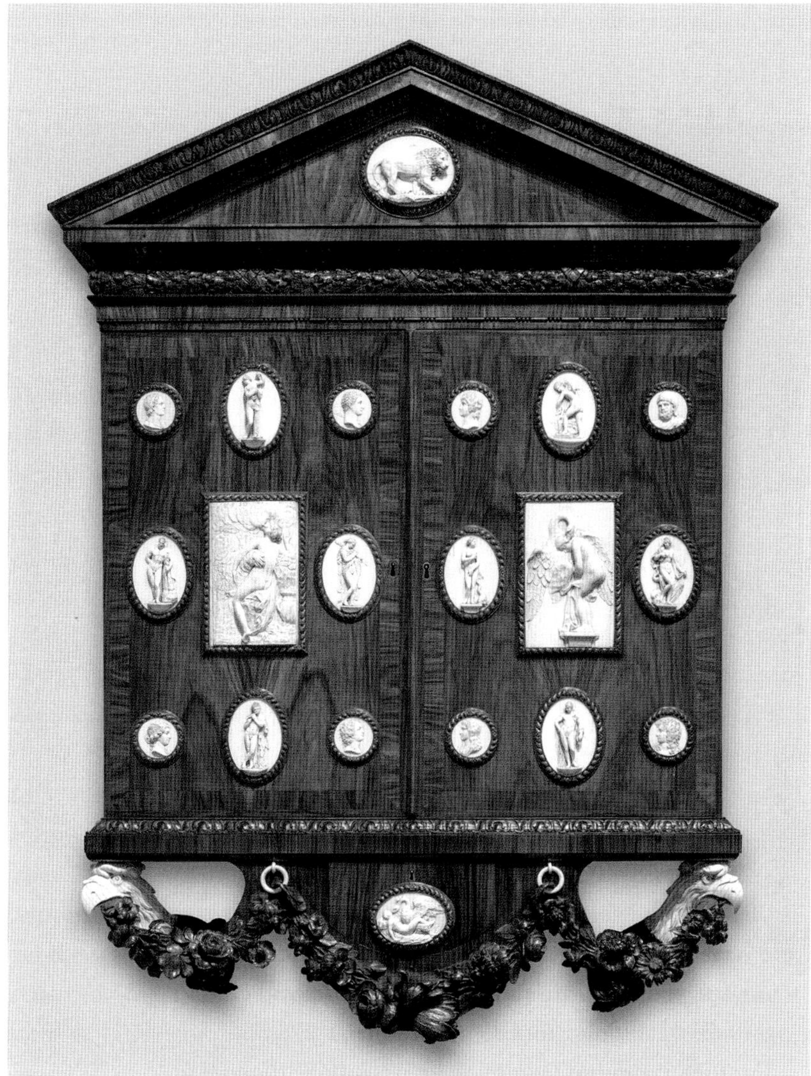

Fig. 61 Pompeo Batoni, *Portrait Miniature of John Chute*, 1745–46. The Vyne, Hampshire. Photo © National Trust Images / Derrick E. Witty.

Fig. 62 The Brand Cabinet, designed by Horace Walpole and probably made by William Hallett, ca. 1743. Photo: Art Institute of Chicago / Art Resource, New York.

by Johann Heinrich Müntz).[26] Inside the cabinet of miniatures, the hermaphrodite miniature becomes an allusion to a shared homoerotic code and a testament to a shared history between two men. Via Winckelmann and others, Walpole inherited the notion that the exchange of homoerotica between men descended from an antique tradition of intergenerational male-male relationships.[27] Referencing Susan Stewart's theorization of the dollhouse, George Haggerty usefully describes the cabinet as a "house within a house . . . [with] its promise of an infinitely profound interiority."[28] The rhetoric of Walpole's cabinet as a container for specific sexual images stands in contrast with its twin, a cabinet designed by Walpole for his friend Thomas Brand, a member of the Dilettanti, also in 1743 (fig. 62). "Considerably less sedate in subject matter" than Walpole's cabinet,[29] the outer faces of Brand's cabinet bear a selection of contemporary ivory carvings of erotic imagery with a principally (but not exclusively) heterosexual orientation derived from classical mythology:

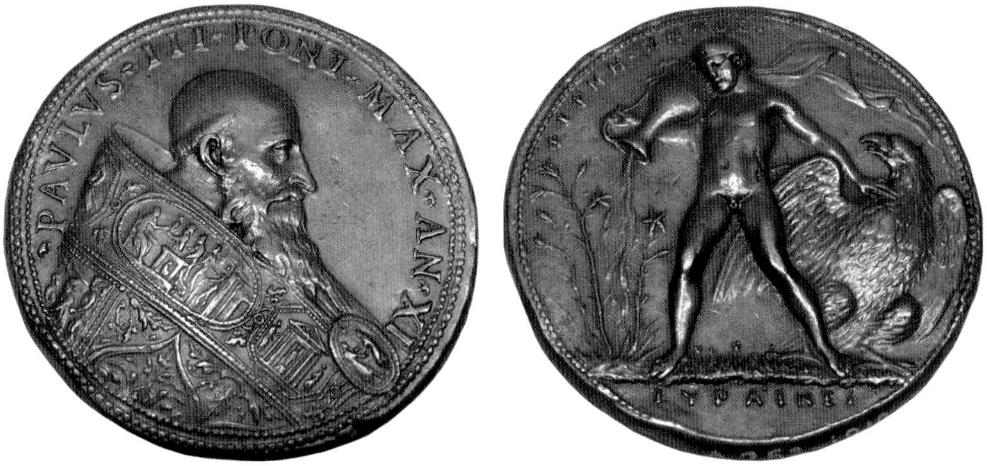

Fig. 63 Bronze medal of Pope Paul III (obverse) with Ganymede and Jupiter as eagle (reverse), second quarter of sixteenth century. Victoria and Albert Museum, London A.253–1910. Photo © Victoria and Albert Museum, London.

Jupiter and Io, Leda and the Swan, Hercules and Omphale, the Belvedere Antinous, Cupid and Venus. The imagery of Brand's cabinet was a natural extension of the erotic but erudite libertinism of the Dilettanti and their troping of sexuality via antique narratives.[30] The comparison of Walpole's cabinet with Brand's usefully highlights Walpole's concept of a cabinet as a place for erotic imagery but also indicates the minimal and particularly secretive nature of his own homoerotica in contrast to Brand's more overt display.

Walpole's homoerotic miniatures, like his homoerotica generally, possess a dual queer genealogy: they derive from a well-established canon of queer imagery but also articulate a tradition of gift giving, an economy of shared appreciation of homoerotica and its meanings within an intimate social web. In this sense, these objects become queer family "heirlooms." A useful example is a medal that Walpole displayed in his Library, which he describes as follows: "Fine gilt coin of pope Paul III. Reverse, a Ganymede, admirably drawn: this beautiful coin was the work of Michael Angelo Buonaroti [*sic*]. From the collection of baron Stosch." The provenance of the medal Walpole acquired from von Stosch has not been traced, but it may be that now in the Victoria and Albert Museum (fig. 63).[31] Relating the story of Jupiter abducting a beautiful youth to use as his cupbearer, the Ganymede story had a lengthy history in homoerotic narratives as a code for intergenerational male sexuality. In this capacity, it regularly appeared as a mise-en-scène in contemporary satiric and graphic representations lampooning homoerotic behavior.[32] One such representation, from Walpole's own collection of satires now in New York, is "Miss Prettyman in Clover" of 1785, in which an image of the Abduction of Ganymede on the wall behind the protagonists provides an appropriate visual gloss upon a gentlemen's conquest of Miss Prettyman (fig. 64).[33]

Like the imagery of hermaphrodites, a medal featuring Ganymede could potentially be found in many antiquarian collections. What is significant is Walpole's explicit linking of the object to von Stosch. A famous Prussian antiquary, collector, and author of *Gemmae Antiquae Caelatae* of 1724 (a copy of which Walpole owned), von Stosch lived in Florence and Rome and

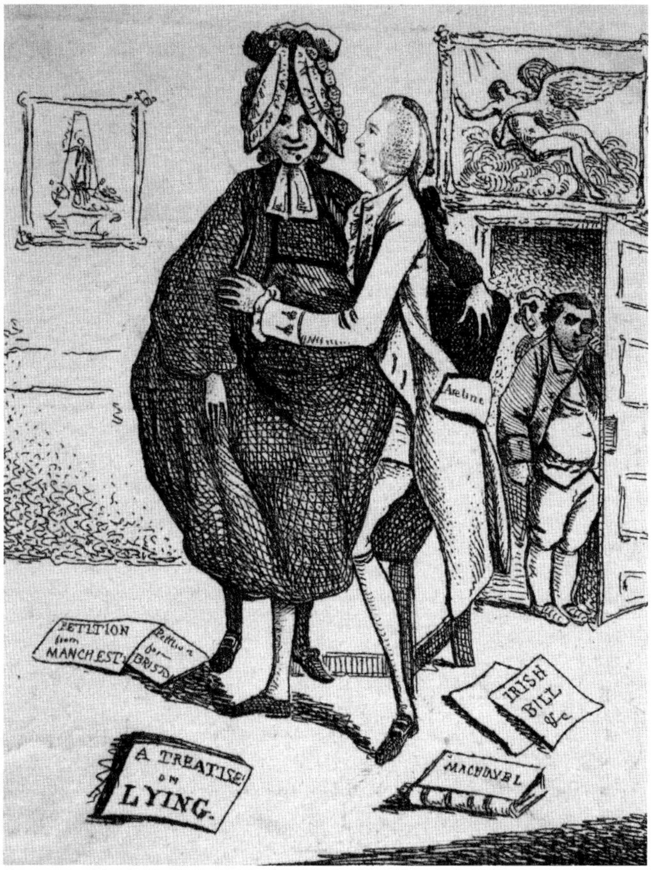

Fig. 64 I. Truepenny, "Miss Prettyman in Clover," London, 30 March 1785. From Horace Walpole's collection of satires, now New York Public Library, NYPL MEZYRKZ, fol. 78r. Photo: author.

operated within the homoerotic antiquarian circles of Joachim Winckelmann, Baron d'Hancarville, Horace Mann (who helped Walpole acquire the medal and was a friend to von Stosch and executor of his will), and others. Von Stosch's Florence home and collection was a regular destination for Englishmen on the Grand Tour with antiquarian leanings and was personally known to Chute, Richard Bentley, and Walpole. Collecting images of Ganymede was common within these circles, serving as a shared iconographic code among homoerotically inclined collectors.[34] Walpole was manifestly intrigued and repelled by von Stosch, whom he prudishly called "a person of infamous character" and about whom he delighted to get updates on his activities in artistic and sexual commerce. Von Stosch was known for his love of youths and his apparently brazen displays of sexuality (Mann reports to Walpole, for example, that von Stosch proclaimed that the human soul resided in the rectum).[35] Seemingly celebrating his notoriety both as a scholar and as a homoerotic libertine, Pier Leone Ghezzi in 1725 drew von Stosch as a monocle-wearing scholar facing pedestaled marble buttocks (fig. 65).[36]

Writing to the young Horace Walpole in 1744, Mann reports:

> Another fracas of loves of a different kind is likely to make great noise. Cyclops the antiquarian [von Stosch's nickname, given because he wore a monocle] has been too rough with a tender Ganimede [*sic*], who has been obliged to retire to the hospital for the assistance of the surgeons there. His disorder is well known here by the name of *creste* [prolapsed anus]. Before he took the resolution of going to this public place of cure he made known his case to his Jupiter, who gave him three *crazie* and dismissed him. A formal deposition has been taken, in which he has not concealed the author of his pleasure and pain, who if matters are carried with rigour would be glad to give his Meleager or Gladiator to be well off [medals Walpole wished to acquire].

Mann's letter then turns from prose to poetry:

Did you ever see these verses:

Ils seront sourds à la trompette
Les bougres au jour du jugement
Il faudra qu'un bel ange pette
Pour les tirer du monument.

Which a friend of yours [probably John Chute] has translated thus:

All men but *bougres* [buggers/sodomites] at the day of doom
Roused by the trumpet shall forsake the tomb
These will remain some minion angel's care
To break their slumbers by a rousing *pet en l'air*.

Or

There will remain some angel's part
To break their slumbers with a rousing f——t.[37]

Recounting a graphic story of apparently pederastic sodomy (albeit one couched in familiar terms of classical myth) and then leading into seemingly lighthearted scatology, it is delicious gossip conveyed via a hardly subtle homoerotic lexicon. The identity of "Cyclops the antiquarian" (perhaps with attendant phallic double entendre) was understood by Walpole and required no explanation. So too was the framing of this sexual relationship with the narrative of classical myth in which a young male who engages in passive sodomy was a "Ganimede" and his elder lover a "Jupiter." Mann concludes this anecdote by returning to a shared passion for collecting and the possibility that Walpole may benefit from von Stosch's current predicament. Mann's letter follows from a crossing of swords between Walpole and von Stosch two years previously, when, again via Mann, Walpole tried unsuccessfully to acquire the two medals (of a Gladiator and a Meleager) that von Stosch refused to sell.[38] In the context of epistolary exchange, von Stosch's sexual libertinism becomes a fault that tips the scales in Walpole's favor, offering a potential victory for the young collector. Not only does Walpole's *Description* offer an illustrious provenance for his Ganymede medal in the (in)famous collection of an important collector, but it also locates the medal within a genealogy of queer collections, one that was bridged, mediated, and arguably interpreted by Horace Mann. While Walpole did not record his impressions of the medal, it would seem impossible for him not to have connected the medal with the graphic story recounted in Mann's letter.

Understanding the status of the Ganymede myth in Walpole's circle as a code for male homoeroticism may be useful in understanding other discursive trails that connect these men with the objects they collected and reveal how they interpreted them. A case in point is the Boccapadugli Eagle (fig. 66), a first-century C.E. Roman sculpture found within the precincts of the Baths of Caracalla in Rome and displayed in the center of the Long Gallery at Strawberry Hill.[39] Walpole not only had it engraved for publication in the *Description* but also had it represented in Joshua Reynolds's 1756 portrait of him (fig. 67): in the guise of a gentleman scholar, Walpole leans on a table, descending from the edge of which the eagle appears unfurled on a sheet of paper, indicating not only Walpole's pride of ownership but also something more self-reflexive, a double

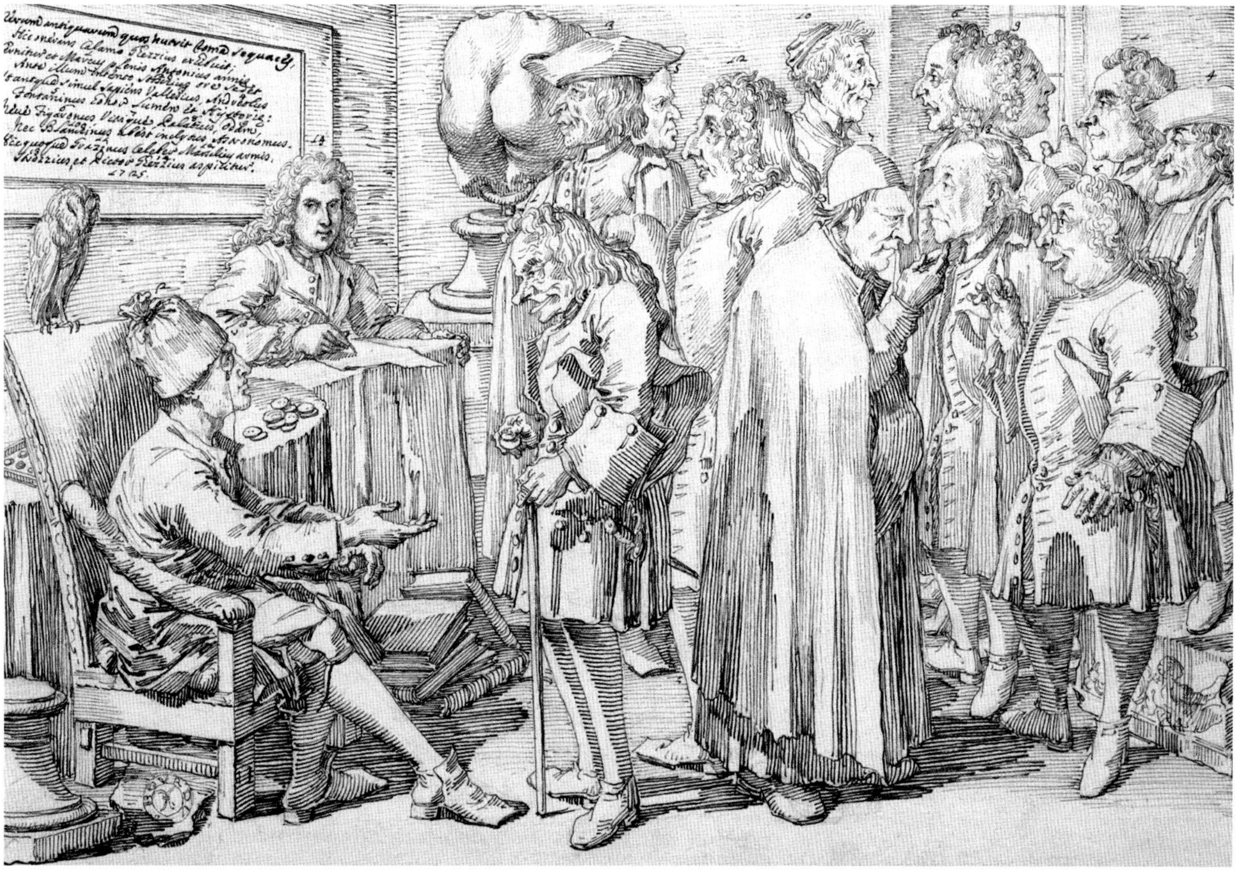

Fig. 65 Pier Leone Ghezzi, *Baron Philipp von Stosch Receiving Roman Antiquaries*, 1725. Photo © The Albertina Museum, Vienna.

or avatar.[40] Viewers were intrigued by the significance of the eagle: viewing a copy of the Reynolds portrait, Madame du Deffand in 1767 insisted on knowing its significance, but Walpole did not answer.[41] Unearthed in Rome in 1742 and purchased in 1745, the eagle was successfully acquired due to the shared labors of Walpole and his friends, in this case John Chute, who first came to know of the sculpture, and then Horace Mann, who announced it to Walpole in a letter and encouraged him to buy it. Chute, via Mann, was clear that the eagle was "far superior to that of Benv[en]uto Cellini which Ganimede keeps [at the Uffizi]"—a sculpture both men knew from the Grand Tour.[42] Chute thus considered it finer than one of the most overtly erotic representations of the story, the Uffizi *Ganymede*, reworked by Benvenuto Cellini (1500–1571) in 1545–46 (fig. 68), in which the eagle's wing tenderly embraces the youth. In terms of conventional iconography, the Boccapadugli Eagle has no obvious connection to the Ganymede myth; it descends from a tradition of freestanding eagle sculptures from Roman antiquity, including a recently excavated example now in the Museum of London and one acquired by William Hamilton (1730–1803) while on the Grand Tour, which may or may not have signified Jupiter to Roman viewers but certainly did not allude to Ganymede.[43] Nevertheless, in this first reference to the eagle, Mann and Chute located it within an established homoerotic iconography and within a homoerotic genealogy of art objects from Roman antiquity to the present.

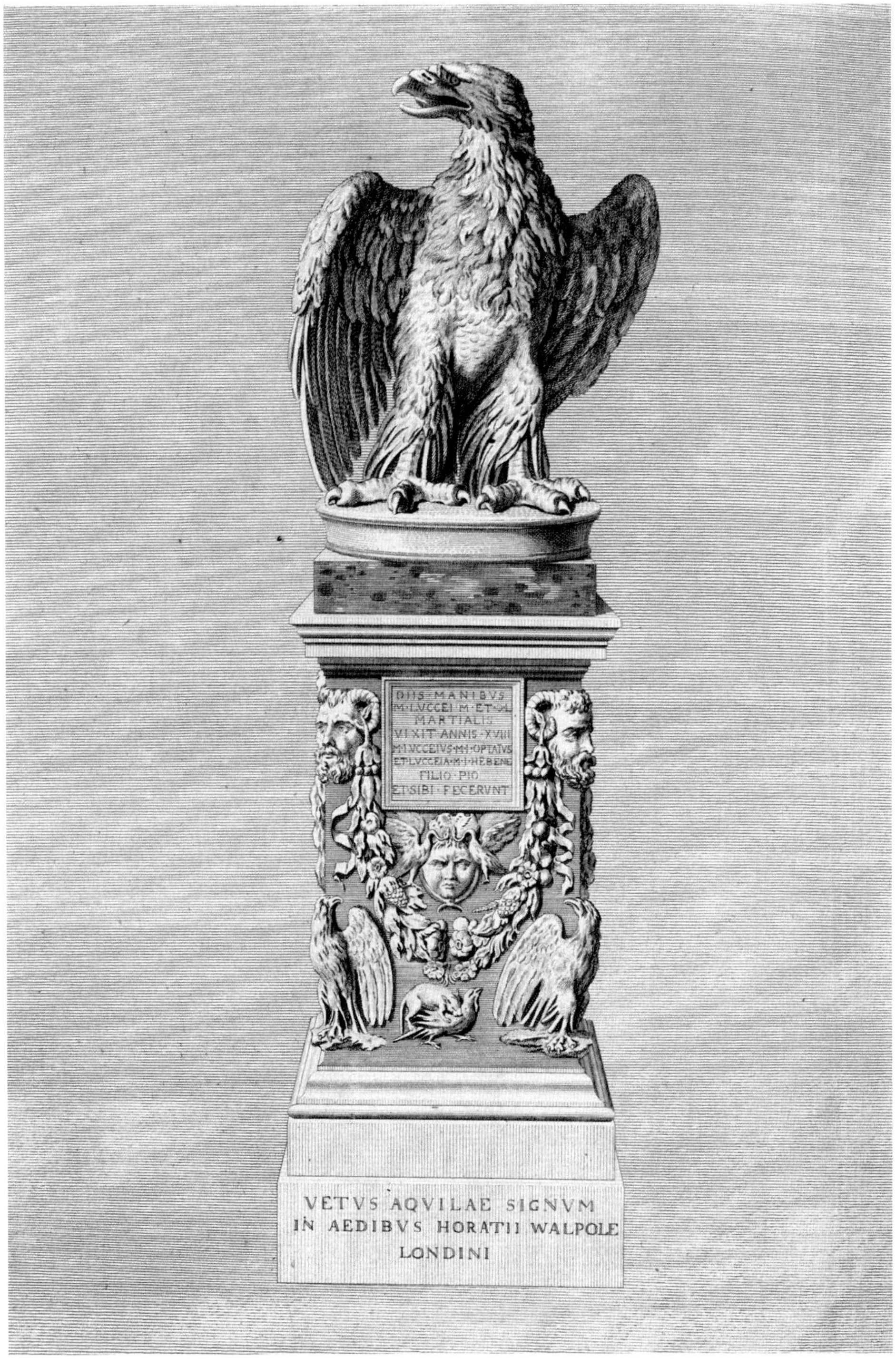

Fig. 66 Marble eagle on an altar base (Boccapadugli Eagle), originally displayed in the Long Gallery at Strawberry Hill. Roman, first century A.D. Engraved for Walpole's *Description*, LWL 33 30 Copy 11 Folio, p. 141. Courtesy of The Lewis Walpole Library, Yale University.

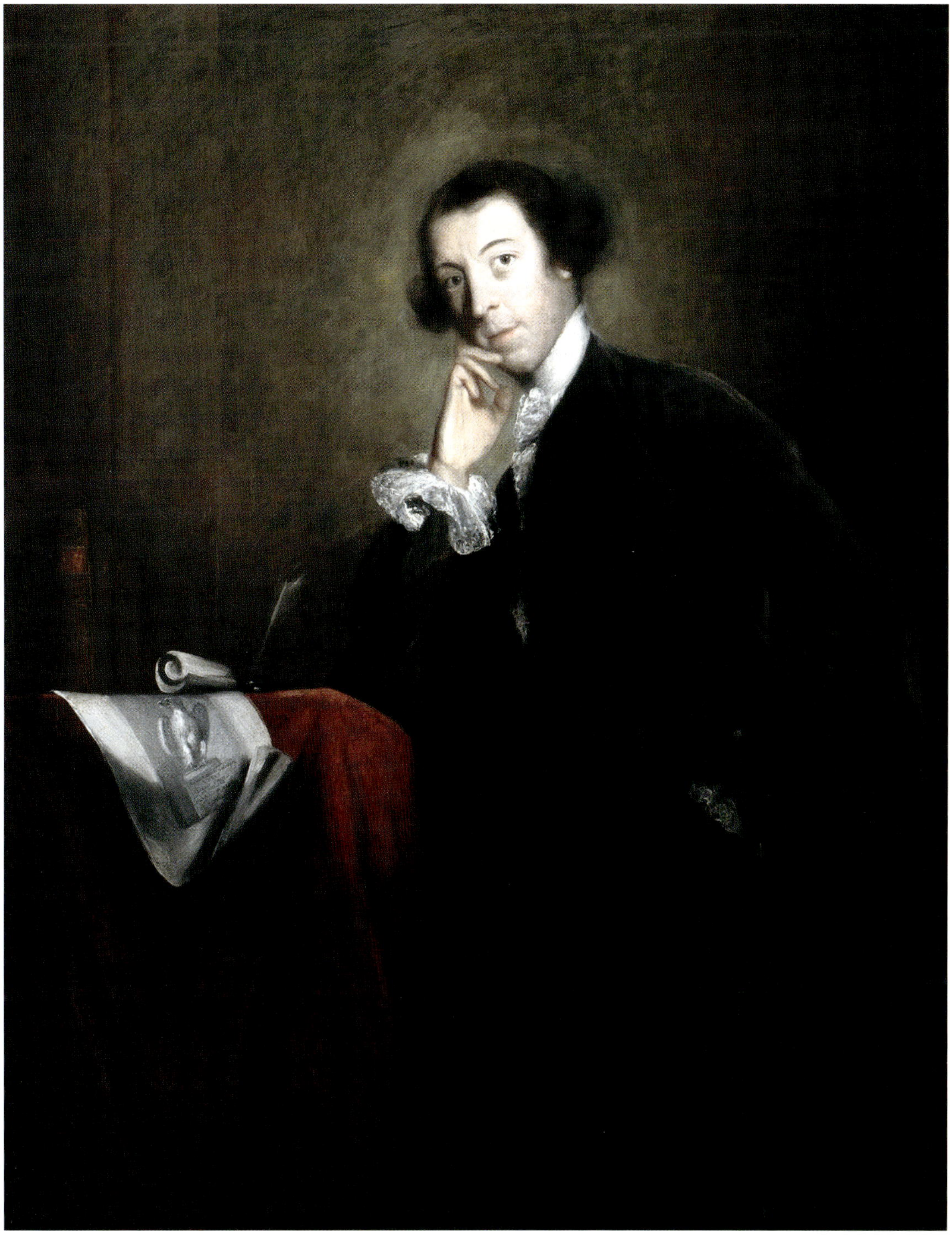

Fig. 67 Joshua Reynolds, *Horace Walpole*, 1756. Oil on canvas. National Portrait Gallery, London. One of three autograph copies of Reynolds's portrait of Walpole produced by the artist between 1756 and 1757. Photo © National Portrait Gallery, London.

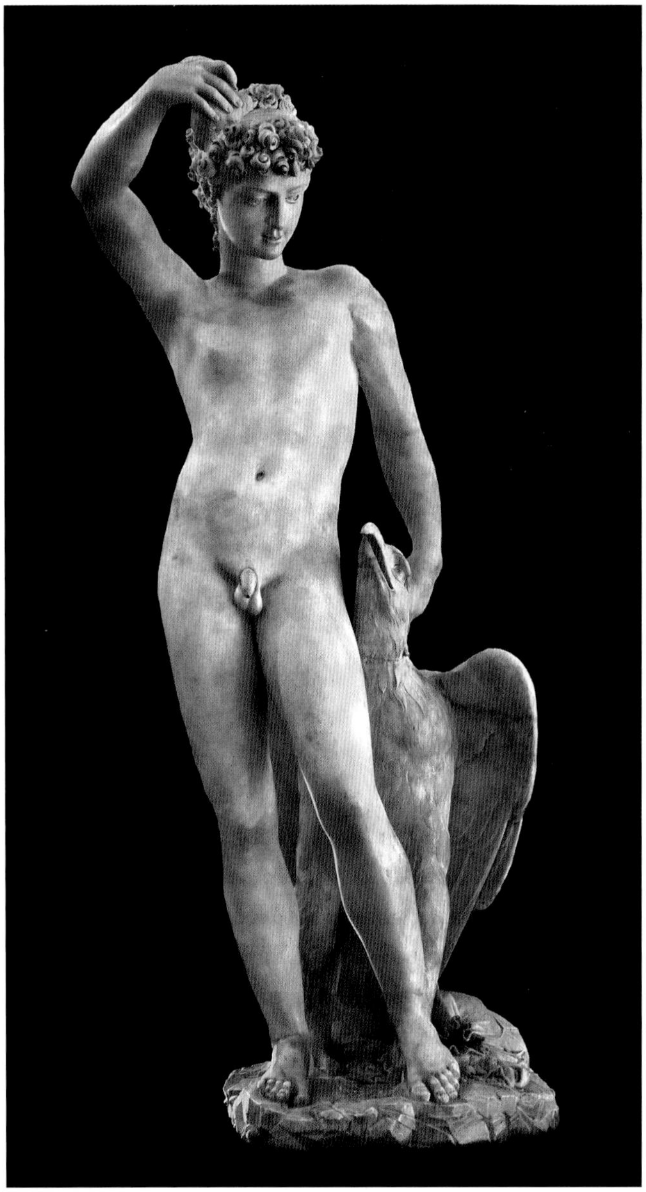

Fig. 68 Benvenuto Cellini, *Ganymede and Jupiter*, reworked Roman copy of a Greek sculpture of the third century B.C.E. Museo Nazionale del Bargello. Photo: Peter Horree / Alamy Stock Photo.

What is interesting is that Cellini did much the same thing. The Roman torso around which the statue was built, to which he added a head, arms, feet, and the eagle, likewise had no obvious connection to the Ganymede myth. According to his autobiography, it was Cellini who proposed to transform an antique torso into a Ganymede.[44] In this light, Walpole's eagle becomes a double fabrication, a projected or invented queer genealogy through objects that were not, originally at least, queer at all. Walpole's circle thus engages in a highly subjective interpretation of form that in many respects challenges and even upends "objective" iconographical analysis by insisting on the radically subjective nature of interpretation and the ability of the Ganymede myth, in this case, to transform images/objects into homoerotic substitutes. Here too there was a context for these ideas in queer collections. During this time Joachim Winckelmann would impose the same myth on an apparently iconographically unrelated work of art, thereby positing the self and the image as substitutes for the relationship of Jupiter and Ganymede. For Winckelmann, the antique faun in his collection was called "my Ganymede," whose face he might "kiss without offense before the very eyes of the saints."[45] Walpole's writings, of course, never get so close to an eroticization of the eagle, and so it remains a matter of speculation whether the Zeus/Jupiter–Ganymede paradigm is meant to reference Walpole's relationship with Chute (who was sixteen years senior to Walpole). Yet it is notable that to Walpole is attributed the gift of similar stone eagles to Chute for the Vyne, where they were placed on the exterior of the house (discussed in chapter 5). Whether or not these were gifts of Walpole's, the development of shared codes to articulate aspects of common sexual subjectivities and practices in the art patronage of his circle can be paralleled in other productions, particularly in their letter writing.[46]

"The Castle of My Ancestors": Family Genealogies at Strawberry Hill

Focusing on the homoerotic imagery of Strawberry Hill is an important, if limited, approach to understanding the queer significations of Strawberry Hill's collections and ornamentation. Walpole was neither a libertine nor a pornographer: his sensibilities oriented him toward subtler and more psychologically complex articulations of homoerotic bonds in his art patronage. I turn now to consider another aspect of the Strawberry Hill collections, namely their implicit and frequently explicit construction and juxtaposition of his biological family and his "queer family" of friends and associates, evident in the display of heraldry in stained glass and wall painting, on the house's ornament and its furniture, and in the portraits that hung in the house in carefully structured family groups. The genealogical displays of heraldry and portraiture at Strawberry Hill were integral components of the house and of what Walpole took to be "Gothic" about it.[47] They were based on a conception of medieval architecture, and the aristocratic family seat in particular, which was filled with heraldic blazons and other emblems of family lineage. A passage in the *Gentleman's Magazine* of 1739 provides an established contemporary image: "Methinks there was something respectable in those old hospitable Gothick halls, hung round with the Helmets, Breast-Plates, and Swords of our Ancestors; I entered them with a Constitutional Sort of Reverence and look'd upon those arms with Gratitude, as the Terror of former Ministers and the Check of Kings."[48] By the time Strawberry Hill was begun, the Gothic already enjoyed a status in England as an anachronistic style that articulated dynastic ambitions, as in the building of Welbeck Abbey, Nottinghamshire, by Henrietta Cavendish Holles Harley, Countess of Oxford, from 1742.[49] Viewing Welbeck in 1756, Walpole drew particular attention to the Gothic house as a setting for dynastic display: "It is impossible to describe the bales of Cavendishes, Harleys, Holleses, Veres, and Ogles: every chamber is tapestried with them; nay, and with ten thousand other fat morsels; all their histories inscribed; all their arms, crests, devices, sculptured on chimneys of various English marbles in ancient forms."[50]

As at Welbeck, at Strawberry Hill Walpole's construction of his own genealogy was indebted to his antiquarian endeavor into the history of his own family—the Walpoles on his father's side and the Shorters on his mother's. But heraldry and genealogy, as components of Walpole's construction of the Gothic, were as much subject to play, creative license, and subjective revision as the forms of Gothic architecture itself. In 1756, for example, Walpole had an "out-of-town party" at Strawberry Hill with Richard Edgecumbe (Strawberry's "chief herald painter"), George Selwyn, and others, in which they composed a coat of arms for White's (a London club) featuring claret bottles and gaming dice among standard blazons (John Chute retained his title of "Strawberry-King-at-arms").[51] Walpole was not above the playful invention or supposition of ancestry via the display of reused heraldry or repurposed objects to suggest pedigree even if none was actually implied. In 1750 he purchased almost 450 pieces of Netherlandish glass for Strawberry Hill from the agent "Asciotti" (introduced to him by Dicky Bateman, who had employed Asciotti to acquire glass for Old Windsor), including armorials, which he described as "the achievements of the old Counts of Strawberry" (although he admitted that they "have no relation to the Family"), thereby suggesting a further genealogical line of invented ancestors who populated Strawberry Hill's fictive medieval history.[52] He

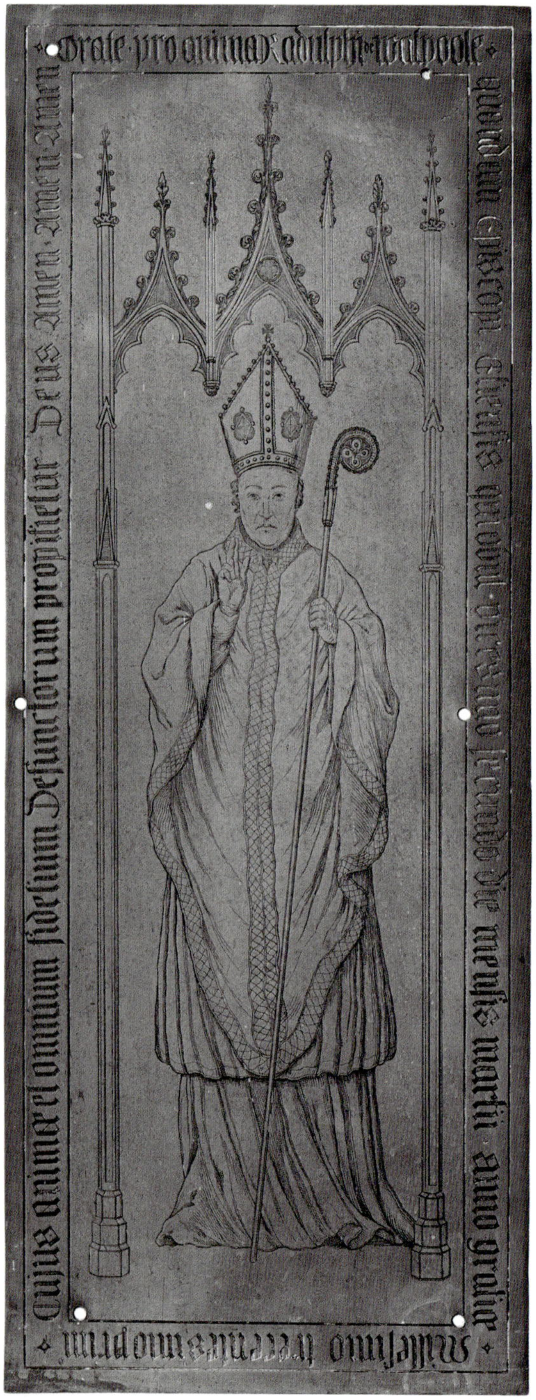

Fig. 69 J. H. Müntz, monumental brass of Ralph Walpole, bishop of Norwich and Ely, ca. 1758. This remarkable neo-Gothic brass was originally housed in the Little Cloister at Strawberry Hill. Collection of Dame Gillian Wagner.

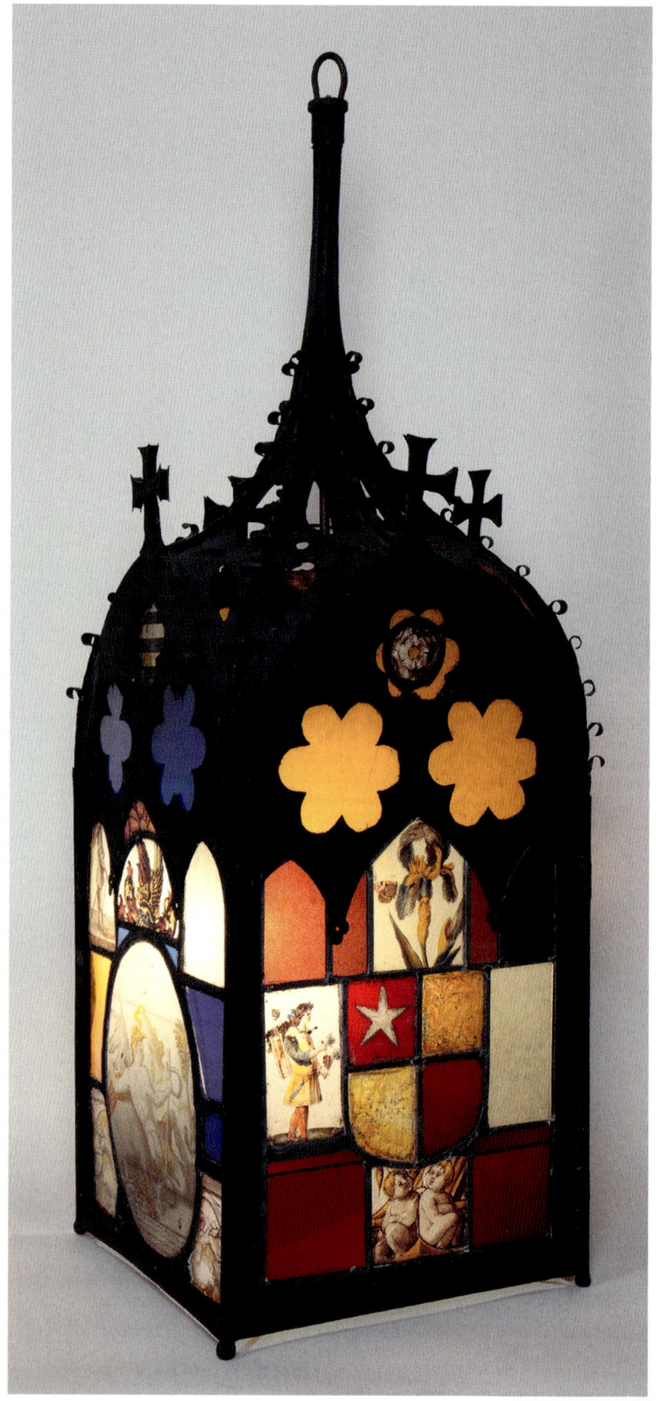

Fig. 70 William Hallett Sr., Gothic lantern from the main staircase at Strawberry Hill, with reused glass, designed by Richard Bentley, ca. 1755. LWL. Courtesy of The Lewis Walpole Library, Yale University.

referenced these "ancestors" often, noting, for example, that the Armory "bespeaks the ancient chivalry of the lords of the castle."[53] Walpole's use of the word "castle" is significant: in the eighteenth century this term connoted ancient family seats and encouraged associations with England's great ancestral mansions, an evocation of the patriarchal structures of the Middle Ages.[54]

Various individual objects and images within the house attest to Walpole's articulation of his biological ancestry. The monumental brass of Ralph Walpole, bishop of Norwich and Ely (1299–1302), that Walpole commissioned to display in the Little Cloister (fig. 69) celebrates an illustrious medieval ancestor on his father's side (Ralph Walpole's heraldry, where the See of Ely impales the Walpole family, was also painted in the Armory). Walpole claims to have based the monument upon an engraving of a brass of Robert Derby, bishop of Durham, in John Dart's *Westmonasterium*, although the memorial is in fact more closely modeled upon that of Robert de Braybrooke, bishop of London, from the engraving in Dugdale's *History of St. Paul's*.[55] Designed by J. H. Müntz, the brass is an extraordinary example of eighteenth-century Gothic design in its own right, since it employs the materials of medieval commemorative monuments and borrows a standard formula for funerary inscriptions in Gothic letters ("Orate pro anima Radulphi Walpoole quondam Episcopi Eleinsis . . ."). The Walpole arms—"on a fesse between two chevrons sable, three cross crosslets of the field"—appear throughout the house and in its stained glass, notably in the windows of the Long Gallery and the Great North Bedchamber.[56] Glossing such familial displays at Strawberry Hill, Walpole often mused that he was building a new "family seat," a replacement of sorts for his father's former estate at Houghton. Writing to his friend George Montagu in 1753, Walpole describes Strawberry Hill as "the castle [. . .] of my ancestors" (a statement he does not qualify), and he goes on to describe the Gothic lantern ("lanthorn") in the main staircase, designed by Richard Bentley (fig. 70), into which he set a stained-glass armorial blazon of the de Vere family (earls of Oxford) to suggest that, despite its recent facture, it derived from the twelfth-century Castle of Hedingham.[57]

Strawberry Hill's heraldry and portrait displays have typically been interpreted as evidence of Walpole's attachment to traditional aristocratic values. For David McKinney, Strawberry Hill was a "family seat . . . [that] was created to pay tribute to the institutional family," and its apparently anachronistic style "exemplified the legacy of English heroism."[58] In this reading, Strawberry Hill became the next "family seat" of the Walpoles. Apparently intended as a "dynastic symbol," it functioned as an idealized replacement for the Walpole family seat at Houghton Hall, which declined after his father's political disgrace in a motion of no confidence in Parliament in 1742 and his death three years later. Nuancing this line of argument, Stephen Bann has usefully considered Strawberry Hill a "compensatory fantasy," a means of overcoming a range of anxieties about patriarchy and familial succession.[59] There is of course something to recommend these views: Walpole and the Strawberry Committee were actively interested in genealogy and heraldry, and they employed Strawberry Hill and other homes built by them as settings to display and order their various emblems of collecting and genealogical research. But here, as in other aspects of Walpole's Gothic, there is a critical double edge that seems to question, if not substantially overturn, literal readings. From my perspective, a literal reading of Walpole's various constructions of family genealogy fails to glean the subversive humor that underlay his Gothic project as a whole. Family structure (what would now be called "family dynamics"), genealogy, and patriarchy were among the most contested concepts in Walpole's thought, and they were explored, deconstructed, and ultimately parodied in his many writings.

Studies of Walpole's Gothic literature—what have been called his "family romances" (*The Castle of Otranto* and *The Mysterious Mother*)—have employed psychobiographical approaches to interpret these narratives as ciphers for Walpole's own complex family dynamics (what he allegorizes as "the bloody civil wars of the house of Walpole").[60] In these narratives, sexual sin—particularly incest—consistently thwarts natural patterns of patriarchal succession as the fundamental mode of transmitting power between fathers and sons. As I have already suggested, *The Castle of Otranto*'s traumatic opening, in which the effeminate Conrad is suddenly crushed to death by a gigantic helmet, introduces not only the impossibility of an effete boy's marrying well, producing heirs, and succeeding his father, but the inevitability of the father's exposure as the tyrannical usurper of the principality in the first place. This is announced in the prophecy that the "castle and lordship of Otranto should pass from the present family, whenever the real owner should be grown too large to inhabit it,"[61] thereby anticipating the explosion of the castle at the end of the novel. Exploring Walpole's use of the biblical trope of "the sins of the fathers," psychobiographical readings of *Otranto* have pointed to an Oedipal relationship between Horace Walpole and his father as a template upon which the story is constructed. Domineering fathers are vanquished at the feet of sympathetic mothers.[62]

As Walpole's new "family seat," Strawberry Hill, as well as its collection and imagery, is deliberately encoded with a series of paradoxes. Despite its anachronistic character, the house was an "ancient" family seat without a history and, to a large extent, without a family. If it was intended to be the new "seat" of the Walpoles, then it was one that was self-consciously antithetical in style and meaning to his father's Palladian estate at Houghton, as many contemporaries noted. Style serves to break paternal succession in the Walpoles' architectural genealogy. More important still, Strawberry Hill was the "family seat" of a resigned bachelor whose sexuality meant that he was unlikely to produce heirs (as he and his circle manifestly understood), thus suggesting that Walpole intended to embrace both biological and queer families at Strawberry Hill. Musing on this in a letter to Henry Conway concerned in part with "matrimonial satire," Walpole recounts an early visit to Strawberry Hill from his sister Lady "Mary" (i.e., Maria) Walpole and her husband, Charles Churchill: "I only tell you this, to hint that my house will hold a married pair: indeed it is not quite large enough for people who lie like the Patriarchs with their whole genealogy, and manservants and maidservants and oxes and asses in the same chamber with them."[63] Employing his well-worn trope on the house's diminutiveness, Walpole puns on the possibility—thus underlining the impossibility—that Strawberry will hold a married couple. We can trace these ideas in Walpole's poetry. His poem "The Entail, a Fable," of 1754, provides a comic vision of property ownership when a butterfly "takes possession" of a rose as his new abode (note that "butterfly" and "butterfly men" were codes for the third sex):[64]

> In a fair Summer's radiant morn
> A Butterfly, divinely born,
> Whose lineage dated from the mud
> Of Noah's or Deucalion's flood,

Long hov'ring round a perfum'd lawn,
By various gusts of odours drawn,
At last establish'd his repose
On the rich bosom of a Rose.

Beneath this passage comes an explanatory footnote, stating: "This piece was occasioned by the author being asked (after he had finished the little castle at Strawberry-hill and adorned it with the portraits and arms of his ancestors) if he did not design to entail it on his family?" The poem then turns to the problem of succession, with the introduction of a "subtle slow Conveyancer" in the form of a caterpillar, and Walpole laments (comically, perhaps) the current problem of homes falling into the hands of nouveau riche buyers when they should, through suitably medieval rituals, succeed to sons to continue England's noble families. But the beautiful habitation and its butterfly meet an unexpected end before the drafting of a will by the lawyer-caterpillar, when a boy at play "[crushes] the proud Tenant of an hour / And [sweeps] away the Mansion-Flow'r."[65] Walpole's poem provides a subtle and characteristically subversive answer to his own footnotes. Its conventions—scalelessness, thwarted patriarchal succession, and the eventual destruction of a grand (if diminutive) habitation—are motifs that run through many of Walpole's cultural productions, including Strawberry Hill.

With this in mind, it is not surprising that Strawberry Hill's displays of heraldic and genealogical imagery undercut or parody some of the very patriarchal significations of the Gothic mansion. The decoration of the Library—itself the setting for his grandest genealogical display at Strawberry Hill, exhibiting both paternal and maternal heraldry and imagery—provides a useful starting point.[66] The trompe l'oeil ceiling in the Library was designed by Walpole and Bentley and painted by Andien de Clermont in 1754 (fig. 71). Walpole describes it thus in his *Description*: "In the middle is the shield of Walpole surrounded with the quarters borne by the family. At each end in a round[el] is a knight on horseback, in the manner of ancient seals; that next to the window bears the arms of Fitz Osbert, the other of Robsart. At the four corners are shields, helmets, and mantles: on one shield is a large H, on another a W, semée of cross crosslets, in imitation of an ancient bearing of the Howards in Blomfield's Norfolk."[67]

The heraldic blazons and replications of sillographic images of knights celebrated his medieval (and as Walpole believed) Crusader ancestry, linking his arms and initials with the Fitz Osberts and the Robsarts.[68] His early genealogical research (what W. S. Lewis called "dredging the past for distinguished ancestors") discovered the medieval relations of the Walpoles in the Robsarts, a significant Norfolk family that Horace presumably first encountered in William Musgrave's 1738 *Brief and True History of Sir Robert Walpole and His Family*.[69] The Robsarts were the medieval relations of the Walpoles (Sir Terry Robsart was the maternal grandfather of John Walpole, Sir Robert's great-great-great-grandfather). The Robsarts offered a number of distinguished ancestors, but Walpole focused particularly on the figure of Terry Robsart, a Knight of the Garter, whom he took to be a famed Crusader, a chivalric champion from the wars of Richard II. Willfully perhaps, Walpole confused Sir Terry Robsart (knighted 1483 and d. 1496) with Sir John Robsart, who fought under Richard II (1367–99). The devices of the Walpole arms and crest were cleverly dismantled and reemployed in a decorative frieze running along the top of the bookcases in alternating cross crosslets and Catherine wheels (figs. 51, 71). Centered above

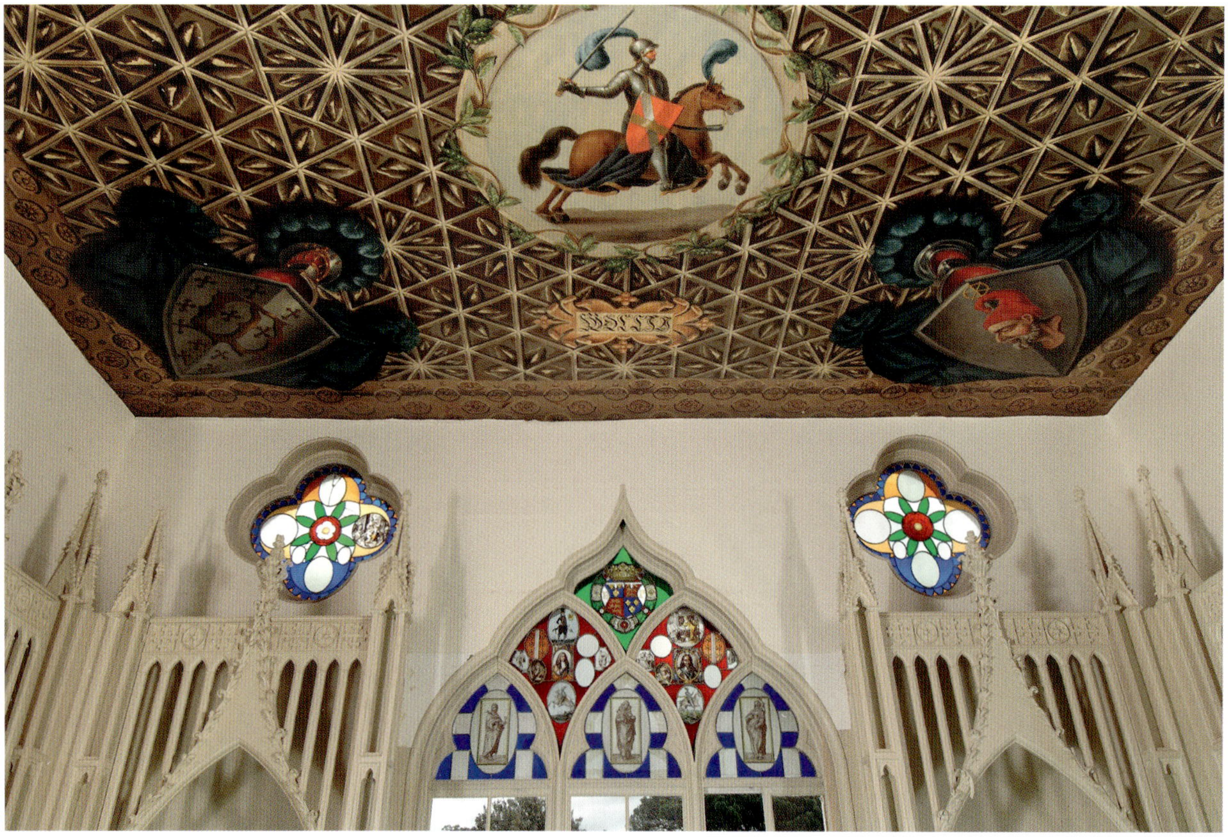

Fig. 71 Strawberry Hill Library ceiling. Photo: author.

each of John Chute's imitation Gothic bookcases was a portrait set within a roundel and framed by a pointed arch—thirteen in total, celebrating the Shorter family, Walpole's legitimate aristocratic lineage on his mother's side. The Shorter portraits constitute the dominant cycle of images in the Library. As Peter Lindfield has recently shown, Walpole in the early 1750s imagined a second paneled room filled principally with the Shorter arms, but it was never realized.[70] Framing this display of family lineage were stained-glass portraits of Charles I and II and the royal arms of England, as well as a late fifteenth-century wedding portrait over the fireplace that Walpole took to be the marriage of King Henry VI (now attributed to an anonymous Flemish master and titled *Marriage of a Saint*).[71]

In the genealogical displays of the library, Walpole would seem to have privileged his mother's aristocratic line over his father's "notoriously common" ancestry, which could boast only of the belatedly knighted prime minister, Sir Robert Walpole. At Strawberry Hill a "family romance" in the Freudian sense can be detected in Walpole's denigration of his father, whose relatively common heritage was trumped by his mother's aristocratic pedigree. Walpole's affections for his mother were well known during her lifetime and afterward, manifest, for example, in his design of her tomb at Westminster Abbey, with a monumental image based upon the classical Roman statue of Modesty (*Pudicitia*), a copy of which would also feature in the Tribune.[72] Sir Robert Walpole's presence and the Walpole family line in general are acknowledged and partially replaced by the figure of Sir Terry Robsart. Indeed, as often as not at Strawberry Hill, Walpole referenced the fabled Crusader as a cipher for his father's family. It is notable that Horace's presence was felt even less at Houghton Hall: a finished pastel study by Rosalba Carriera (1673–1757) of Horace from the Grand Tour of 1741 hung alongside his brother's portraits in the Yellow Drawing Room as the sole visual testament to Horace's place in Sir Robert's paternal home.[73] Discussing Strawberry Hill's heraldry, Emma Clery has described it as "an ingenious form of revenge" on Sir Robert.[74] Horace would comment somewhat acidly that his motto, *Fari quae sentiat*—which appeared on the Library ceiling—was "the best legacy my father left me."[75] This clever rethinking of ancestry and its representation through manifestly dubious simulacra or attributions has been called by Clery "a 'theme park' treatment of aristocratic ascendency. . . . As the feudal origins of the aristocratic order were turned into the plaything of a whimsical hobbyist, its present legitimacy was symbolically diminished."[76] Walpole's use of heraldry and dynastic portraiture—a thoroughly Gothic concept in Georgian England—largely evacuated from a hallowed medium its established or normative content. While Clery may exaggerate in framing these productions as manifestations of "a whimsical hobbyist," her focus on humor and parody is surely correct. It agrees with recent accounts of Walpole's literary family romances that likewise point to parody and theatricalization as tools to critique the aristocratic order and the sentimental bonds of the bourgeois family in contemporary England.[77] Walpole's overt, occasionally ridiculous, and often saccharine representations can be understood within the terms of "camp," as I have argued above with respect to Walpole's Gothic architecture.

Underlying Walpole's subversive structuring of family romance may have been his own contested parentage. As Anne Williams has recently discussed, there was much doubt during his life that Horace was indeed a Walpole.[78] His mother's fabled indiscretions, recounted in a variety of sources, including the letters of Lady Mary Wortley Montagu and a passage in Jonathan Swift's *Gulliver's Travels*, indicate the possibility that Horace was in fact the son of Carr, Lord Hervey (the elder half-brother of John, Lord Hervey, the subject of Horace's famous critique of the third sex). Lord Hervey had a liaison with Lady Mary Walpole while she was living estranged from Sir Robert, then living with his mistress, Maria Skerrett. Adulteress though Horace's mother certainly was, his sympathies remained with her. Although it is clear that Horace was aware of the rumors of his contested parentage, it is not clear whether he substantially believed them, though many in the period certainly did. In either case, as Williams suggests,

> [Horace's] manifold works testify to his troubling anxieties about himself and his parents—the paradoxical good mother, who undoubtedly was his mother and yet was "bad" according to cultural standards, and the equally paradoxical "father" who was not his father and a monster besides, but who had been good to him. Such fears would account for Horace's lifelong obsession with the past, with genealogy, with family secrets, with deceptive situations and with disguise and the counterfeit. . . . It explains his career, which may be seen as a lifelong drive to "materialize" "Horace Walpole."[79]

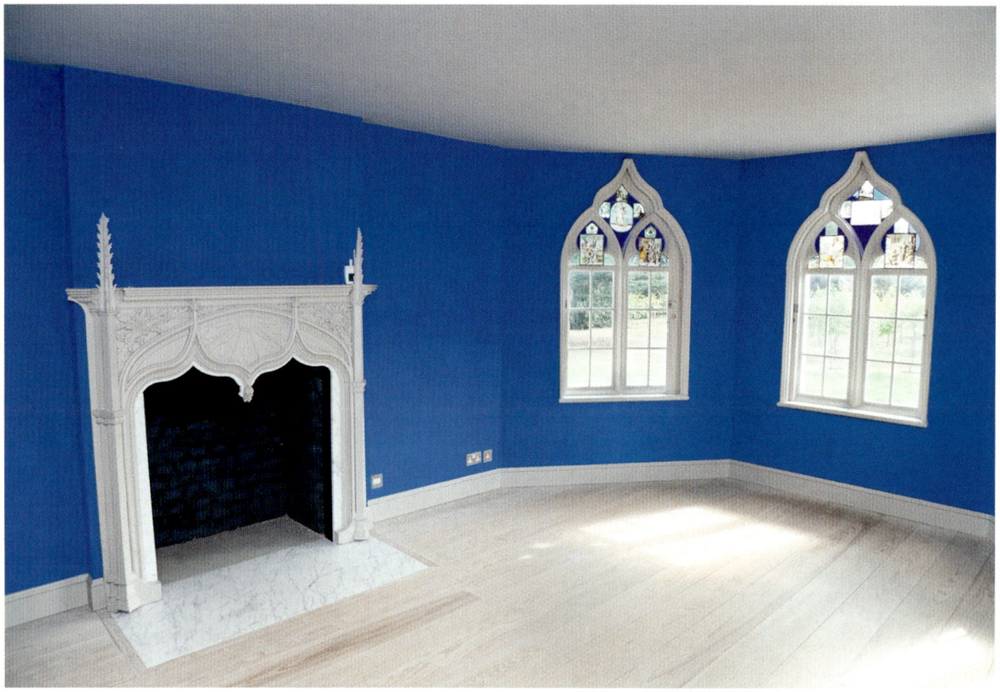

Fig. 72 Blue Bedchamber after restoration, Strawberry Hill. Photo: Alamy Stock Photo.

Williams's reading may be extended to gloss Walpole's construction of ancestry at Strawberry Hill, and perhaps also his Gothic texts—notably *The Castle of Otranto*—which thematize illegitimate succession. More germane to my current interests, Walpole's unwriting of "family romance" in the displays of heraldry and imagery at Strawberry Hill decisively and deliberately created a space for the construction of alternate, "queer" genealogies in the house.

Queer Family Portraiture

At Strawberry Hill the images of "family romance" in the quasi-public and scholarly space of the library contrast with images of "queer family romance" in the more private spaces of the Blue Bedchamber and the Round Room. The Blue Bedchamber (fig. 72) was reached via the stairway and was the grandest of a suite of south-facing rooms opposite the Library and Armory. As Michael Snodin has suggested, its hang was "conceived as a complement" to the ancestral display in the Library,[80] but it was a complement that alluded to biological *and* sexual forms of family. The hang comprised seven paintings principally by the society portraitist John Giles Eccardt commissioned by Walpole between circa 1746 and 1755.[81] Over the Gothic fireplace (designed by Richard Bentley) hung a posthumous image of Sir Robert Walpole and his first wife, Catherine Shorter (ca. 1746; fig. 22), set in a frame of circa 1680 in the style of Grinling Gibbons (Robert Walpole had died in 1745 and Catherine Shorter in 1737).[82] Against the backdrop of Houghton Hall, this portrait celebrated Walpole's maternal and paternal ancestry and his parent's shared legacy of Houghton, but it also implied an erasure of his father's very public affair with his mistress, Maria Skerrett, whom he married in 1738, very shortly after his wife's death, much upsetting Horace. The imagery for Robert Walpole and Catherine Shorter was based upon George Vertue's engravings, which Horace featured in his first edition of *Aedes Walpolianae*, themselves retrospective images that reinstated Sir Robert's marriage to Catherine Shorter and denied his later union.[83] Reflecting Walpole's own revisionist approach to his family in the Library, here surely was testimony to Walpole's "desire to veil the miscarriages of my race," in his own words.[84] Also by Eccardt were images of Walpole's half sister (born to Skerrett), Maria Walpole, and her husband, Charles Churchill.

The subjects of the remaining portraits in the room were related in one way or another to Walpole's "romantic and erotic camaraderie":[85] Henry Seymour Conway; the poet and playwright Sir Charles Hanbury Williams, described as "witty but licentious," who holds a copy of "Isabella, or the Morning"—a clever satire on the third sex featuring their mutual friend Dicky Bateman, possibly Horace Walpole himself, and other men in their circle (fig. 73);[86] the scholar and poet Thomas Gray, who holds the text of his "Ode on a Distant Prospect of Eton College" (fig. 74),[87] with whom Walpole went to Eton and had a youthful romantic liaison on the Grand Tour; Richard Bentley (fig. 75), a member of the Strawberry Committee; and Walpole himself, positioned in front of Strawberry Hill (fig. 76).[88] With the exception of his parents' portrait, the other portraits in the room participated in the current fashion of historicized family portraiture in which subjects appeared in the style of past masters and frequently in anachronistic costume.[89] Walpole stated that his own portrait, Bentley's, and Gray's were modeled after Van Dyck, while Conway's was based on Watteau and Maria Walpole's on Rubens. Elsewhere Walpole describes "Vandyck dress" as the costume of the "Macaronies."[90] This created what most eighteenth-century observers would have understood as a "family-portrait gallery," particularly those attuned to grand displays of similar historicizing family portraits, familiar from the country-house tour. Emphasizing this continuity, Walpole enclosed the portraits (again, his parents' portrait excepted) in black and gold frames "carved after those to Lombard's prints from Vandyck, but with emblems peculiar to each person."[91] Employing the technologies of family portraiture, Walpole's hang in the Blue Bedchamber provided a clever rethinking of the genealogical display in the Library to express the familial bonds between himself and his intimate coterie: a queer family romance.

The hang in the Blue Bedchamber was one of a number of articulations of Walpole's homoerotic circle in the objects and imagery of Strawberry Hill. Another was in the Round Tower, which held "six curious and interesting sketches, drawn at Venice, Portraits of the Earl of Lincoln, Horace Walpole, John Chute, Joseph Spence, Mr. Chaloner and Mr. Whitdsend [i.e., Francis Whitehead], by Rosalba [Carriera]," the prominent Venetian pastelist, which were made when Walpole and his friends were on the Grand Tour in 1741.[92] The marginal annotations in the copy of Walpole's 1784 *Description* owned by Thomas Kirgate (1734/35–1810), Walpole's printer and amanuensis, add a little to the end of this description, noting that the images were taken "when those Gentlemen were in Italy, unknown to them, when at some public Place; yet very like." These sketches were set within "Old Carved Frames," but nothing further is known about how they were displayed.[93] Some of these sketches may have been preparatory drawings

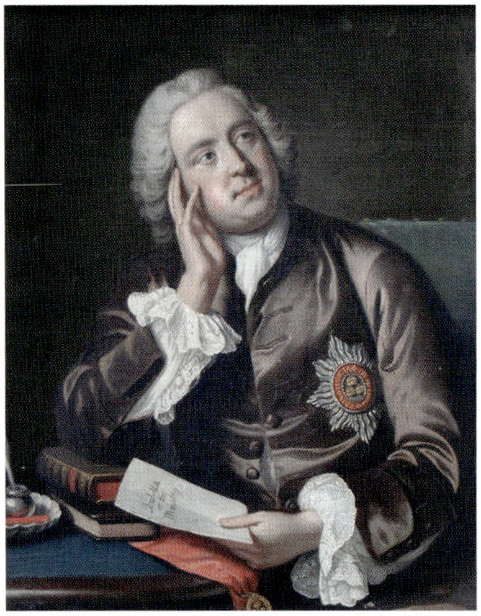

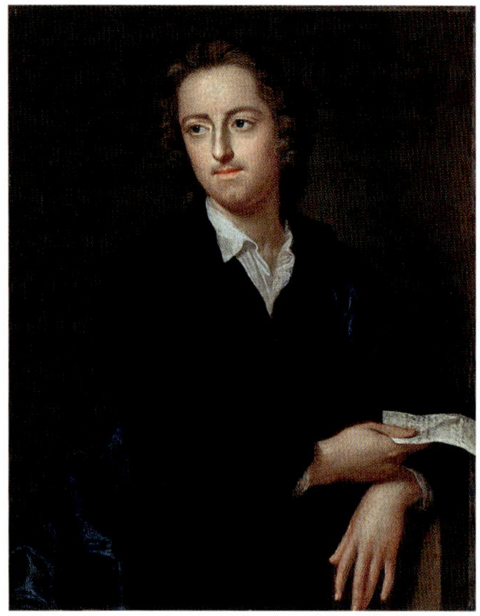

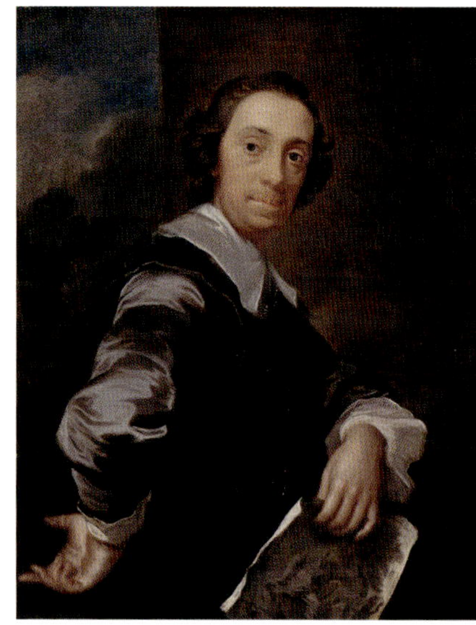

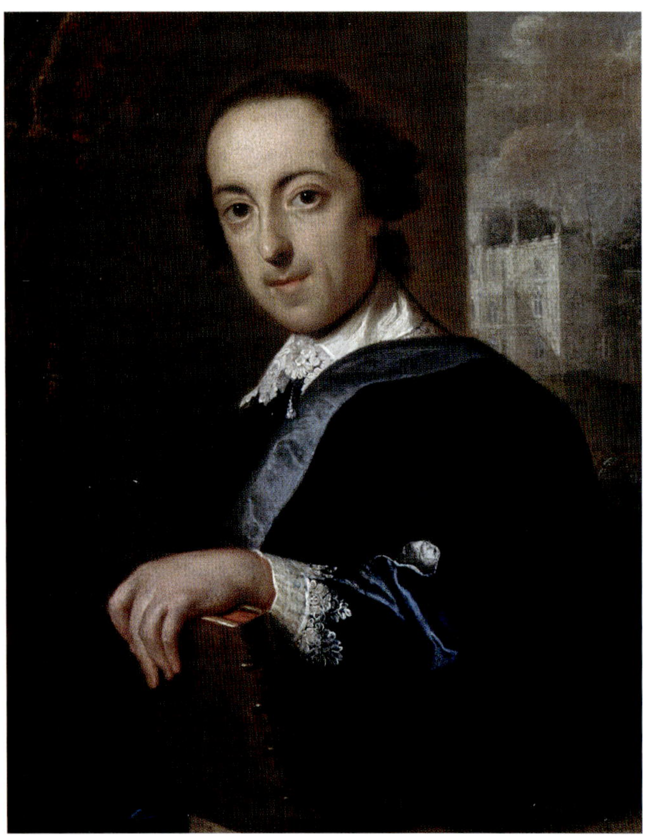

Clockwise from top left:

Fig. 73 John Giles Eccardt, *Sir Charles Hanbury Williams*, ca. 1754. Fingask Castle, Perthshire. Photo: Andrew Threipland.

Fig. 74 John Giles Eccardt, *Thomas Gray*, 1747–48. Photo © National Portrait Gallery, London.

Fig. 75 John Giles Eccardt, *Richard Bentley*, 1753. Photo © National Portrait Gallery, London.

Fig. 76 John Giles Eccardt, *Horace Walpole*, 1754. Photo © National Portrait Gallery, London.

for later pastels, including those of Horace Walpole at Houghton Hall or Francis Whitehead at the Vyne.[94] Carriera's sketches and finished originals form part of a current convention of commemorative portraiture popular among British Grand Tourists. Carriera, George Knapton (1698–1778), and Pompeo Batoni (1708–1787) were popular choices for tourists who commissioned individual or sequential portraits to commemorate their Italian journeys. In this sense, they might be compared to those of the Society of Dilettanti in the 1740s, some of which employ the same retrospective conventions as Walpole's portraits by Eccardt (especially Van Dyckian

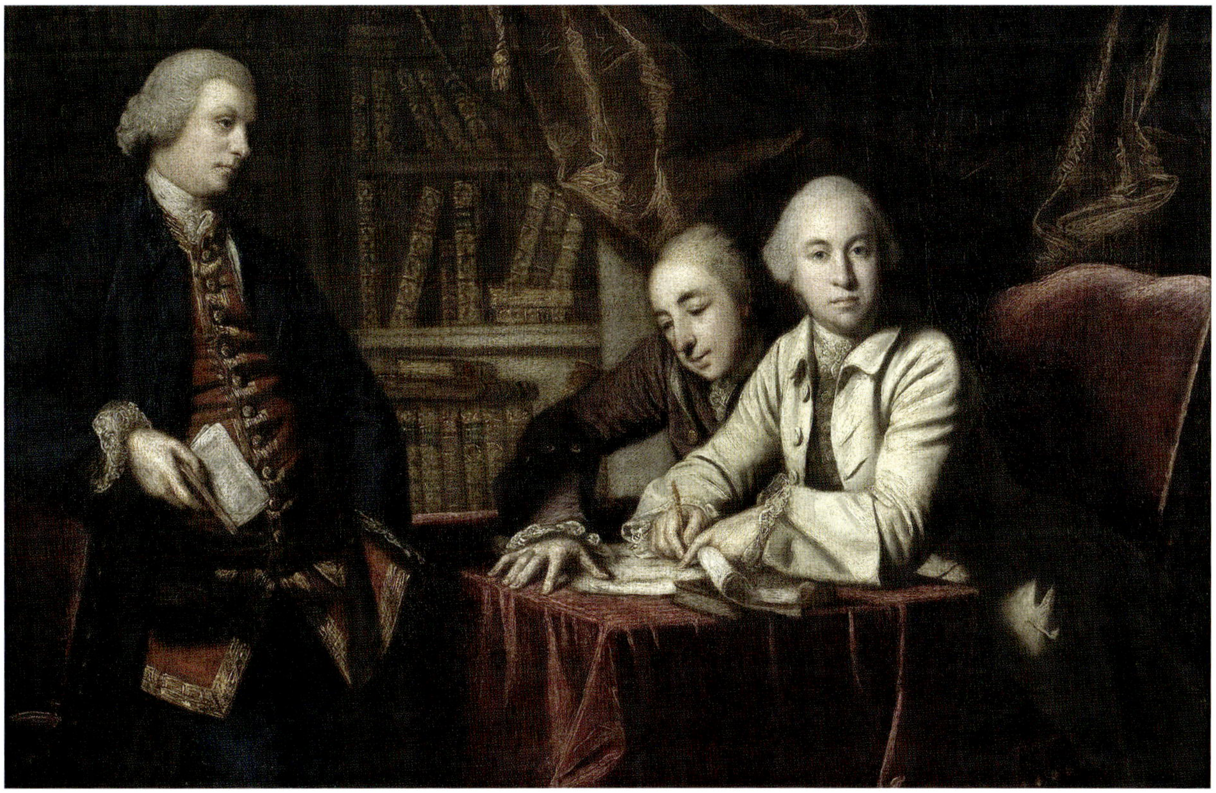

Fig. 77 Joshua Reynolds, *The Out of Town Party*, 1759–61. Set in the Library at Strawberry Hill, the painting shows (from left to right) George Selwyn, George James Williams, and Richard Edgecumbe. Bristol City Museum and Art Gallery, F. P. M. Schiller bequest, 1946. Photo: Bridgeman Art.

costume) but go considerably further in their use of elaborate impersonation through costume, crude sexual innuendo, and sacrilegious symbolism, as I have noted above. Although these images may not have had the same overtly parodic and sexual tenor, they nevertheless functioned in a similar fashion in their "consolidation of a coterie," to use Bruce Redford's useful epitome.[95] Whatever the nature of this series, they can only have recalled the heady days of Walpole's Grand Tour, which, as George Rousseau suggests, "evolved to a large extent out of his homoerotic needs" and "virtually institutionalised [his] homosocial relationships."[96]

Many other objects or images in the Strawberry Hill collection are worthy of further consideration in understanding its homoerotic intelligibility. In the Refectory, or Great Parlour, for example, which functioned as Walpole's dining room, Walpole complied with custom by structuring hangs of portraits of his immediate family, each positioned according to status (fig. 41).[97] The most privileged space in the room, however—the space above Richard Bentley's Gothic fireplace—was devoted to images of Walpole's queer family. Here hung Joshua Reynolds's *Out of Town Party* (commissioned by Walpole, 1759–61), which features Richard Edgecumbe, George (Gilly) Williams, and George Selwyn posed in the Library at Strawberry Hill (figs. 77, 41—the painting is visible at left). Such "out-of-town" parties took place with these men at Strawberry twice a year, at Easter and Christmas. In the painting, Selwyn holds a book and gazes inward toward his companions, while Williams leans in to look at and possibly select a drawing made by Edgecumbe, who in turn looks out of the painting as though interrupted by the entrance of their host, Horace Walpole. As Mark Hallett suggests, "the well-used shelves of the library are crowded with books that lean against each other with an intimacy and informality that echoes the easy interaction of the men themselves."[98] While Reynolds's group portrait surely depicts a singular meeting at Strawberry Hill, from Walpole's perspective the image commemorated a tradition of "out-of-town parties" at the villa. Anticipating their Christmas 1754 meeting, Walpole confided to Bentley, "when I do admit anybody within my cloister, I choose them well."[99] Edgecumbe, probably bisexual, helped produce a comic heraldic blazon for White's gambling house in London (a copy of which hung at Strawberry Hill); Selwyn was accused by contemporaries of "a sort of sentimental sodomy" because of his relationships with William Douglas, third Earl of March, and Frederick Howard, fifth Earl of Carlisle (who was twenty-nine years his junior); and Williams (cousin to Sir Charles Hanbury Williams) has latterly been called "a gay bachelor," for although he did wed in his thirties, the marriage produced no offspring.[100] In Stephen Bann's commentary on this image, he rightly considers it "a testimony to the fact that Walpole wished such cultural bonds to be placed on record."[101]

Like the villa that housed it, the Strawberry Hill collection was unique. As I have argued here, one of the "discursive trails" that runs through the collection articulated the complex bonds that Walpole shared with his homosocial circle, or "queer family." The Gothic house, complete with its heraldic blazons, ancestral portraiture, and even its own historicity as an architectural entity *supposed* to be built over several generations by a single family, offered Walpole a fitting space to explore and reimagine the patriarchal core of the Gothic castle. Images such as Eccardt's portraits in the Blue Bedchamber or Reynolds's *Out of Town Party* offer essays in queer family romance and can usefully be understood as visual corollaries to Walpole's clever invention of coterie labels, including "the Strawberry Committee" at Strawberry Hill and the "Quadruple Alliance" at Eton, composed of Horace Walpole, Thomas Gray, Richard West, and Thomas Ashton. But collecting, arranging, displaying, and exchanging art and architecture was only one possible venue for creating queer family romances. As I suggest in subsequent chapters of this book, another was found in the built environment.

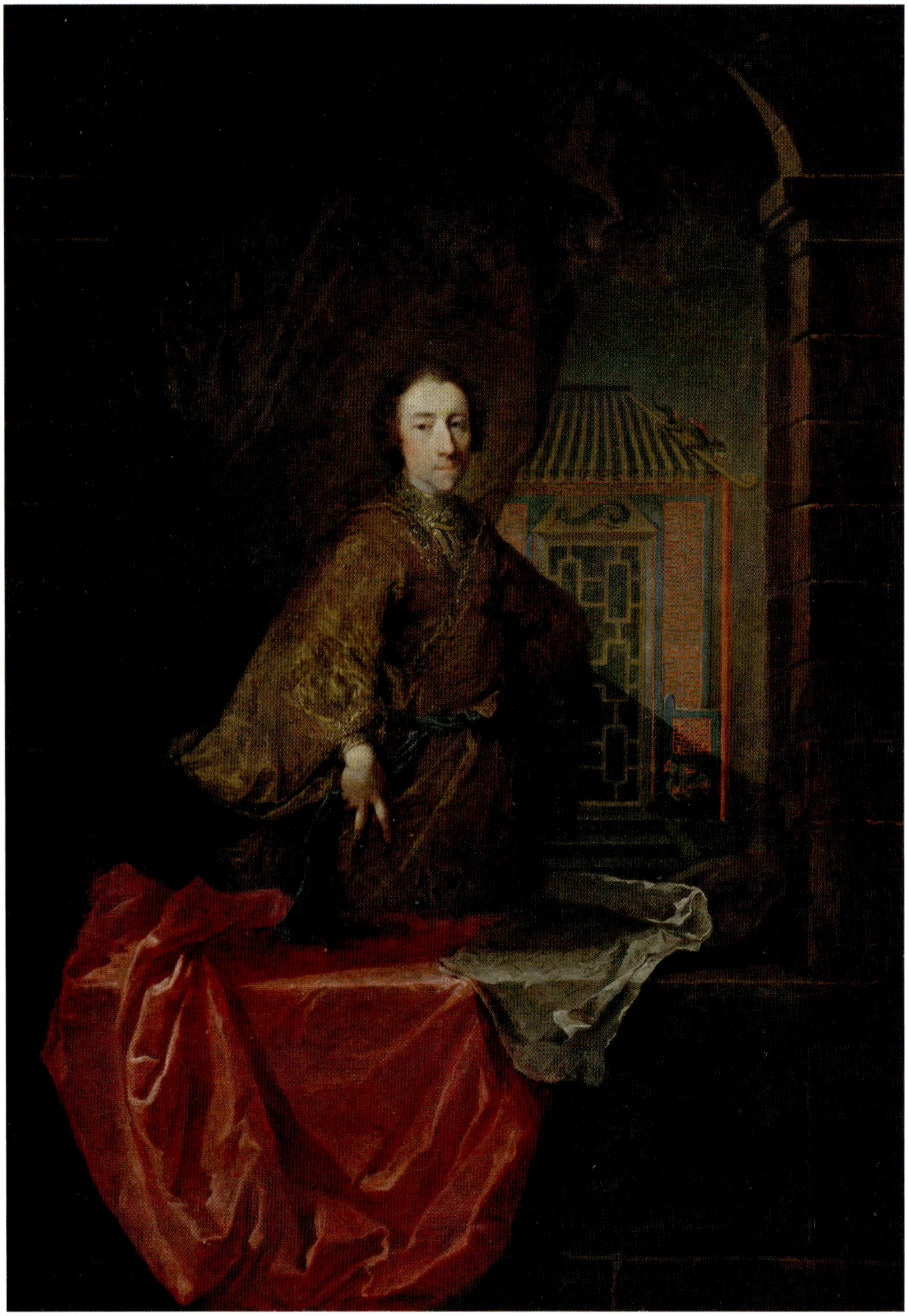

Fig. 78 Robert Levrac-Tournières, *Richard Bateman*, 1741. Birmingham Museum and Art Gallery. Photo: Birmingham Museums Trust.

4 Dicky Bateman and the Gothicization of Old Windsor

Mr Dicky Bateman was a typical eccentric, who resembled his friend Horace Walpole in his Gothic affectation, and [John] Wilkes in his impious buffoonery.

—Mrs. Delany

One figure that Horace Walpole may have helped to erase from the historiography of eighteenth-century Gothic art and architecture was Richard (Dicky) Bateman (1705–1773),[1] along with his Gothic villa at Old Windsor, up the Thames from Strawberry Hill (fig. 78). Twelve years senior to Walpole, Bateman was a leading man of taste and fashion in London during Walpole's youth, and his villa would be an important influence on Walpole and Strawberry Hill.[2] Bateman acquired the villa around 1730 and substantially transformed it into the Strawberry Hill Gothic mode between 1758 and 1768. Although a cause célèbre in the period, Old Windsor has been very little studied, and its place in the development of the Gothic has, until recently, been little understood.[3] Because the villa has been in private hands from Bateman's death to the present and has been subject to regular interventions, the standing fabric and its internal divisions retain little that is original to his campaigns, with the notable exception of the Gothic dining room (fig. 79). Fortunately, our understanding of the house and its collection is supported by extensive contemporary drawings and descriptions and a catalogue of its contents sale of 1774.[4]

One reason why Bateman and Old Windsor have not enjoyed a more prominent place in our understanding of eighteenth-century Gothic is that Horace Walpole, the Gothic's main interlocutor, said little of Bateman's Gothic buildings and framed him instead as "the founder of the Sharawadgi [Chinese] taste in England."[5] Walpole went further by calling Chinoiserie "Bateman architecture," an architecture of "weak nerves,"[6] thus employing the body-building analogy to describe Chinoiserie as a plastic expression of Bateman's own queer physicality. Recent accounts of Chinoiserie in England have shown that this glossy, fussy mode was patronized particularly by women and appealed, broadly speaking, to a female subjectivity. Bateman was not, of course, the founder of a Chinese taste in England, but he was clearly a

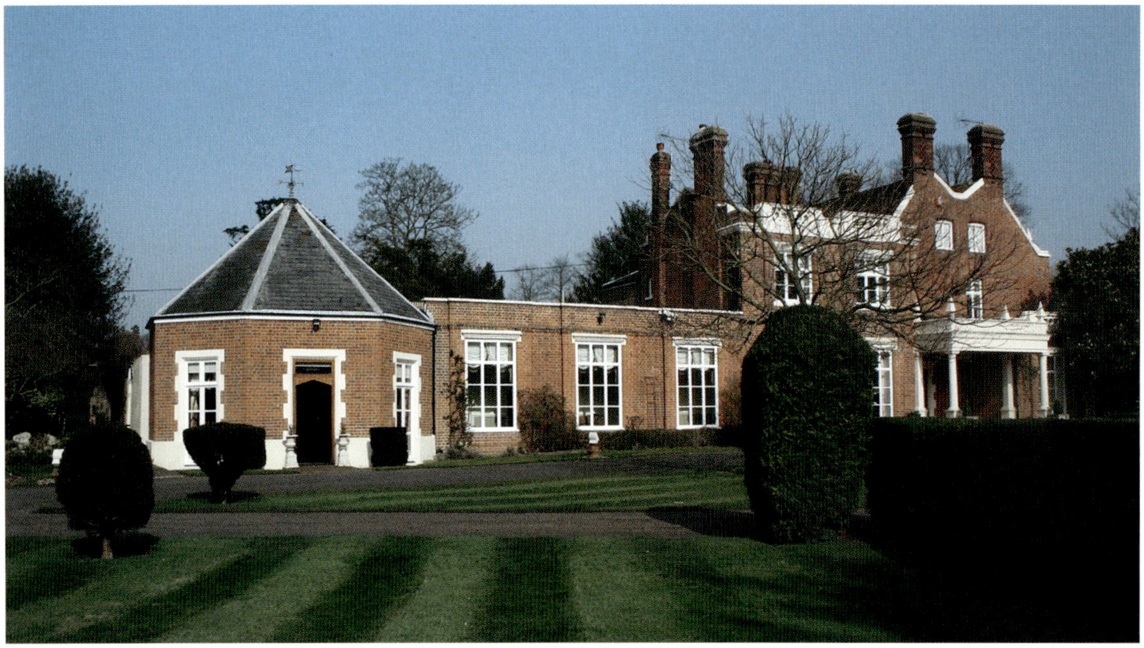

Fig. 79 Dicky Bateman's Old Windsor, Berkshire, showing the original house and dining room. Photo: author.

leading proponent of it. His Chinese enthusiasms were celebrated in his 1741–42 portrait by Robert Levrac-Tournières, in which he is represented as a Mandarin dressed in a silk robe in front of a Chinese building or screen with carved dragons while pointing to a Chinese calligraphic scroll (fig. 78).

But Bateman was also a significant patron of the Gothic, commissioning plans for the extraordinary new church at his family's estate at Shobdon, Herefordshire, in 1746 (not built until 1752–53). Purchased by his father, Sir James Bateman, a prolific merchant financier and director of the Bank of England, Shobdon was the country seat of a London banker who built a grand Palladian mansion by 1717. Upon his death in 1718, the estate went principally to William Viscount Bateman, elder brother to Dicky, although Dicky, from London, oversaw subsequent renovations to the interior and grounds of the estate. Dicky's commissioned designs for the new church were based upon the influential Gothic designs of William Kent but were probably executed by Henry Flitcroft, who had been remodeling Shobdon Court from 1746.[7] Shobdon church and its furniture constitute one of the most remarkable essays in Gothic design conceived in England in the 1740s (figs. 80, 81): its radical elaborations of form and its fictive materials preface much of Walpole's work at Strawberry Hill, conceived a decade or more later.[8] Bateman's rebuilding of the church at Shobdon in the Gothic style also involved the demolition of the Romanesque Abbey of St. John the Evangelist built by Oliver de Merlimond in the 1130s and 1140s and the creation of a second medievalist project, the so-called Shobdon Arches (1752). Rebuilt from the chancel arch and two portals of the abbey, the Shobdon Arches were conceived as an "eye-catcher," or Gothic folly, on the

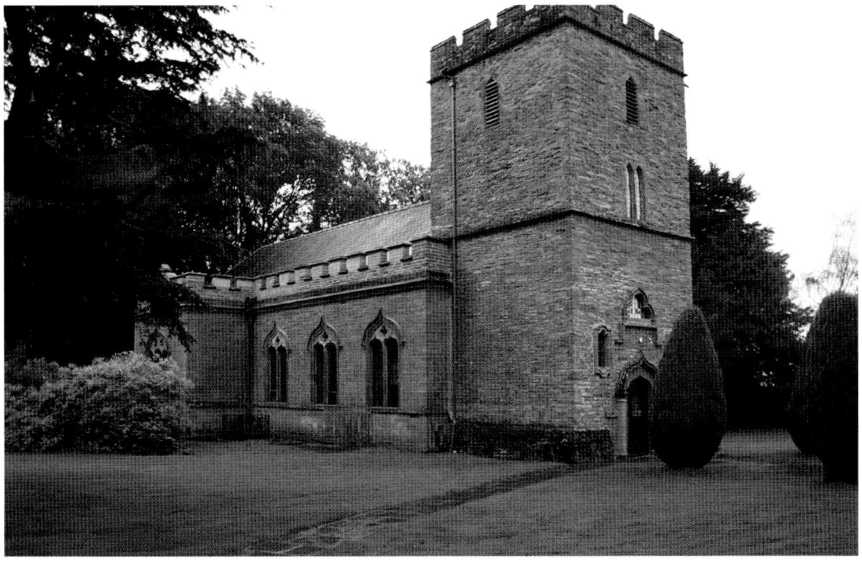

Fig. 80 Shobdon church, Herefordshire, exterior. Photo: author.

Fig. 81 Shobdon church, Herefordshire, interior. Photo: author.

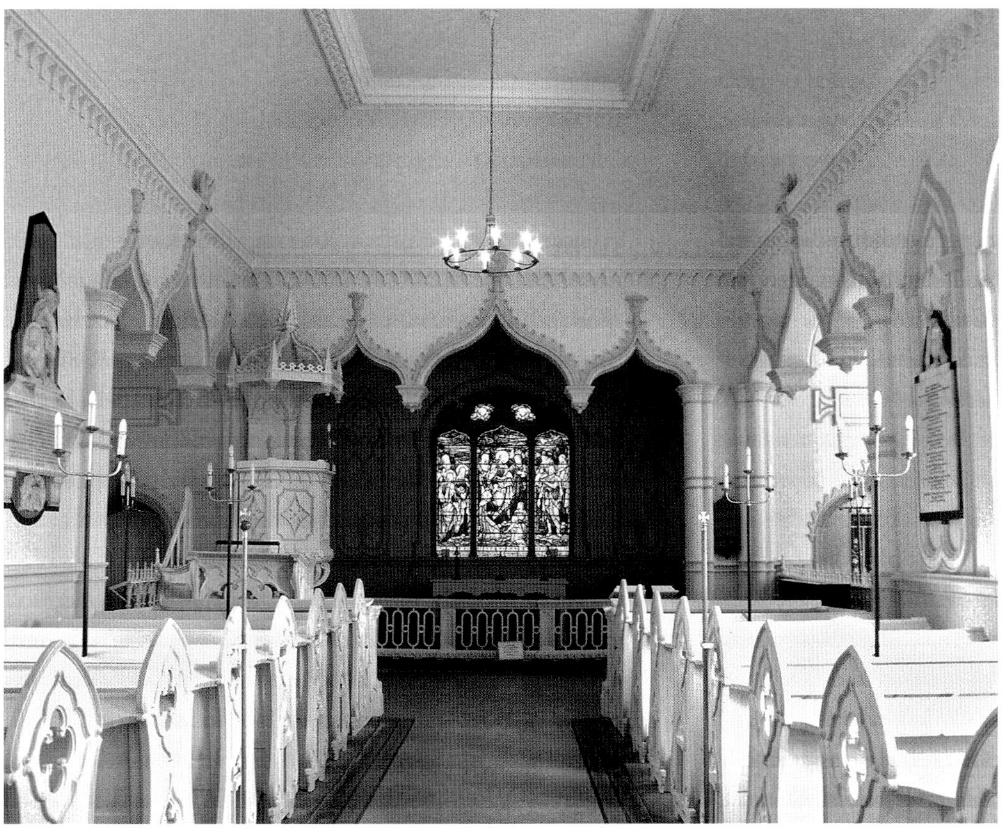

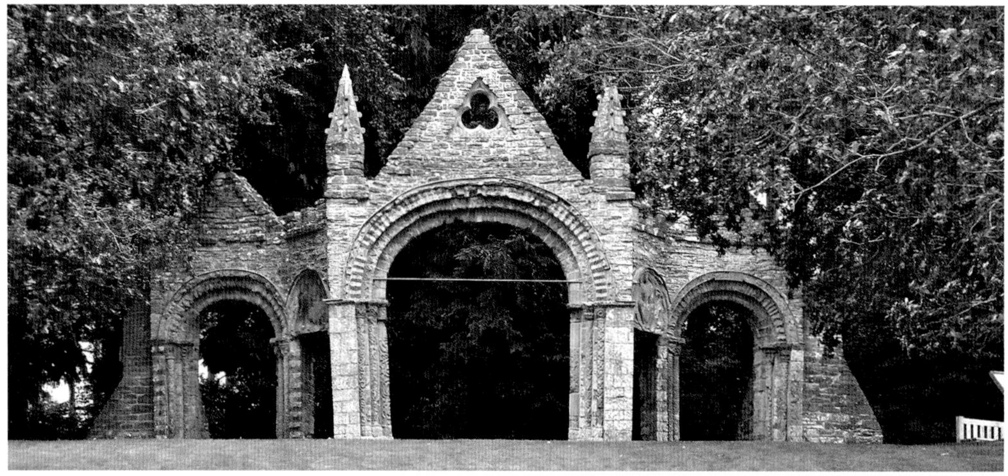

Fig. 82 Shobdon Arches, Herefordshire. Photo: author.

grounds of Bateman's estate (fig. 82). But such titles obscure what was a significant exercise in medievalist archaeology. Certainly imagined before the dismantling of the façade, the Shobdon Arches were a monumental work of Gothic architecture reconstructed almost entirely from stunning Romanesque architectural spolia, something Walpole never imagined in any of his Gothic projects.[9] Whether Kent's designs influenced the Shobdon Arches is unknown, but it is significant that by the 1740s he had already built similar three-bay Gothic "eye-catchers" at Rousham (ca. 1739) and Steeple Aston (1738–41), albeit not out of medieval spolia.[10] Unfortunately, Shobdon left little mark upon eighteenth-century English architecture: its location in rural Herefordshire meant that it did not receive the praise it was due as a significant statement of the Gothic taste circa 1750. While Walpole appears never to have visited Shobdon, his close relationship with Bateman means that he surely knew of the project and could well have seen the designs.[11]

Walpole did, however, provide some of the most valuable information on Bateman's rebuilding at Old Windsor, even if his discussions of the project conceal as much as they reveal. In a once-famous episode in the history of eighteenth-century architecture, Bateman transformed his residence from a small seventeenth-century house that he decorated in a hybrid Chinese-Gothic rococo taste in the 1730s and set in extensive gardens ("Grove House") into a Gothic villa (the "Nunnery")—or, in the words of one critic, into "an old monastery (for such it is to represent)."[12] Old Windsor was surely intended to be one of the Thames-side villas in the new Chinese and Gothic styles that Walpole describes as the "new face" that adorned the country, with "generally Gothic or Chinese [buildings that] give a whimsical air of novelty that is very pleasing."[13] Walpole describes the villa's transformation in two characteristically witty turns of phrase. In the first, written to the amateur architect William Wentworth, Earl of Strafford (1722–1791), he asserts, "[I] converted Dicky Bateman from a Chinese to a Goth. . . . I preached so effectively that his every pagoda took the veil."[14] His discussion of Bateman follows discussion of another "disciple" of Walpole's—Mr. Storer—who was a fellow "scholar" of the famed ballet dancer Gaetano Vestris and who had become an antiquary ("the last patina I should have thought a Macaroni would have taken").[15] In this flippant passage, Walpole emphasizes his own wit and authority over these men and positions himself as a teacher and Bateman as a "disciple" whom he has convinced to change his tastes from Chinoiserie, "the fashion of the instant," to the Gothic, the style "of the elect." Here "the elect" is not simply a socioeconomic category but a tongue-in-cheek reference to Walpole's own circle of friends and associates and their shared Gothic idiom. His second significant commentary appears in a 1762 letter to George Montagu, in which he describes the change of the style of Bateman's house in terms of spiritual affiliation: "I did not doubt but you would approve Mr Bateman's since it has changed its religion; I converted it from Chinese to Gothic."[16] Walpole's clever allegory of stylistic change as national and religious conversion was based in part on the fact that he made it possible for two of his closest designers in the Strawberry Committee—Richard Bentley and Johann Heinrich Müntz—to design the new Gothic additions. Rebuilt and expanded by its designers in the fashionable mode of Strawberry Hill, Bateman's works at Old Windsor, from Walpole's perspective at least, served to reinforce his role as arbiter of the Gothic taste and Strawberry Hill as its paradigm. Walpole would later describe such emulation of Strawberry Hill in his friend's homes in terms of biological lineage, the homes as "child[ren] of Strawberry." Premised on friendship and facilitated by common designers and motifs, Gothic architecture, particularly that rooted in the designs and experiences of Walpole's circle, became a form of queer family romance in and of itself.

Dicky Bateman

By the time Walpole returned from the Grand Tour in 1741—the year Levrac-Tournières painted Bateman's portrait (fig. 78)—Bateman was a well-established man of taste in London. He was regularly celebrated and caricatured in letters and print and on the stage for his outrageous effeminacy and the artistic tastes to which it was connected. He was a member of the homoerotic coterie of Stephen and Henry Fox, Lord Hervey, and Bateman's own brother, Viscount Bateman, who was exiled to France for homosexual offenses in 1738.[17] In contemporary documentation he appears regularly as a consultant for a number of aristocratic clients—particularly women—purchasing Chinoiserie and probably also works in the hybrid Gothic-Chinese manner he favored in the 1740s through mid-1750s. Bateman appears to have acted as an "interior designer" for his aristocratic friends, for whom he purchased, shipped, and advised upon a range of furnishings (fireplaces, sculptures, wallpaper, etc.), most notably at Redlynch for Lord and Lady Ilchester.[18] Typical of this, Bateman in 1748 offered his services to Princess Caroline "to build Benches, China rooms, and whatever she [thought] upon."[19]

Dicky's queer affect and his role as an arbiter of the modern styles were subjects of numerous jabs and critiques. Writing to Charles Hanbury Williams in 1744, for example, Henry Fox pokes fun at Dicky and his reputation as an arbiter of taste: "Dicky Bateman . . . has sent the very finest Chinese Portico and RAIL for the Whitehall Garden, that was ever seen on this side of the Ganges, and yet goes to Ingelfield Green [Englefield Green, Surrey] ev'ry now and then still, which I agree with you, if both last, will show him *un habile courtizan*." Fox refers to Bateman's Chinese designs as expressions of a "skilled courtizan," an allusion to not only Bateman's apparent licentiousness but also, it seems, the effeminized ostentation of Chinoiserie as a style. Some sense of the nuance implied here is provided by the ending of the letter, in which Fox urges Williams not to publish a recent poem that clearly describes in some ways Dicky's sexual persona and that of his brother:

"Don't shew your verses, till you determine not to print them, which, if it may be, I am always much for. Pray work prudence, in the right place (I mean the elder brother) and nobody see it by you and I."[20]

Bateman's mannerisms and tastes in art, and those of his close circle, were the subjects of Hanbury Williams's "Isabella, or the Morning" (1740), in which, for example, Lord Lovel is reputed to "admire no woman but the four queens in a deck of cards." Bateman is given a fuller treatment as a foppish purveyor of Chinese novelties:

> "'Tis Mr. Bateman, ma'am, in his new chair:
> Dicky's new chair! the charming'st thing in town,
> Whose poles are lacker'd, and whose lining's brown!"
> But see, he enters with his shuffling gait;
> "Lord," says her Grace, "how could you be so late?"
> "I'm sorry, madam, I have made you wait,"
> Bateman reply'd; "I only stay'd to bring
> The newest, charming'st, most delightful thing!"[21]

Hanbury Williams's portrait of an effeminate connoisseur and collector was expanded and refined in David Garrick's probable caricature of Bateman as Mr. Fribble in his wildly successful 1747 satire *Miss in Her Teens: Or, The Medley of Lovers; A Farce in Two Acts*, performed in London's West End. This play was understood as a comic satire on Bateman and his circle, including Lord Hervey and possibly Horace Walpole.

Although Walpole would never have admitted it, Bateman presented the younger man an attractive role

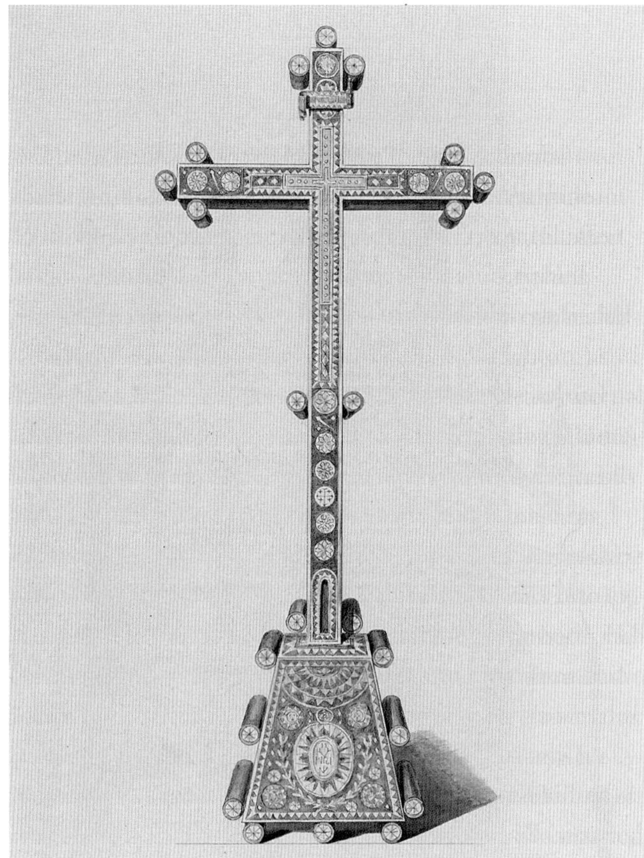

Fig. 83 John Carter, "The Crucifix under the Shrine in the Chapel. Made of Box inlaid with Gold and Mother of Pearl." LWL 33 30 Copy 11 Folio, p. 231. The depicted crucifix was purchased by Horace Walpole at Richard Bateman's 1774 sale and displayed in the chapel. Courtesy of The Lewis Walpole Library, Yale University.

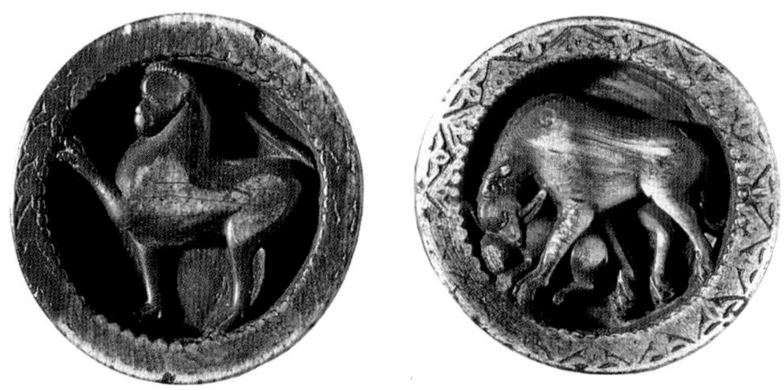

Fig. 84 Walrus-ivory draughts piece, German, late twelfth century. British Museum, London, 1892,0801.26. Purchased by Horace Walpole at Richard Bateman's 1774 sale and displayed in the Great North Bedchamber at Strawberry Hill. Photo © Trustees of the British Museum.

model. When Walpole returned from the Grand Tour, he actively sought a place within Bateman's clique. The unpublished correspondence of Charles Hanbury Williams presents Horace Walpole as an outsider to this older fashionable world, with his face pressed up against the glass. Henry Fox, for example, wrote to Hanbury Williams in 1744 stating that he had decided to delay his visit to Houghton, which was (tiringly, it seems) "Horry Walpole's daily expectation."[22] Walpole would purchase substantial lots from Bateman's contents sale of 1774 for Strawberry Hill, from Catholic liturgical *ornamenta* (fig. 83) to Romanesque ivory draughts pieces (fig. 84), furniture bearing Bateman's heraldry, porcelain, and Indian flower tubs, leaving no doubt that Walpole envied and admired Bateman's illustrious example.[23] "Visited by the best of company,"[24] Bateman's Old Windsor was the home of a senior man of taste, the center for his own homosocial circle. Emulation of Bateman undoubtedly informed Walpole's thwarted attempt in 1746 to acquire the White House at Old Windsor directly beside Bateman (then owned by Charles Hanbury Williams), before purchasing Strawberry Hill.[25] And Walpole was, following Bateman's flamboyant lead, enamored with the more florid manifestations of Chinoiserie from circa 1735, when Lord Hervey gave him a copy of Jean-Baptiste Du Halde's *General Description of China*, a text that had so profound an effect on the young Walpole that Hervey advised him "to continue [to be] an Englishman" rather than become "Chinese."[26] This infatuation persisted into the earliest phases of the design of Strawberry Hill, around 1750, which included a goldfish pond called Po Yang (based on a reference in Du Halde) and a Chinese pavilion that was never executed.[27]

From Grove House to the Convent: The Patronage of Dicky Bateman

When Bateman acquired Old Windsor around 1730, the estate consisted of a small seventeenth-century red brick house with an adjoining property of fourteen acres located on the Thames. Bateman's earliest renovations to the property appear to have been to the gardens: forming an early ferme ornée, or toy farm, the gardens were punctuated by garden and farm buildings described by Richard Pococke in 1754 as being "in the Chinese taste."[28] In fact, by circa 1735, when four anonymous views of the property were painted, Bateman's estate had been built in a hybrid manner, synthesizing Chinese, Gothic, Indian, and antique styles.[29] Emblematic of this hybridity was Bateman's farmhouse, aptly characterized by John Harris as "a freakish confection of styles" (fig. 85).[30] The earliest evidence for renovations to the house derives from views executed around the 1740s. One view shows the exterior of Bateman's house in an unaltered state circa 1735 (fig. 86), while a pair of later but undated views by Thomas Robins (present location unknown) shows Bateman's first alterations, between circa 1735 and circa 1748 (figs. 87–88).[31] Robins's first view, showing the rear façade of the house, facing the road, indicates that the fenestration was altered with the addition of fanciful ogee arches. Set close to the house and nearly kitty-corner, a barn (likely what Pococke referred to as the "offices")[32] was added, which was dressed in spiky Gothic pinnacles and early Gothic shafting, it and the house forming one angle of a courtyard entered via a Gothic entrance arch. Contemporary viewers considered it a "Gothick front" or "in the Gothic stile."[33] Robins's second view shows the front of the house, which faced the Thames. The "show front" received a different treatment: extending the

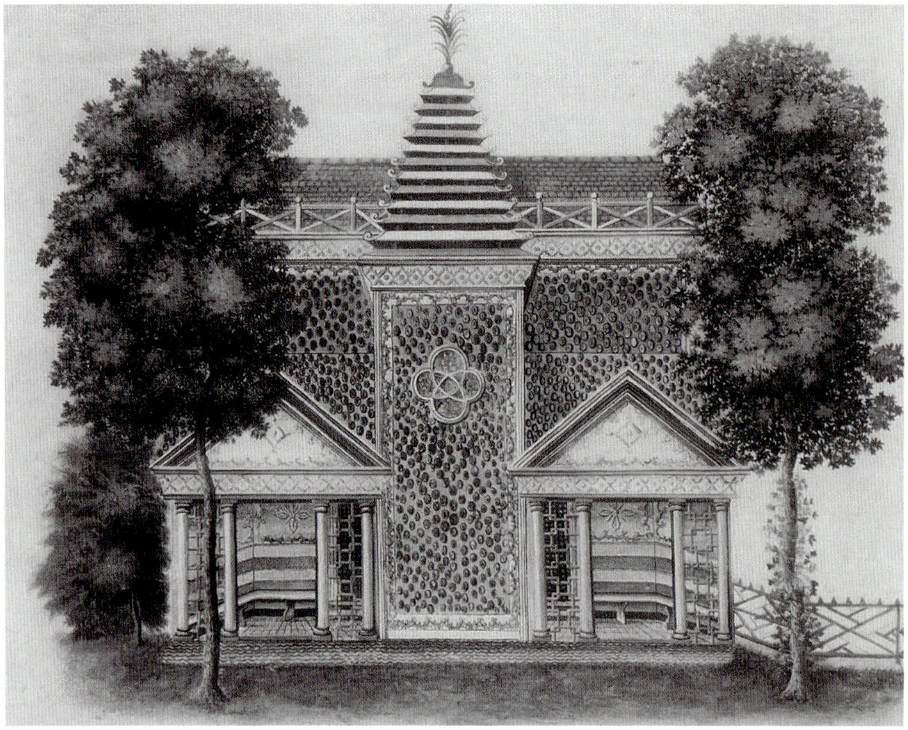

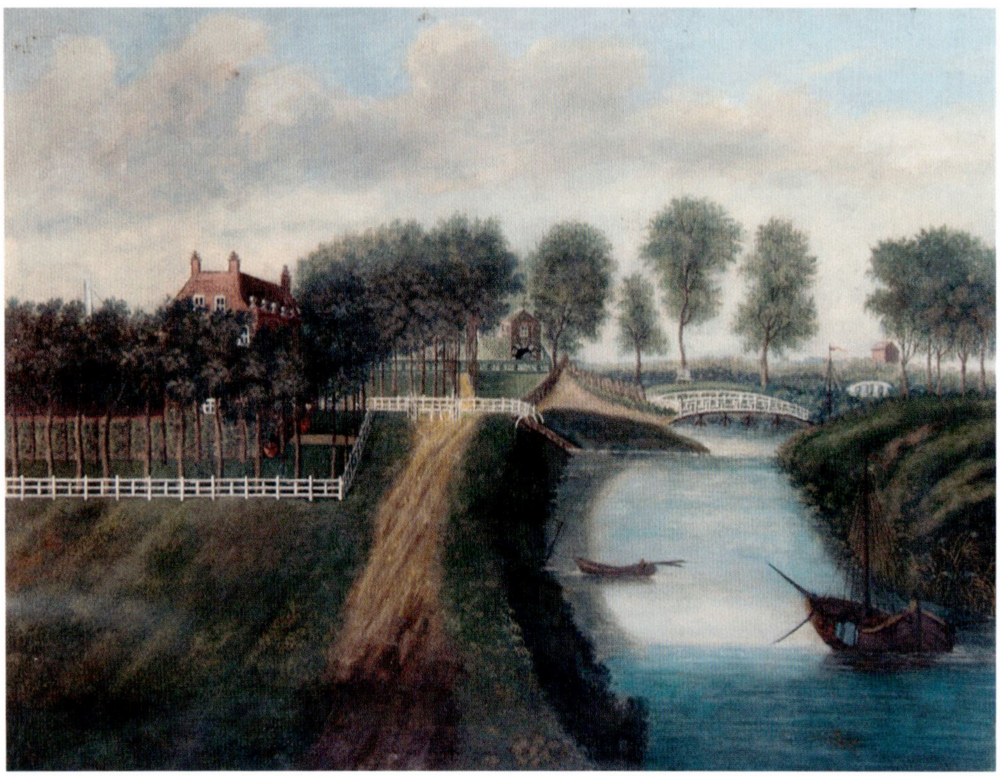

Fig. 85 View of the farmhouse, Old Windsor, English, 1730s. Private collection.

Fig. 86 View of Grove House, Old Windsor (in an unaltered state), English, 1730s. Private collection.

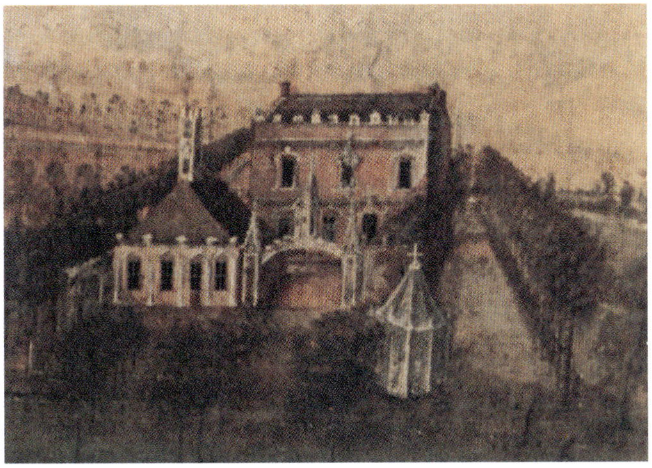

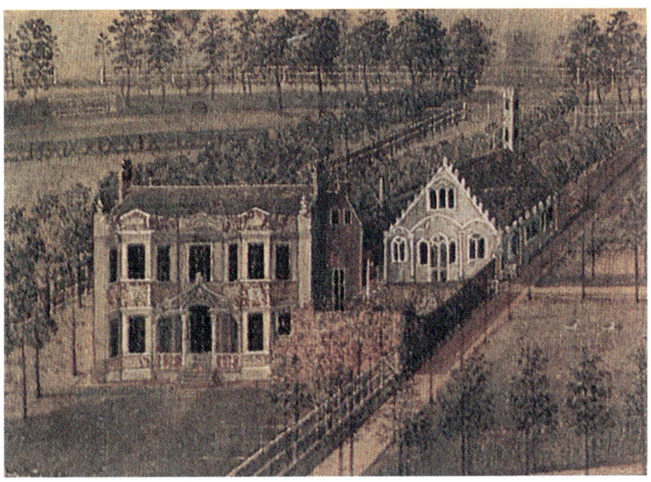

Fig. 87 Thomas Robins, *Prospect from the Meadow, Grove House, Old Windsor*, 1750s, detail. Private collection. From J. Harris, *Gardens of Delight* (1978).

Fig. 88 Thomas Robins, *Prospect from the River, Grove House, Old Windsor*, 1750s, detail. Private collection. From J. Harris, *Gardens of Delight* (1978).

façade, Bateman added two canted bays and a projecting porch that were seemingly built in a Chinese or Chinese-Gothic manner, including bells, nodding mandarins, and windows with fretted glazing bars.[34] Some tentative evidence suggests that this front was in place by 1741.[35] Bateman's early works on the interior of the house are not possible to date with precision, but it is clear that some work was under way by circa 1750, if not previously. In that year he acquired painted glass from an Italian merchant named Asciotti (whom, via Bateman, Walpole was subsequently to employ to acquire glass for Strawberry Hill), which is described in situ in 1768.[36] Richard Pococke recounts the presence of "painted and gilt ceilings," an eccentric collection of furniture, and a "long gallery" in miniature. Pococke also confirms that offices behind the house then contained much of Bateman's collection of "Japan, China, and porcelane [*sic*] wares."[37]

The authorship of the early works at Old Windsor is an important, if at present unanswerable, question. In the documentation, no architects are associated with Bateman's early work, and the visual evidence is insufficient to allow for anything other than loose stylistic affiliations. Bateman had intimate knowledge of the Gothic work of William Kent from the late 1740s, demonstrated in his commissions at Shobdon.[38] As noted above, current opinion suggests that Henry Flitcroft was responsible for the work at Shobdon, following Kent's designs. Is it possible that Old Windsor was a testing ground for Flitcroft's later work for Bateman at Shobdon? In the 1730s and 1740s Flitcroft was the favored architect among Bateman's close friends: for example, in 1740 Flitcroft prepared Gothic designs for Bateman's friend Thomas Foley, who planned to rebuild the church at Stoke Edith, Herefordshire, and Flitcroft or his designs appear to have been employed at Redlynch in the 1740s, where he would build Gothic gates for Stephen Fox in 1755.[39] As a significant architect in the Gothic style who had worked within Bateman's circle during the earliest phases of work at Old Windsor, Flitcroft is surely worthy of consideration as its architect. If this is the case, then the later work at Shobdon might be a reflection of the earlier campaigns at Old Windsor.[40]

Bateman's earliest works at Old Windsor before what Walpole called his "conversion" were already an important statement of Gothic taste, albeit one that freely blended with Chinese, Indian, and antique styles. The house's stylistic heterogeneity was described by Lord Lyttelton in August 1759 as "half Gothick, half attick, half Chinese and completely fribble."[41] The transformations begun in 1758 were profound for contemporary viewers: they were described by Mrs. Delany in 1760 in Ovidian terms as having "metamorphosed out of the Indian into the Gothic."[42] Revisiting the house in 1768, Delany commented on the Gothicization in its completion: "Its outward appearance is venerable—arched porticos and windows, Gothic towers and battlements, encompassed and shaded with large trees." She continues, "Were I to particularize all I saw within and without the house—the vestibules, the 'refectories,' the 'monuments,' &c., &c., you would think I was quoting old [William] Dugdale."[43]

No interior or exterior views of the house after 1758 have come to light to confirm Delany's description.[44] In all likelihood, however, the "Gothic towers and battlements" were additions to the existing house, created, like those at Strawberry Hill, in lath and plaster. Delany compares some of the ornament to the engravings by Wenceslaus Hollar in Dugdale's influential seventeenth-century antiquarian texts *History of St. Paul's*, *Monasticon Anglicanum*, and *Antiquities of Warwickshire*, which were employed by Walpole and the Committee in the design of a long list of monuments at Strawberry Hill, effectively popularizing them as sources for eighteenth-century Gothic designs. This points to the likelihood that, as at Strawberry Hill, Bateman's interiors were based in part upon antiquarian engravings and that elements of the house (fireplaces, bookcases, etc.) were designed as recognizable "quotations" of medieval monuments. This was the cause of a common enough lament voiced by critics of the new medievalism: in John Gilbert Cooper's *Letters Concerning Taste* of 1757, one writer describes the London villas as containing "monstrous Marble Chimney-Pieces, that look like Family Monuments in a Cathedral."[45] In the absence of more specific documentation, Bateman's building works can be bracketed on one side by the employment of Richard Bentley in 1758 and on the other by Mrs. Delany's 1768 description and that in *Windsor and Its Environs* the same year.

Bateman's unpublished correspondence from the period casts some light on the transformation of his home and the related medievalizing topoi he used to describe it. A letter of 18 September 1760 expresses his thanks for an ancient bell that Lady Ilchester gave to him for his newly renovated home: "I have been just writing to Lady Ilchester to thank her for the Bell which I am so glad is found, and so glad is given to me that I cannot express how much the Convent of Old Windsor is obliged to the House of Ilchester. Its bearing such undisputed marks of antiquity about it makes it to me most valuable, and its form and size suits the chapel where tis to be placed so exactly that I entirely agree . . . in calling it a dear little sweet thing."[46] Epistolary evidence such as this allows a unique insight into Bateman's perspectives on the Gothic and the sense of play involved. Bateman's conception of the change of his house's identity (or "religion," as Walpole would have it) is palpable. Closing the letter with thanks, Bateman continues to trope his home in medievalizing terms, declaring that he will make an "offering at the Shrine of the Madonna at Old Windsor."[47] As noted above, Bateman's home was not the only medieval or medievalizing home in the period to bear the title "Convent": the name was used for Strawberry Hill and for Sir Francis Dashwood's "Order of St. Francis" at

Medmenham, a curiously feminized label to articulate and cloak the estate's true nature as a notorious place of licentious sexual ritual.

It is not a coincidence that Walpole was staying with Bateman in July 1758. In that year Richard Bentley was employed by Bateman to design alterations for the "offices," which, I have suggested, are consistent with the barn shown in Robins's river view (fig. 88).[48] By far the most significant change to the house was the addition of an octagonal dining room connected to the main house by a cloister range (figs. 79, 89, 90, 91). The dining room is still extant (although much of the exterior stonework has been altered, the buttresses removed, and the Gothic window heads replaced with square-headed sashes), but

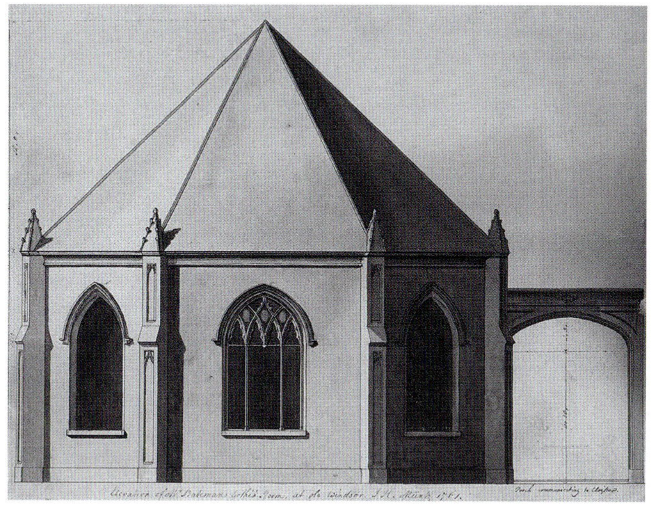

Fig. 89 J. H. Müntz, "Elevation of Mr. Bateman's Gothik Room at Old Windsor," 1761. LWL 75 M92 761. Courtesy of The Lewis Walpole Library, Yale University.

Fig. 90 J. H. Müntz, "Section of the Honble. Rich. Bateman's Octagone [*sic*] Room at Old Windsor." LWL 75 M92 761. Courtesy of The Lewis Walpole Library, Yale University.

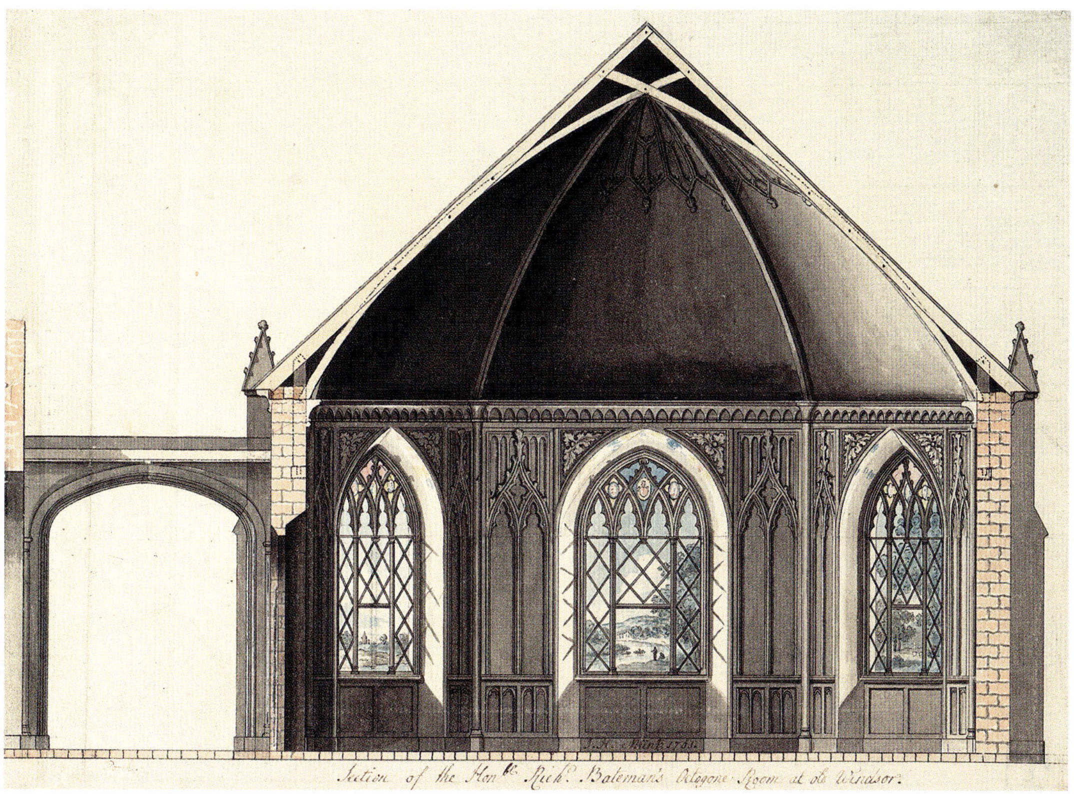

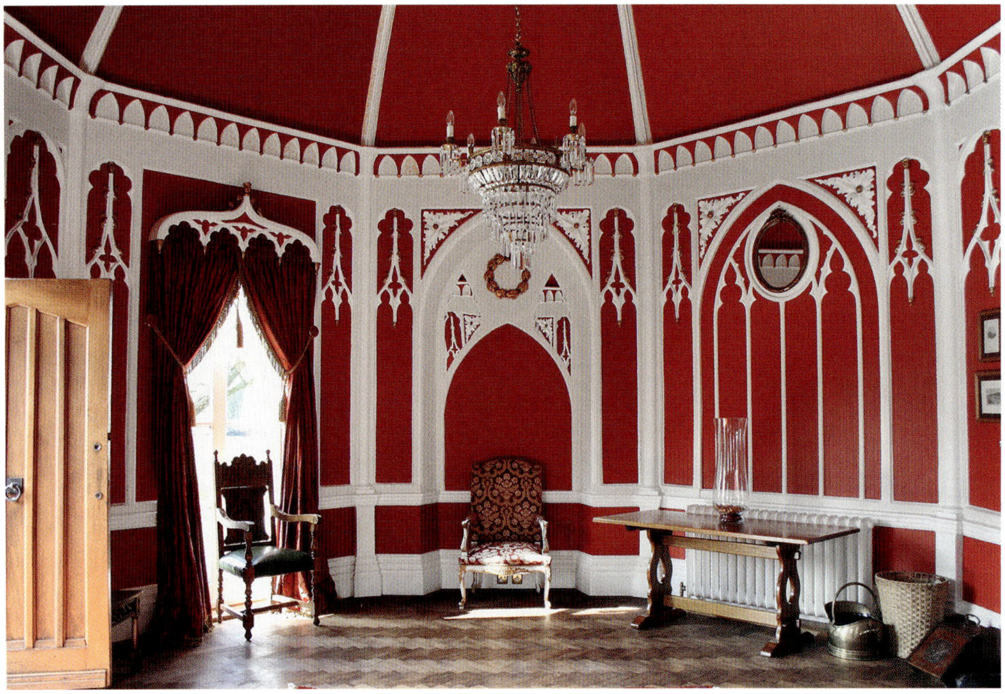

Fig. 91 Bateman's dining room at Old Windsor. Photo: author.

Fig. 92 J. H. Müntz, elevation of a cloister for Grove House, Old Windsor, 1761. LWL Folio 75 M92 761. Courtesy of The Lewis Walpole Library, Yale University.

Fig. 93 Richard Bentley, "Gothic Cloyster designed by Mr. Bentley," 1759. LWL 49 3585c Folio. Courtesy of The Lewis Walpole Library, Yale University.

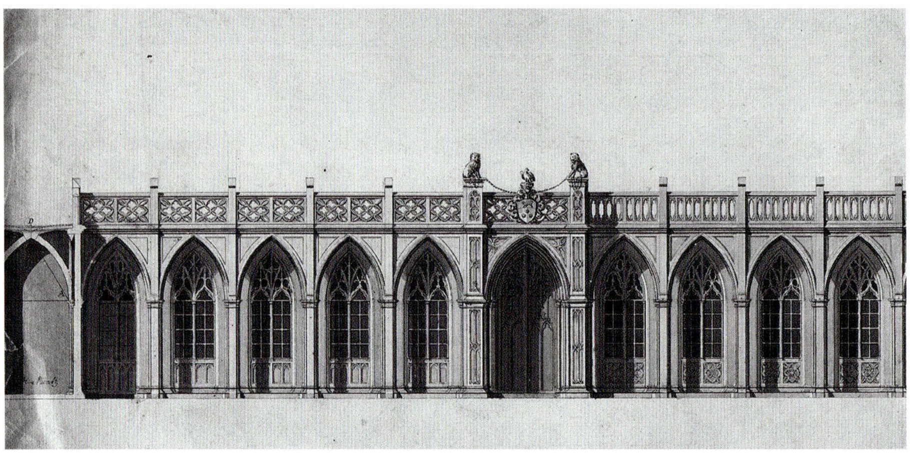

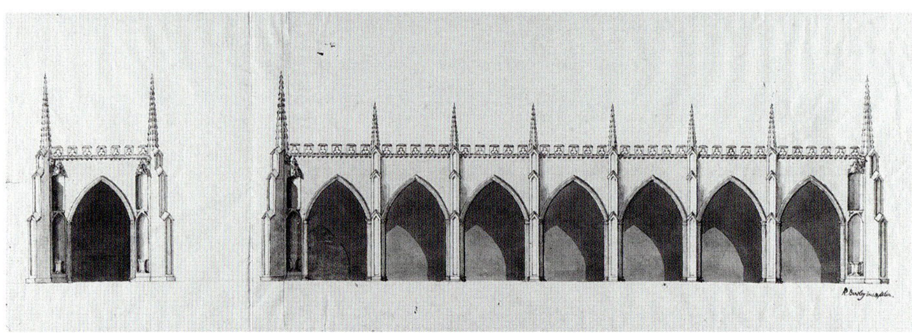

the cloister was replaced with the current brick structure shortly after Bateman's death. Walpole was clear that the original cloister was built to the designs of Richard Bentley, which is to be regretted, since Müntz produced designs for a magnificent cloister that must have been intended for Old Windsor (fig. 92).[49] A bitter disagreement between Müntz and Bentley caused Walpole to dismiss Müntz from his employment, which may have influenced Bateman's choice of Bentley's cloister design.[50] Bentley's presentation drawing for the cloister at Old Windsor is almost certainly that now in the Lewis Walpole Library at Yale dated to 1759 (fig. 93).[51] Müntz's presentation drawings (also at the Lewis Walpole Library) must have pleased Bateman, because the design of his dining room, punctuated by blind Decorated tracery designs in plaster, follows them very closely.

Based loosely on medieval chapter-house designs, the dining room and cloister endowed Bateman's residence with many of the obvious signifiers of a late medieval religious house, as Mrs. Delany noted. This association was emphasized through the display of medieval and medievalizing objects. The exterior of the dining room bore "several Orders of Monks and Fryars," perhaps wall paintings or images in stained glass.[52] The cloister featured a painted genealogy of the kings of England from William the Conqueror to James I, as well as images of other British worthies, including Sir Thomas More.[53] Also installed in the cloister was the tomb of the Welsh abbot Caducanus, bishop of Bangor (1215–36; fig. 94) which Bateman had removed from Abbey Dore, Herefordshire, close to his family estate at Shobdon. The tomb chest and effigy appear to be original, while the canopy is manifestly an invention of Müntz and may reflect a commission by Bateman. Upon the tomb were positioned a series of "medieval"

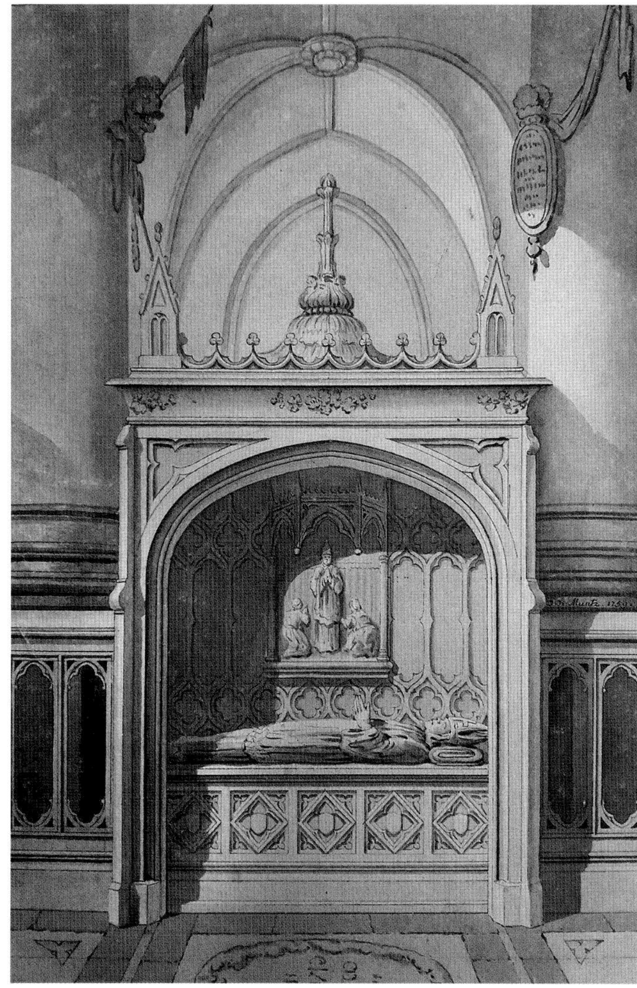

Fig. 94 J. H. Müntz, the tomb of Caducanus, Old Windsor. Royal Museum of Fine Arts, Brussels, no. 4060/ 2674. © Royal Museums of Fine Arts, Belgium.

objects attributed to Caducanus, including a mitre, a crozier, and a copy of the *Looking Glass for Christians*.[54] Also from the Welsh environs of Bateman's family estate and set within the Old Windsor cloister was a series of triangular chairs that were believed by Bateman and others to be medieval in date.[55] Walpole described the passage as Bateman's "cloister of founders," and he expressed his envy of the tomb and chairs in private correspondence.[56] Emulating Bateman's cloister as a set piece, Walpole not only acquired the chairs at the 1774

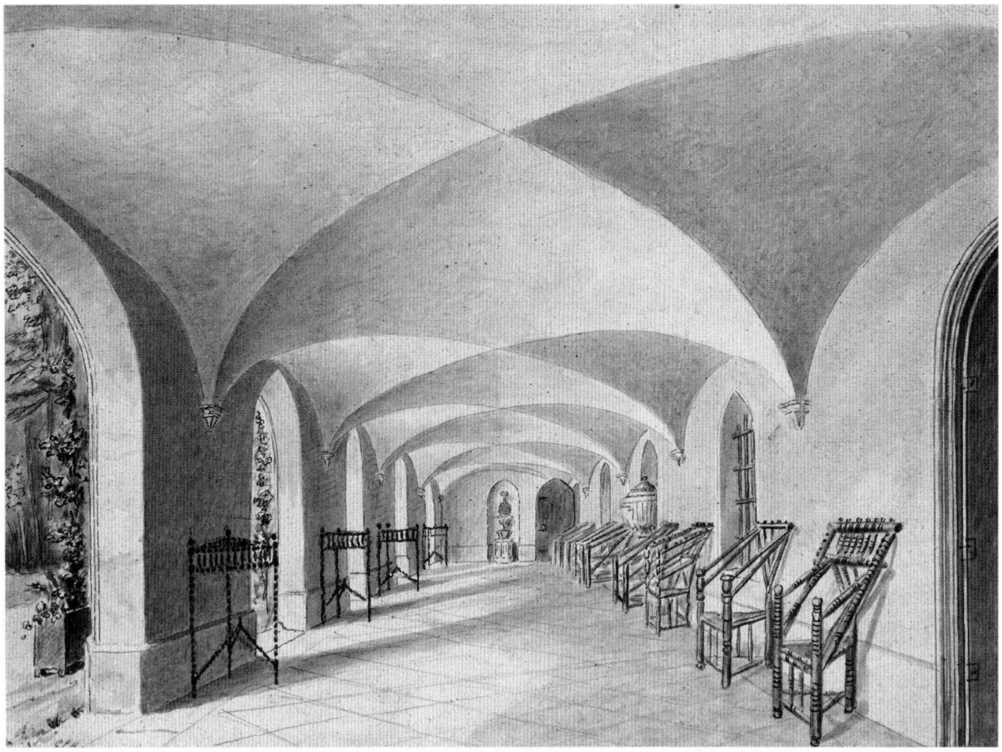

Fig. 95 George Perfect Harding, Great Cloister at Strawberry Hill, showing chairs acquired from Dicky Bateman in 1774. LWL SH Views H263 no. 1 Box 105. Courtesy of The Lewis Walpole Library, Yale University.

sale but placed them in his own cloister at Strawberry Hill (fig. 95), where he set them alongside images of his own "founders," namely the neomedieval monumental brass of Ralph Walpole, bishop of Ely, designed by Müntz (fig. 69). Bateman's renovations included a new garden feature entitled Brian's Cave, which commemorated the Irish hero Brian Boru (ca. 941–1014), featuring a cast-iron statue of the hero and images of his deeds based upon Geoffrey Keating's seventeenth-century *History of Ireland*.[57]

The Gothicization of the exterior between 1758 and 1768 also extended to the interior of the house, although, aside from the reference to Richard Bentley's redesigning the offices in 1758, it is not absolutely certain that Müntz or Bentley was responsible.[58] The best evidence for the interiors is the eight-page account in *Windsor and Its Environs* (1768), which provides a detailed, room-by-room description, much of which is corroborated by Mrs. Delany's letter of the same year. She indicates that "the walls are embossed with undescribable oddities brought from all corners of the world," "an innumerable collection of china, japan, and knick-knacks" (much of which must have been moved from the offices, where this collection was noted by Pococke in 1754), and that the windows were "glazed with as much variety as a glazier's sign," undoubtedly with the glass Bateman acquired in 1750.[59] The ground floor included a hall "hung with a large collection of foreign prints" and Chinese weaponry and was illuminated by "a curious Chinese Lanthorn."[60]

Bateman's dressing room was located on the bottom floor (due perhaps to his affliction with gout)[61] and was richly decorated, featuring a substantial Catholic chapel fitted with liturgical paraphernalia (into which the Gothic bell from Lady Ilchester was set). It received particular attention in Delany's account of Old Windsor:

It is not above eight feet square, or rather an octagon; it is an exact representation of a popish chapel expensively decorated . . . it is like peeping through a show-glass in a box. There are many crucifixes in it, ivory figures of saints, crowns, and crosses set with sapphire, a little case called the treasury filled with rosaries, crosses, and a thousand things relating to ceremonies that I don't understand; and it is so adorned, so crowded, that it is almost impossible to distinguish one thing from another, but what must offend every serious observer must be the intent of this chapel, for if he does *not* make use of it in *good earnest*, his making a joke of it is *shocking*; and at least he should have omitted the *sacred figure*, which ought to strike us with awe and reverence, besides nobody can justify turning any religion into ridicule, though some ceremonies may be trifling and absurd, but I don't suppose he desires to be thought a papist, and perhaps he would rather be thought a heathen![62]

Dicky Bateman was a significant collector of medieval and later religious art, and likely many of the objects now known from his 1774 sale catalogue were stored within his "chapel." Among them were the so-called Malmesbury Châsse (ca. 1200; fig. 96), apparently purchased by Bateman in Wiltshire (subsequently purchased by the antiquarian Richard Astle and now in the Royal Ontario Museum), and a "crucifix inlaid with mother of pearl" that Walpole purchased in 1774 for his "Chapel in the Wood" at Strawberry Hill (fig. 83).[63] Also in his chapel were actual relics, or "old bones"

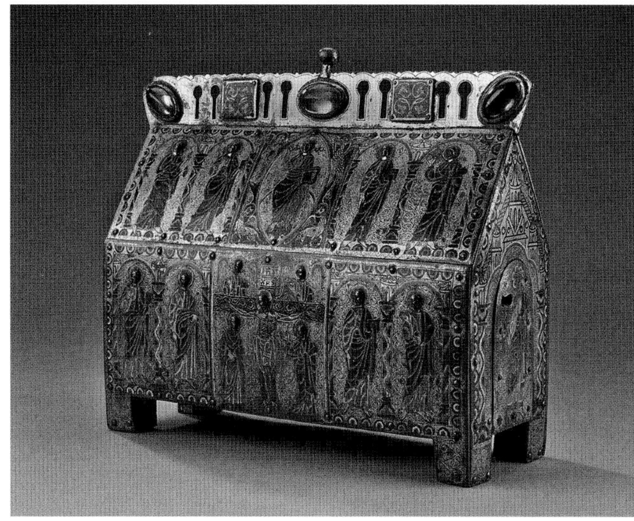

Fig. 96 Malmesbury Châsse, champlevé enamel reliquary, ca. 1190–1200. The Thomson Collection, Art Gallery of Ontario. AGOID.29082. Image © Art Gallery of Ontario.

(presumably contained in a reliquary), that he acquired in France in 1765, which added "much to the antiquity of the place."[64] Although Bateman's chapel was not a dedicated room or freestanding structure but instead a centrally planned space set within a bedchamber, it deserves to be understood as one of a number of "popish" chapels built within Walpole's circle, including Walpole's own Tribune, which possessed "all the glory of popery," and his "Chapel in the Wood" (based upon the chantry of Bishop Audley at Salisbury).[65] Elsewhere in this study I have emphasized the erotic appraisal of Catholicism and the Catholic rite, which appealed to Walpole and his circle and formed an important part of their appraisal of the Gothic. In this context Delany's account of Bateman's chapel and its Gothic/Catholic art is extraordinarily interesting. Her conservative, even doctrinaire, religious sensibilities were manifestly not those of Bateman or Walpole.[66] Alluding to Catholicism as an alternative subjectivity whose art could lead the viewer to idolatry (among other sins), its erotic appeal seemingly lost on her (perhaps willingly), she interprets the chapel instead as a kind of derisive, even heretical, joke.

Access to the upper floor of the house was granted by a single staircase painted with what must have been a stunning display of twenty coats of arms of the baronial signatories of Magna Carta, King John, and the mayor of London, as well as stained glass with imagery from the Old and New Testaments. The immediate inspiration was very possibly Strawberry Hill, where in 1756 Walpole had hung in his bedchamber copies of Magna Carta and the warrant for Charles I's execution, upon which he had written "Major Charta."[67] The display of heraldry likely also referred to the history of Old Windsor itself, since Magna Carta was signed there and Bateman's property was thought to have been built upon a royal residence from the time of William the Conqueror.[68] The staircase led directly to the "Monk Rooms," or "Monkish Chambers." These were two small bedrooms in the Gothic style that had stained glass in the window heads and contained antique beds hung with "Pictures of Several Monks."[69] These rooms now retain some of the only visible evidence of Bateman's work, in the form of pointed-arch doorways and slender Gothic shafts running up the wall in the staircase vestibule. The other rooms on the upper floor included the "Half-Mourning Room," in which "The Bed, Furniture, and every Thing . . . [were] in Half-mourning," and further bedchambers, including Bateman's, which had images of the Twelve Apostles, "a set of Chinese Pictures," and a small ivory crucifix by the side of the bed.[70] The overtly monastic and Catholic nature of Bateman's Gothic residence was noted by a number of commentators beyond Mrs. Delany, including the author of *Les delices de Windsore*, according to whom it had "the appearance of a tendency to the superstitious Tenents [*sic*] of Popery."[71]

Fortunately, *Windsor and Its Environs* provides a more detailed account of at least one picture hang at Old Windsor, namely that in Bateman's octagonal dining room (figs. 90, 91). Like the picture hangs at Strawberry Hill, those in Bateman's residence articulated bonds the proprietor shared with others in his circle, structuring a queer family romance. According to *Windsor and Its Environs*, the pictures in the room were as follows:

> Its pictures are, over the Door,
> Lord *Bateman* [Dicky's older brother, Viscount Bateman]
>
> Over the Chimney,
> Lady *Harvey* [Mary Lepel, Lady Hervey]
> Lord *Ilchester* [Stephen Fox]
> Lord *Foley* [Thomas Foley]
> Lord *Holland* [Henry Fox].[72]

While the description does not explicitly limit the portraits in the room to those on its list, Bateman's portrait gallery as described appears to reflect a specific coterie of interconnected friends who were either of the third sex or women. Bateman's correspondence is full of letters between these figures, whom he describes as "my acquaintances."[73] "Lord Bateman" is Dicky's brother, Viscount Bateman of Shobdon Court, who, as I noted above, caused a scandal for homosexual offenses and was exiled to France, where he retained close ties with Dicky. As Mrs. Delany opines in a characteristically catty letter, "Lord Bateman has sometimes been famous for a male seraglio."[74] Horace Walpole, in his raunchy 1740s poem "Little Peggy," likewise takes a jab at the Bateman brothers—"Another Bateman [i.e., Dicky] shall debauch the boys / and future Sapphos practice mimic joys"—thereby implicating both brothers in sexual acts with younger males.[75] Bateman's apparent predilection for youths may have been alluded to in a series of homoerotic objects at Old Windsor, including "a fine bust of Antinous, by Bernini," a bronze of "Antinous and its companion," and "an antique figure of a Priapus."[76] Lord Foley (of Witley Court in Worcestershire) was a close friend and shared some of Bateman's tastes in art (Dicky imported French art for him in 1742), and he likewise patronized the architect Henry Flitcroft.[77] Henry Fox and Bateman served as the receivers general of South Wales, and he was a regular visitor to Old Windsor. Henry and his brother Stephen Fox were both intimates of Lady Hervey's husband, Lord John Hervey.[78] Stephen and Lord Hervey developed an infamous romance between 1726 and 1736. As I have noted elsewhere, Hervey's sexuality has come to form the very archetype of the third sex, based upon Lady Mary Wortley Montagu's observation that the world consists of "men, women, and Herveys" and on Walpole's own characterization of him as being of the "third sex."[79] Lady Hervey's portrait can be identified as that by Allan Ramsay of 1762. She was a lifelong friend to Bateman and Walpole: the three regularly dined together at Bateman's and at Strawberry Hill, and Walpole dedicated his 1762 *Anecdotes of Painting* to her.

Bateman's picture hang proposes an alternative family of men (most, if not all, of whom had some homoerotic leanings) and one woman from a common elite milieu, who shared tastes in art and architecture. Bateman's alternative family here is not of course *about* sexuality. Rather, it indicates a common subjectivity in which sexuality, aristocracy, and taste freely blended. If the list of paintings is complete, then it is of interest that Horace Walpole did not feature in the portrait gallery. His omission here may underscore a point I made earlier about his own construction of himself as a dominant arbiter of taste: rhetorically useful as it was for Walpole to promote himself and his influence, it does not mean that others necessarily agreed with that projected image. It may also be significant that Walpole purchased Lady Hervey's portrait after Bateman's death, along with the chairs he admired and other objects for display at Strawberry Hill, apparently to "keep for the founder's sake," thus commemorating Bateman's role in the "foundation" of the Priory and, perhaps, inserting himself into a genealogy of objects that Bateman had a role in first creating.[80]

With a fuller account of the architectural history of the house in place, we may revisit Walpole's pregnant characterization of Bateman's "conversion" by which "every pagoda took the veil." First, however notable the transformation from a Chinese or "Indian" villa into a Gothic monastery was for contemporaries, it is clear that the pre-1758 house featured Gothic designs and that the post-1758 house and its collections still bore some mark of Bateman's Chinese enthusiasms. In the Gothicization of Old Windsor, the selective application of Gothic ornament to a seventeenth-century house shifted to a more comprehensive adaptation of the Gothic idiom by which the house could be understood to "represent" a Gothic monastery. Second, despite Walpole's claim to have converted Bateman to the Gothic taste, Bateman's works at Shobdon indicate he already had a developed appreciation of the Gothic idiom. Artistic influence manifestly flowed in both directions between Walpole and Bateman, even if Walpole was quick to claim otherwise. Here, as elsewhere in his architectural criticism, Walpole's views were vigorously partisan and were regularly revised to reflect his own changing opinions or the sensibilities of different audiences. Frequently informing Walpole's aesthetic judgment of a building was an emotive connection with its patron or designer, a connection that could also, as in the case of Dicky Bateman, extend to rivalry—and even bitchy critiques of Bateman's own sexuality.

The 1750s was the crucial decade for the development of Gothic taste for both men. Although he is quick not to mention it, Walpole too was enamored of the stylistic heterogeneity characterizing the earliest campaigns at Old Windsor in the 1740s, and his tastes may well have been inspired directly by them.[81] By 1755, however—a few years before Bateman's "conversion" of Old Windsor—Walpole had vigorously repudiated the appeal of Chinoiserie and of stylistic hybridity in architecture in general.[82] In a letter to Richard Bentley of that year, which very possibly alludes to Bateman's residence, he notes, "When I every day see Greek, and Roman, and Italian, and Chinese, and Gothic architecture embroidered and inlaid upon one another, or called by each other's names, I can't help thinking that the grace and simplicity and truth of your taste, in whichever you undertake, is real taste."[83]

Related critiques can be found throughout the writings of Walpole's circle in the same years. As David Porter has shown, Walpole's repudiation of Chinoiserie was part of a complex change in his taste in the 1750s. These years saw Walpole's adaptation of the Gothic as his personal style and his earliest movements to fashion himself into England's dominant arbiter and mythmaker of the Gothic. This change was bolstered by an increasingly holistic vision within his art historiography, culminating in his *Anecdotes of Painting* of 1762, in which Chinoiserie and the influence of the East on English art could have no place.[84] In the absence of any documentation, Bateman's own patronage and his collection of English worthies at Old Windsor provide only a hint of his own leanings in this direction.

"Fribblish as Himself": Critiquing Bateman's Old Windsor

Although much of the character of the house during Bateman's ownership is lost, contemporary viewers manifestly understood it as a novelty and critiqued it as such. Significant patrons in their own right, Lord Lyttelton and Mrs. Delany indicate in their commentaries a sensitivity to the visual effects of the house and to its sexual and ethical meanings. As noted above, Lyttelton's account of the Priory as "Mr Bateman's half Gothick, half attick, half Chinese and completely fribble house"[85] appears in a letter dated to August 1759. In it, Lyttelton—a man of conservative Palladian tastes and heterosexual inclinations—recounts "a most complete party of pleasure" at the Priory, with his "Old Love," Lady Hervey, and his "New Love," Mrs. Hancock. Mrs. Delany's account occurs in a 1768 letter to her sister: "his library is indeed as *fribblish* as himself, and so furnished with looking glass that had it the property of representing to him his inside as well as outside, it might read him a better lesson than he could find in his whole collection of books, and shew him his own insignificancy."[86]

Both authors employ the same adjective, "fribble" (or "fribblish"), to describe Bateman's Gothic interiors. This adjective does not seem to be used elsewhere in the period to describe architecture, so its use in multiple commentaries on the same building is significant. Although the word had a range of possible significations, including flippancy, physical weakness, and effeminacy, "fribble" is employed here as one of a number of new terms developed in the eighteenth century to describe men of the third sex. The 1753 *Dictionary of Love* states that "fribble" "signifies one of those ambiguous animals, who are neither male nor female; disclaimed by his own sex, and the scorn of both."[87] The fribble (seemingly a combination of "frivolous" and "ribald") was an effeminate man who enjoyed the friendship of women and shared "female" tastes in the arts, but the bonds embraced by the fribble were social and artistic and did not extend to sexual or legal unions.[88] The pronounced domesticity of the fribble—his tastes in fashion and fabrics, collecting and interior design, lapdogs and scented powder—was understood as an unmanly usurpation of female taste that emasculated him, and he was satirized as such in later prints (fig. 97). The term was used by William Warburton in a homophobic attack on Horace Walpole's affections for Gothic architecture and on his "fribble tutor" in taste (likely Bateman), "as sicklied over with affectation as himself": both were affected fops, "half wits," and (quoting Dryden) "so little and so light / One should not know they liv'd but that they bite."[89]

But the meaning of "fribble" employed by Lyttelton and Delany is tied directly to David Garrick's popular 1747 satire *Miss in Her Teens*.[90] The play recounts a comic courtship between Ms. Biddy Bellair and a range of suitors, each playing on established models of masculinity to comic effect (fig. 98). The character of Fribble—played by Garrick—is the comic foil for the

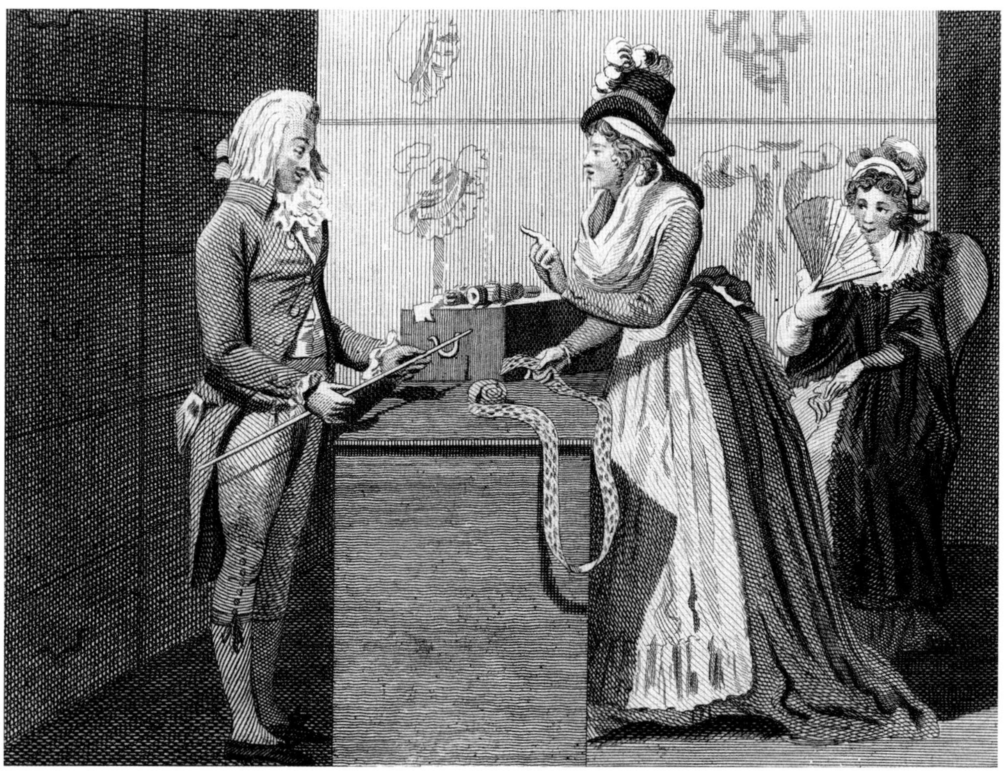

Fig. 97 "The Man Milliner," satiric print featuring Mr. Fribble published by Robert Sayer and Co., Fleet Street, London, 1793. "Indeed Mr. Fribble I am not to be done in this manner, your Yard is to [*sic*] short by an Inch[!]." LWL 793.12.16.03. Courtesy of The Lewis Walpole Library, Yale University.

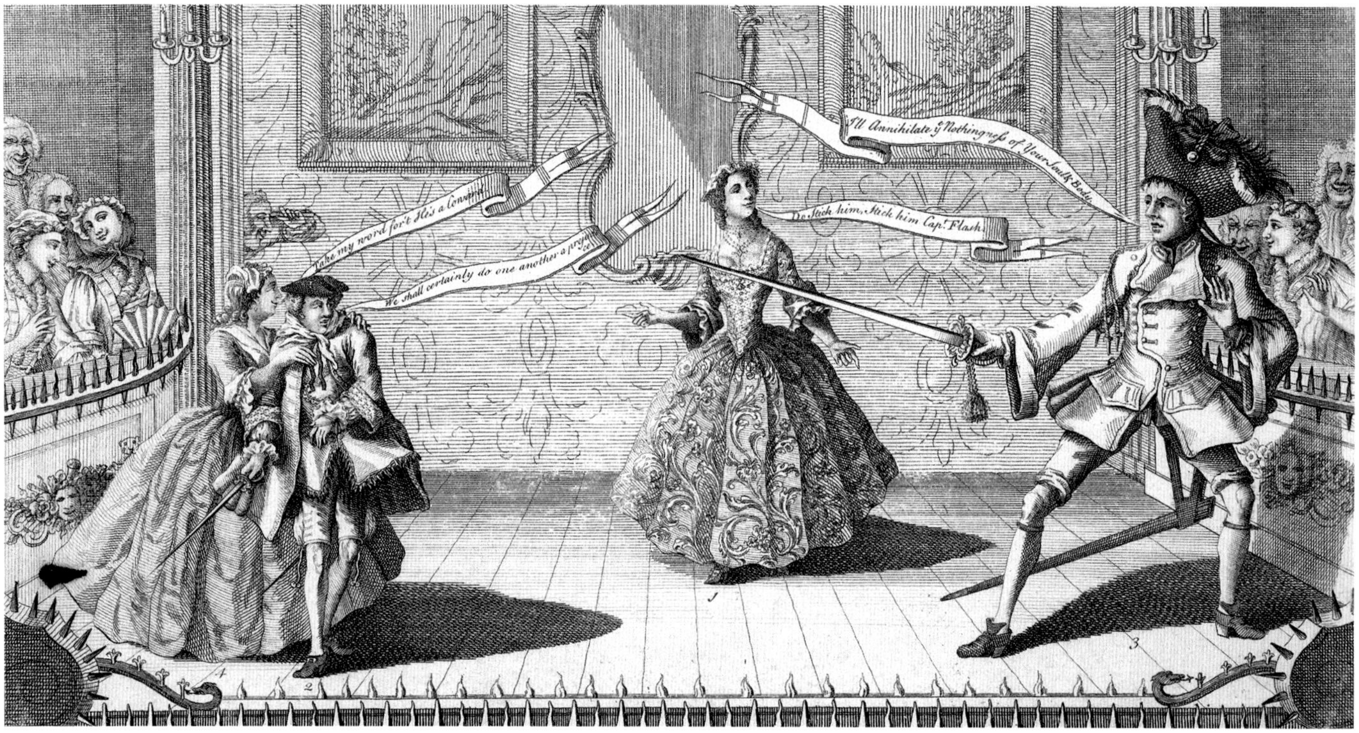

Fig. 98 "The Modern Duel, Taken from Miss in her Teens, as it's now Acted at Covent Garden." From *London Magazine*, February 1747. Photo © Trustees of the British Museum.

story: celebrating the incongruity of an outrageously camp man of taste's aspiration to wed a young belle, he tells Biddy that in marrying him she will "have love's better part, / His downy Wing, but not his Dart."[91] Positioned as an antithesis to the virile masculinity of his rival suitor, Captain Loveit, Fribble is set up as a subject of mockery for the audience, expressing popular homophobic sentiments. Fribble relates how a coachman broke his fingernail while insulting him, stating, "I'll carry you and your doll too, Miss Margery, for the same price" ("Margery" was common slang for sodomite).[92] "Fribble" quickly entered contemporary parlance as a term for a queer sexual subjectivity, possibly anticipating "queen" within the modern construction of homosexuality. An anonymous pamphlet of 1747 entitled *The Pretty Gentleman, or Softness of Manners Vindicated from the False Ridicule Exhibited Under the Character of William Fribble, Esq.* provided a comic defense of the fribble, whose "System is of a finer Turn, [with] superior Accuracy of Fabric, insomuch that it looks as if Nature had been in doubt, to which Sex she should assign *Him* . . . The Happy Metamorphosis,—Or, The Gentleman turned Lady."[93] In the 1749 satire *Tittle Tattle; or, Taste A-la-Mode*, by Timothy Fribble, the fribble is an advisor on manners to young women who warns against intellectual pursuits (including reading Addison's *Spectator*) and advises instead that ladies adopt the extraordinary elaborations of gesture and pose apparently embodied by Fribble himself.[94] The fribble had a lengthy history in moralizing critiques disdaining the modern present: John Brown's *Estimate of the Manners and Principles of the Times* (1757) considers the fribble the paradigmatic image of modern effeminacy, which, sadly (he opined) inspired "peals of laughter and applause" from fribbles and nonfribbles alike, who were absolutely blind to what he felt was a moralizing, anti-exemplary image.[95] Here, as elsewhere, the fribble and homoeroticism were linked, if not frequently synonymous, as in Charles Churchill's "Rosciad" (1763), which specifically connects the effeminate fribble as an arbiter of taste with the new third sex, which the author defines as a clear sexual category and a social coterie: "the Fribble Tribe."[96]

Writing to her sister in 1747, Delany provides a private insight into Garrick's play as a satire not only on a specific new class of urban gentlemen of the third sex but particularly on Dicky Bateman and his close acquaintances: "It is said [Garrick] mimics *eleven* men of fashion—Lord Bate——n, Ld Her——y, Felton Her——y, some others you don't know, and our friend Dicky Bate——n, I must own the latter is a *striking likeness*; but do not name to any body these people, for I don't love to spread such tattle, though I send it for your private amusement, and that you may not be ignorant of the ways of this world."[97] As T. Eustace Harwood has noted, the character of Fribble was probably modeled directly on Dicky Bateman, which is underscored by Delany's notion of "a *striking likeness*."[98] Edmund Malone suggested that the character of Fribble may have been based upon Horace Walpole and his newly affected postures and tastes, acquired on the Grand Tour.[99] Lyttelton and Delany, however, do not mention Walpole, so aside from a broad allusion to a shared affect among the men (and shared tastes in art and architecture), the connection in their writings would seem to be largely or exclusively with Bateman and Old Windsor. Operating within a highly nuanced medium of epistolary exchange, Lyttelton and Delany employ "fribble" as both a sexual type and a nickname. Articulating a tension between acceptance and ridicule of Bateman's sexuality within a common elite milieu, Delany's and Lyttelton's commentaries provide sophisticated readings of the perceived ethical and sexual character of Bateman's house. Eliding patron and building with a stereotype of the third sex, these commentaries reflect the displacement of a theatrical trope from the stage to the built environment, from theatrical domesticity to real domesticity, from an abstract type of man to a physical manifestation of his tastes.

In this, "fribble" proved a malleable adjective to describe architecture. Writing in 1759, on the cusp of Bateman's Gothicization, Lyttelton employed the term to describe the unseemly mixture of architectural styles at Grove House. Characterized by ornamental excess and extravagance ("half Gothick, half attick, half Chinese"), Bateman's residence was unnaturally abundant in signification—literally more than the sum of its parts—a ridiculous corruption of form that delighted but disoriented Lord Lyttelton.[100] He aligned Bateman's house with current debates about the villa that were taking place in the popular press, in which the new hybrid villas were understood as debased modern aberrations of architectural form. A well-known man of letters, there can be no doubt that Lyttelton knew these critiques. A famous satire in the *World* for 1753 recounts how Squire Mushroom acquired an old farmhouse and "he fell to building . . . with all the rage of taste. The old mansion immediately shot up into Gothic spires, and was plastered over with stucco; the walls were notched into battlements. . . . Thus while one-half [of the house] is designed to give you the idea of an old Gothic edifice, the other half presents to your view Venetian windows, slices of pilaster, balustrades, and other parts of Italian architecture."[101]

Other critics, such as John Gilbert Cooper, railed against the "splendid Impertinence," "unmeaning Glitter," and "tasteless Profusion" of the new villas discovered on a stroll on the Thames. Very possibly with Bateman's Old Windsor in mind, Cooper writes acidly: "we found an old *Gothic* Building encrusted with Stucco, sliced into *Grecian* Pilasters, with gilded Capitals; superbly lined with Paper disfigured all over with the fat Deities of China. . . . But in all these notable Distortions of Art, I perceived the poor, prostituted word Taste, was constantly made use of to express the abortive Conceptions of a distempered *Fancy*."[102] Centering his critique on stylistic hybridity, Cooper considers taste for the modern styles to be a disfiguration of the purity of the Palladian mode and the tradition of disinterestedness to which it is connected. Hybrid architecture becomes the product of debased modern "taste," itself the product of "distempered *Fancy*." In his view an aesthetic subjectivity that embraces the stylistically heterogeneous, opulent, and overtly ornamental modern styles is a product of a stunted or degenerated imagination incapable of conceiving of architecture within a tradition of disinterestedness, a subjectivity that will be significant in a nascent queer aesthetics. A comic version of this critique is pictorialized in "A Common Council Man of Candlestick Ward and his Wife on a Visit to Mr Deputy at his Modern Built Villa near Clapham" of 1771 (fig. 5), in which the ridiculous disorder of a hybrid villa with Gothic, Chinese, Palladian, and classical elements is the mise-en-scène for the physical and social inversion of a carriage tumbling to the ground and the horse wearing the councilman's wig.

It is significant that these debates about the new styles regularly employed corporeal metaphors to describe architectural hybridity. Writing in 1753, for example, a critic of the Gothic style complains of the "disgrace" of the newly built Gothic villas around London: "in front of the same edifice [of a Gothic villa] to find a Grecian plan adulterated and defiled by the unnatural and impure mixture of Gothic whimsies." The author goes on to employ Horace's well-known description of a siren or mermaid from the *Ars Poetica*: "Desinit in piscem mulier formosa superne" (A woman, beautiful above, has a fish's tail).[103] The critic describes a classical or Palladian villa that has been "Gothicized," no doubt with crenellations, ogee-headed windows, pinnacles, and other features common in the period. To translate his Ovidian allusion to architecture: the masculine body of the "Grecian" villa has been defiled by feminine Gothic ornament, creating an "unnatural" and "impure" architecture. Blending male and female characteristics in the same form, the villa becomes, quite literally, an intersexual architecture, a hermaphrodite of the built environment. Here, as elsewhere in this study, Gothic architecture and the third sex share common critical tropes. Men of the third sex were regularly labeled "hermaphrodites," and fribbles were defined by their "male" bodies adorned with "female" finery and manners. Charles Churchill's "Rosciad" describes "A Motley Figure, of the Fribble Tribe, . . . Nor Male, nor Female; Neither, and yet both; Of Neuter gender, tho' of Irish Growth; A six-foot suckling, mincing in Its gait; Affected, peevish, prim, and delicate," while David Garrick's *Fribbleriad* (1761) opens with the Latin tag "Faemina, Vir, Neutrum" to describe the hermaphrodite.[104] Writing in the context of such critiques, Lord Lyttelton suggests that Bateman's home is like his sexuality, or fribblishness: being neither wholly Gothic, Chinese, nor antique, it is, like Bateman's own sexual hybridity, a corruption of natural form.

Most telling of the aesthetic character of the fribble and its possible architectural analogues is Johann Kaspar Lavater's influential *Essays on Physiognomy*, which illustrates the "Contrasted attitudes of a man and a fribble" (fig. 99). Considered a "harebrained coxcomb," the

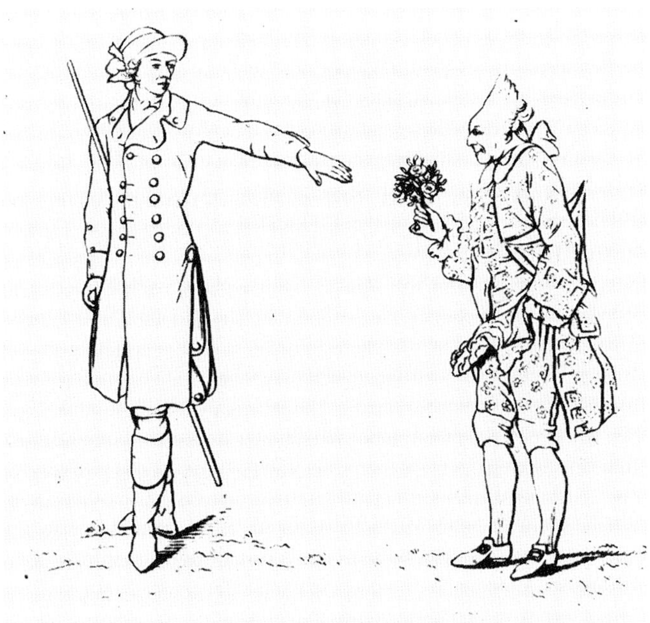

Fig. 99 Thomas Holloway, "Contrasted attitudes of a man and a fribble." From Lavater, *Essays on Physiognomy* (1789), 3:213.

fribble is an infantilized male "who will pass his whole life in eternal childhood." "Incapable of feeling either the great or the beautiful, or the simple and natural" (i.e., the grand manner of neoclassicism interpreted via disinterested contemplation), the fribble is trapped in adolescence and is accordingly engaged with the ephemeralities of the world (the theater, the court) and is perpetually transfixed by his own image in a looking glass.[105] In Thomas Holloway's engraving, the fribble is a gaudily dressed old letch whose richly ornamented exterior and accoutrements (a bouquet of flowers and a codpiece that simulates a giant phallus) signify affected decadence, and his stooped posture and age suggest moral and physical decay in contrast with the erect virility of the youthful and overtly chaste "man." Visualizing alternative modes of contemporary masculinity, this image might be understood as an analogue to contemporary paradigms on the gender of architecture in the Vitruvian tradition, in which the unadorned and upright form of the "man," as an analogue for the classical orders (particularly the "manly" Doric), may be understood to embody the aesthetics of contemporary classicism. The fribble, by contrast, reflects the ornamental vocabulary of the modern styles of Chinoiserie and the Gothic, with their gaudy surfaces, rich patterns, and frequently fictive simulations in wood, papier-mâché, and paint. As styles conceived principally as ornament that often graced (or defiled) preexisting structures, rather than styles conceived as structural systems in their own right, the modern styles were considered "decoration" and were susceptible to the same moralizing critiques of the whims of sartorial fashion. In this sense, the fribble's richly patterned and attenuated clothing provides a ready parallel (as Lyttelton would have it) with the fancy dress, or "*gaudy gout*," of the modern interior.[106]

In Delany's 1768 commentary on the Priory, "fribble" has a different range of meanings. Focusing on the mirrored surfaces of his library—something that was relatively new to the English interior and therefore worthy of commentary—she too characterizes Bateman's house and its illusionistic surfaces as a double, or a second self. The stylish, pretentious, and effete surfaces of the man and the building become synonymous; these surfaces act like a veneer that exists independently of a hidden inner self, which Delany clearly derides, even if she has called him "our friend" and has emulated his Chinese designs.[107] Delany provides a queer interpretation of an eighteenth-century trope of the mirror in which the "subject becomes artificial by overinvesting in the [mirror's] image: the subject disappears behind the character he produces and takes pleasure from himself as he would from a realized fiction."[108] The mirrors, in other words, are understood to reflect not Dicky Bateman, but his "fribble" persona. Unfortunately, we know much less about the original appearance of the room than we would like, but mirrors were certainly dominant ornamentation in it, since mirrors or "looking glass[es]" were also noted in the contemporary account in *Windsor and Its Environs*, which confirms that the library was "in the *Chinese* Taste, which, by Means of Glasses, [gave] a double Reflection." This suggests that the mirrors were, like those of the famous Villa Palagonia in Sicily or the slightly later mirrors from Robert Adam's Northumberland House of circa 1773–74, integral components of the wall surfaces rather than hanging mirrors in the Chinese style, such as those by Chippendale or Ince and Mayhew.[109] More directly relevant to Old Windsor, many of the villas built along the Thames employed the newly affordable mirror in their interiors and used them similarly to guide or even distort vision.[110] In the library, books were not read, mirrors usurped the role of painted and graphic representations, and the multiplied human subject became the image for meditation and analysis (more so perhaps than the books, to follow the drift of Delany's critique).[111] Mirrors were central to Bateman's design of the interior spaces of the Priory: elsewhere he toyed with optical illusion and manipulated its spatial properties, including "Windows [mirrors] . . . so contrived as to shew the Company on their Heads," thus suggesting the use of concave mirrors to provide inverted, anamorphic images of their subjects.[112] In its style and in its fictive, unreal surfaces, Bateman's house literally and figuratively inverted contemporary nostrums of English decorum.

Paralleling a perverse architectural interior with a perverse or morally corrupt character, Delany suggests that if the surface of the mirror could expose Bateman's *inner* character, it might "shew him his own insignificancy." Just as the beautiful face of Oscar Wilde's Dorian Gray disguises his real, inner character (displaced to a painting), so are the surfaces of the Priory and the mirrors in particular doubles that fail to signify a morally or sexually corrupt inner self. They are, so to speak, pure fashion. "Insignificancy" here codes male effeminacy—a lack of physical, and by extension moral, prowess.[113] Since the Priory was created predominantly in the Chinese taste, which was broadly associated with femininity, frivolousness, and the corrupt, effeminate luxury of a mercantile world besieged by glossy but morally dubious foreign imports, Delany's comment is well placed.[114] She also hints at narcissism in her discussion of the library interior. Narcissism was a common trope of contemporary male effeminacy and the third sex in particular: Lavater's Fribble and characters such as Sir Novelty Fashion from Colley Cibber's *Love's Last Shift, or The Fool in Fashion* (1696) and Sir Fopling Flutter in George Etherege's play *The Man of Mode* (1676) were often figured obsessing over themselves in mirrors, enamored with their own reflections, thus justifying Thomas King's observation that the fop or the fribble's greatest offense was not his excessive display but rather his radical self-sufficiency.[115] Unsurprisingly, perhaps, after Bateman's death Delany's single response to the house was to "[moralize] on the vanities of human life."[116]

The fribble's aesthetic attraction to overtly ornamental, decorative art forms is a result of his own arrested development: his infantile, childlike imagination is enamored with surface decoration and is, within the logic of the critique, apparently incapable of conceiving of art in the grand manner of classicism consonant with disinterested contemplation. Such a critique was ultimately grounded in current physiology, in which it was believed that human sexual development emerged from a single female sex that matured as male or female at puberty. The fribble's childlike attraction to glamorous, superficial "bling" positions him squarely in an early phase of physical and sexual development, before the development of, in his case, "male" aesthetic judgments.[117] The lavish attention devoted to the house, the fastidious care in its design and arrangement, and the erotic attachment to objects displayed therein—its fribblishness—are suggestive of a particular construction of narcissism linked to a "homosexual" subjectivity in the eighteenth century and beyond.

There is much that feels familiar to twenty-first-century readers of these critiques. Their two dominant strands—first, recognition of the erotic identification with the self and of the doubling of one's ego in images or in buildings (i.e., narcissism), and second, perception of queer aesthetic judgments as products of infantile or arrested psychic and sexual development—were manifestly at play in aesthetic discussion during the eighteenth century, but they awaited codification in the sexological research of Sigmund Freud and Isidor Sadger more than a century later.[118] Delany's and Lyttelton's commentaries on architecture (and later texts such as Lavater's) thus significantly anticipate some of the tropes of homosexuality that would be codified in sexological (and particularly psychoanalytic) discourses over the next two centuries and would form much of our current construction of "homosexuality."

Conclusion

Upon Dicky Bateman's death in 1774, ownership of the Priory went to his nephew John Bateman (1721–1802), who seems to have had no love for his uncle's famous home. He pulled down parts of the house and sold its contents in the Christie's sale the same year. Walpole provided an emotional response: writing to William Cole, he urges him to come to visit Strawberry Hill soon because "Strawberry is almost the last monastery left, at least in England. Poor Mr Bateman's is despoiled: Lord Bateman has stripped and plundered it[!]." He continues, "I was hurt to see half the ornaments of the chapel, and the *reliquaires*, and in short a thousand trifles exposed to sneers. I am buying a few to keep for the founder's sake. . . . I suppose Strawberry Hill will have the same fate!"[119] Walpole's rich passage provides a lament for a lost *environment*—a queer culture that was located within and normalized by Old Windsor's Gothic setting and collection. Central to his lament is the fragmentation of the very code that bound this culture to its setting and of the many medievalist tropes that informed it. Commemorating the "founder" of another Gothic "monastery" in this passage, Walpole reflects upon what he understands as a spiritual continuity between the two buildings and between the two men and upon Strawberry Hill as the last bastion of a shared taste. In purchasing "a few" objects, Walpole becomes the protector of Bateman's queer Gothic legacy against the vulgar, grasping, unknowing bidders who would otherwise degrade these emblems of a shared taste to the status of trifling commodities; and Strawberry Hill becomes an environment that normalizes Bateman's Catholic art, which is otherwise received with sneers. Walpole echoes similar sentiments in a letter to Lady Ossory describing the sale: "It was a melancholy sight to me in more lights than one. I have passed many pleasing days there with him [Dicky Bateman] and Lady Hervey, and felt additional pain by reflections on my child Strawberry!"[120] Walpole's grief over the loss of his friend and his friend's residence is palpable. Considering Bateman's house to be a "monastery" that is spiritually connected to Strawberry Hill by a common "religion," he is afraid that his own "child"—which gave birth to Bateman's residence—will suffer the same fate. To some extent at least, he was right.

5 "The Spirit of Strawberry-Castle"

DONNINGTON GROVE, THE VYNE, AND LEE PRIORY

[Thomas Barrett] gave himself up to it with so much enthusiasm, that it almost engrossed his attention. He could think or dream of nothing but *Gothic architecture*. His taste was refined and elegant even to fastidiousness: and every thing about his house had a studied regard to polish and refinement.

—T. F. Dibdin, *The Bibliographical Decameron* (1817)

On 18 September 1754 Thomas Gray wrote to the medievalist Thomas Warton about the transformation of his London home on Coleman Street: "I rejoice to find you at last settled to your heart's content, and delight to hear you talk of giving your house some *Gothic ornaments* already. If you project any thing, I hope it will be entirely within doors, and don't let me (when I come gaping into Coleman-street) be directed to the gentleman's at the ten Pinnacles, or with the church porch at his door. I am glad you enter into the spirit of Strawberry-castle;—it has a purity and propriety of Gothicism in it, (with very few exceptions) that I have not seen elsewhere."[1] Gray expresses what were often-articulated concerns within the Strawberry Committee about stylistic hybridity and the tacky commodification of Gothic ornament—that is, the awkward addition of a Gothic porch to a London townhouse—and he advises Warton to focus on altering the interiors of his London home. Although advising on architectural transformations, Gray's commentary suggests that an aesthetic transformation first took place within Warton, in which he "enter[ed] into the *spirit* of Strawberry-castle" (my emphasis), aligning his aesthetic subjectivity with the perceived significations of Strawberry Hill. Warton had recently seen the house, and he would return over the years. What the "spirit" of Strawberry Hill meant to both men was never stated, largely because it was readily understood by writer and reader. It undoubtedly signified a series of ideas and orientations: a preference for the medieval over the classical past, a predilection for antiquarian and literary endeavor, the complex psychology of the collector, elite sociability, and, most profoundly, the house as a projection or even personification of an alternate self. Warton's London home long ago disappeared, but it was one of a list of buildings that emulated Strawberry Hill in the eighteenth century and beyond. From the mid-1750s,

Walpole's famous home suggested a template for subsequent Gothic homes, and the increasing prominence of Walpole and Strawberry Hill within English culture during the century meant that it suggested the most significant single model for Gothic houses built during and even after his lifetime.

This chapter explores the influence of Horace Walpole, Strawberry Hill, and the Strawberry Committee on three significant homes built between circa 1760 and 1790: James Pettit Andrews's construction of Donnington Grove, Berkshire, designed by John Chute in 1763 and complete by 1772; Chute's own additions and alterations to the Vyne, Hampshire, from circa 1770 until his death in 1776; and Thomas Barrett's remodeling of Lee Priory in Kent, designed by James Wyatt and John Carter (ca. 1780–90). These buildings have long been understood to illustrate the development of the Strawberry Hill Gothic mode of design via the men in Walpole's circle and by the architects and designers that worked at Strawberry. While this is surely true, none of these buildings reflects anything like a slavish copy of Strawberry Hill. Each building employs the Gothic in a unique fashion, in response either to the physical constraints of existing fabric or to the particular desires of patron or designer. Their employment of the Gothic style and common architects and designers aside, these buildings all specifically reference or quote Strawberry Hill in their ornamentation, picture hangs, and other features. Such gestures cannot be read simply in terms of "style," at least in an unqualified sense. In referencing Walpole's famous home in their subsequent buildings, the owners of these buildings positioned themselves and their homes in a particular relationship with Strawberry Hill. As Bruno Latour and Adam Lowe might suggest, Strawberry Hill's very originality—its status as a famous monument—is fundamentally dependent on its originary position in a chain of replications or *versions* of it. These replications began the process of establishing Strawberry Hill as a canonical building, becoming in essence the retinue of its "continually rewritten biography."[2]

Horace Walpole was involved in one way or another in each of these building campaigns. Careful study of them illustrates that his influence was both more and less profound than he suggests in his commentaries. As in all of his art criticism, his own aesthetic judgment, his *interestedness* in specific objects or buildings, cannot be detached from his personal relations with them and their patrons. Walpole developed a range of conceits to describe these buildings in relation to Strawberry Hill. In the case of Lee Priory, he spoke in overtly familial terms, describing Lee as "a child of Strawberry prettier than its parent," "my Gothic child," and saying that "if Strawberry were not its parent, I would be jealous."[3] He thus posited a genealogical relationship between architectural parent and child and between a senior arbiter of taste and a young disciple. Walpole only ever describes Lee directly in these terms, but some sense of his perception of the other houses as relatives or progeny of Strawberry is suggested by the display of images of them in his home. He displayed an image of Donnington Grove in his own bedchamber, calling it "Chaucer's Grove," and he ascribes the authorship to Chute (fig. 100).[4] Further images of Donnington were in the Beauclerc closet. An image of Lee Priory hung in the Breakfast Room, while images of the Vyne by Müntz and Chute were hung in Walpole's bedchamber.[5] These images functioned as architectural analogues to the portraits of Walpole's circle that hung in the house. From Walpole's perspective, and from that of many in his circle, the Gothic buildings

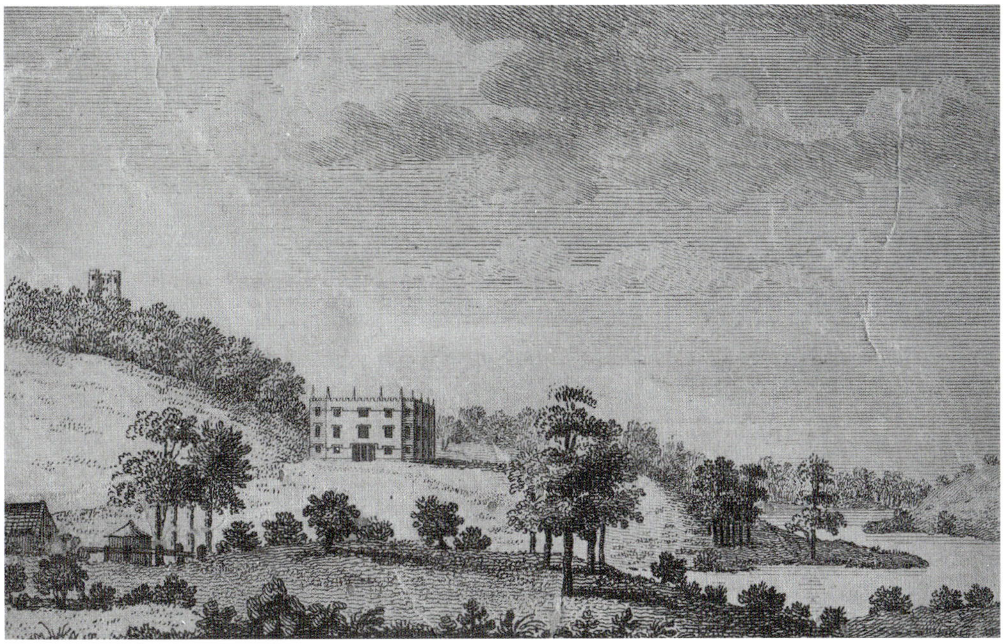

Fig. 100 Peter Mazell, "Chaucer's Grove near Spidehill the Seat of Mr. Andrews, designed by John Chute Esq. of the Vine. Above is the View of Donnington Castle were [*sic*] Chaucer Lived," 1786. Title in Horace Walpole's hand. This work hung in Walpole's own bedchamber at Strawberry Hill. LWL SH Views An565 no. 1 Framed, shelved in LFS Bin 36. Courtesy of The Lewis Walpole Library, Yale University.

built by his friends in emulation of Strawberry constituted a queer family romance in the built environment. Understood to be a "family" of buildings stylistically bound together by a common employment of the Gothic style (and of course by a common group of patrons), they each acknowledge Strawberry's paternity through architectural form or other quotations from Walpole's Gothic oeuvre.[6]

But Strawberry Hill offered an influential and highly malleable template for the Gothic house to subsequent patrons, both within and outside of Walpole's circle. Lady Eleanor Butler and Miss Sarah Ponsonby—the so-called Ladies of Llangollen—built the extraordinary Plas Newydd in Llangollen, North Wales, from 1780, based in part on the Strawberry Hill model (fig. 101). The house translated some of Strawberry's metropolitan Gothic forms into Welsh woodwork and was filled with Catholic religious art and objects, including stained glass from Valle Crucis Abbey and a medieval High Cross from Chester.[7] The antiquary Francis Grose (1731–91) manifestly understood the house's allusions,

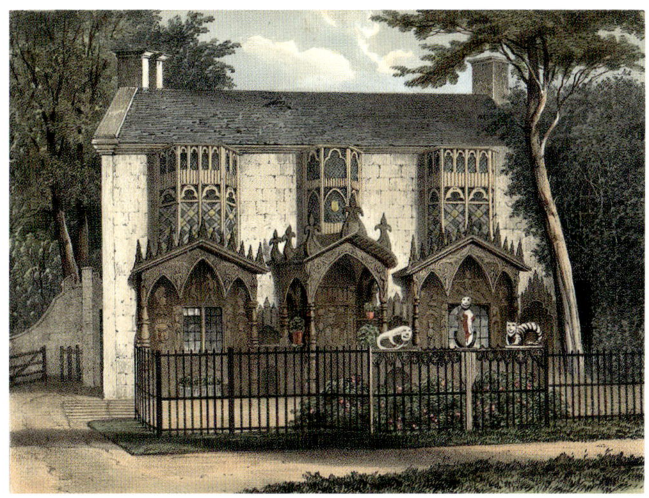

Fig. 101 Edwin W. Jacques, "Plas Newydd, near Llangollen the seat of the late Lady Eleanor Butler and Miss Ponsonby," 1840. Llyfrgell Genedlaethol Cymru—The National Library of Wales.

suggesting, "Don't you think that same cottage somewhat of the Strawberry Hill Kind[?] Could houses Marry & propagate, I think a cottage like Langothlin [*sic*] would be the progeny of a Match between Strawberry Hill & the Thicknesses Cottage near Landguard Fort."[8] In other words, the house is another child of Strawberry Hill, albeit one of mixed parentage. William Beckford's Fonthill Abbey also reflects the influence of Strawberry, even if the owner was scathing in his criticism of Walpole and his home. Beckford employed James Wyatt, who had just finished building Lee Priory; he would go on to purchase lots from Walpole's sale; and he employed many of the conventions of the Gothic imagined or popularized by Walpole at Strawberry Hill. Sir Walter Scott's Abbotsford of 1824, a Gothic house in the Scottish Borders, followed the model of Strawberry Hill and was even assembled by his own "committee."[9] Scott penned an influential "Critical Introduction" to the 1811 edition of *The Castle of Otranto* as one component of his literary medievalism; others include *The Antiquary* (1816) and *Ivanhoe* (1820).

A supreme and self-conscious product of English modernity, Strawberry Hill and its collection have been understood as the most significant progenitor of what Clive Wainwright has called "the Romantic Interior," a fashion for medievalizing great houses for literary gentlemen, collectors, antiquaries, and dilettantes in later eighteenth- and nineteenth-century architecture. In this study, I have placed particular emphasis on the sexual subjectivities of its main protagonists. While Strawberry Hill and many related buildings discussed in these pages were imagined by a homoerotic coterie, they were appropriated to a range of subjective ends often different from those of the persons who had imagined them in the first place. Although the sexualities of John Chute and Thomas Barrett are well attested in documentation, that of James Pettit Andrews is unknown (unique among the patrons considered in this study, he married). His own interest in Strawberry Hill may have been related to sexuality, but it might as well have been due to his understanding of the house as a site of antiquarian, literary, and historical endeavor. The patrons of these great buildings shared a broad range of orientations of which alternative sexuality was one component. They were significant artists or authors of literary and antiquarian works and collectors of medieval art and furniture, a category of Georgian men who in contemporary satires would be called "the Gothic Gentlemen,"[10] for whom the Strawberry Hill model was an appropriate architectural model. Complicating this picture, the Ladies of Llangollen were certainly a lesbian couple, thus suggesting the significance of the Strawberry Hill model to a range of sexual subjectivities. As I have consistently argued in this study, we cannot reduce art and architecture to sexuality any more than we can exclude sexuality from considerations of tastes in or for art and architecture. Yet it is notable that the Gothic house, homoeroticism, and creative and literary endeavor share much common terrain during the eighteenth century. As Andrew Elfenbein has so cogently argued, eccentricity, deviation from social and sexual norms, heightened aesthetic sensibilities for art and architecture, and homoeroticism in particular were central features of the myth of the "Romantic Genius" in the period (a title that manifestly applies to some of the men included in this study).[11] In exploring this common terrain, Elfenbein's account of the Romantic genius may usefully inform our reading of other significant cultural productions of the period, including the Romantic Interior. Understood in these terms, sexuality and architecture are interrelated phenomena in the changing contours of English aesthetics.

Donnington Grove and the Patronage of James Pettit Andrews

James Pettit Andrews, F.S.A. (1737–1797), was an antiquary, historian, and author whose publications covered literary anecdotes, multivolume histories of England, satires, children's literature, and antiquarian essays that appeared in *Archaeologia* and the *Gentleman's Magazine*.[12] Yet he has been the subject of surprisingly little research.[13] Andrews's immediate circle comprised some significant literary figures, including his brother-in-law, the poet Thomas Penrose (1742–1779), who was well acquainted with Strawberry Hill;[14] the medievalist Francis Grose, whose *Antiquities of England and Wales* (1772–76) included a foundational essay on the origin of the Gothic;[15] and the poet James Henry Pye (1744–1813). Although some sources claim that Walpole and Andrews were great friends and that Andrews was inspired by Walpole's home, Andrews does not appear in Walpole's letters, even if his own records make it clear that he had visited Strawberry. In any case, Andrews was sufficiently close to Walpole's circle to acquire the talents of his closest designers and to commission a home that self-consciously emulated Walpole's example.

Andrews purchased Donnington in 1762, and Chute prepared designs by the following year (fig. 102). A range of early drawings by Chute now at the Lewis Walpole Library at Yale chart the evolution of the design for the house (e.g., fig. 103).[16] Two further drawings have recently come to light in Andrews's papers; these are not signed but are certainly by Richard Bentley (fig. 104).[17] These are proposals for different designs for the house: the one shows a two-level house with a Gothic louver on the roof, ogee-headed arches over the doors,

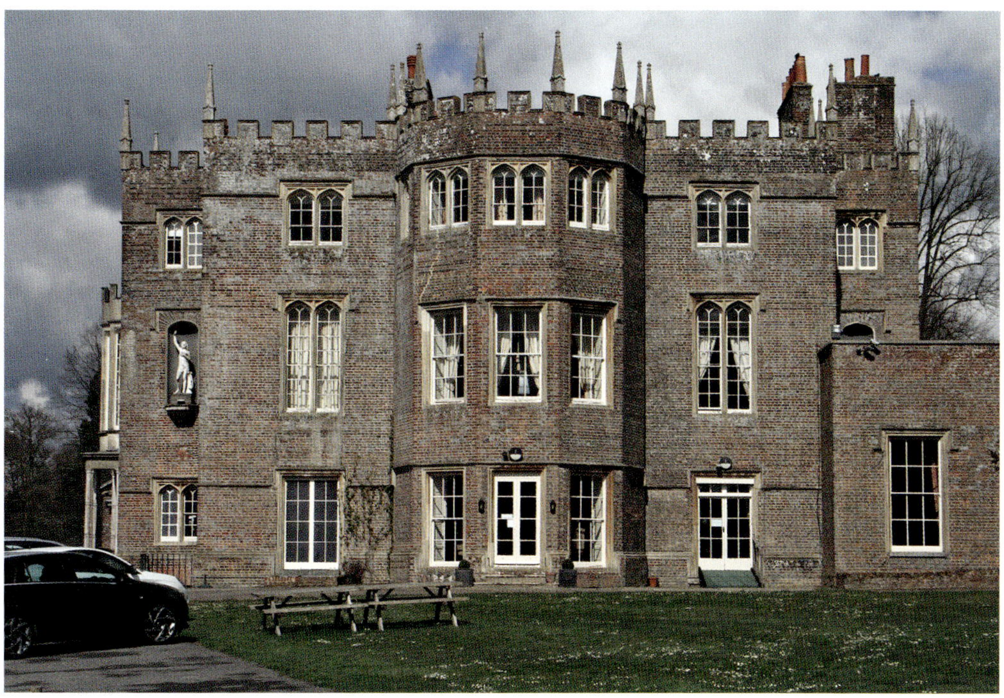

Fig. 102 Donnington Grove, Berkshire. Photo: author.

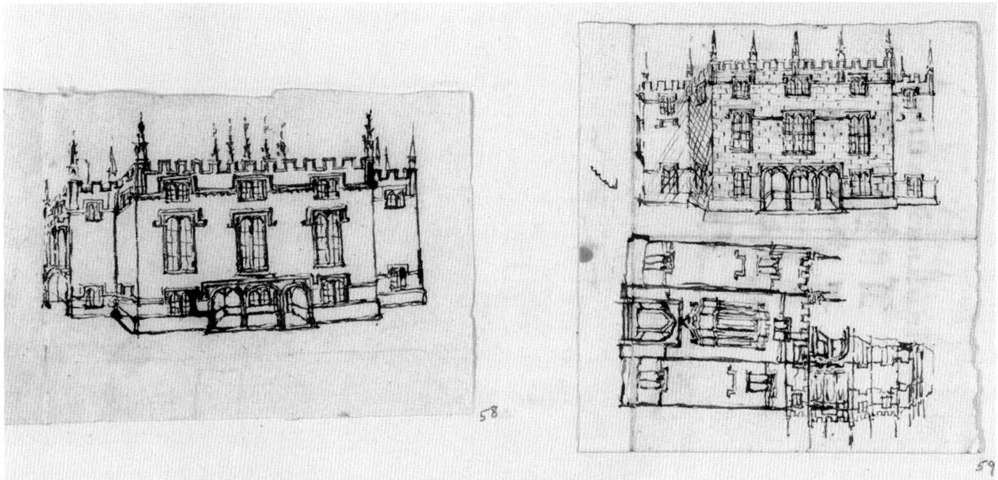

Fig. 103 John Chute, "Designs of a Gothic House for Mr Andrews in Berkshire." LWL 49 3490, sketches 58–59. Courtesy of The Lewis Walpole Library, Yale University.

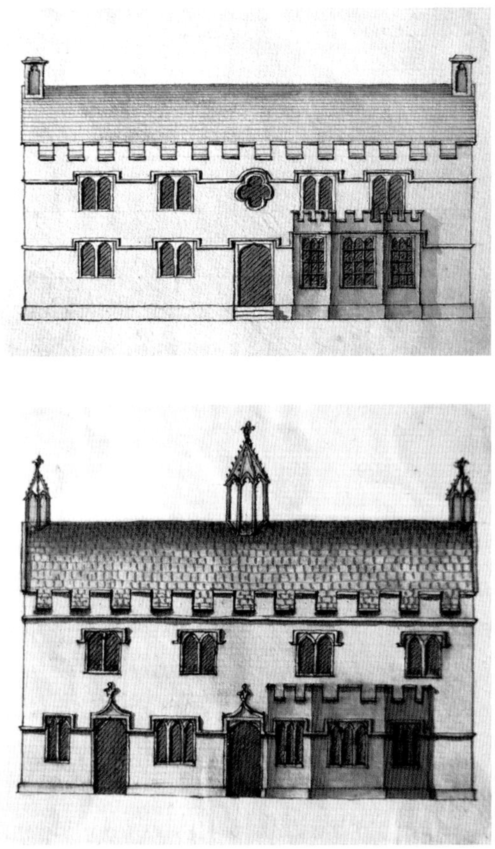

Fig. 104 Richard Bentley (attrib.), preliminary drawings of Donnington Grove. Bibermühle, Collection Heribert Tenschert, Switzerland, MS "Dessins Grotesques," vol. 3 (unpaginated). Photo: Antiquariat Bibermühle.

and a canted bay on the right side; and the other is a simplified design punctuated by a quatrefoil window above a centrally placed ground-floor door (the glazed quatrefoil can be readily paired with the early work at Strawberry Hill). The circumstances surrounding Andrews's commissioning of Walpole's draughtsmen are unknown. Bentley and Walpole had an acrimonious split the year previously, thus raising the possibility that Bentley had worked independently or had perhaps produced the drawings before Chute.

Whatever the situation, Chute's designs were selected over Bentley's, and deservedly so. Donnington was Chute's first whole completed Gothic house, making it a significant demonstration of the Gothic designs worked up over the 1750s and 1760s at Strawberry Hill. He had designed Chalfont House, Buckinghamshire, in 1755, a Gothic country home for Walpole's niece Lady Maria Walpole and her husband, Charles Churchill, which, seemingly, was never realized.[18] Donnington was complete by 1772, when a brief account was given in the *Gentleman's Magazine*. Work was clearly done in the gardens at the same time, including "a rustic Gothic temple in flint" whose image appears in Andrews's papers (fig. 105).[19] Andrews was undoubtedly drawn to the site by its literary and historical associations: positioned

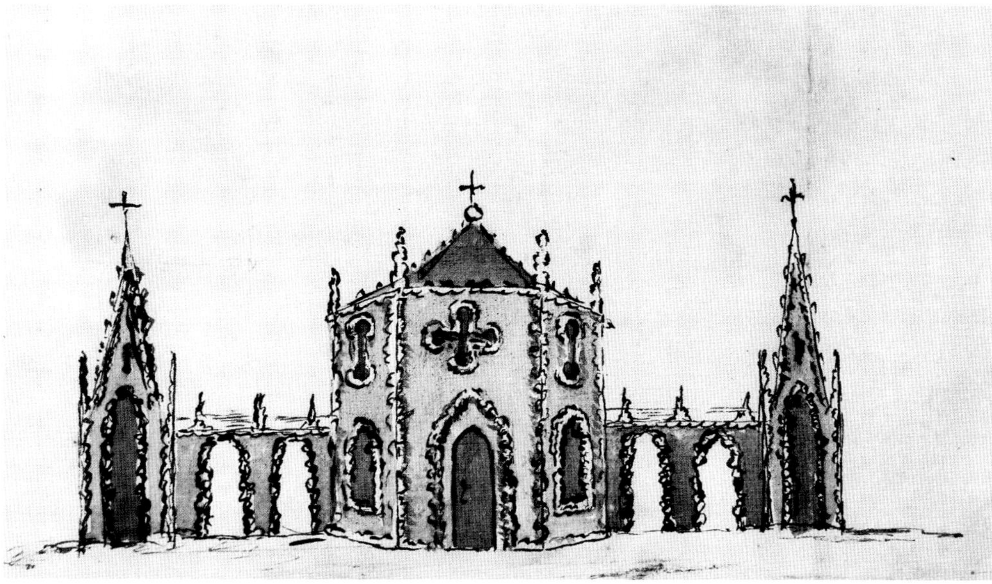

Fig. 105 John Chute (attrib.), probably Chute's design for "a rustic Gothic Temple in flint" at Donnington. Bibermühle, Collection Heribert Tenschert, Switzerland, MS "Dessins Grotesques," vol. 3 (unpaginated). Photo: Antiquariat Bibermühle.

Fig. 106 Donnington Castle, showing the remains of the curtain walls and the two-towered gatehouse from the interior. Photo: author.

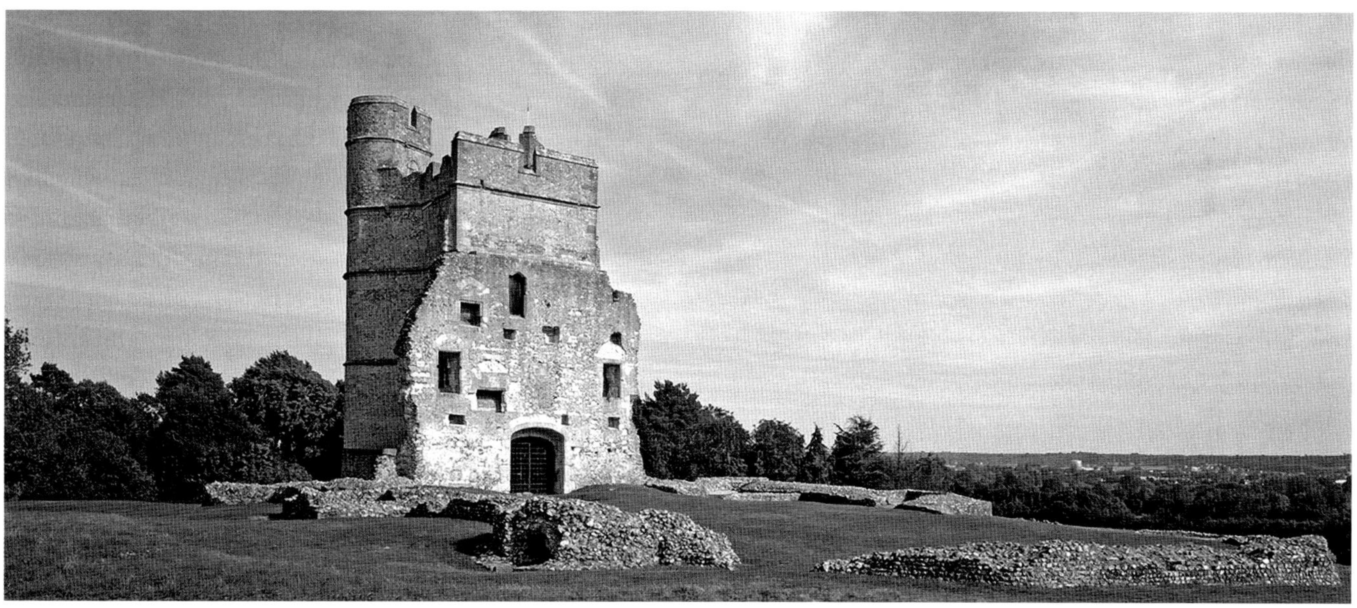

to view the fourteenth-century gatehouse and walls of Donnington Castle (figs. 100, 106) as an "eye-catcher," or folly, the site not only was understood to have been lived in by Geoffrey Chaucer (in fact his son Thomas) but had also been the site of a major siege during the Civil War.[20] Unfortunately, the house spent only twenty years in Andrews's possession. The costs of maintaining it were too great, and Andrews auctioned the contents and sold it to William Brummell in 1783.[21] While Brummell added significantly to the estate and gardens, his only major alterations were the back "offices," added to the rear of the house, and the new entrance porch, leaving Andrews's home otherwise original.[22]

Even without a "brief" for Donnington, it is clear that Chute loosely based his designs upon the earliest phases of Strawberry Hill. The house is centrally planned around a staircase and has projecting canted and flat bays at its cardinal points. The three-level staircase sweeps through the house and terminates in a cantilevered upper gallery (fig. 107). Lit by a raised skylight with blind Gothic paneling carried on slender quatrefoil shafts, the gallery is one of the most majestic statements of later eighteenth-century Gothic architecture and one that clearly owes a nod to Strawberry Hill (fig. 108). And yet the design is Chute's own, and it reflects his sharp, draughtsmanly approach to architectural form. Walpole captures something of this in his description of Donnington: "as chaste a specimen of Gothic architecture as exists any where."[23] Based in part on the possibilities of a *de novo* design and on Chute's own stylistic predilections, Donnington denies much of the stylistic heterogeneity of Strawberry Hill, with its many "quotations" from Gothic buildings taken out of a geographic or temporal sequence. Chute's drawings of the façades are all symmetrical elevations with square-headed Perpendicular windows

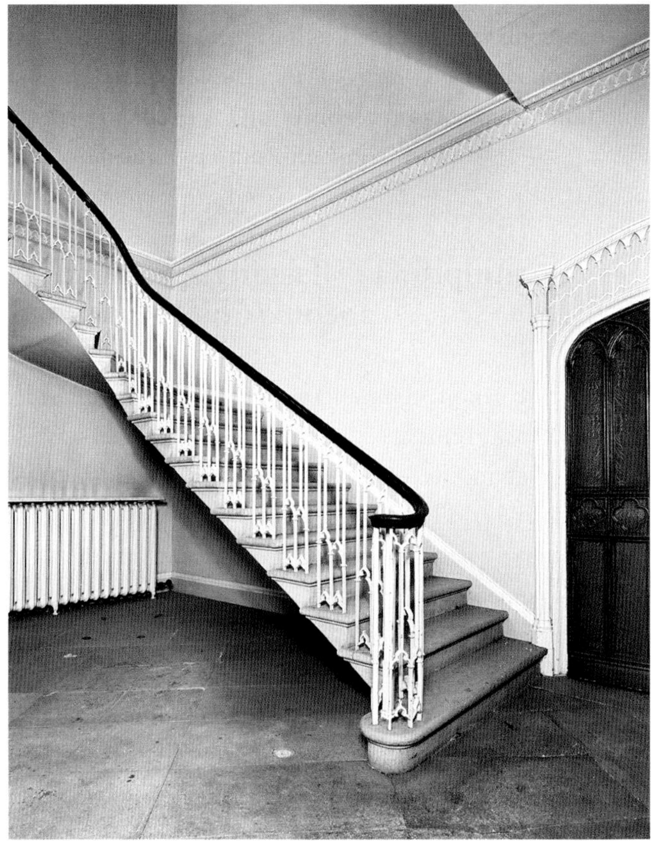

Fig. 107 Donnington Grove, staircase. National Monuments Record. Photo by permission of Historic England Archive.

and label stops. Chute's designs created a crisp new Gothic house and did not aim to achieve anything like the fictive architectural history of Strawberry Hill. Also unlike Strawberry but akin to Lee Priory and Grove House, Donnington pursued the fashionable approach to stylistically mixed interiors: although much of the interior was Gothic, a room leading off the main entrance was Chinese, with Chinoiserie paper and a playful fireplace mantel with Chinese-inspired motifs, all beneath a gilded crown molding simulating bamboo. Andrews's library can now be situated within the long first-floor drawing room, with

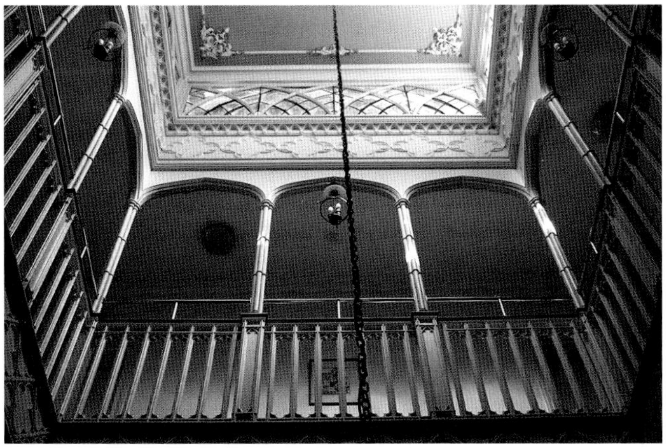

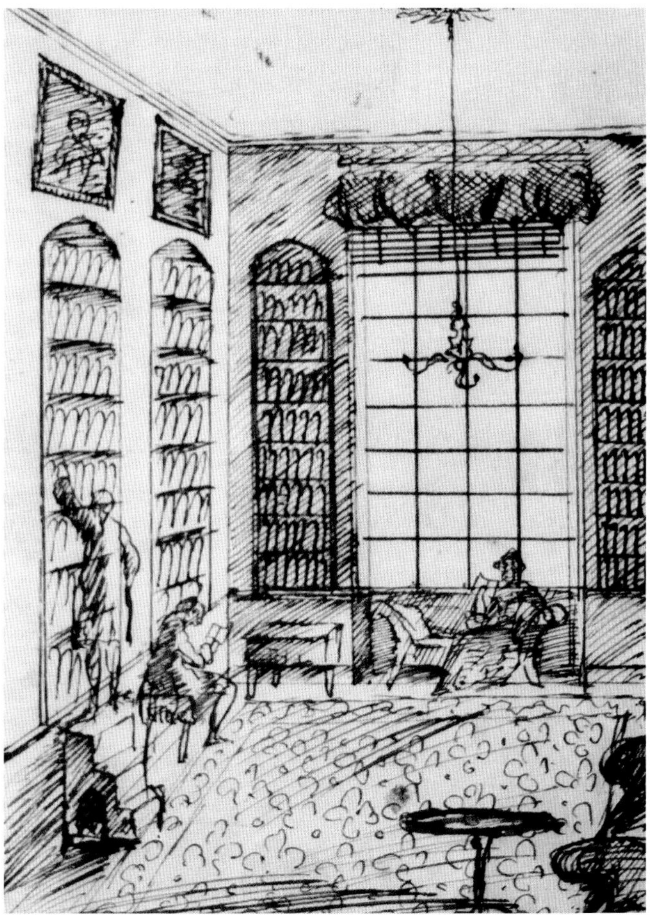

Fig. 108 Donnington Grove, upper gallery. Photo: author.

Fig. 109 James Pettit Andrews, the library at Donnington Grove. Bibermühle, Collection Heribert Tenschert, Switzerland, ms "Dessins Grotesques," vol. 3 (unpaginated). Photo: Antiquariat Bibermühle.

its stunning Gothic pendants, due to a sketch by Andrews himself of a scholarly *convivium* within the room, then decorated with tall Gothic bookcases (fig. 109).

Comparing the architecture of Donnington with that of Strawberry Hill is a useful, if limited, approach to understanding the broader conceptual kinship between the two. Donnington was probably the first Gothic house created after Strawberry Hill that had a double, fictive identity reinforced by medievalist literature. As noted above, Walpole based the setting of *The Castle of Otranto* on Strawberry Hill, promoted the house as "my own little Otranto," and staged images and objects to remind viewers of the house's fictive literary status. Following Walpole's influential lead, Thomas Penrose wrote the poem "The Helmets, a Fragment" for Andrews and published it in his 1775 book of poetry *Flights of Fancy*.[24] The narrative of the poem takes place at Donnington, as the poem's preface states: "The Scene of the following Event is laid in the Neighbourhood of Donington [*sic*] Castle, in a House built after the Gothic Taste, upon a Spot famous for a bloody Encounter between the Armies of Charles [I] and the Parliament [i.e., the Battle of Newbury, 1644]. The Prognostication alludes to Civil Dissention, which some have foretold would arise in England, in Consequence of the Disputes with America." Evoking Walpole's tongue-in-cheek view that the narrative of Otranto "was undoubtedly laid in some real castle," Penrose's poem uses Donnington as a setting for medievalist narrative.[25]

The poem adopts many of the conventions of *The Castle of Otranto*, including its opening image of a gigantic plumed helmet. It begins in Donnington when two helmets are struck by lightning and thereby brought to life (an idea that would be popularized by Mary Shelley's *Frankenstein*, 1818). Instantly embodied by the spirits of the armor that had been dormant (rather than the spirits of their wearers), the plumed helmets become personalities from the medieval past given new agency in the present, not unlike the brooms and buckets of Walt Disney's *Sorcerer's Apprentice* (1940, itself based on Goethe's "Zauberlehrling" [1797]): "The Spirits, wandering round this gothic pile / All join their yell—the song is War and Death.— / There will be work anon[!]." Andrews was clearly fascinated by such uncanny animations of inanimate form: his papers contain drawings by

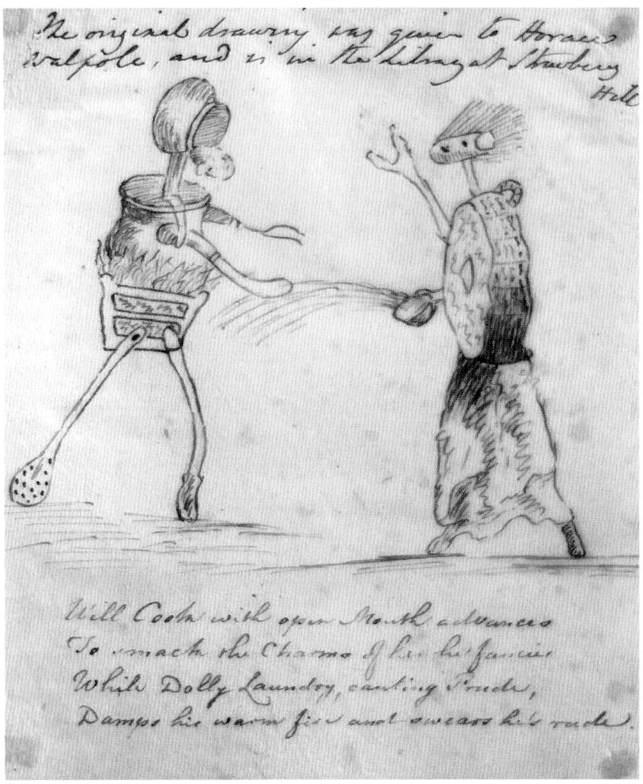

Fig. 110 Thomas Penrose, copies of figures from Walpole's copy of Giovanni Battista Braccelli's *Bizzarie di varie figure* (1624) in the library at Strawberry Hill. Collection Heribert Tenschert, Switzerland, MS "Dessins Grotesques," vol. 3 (unpaginated). Photo: Antiquariat Bibermühle.

Penrose based on Walpole's copy of Giovanni Battista Braccelli's *Bizzarie di varie figure* of 1624, then located in the Strawberry Hill library (subsequently purchased by William Beckford for Fonthill).[26] Featuring figures composed of common household implements and furnishings (chairs, pots, brooms, bladders, etc.), the figures are "readymades," and Andrews (or perhaps Penrose) penned humorous poetry to gloss their various interactions (fig. 110). As Christopher Hussey has rightly opined, the drawings "afford a queer link in surrealism between [Hieronymus] Bosch and [Edward] Lear" (notably, Braccelli's *Bizzarie di varie figure* was appropriated by the surrealists, with a new edition published and prefaced by Tristan Tzara).[27]

Returning to Penrose's poem, the bellicose, melodramatic tenor of the language is the stuff of *Otranto*. With derring-do, one helmet states, "Call armourers, Ho!," while the other, which did not prevent the death of its former occupant, lazily waxes on instead about his inability to do battle and ultimately about his transformation from an object of the medieval past to an object of antiquarian curiosity in the present:

> Bored by a happier mace, I let in fate
> To my once master,—since unsought, unused
> Pensile I'm fixed—yet too your gaudy pride
> Has nought to boast,—the fashion of the fight
> Has thrown your gilt, and shady plumes aside
> For modern foppery;—still do not frown,
> Nor lour indignantly your steely brows,
> We've comfort left enough—The bookman's
>   lore
> Shall trace our sometime merit;—in the eye
> Of antiquary taste we long shall shine:
> And as the Scholar marks our rugged front,

He'll say, This *Cressy* saw, that *Agincourt*:
Thus dwelling on the prowess of his fathers,
He'll venerate their shell.

It could hardly be said that Penrose's poem deserves to be better known on account of its literary merit. But the poem is of interest as a statement on medievalist collections and architecture in the period. Here medieval objects are dissociated from their original heroic functions and become emasculated as objects for speculation; their raw functionalism in the medieval world becomes aestheticized and historicized in the present, a period of "modern foppery" in which armor is unnecessary. Its functionlessness is emphasized by the apparent decline of masculine, martial rigor. Despite his status as a historian and poet of note, Penrose enjoys a jab at contemporary antiquarian practice, in which study, prosopographical analysis, and display diminish the masculine rigor of medieval armor, transforming it from a functional body covering to a purely aesthetic object. The helmet seems happily resigned to the fact that its historicity is now dependent on some flawed but optimistic antiquarian connoisseurship that links it, without historical evidence, to famous battles. That Penrose had in mind Walpole's own collection of armor at Strawberry Hill and its whimsical attribution, in which "all [was] *supposed* to [have been] taken by Sir Terry Robsart in the holy wars," seems likely.[28]

Significantly, Penrose's poem references the actual medievalist interiors that existed at Donnington in the 1770s. Andrews's papers include a watercolor entitled "Armour as it was placed on the staircase at the Grove and the 'Gilded Casque'—in the Revd. Penrose's Poem of 'The Helmets'" (fig. 111). The image shows two symmetrically positioned splays of armor on either side of an image—seemingly a life-sized painting—of a man

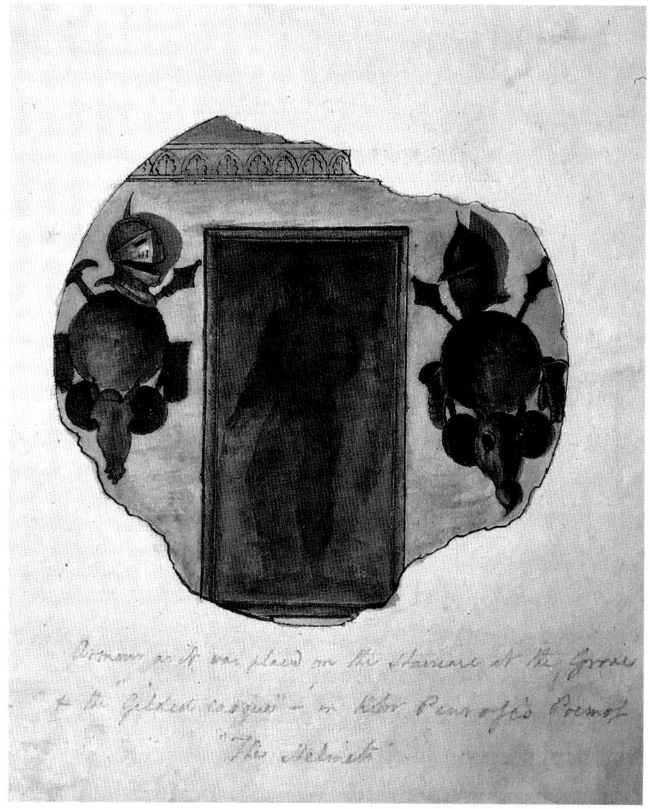

Fig. 111 "Armour as it was placed on the staircase at the Grove and the 'Gilded Casque'—in the Revd. Penrose's Poem of 'The Helmets.'" Bibermühle, Collection Heribert Tenschert, Switzerland, MS "Dessins Grotesques," vol. 3 (unpaginated). Photo: Antiquariat Bibermühle.

in armor. This was the original design for the staircase landing, which is confirmed by the cornice molding, which is the same as that at Donnington. The poem in fact describes a larger display of objects in the armory than is referenced in the image:

Suspended, nodded o'er the steepy stair,
In many a trophy formed, the knightly groupe
Of helms and targets, gauntlets, maces strong,
And horses' furniture—brave monuments
Of antient Chivalry.

Without doubt, Andrews's point of reference for this composition at Donnington is the Armory at Strawberry Hill (fig. 26), analogously placed on the house's staircase landing (the suit of armor on the stair inspired *The Castle of Otranto*, as Walpole would admit). This imagery and its literary amplification are extraordinarily interesting for my purposes. On one hand, they allow me to challenge Michael McCarthy's view that the interiors of Donnington were unrelated to Strawberry Hill[29] through the reconstruction of a significant painted scheme of the eighteenth-century Gothic Revival. But on the other hand, they suggest something of the mobility of the medievalist literary and antiquarian template that Walpole established, and of the imaginative dimensions of the Gothic myth within his circle.

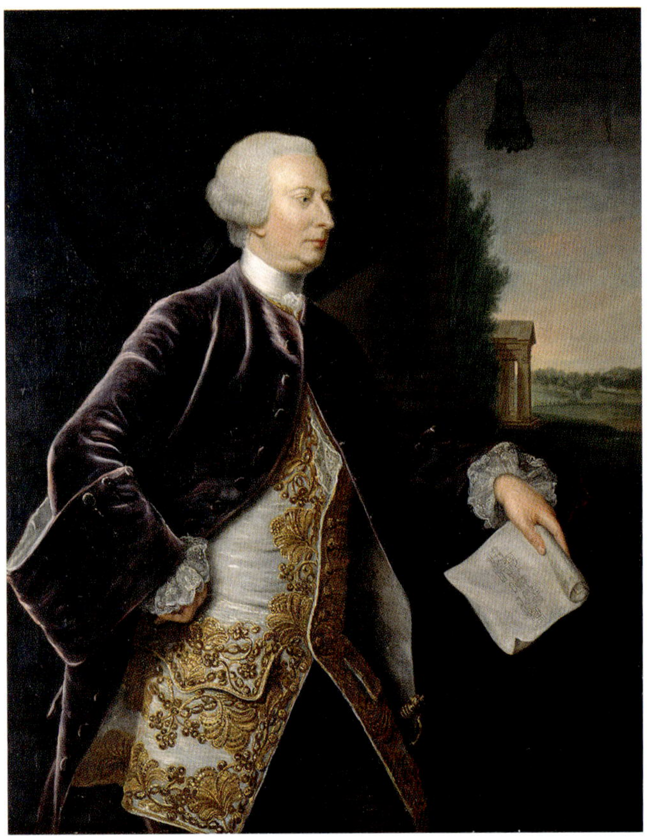

Fig. 112 Gabriel Mathias, *John Chute*, 1758. The Vyne, Hampshire. Photo © National Trust Images.

The Vyne, Hampshire, and the Patronage of John Chute

John Chute (1701–1776) was the most capable but least likely patron of architecture in Walpole's circle (fig. 112). Youngest of ten children, he was not groomed to inherit the family estate—the Vyne in Hampshire—and instead spent much of his early life abroad as a connoisseur and dilettante. Chute's acquisition of the Vyne came about unexpectedly with the death of his brother Francis in 1754, when he became heir presumptive to the extraordinary Tudor house. In Italy he acquired some of the foreign affectations of connoisseurs, such as carrying a fan and wearing a monocle.[30] A part of the homoerotic circle of antiquaries including Joachim Winckelmann, Baron Philipp von Stosch, and Horace Walpole's cousin, Horace Mann, Chute likewise surrounded himself with younger men. At the time of his return from the Grand Tour and the untimely death of Francis Whitehead, in 1751, the younger Walpole and Chute, as noted above, developed a bond that would last the rest of their lives (until Chute's death in 1776), centered around the developing architecture of Strawberry Hill, the Vyne, and other buildings.

Chute's acquisition of the Vyne in 1754 provided a new focus for the medievalist research and designs of the Strawberry Committee (fig. 113). It was the most historically significant building that they would work on, and it naturally appealed to the architectural, genealogical,

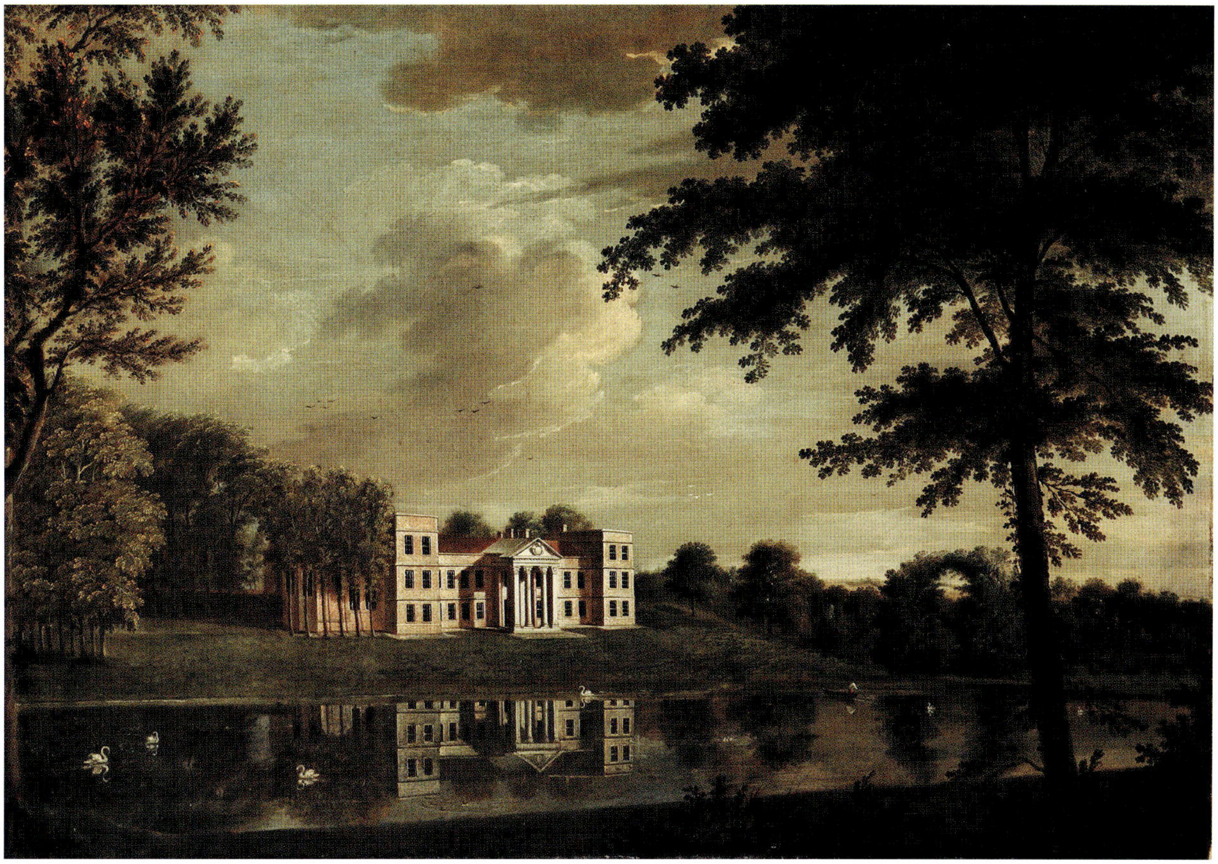

Fig. 113 J. H. Müntz, *The Vyne from the North East*. Photo © National Trust Images.

and antiquarian interests of Walpole and Chute. Created by William, first Lord Sandys (1470–1540), who was chaplain to Henry VIII, the Vyne was a Tudor palace that hosted the king and his court, and Sandys would play a minor part in Shakespeare's *Henry VIII*. Walpole went with Chute right away and encouraged him to begin work at the Vyne.[31] By July of the following year, Walpole had prepared an "Inventionary," which was essentially a list of works that had been voted upon by the Strawberry Committee.[32] The Inventionary essentially proposed to extend the Strawberry Hill Gothic mode to the Vyne, including strategies of ordering and displaying imagery. The Inventionary, for example, proposes that Chute's "great parlour" feature paintings of Chute himself and his Dacre relatives, as well as, "Over the doors, heads of Mr Whithead, Mr Gray, Mr Bentley, and Mr Walpole,"[33] a queer family romance in portraiture analogous in many respects to the portraits by John Giles Eccardt that had just been hung in the Blue Bedchamber at Strawberry Hill. It is not clear whether these were from an extant series of portraits or if, like Walpole, Chute was to commission a new series (Chute's pastel sketch

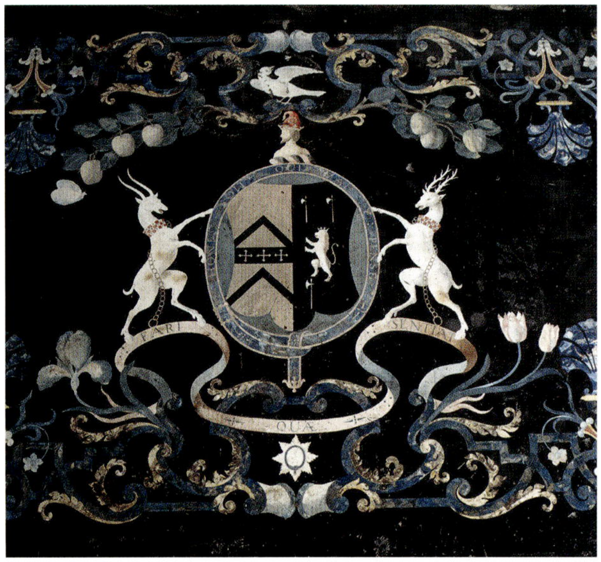

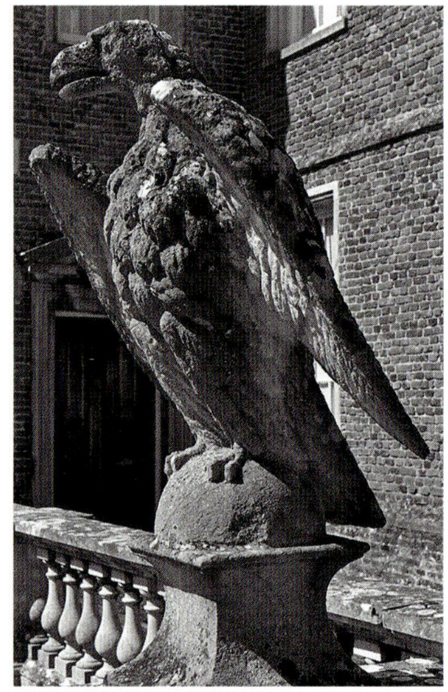

Fig. 114 Detail of the scagliola tabletop in the Oak Gallery at the Vyne, Hampshire, featuring the Walpole arms and motto, *Fari quae sentiat*. Photo © National Trust Images.

Fig. 115 Stonework eagle at the Vyne, Hampshire. Photo © National Trust Images.

of Francis Whitehead by Rosalba Carriera still hangs at the Vyne). Typical of his strategies for referencing related buildings at Strawberry, Walpole advised hanging images of Strawberry Hill in the Vyne's great drawing room. To emphasize his own role in Chute's life and home, he gave Chute furnishings from his own family collection, including the scagliola table with the Walpole arms and motto (*Fari quae sentiat*) from Houghton Hall (fig. 114).[34] Tradition acknowledges the stone eagles on the exterior of the Vyne as a gift from Horace Walpole (fig. 115).[35] If so, the eagles are deeply referential images that lead back to Walpole's own Boccapadugli Eagle as a homoerotic symbol within Walpole's circle (fig. 66). The Inventionary also mentions the first of at least two "Strawberry rooms" that would be built within his circle, which he describes as "the little Strawberry parlour."[36] This is a small wood-paneled ground-floor room that was hung with architectural drawings created inside Walpole's circle, themselves testament to the shared tastes and labor of the two men.

Although the design of the Vyne was an effort shared among Walpole, Chute, and other members of the Committee, many of the ideas that they offered either would not be accepted or would only be executed a decade and a half (or more) later. Chute considered a range of possible projects at the Vyne, including a comprehensive transformation of the south front of the house into a symmetrical Gothic design with square-headed late Gothic windows and labels similar to those he drew for Donnington. His plans for the south front are recorded in a handful of his drawings and in his remarkable portrait by Gabriel Mathias of 1758, in which he appears surveying his estate, holding a sketch of his own designs (figs. 112, 116).[37] In the same years, Walpole urged him to press forward with building works and employed Richard Bentley to design a Gothic columbarium, which was never executed. This was one of two such designs conceived contemporaneously: in 1758 Walpole asked Bentley to design a second columbarium for Strawberry Hill, which was also never executed.[38] Writing to George

Montagu in 1757, Walpole recounts his frustrations: "I have done advising, as I see Mr Chute will never execute anything."[39] For reasons that pertain as much to finance as to Chute's own inherently cautious nature, these early proposals were abandoned, and Chute would not execute any major works until 1770.

Chute's major changes to the Vyne were in the central staircase (fig. 117) and in the chapel. The staircase is a stunning, if compromised, design that Chute worked up over seventy drawings before it was finally built.[40] The end result is a richly textured classical (or "Grecian") staircase in a hall with fluted Doric columns at ground-floor level and Corinthian fluted columns on the first floor. Superficially at least, Chute's remarkable staircase and hall might seem antithetical to his overwhelmingly Gothic tastes. But as a house of historical significance, the Vyne presented a challenge fundamentally different from Walpole's "chopp'd Straw Hall," Donnington, or Old Windsor. Chute's work never attempted to create anything like the fictive medieval interiors of Strawberry Hill or the overtly monastic air of Old Windsor; rather, Chute's work balanced the original influences evident in the fabric of the home he inherited, which were both Gothic and Palladian. Chute's intention appears to have been to echo the forms of John Webb's pedimented north

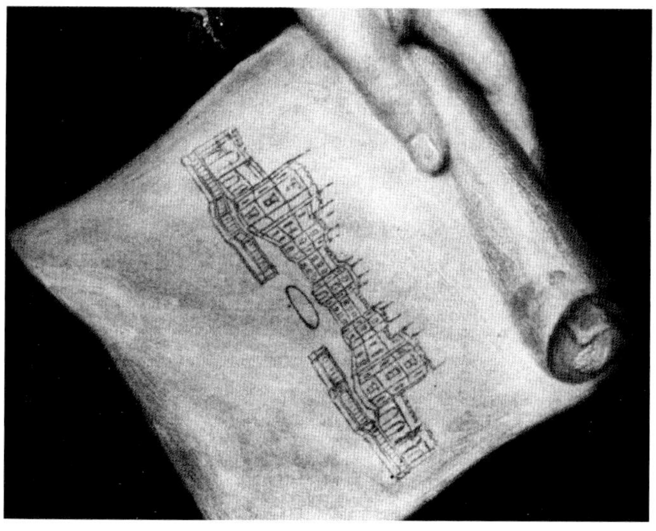

Fig. 116 Façade designs in the hand of John Chute, detail of figure 112. After McCarthy, *Origins of the Gothic Revival* (1987), plate 136.

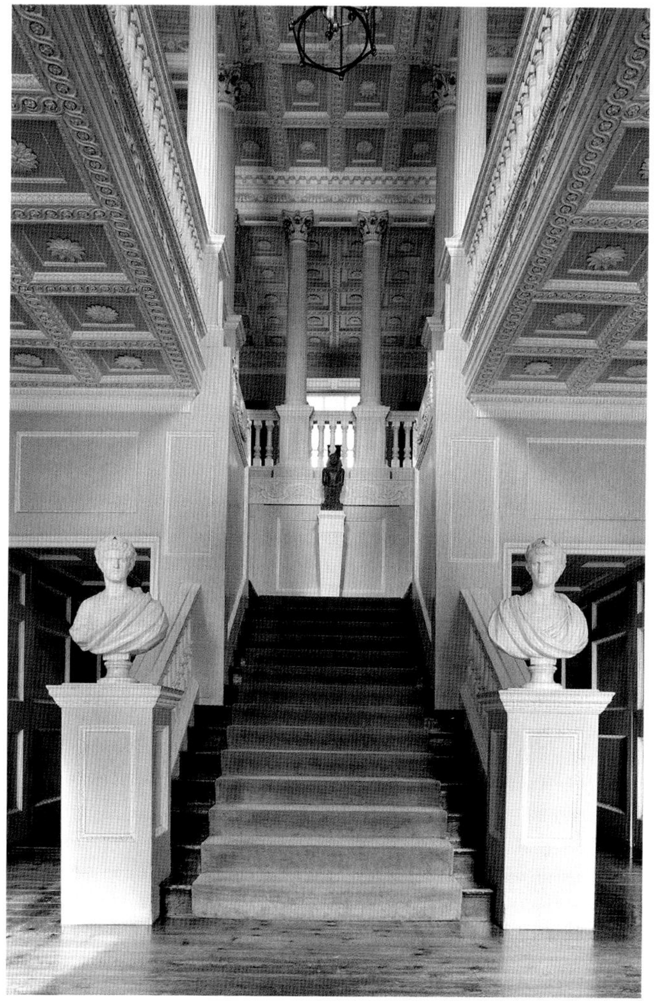

Fig. 117 The staircase hall at the Vyne, Hampshire. Photo © National Trust Images.

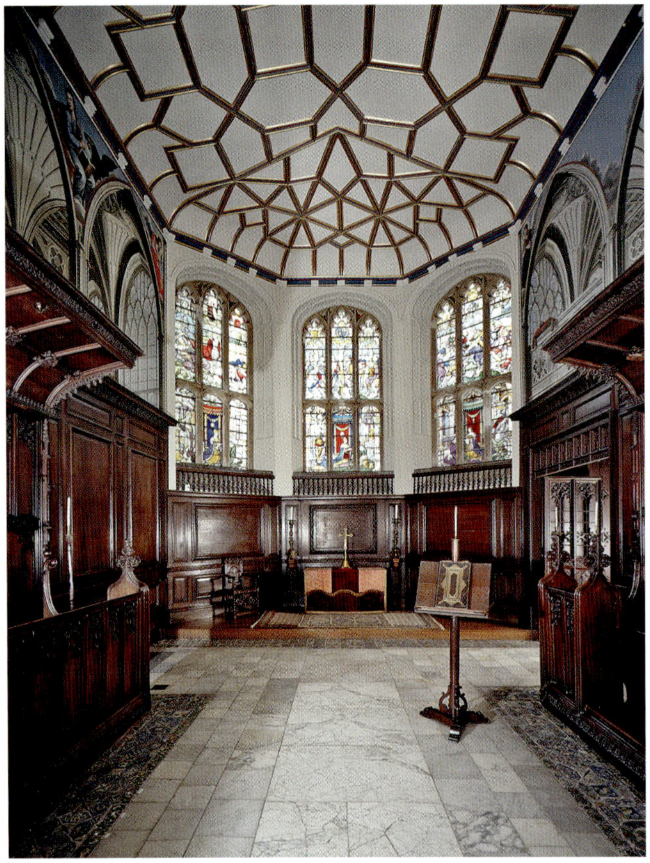

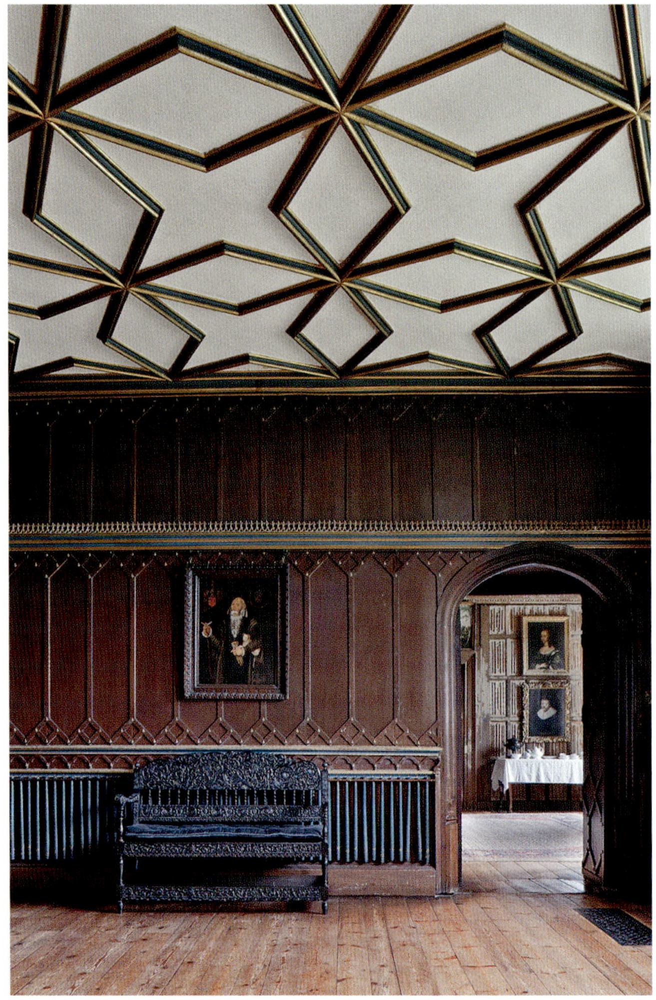

Fig. 118 The chapel at the Vyne, Hampshire, facing east. Photo © National Trust Images.

Fig. 119 The antechapel, the Vyne, Hampshire. Photo © National Trust Images.

front, created in the 1650s for Chaloner Chute. (The seventeenth-century history of the house featured in *Anecdotes of Painting*, in which Walpole rightly revised the attribution of the seventeenth-century portico from Inigo Jones to John Webb.)[41]

Chute's most remarkable work at the Vyne was contained within the Gothic chapel (fig. 118). An altered but integral part of the Tudor palace, the chapel was one of the most beautiful interiors designed within Walpole's milieu. Walpole wrote about it in rapturous terms: "At the Vine [*sic*] is the most heavenly chapel in the world; it only wants a few pictures to give it a true Catholic air."[42] But Chute's work extended beyond decoration: his project was a sensitive transformation of the Tudor chapel that significantly enhanced its liturgical function and its overtly Catholic glamour while also emphasizing continuity with the Gothic fabric and the historical associations with the Chute family. Chute's main contributions to the chapel were the renovation of the antechapel, the addition of a chamber and tomb commemorating Chaloner Chute (d. 1659), who brought the Tudor palace into the Chute family, and the trompe l'oeil painting of the wall space above the choir stalls on the north, south, and west walls. Although plans for all of these works were proposed in the 1754/55 Inventionary, it seems that few, if any, were carried out immediately. In the 1750s Walpole and Chute sought out for the chapel an altarpiece and paintings from Italy (via Horace Mann) and stained glass in England, but they appear to have been stored.[43] A flood of new light has been shed on the chapel due to recent conservation work, and it is now reasonably certain that most of its design and execution did not begin until 1769 or 1770.[44]

Beginning in the chapel antechamber (fig. 119), the Inventionary states that it should "be finished as the end is," meaning that the walls were to be covered in wooden fretwork consistent with the extant paneling in the eastern part of the room,[45] thus suggesting stylistic continuity between old and new. It seems that the Committee's intention to paint trompe l'oeil architecture in the chapel was suggested as early as 1754, the date of Walpole's first visit, when he and Bentley hoped to get Müntz to "paint perspectives, and cathedral-aisles, and holy glooms."[46] The Walpole-Müntz scheme—or, rather, a version of it—was realized in 1769–70 by Spiridione Roma, a Greek painter hired by Chute.[47] Recent conservation has uncovered fragments of Gothic wallpaper, which suggests that the initial scheme was achieved in wallpaper similar to that employed by Walpole, Thomas Warton, and others in the period.[48] Roma's paintings would be executed in oil on canvas, stretched over a wooden substructure, and hung in three panels over the north, south, and west walls of the choir above the choir stalls (fig. 120). The final scheme, with three arched openings along the north and south walls, may have been intended to mirror the original architecture of the chapel, which had had windows along the lateral walls (fig. 121). Designed to privilege the perspective of the viewer at floor level gazing across the chapel, the north and south canvases dissolve the wall space into stunning aisle vaults. The form of the painted fan vaulting and aspects of the window tracery are based upon the fourteenth-century cloister of Gloucester Abbey, a monument known to Horace Walpole and celebrated by contemporary antiquaries such as William Stukeley, who considered them to be evidence of the Gothic's origins in the natural forms of the forest.[49] Roma's west-wall, or screen-wall, painting is a theatrical curtain, open at the center and heavily falling over either side of the Gothic screen that separates the "Closet," or gallery, above the antechapel, which allowed Lord

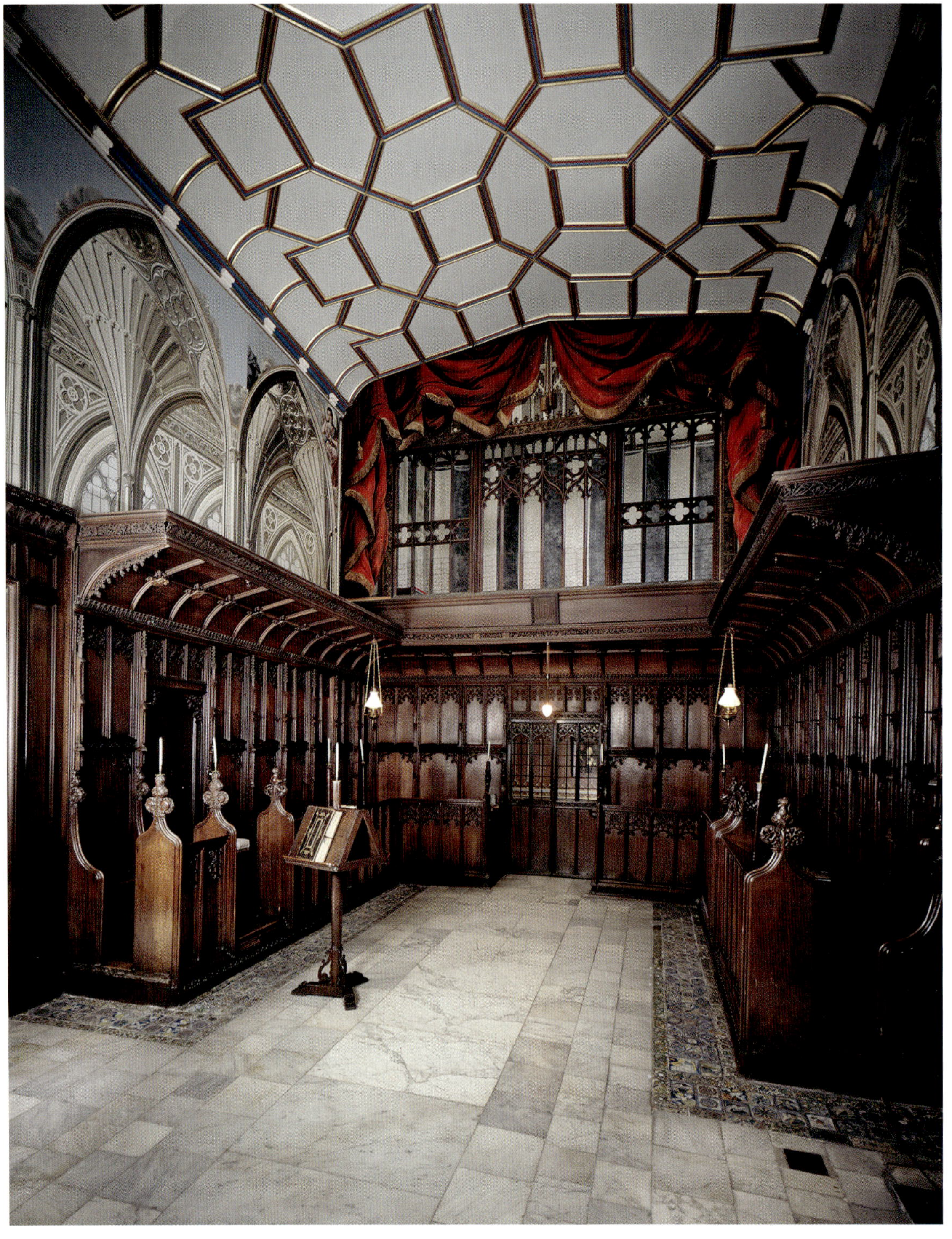

Fig. 120 The chapel at the Vyne, Hampshire, facing west, showing painted scheme by Spiridione Roma (1737–1787). Photo © National Trust Images.

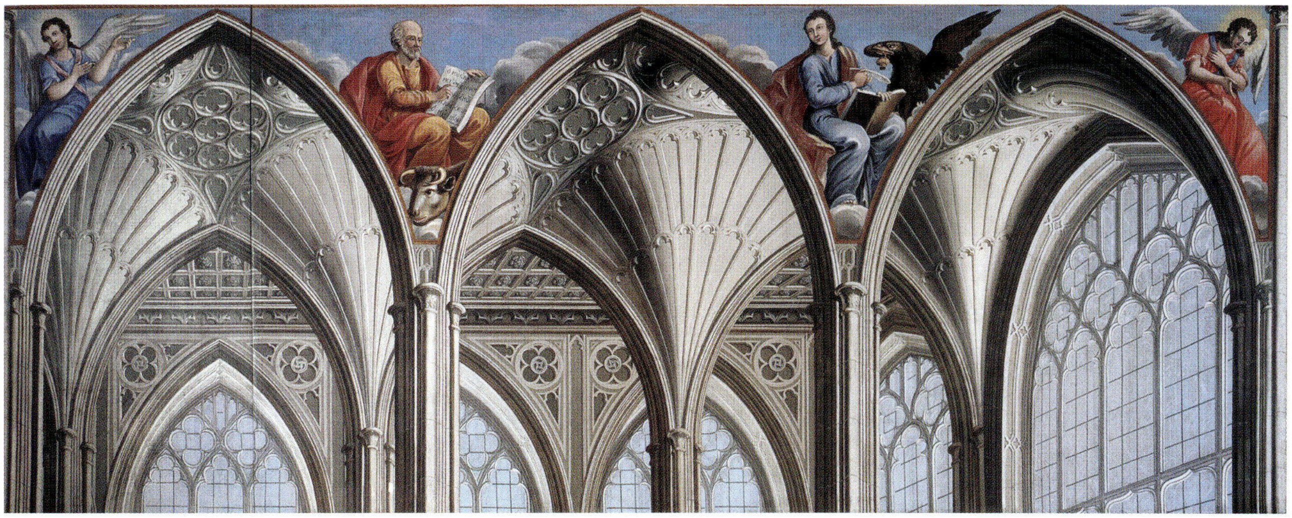

Fig. 121 Decorations by Spiridione Roma on the north wall of the chapel at the Vyne, Hampshire. Photo © National Trust Images.

Sandys and his successors an uninterrupted view of the altar. Technical examination of this canvas shows that the curtain scheme is painted on top of an earlier scheme of fictive Gothic tracery. A palimpsest, the west wall panel was originally painted to reflect the tracery in the eastern wall of the chapel. The curtain designs and the Gothic wooden tracery screen were designed by John Chute as a change to Roma's initial designs.[50] The changes to the paintings may be due to Chute's dismissal of Roma for his idleness after only two years' work. A drawing by Chute in the Hampshire Record Office is clearly an early version of the design (fig. 122). The curtain, or veil, whatever the circumstances of its creation, was integral to the program of the chapel imagined by Chute. Located at the entry to the chapel, the parted veil had a lengthy heritage in Catholic art, signifying the unveiled spirit of revelation.[51] Understood in these terms, the parted veil and the Evangelists in Roma's lateral canvasses suggest the unfolding drama of the life of Christ, terminating in the east window's Tudor glazing scheme of the Crucifixion, whereby the redeeming blood and body of Christ is consumed at the Eucharist at the altar directly below. Such a reading

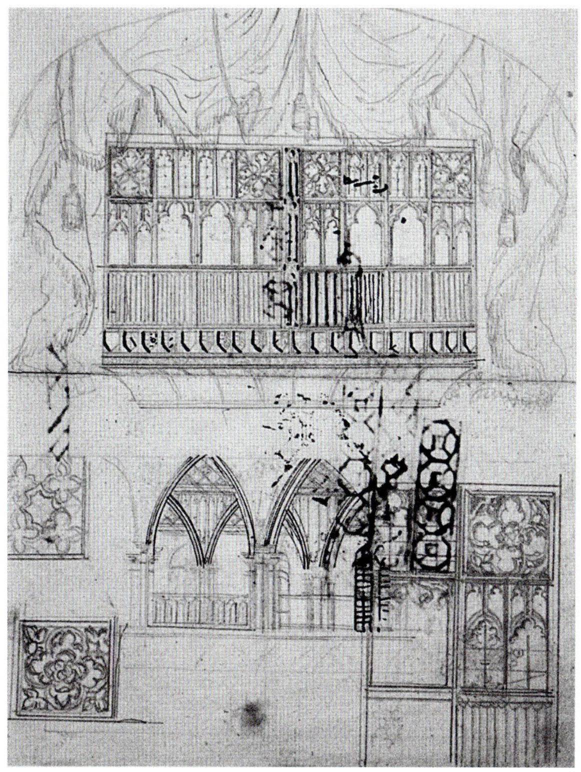

Fig. 122 John Chute's drawing of the west wall of the chapel at the Vyne, Hampshire, showing a scheme for a fictive veil. HantsRO 31M-57/652. Photo: author.

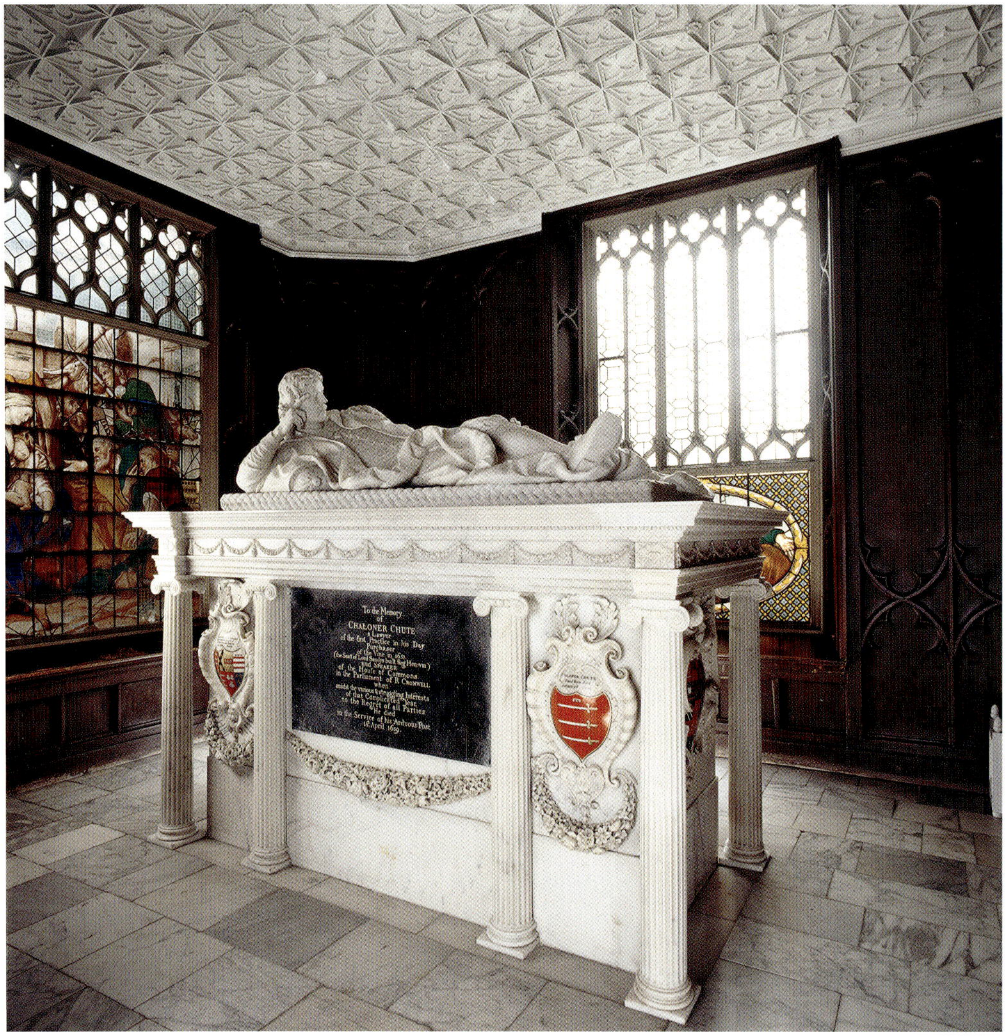

Fig. 123 The interior of the tomb chamber at the Vyne, Hampshire. © National Trust Images.

presupposes a scholarly understanding of the liturgical interior, one that respects and integrates earlier and later imagery into a coherent iconographic whole.

Chute's final commission in the chapel was the tomb and chamber commemorating Chaloner Chute (ca. 1770; fig. 123). At the center of it was the monument to Chute by Thomas Carter (d. 1795), which was not created until 1775–81, after John Chute's death.[52] Although the celebration of family ancestors was common in Walpole's circle—for example, Walpole's commemoration of Sir Terry Robsart and his brass commemorating Ralph Walpole (fig. 69)—the idea of creating a cenotaph to a family ancestor was unprecedented. Chute's decision to honor Chaloner Chute is surely explained by his interest in family genealogy as much as by his ancestor's role as Speaker of the House of Commons and his place in the Civil War. It has also been suggested that Chute's status as an unmarried man without any direct descendants informed his decision to subordinate his own claims to remembrance and direct attention backward toward his illustrious ancestor.[53] The chamber was built upon the foundations of a previous structure in the angle between the south chapel wall and the vestry, and it can be concisely dated to 1770/71.[54] As noted above, Walpole asked Bentley to make drawings for a columbarium at the Vyne in the 1750s, which were praised by Walpole but seemingly not considered by Chute. Bentley never saw the Vyne, and his drawings were made at Walpole's request, which surely explains why they were awkward not only in terms of style but also because they were intended for a family chapel with various niches and urns rather than a dedicatory chapel to a single ancestor, which was Chute's final design.[55]

As Hilary G. Wayment and Michael McCarthy have suggested, the form of the chamber may have been based on the Holy Trinity Chapel at the Chapel of the Holy Ghost in Basingstoke, which was also the likely origin of the sixteenth-century stained glass in the chapel windows (they were probably installed at the Vyne by Edward Chute [1685–1722]).[56] If so, Chute's decisions would be based on keen historical and architectural precedent, since the Vyne and the Holy Ghost Chapel were both erected under the patronage of William Sandys. But even if the form was based on an extant (though partial) structure, the Gothic designs were Chute's own. The repeating round quatrefoils are from the same repertoire of Gothic designs as the wooden screen in the watching chamber, and the wooden paneling in the tomb chamber, with its cinquefoil-headed lancets, is based ultimately on the forms of the chapel's sixteenth-century east windows. Chute's designs for the tomb chamber's ceiling, featuring a grid of intersecting four-pointed stars and sharpened quatrefoils, is most closely related to the design of the Holbein Chamber at Strawberry Hill. A small, intimate space, its east window is filled with a large early eighteenth-century stained-glass window by John Rowell showing the Adoration of the Shepherds, based on Anthony Van Dyck's 1626–28 painting (now Kunsthalle, Hamburg), while its south window has an oval Adoration by William Price (ca. 1750). Ostensibly designing the chapel around glass he purchased in the 1750s,[57] Chute created six-light windows that could be lengthened or shortened to allow for the varying size of the windows. His selection of two windows with a common iconography in the tomb chamber is not easily explained. Both, however, are based on seventeenth-century models and were very likely intended to reflect the period of the chapel's dedicatee, Chaloner Chute.

Aside from Strawberry Hill, Chute's work at the Vyne and in the chapel in particular received the greatest attention from Walpole and the Committee. Although Gothic "chapels" were built at Strawberry Hill and Old Windsor, the chapel at the Vyne was the only actual (potentially) functional chapel conceived within Walpole's circle. In Walpole's many commentaries on the chapel, its Catholic*ness*—its exemplification of what Walpole understood to be a Catholic religious aesthetic—was central. As I noted above, Walpole's intention was to reendow the chapel with "a true Catholic air." He consistently polarized Catholicism and Protestantism, associating them with unreformed and reformed aesthetics: one apparently sensorially rich and mysterious, the other minimal and rational. Horace Mann, for example, could claim: "I will endeavor to get a Last Supper [painting for the Vyne] which shall edify the most delicate Protestant believer"; and Walpole: "we are so conscious of the goodness of our Protestantism, that we don't care how things look."[58] Sharing much of the same terrain with his conception of the Gothic, Walpole's commentary on Catholicism is pitched as social criticism. Catholic aesthetics, its apparently illicit nature polarized opposite the "goodness" of Protestantism, become those of unreformed human sensibilities—the human condition unregulated by social controls.

It is thus not a surprise that the chapel at the Vyne served as a significant space for Walpole and his circle to perform their interests in Catholicism. On his first visit to the Vyne, in 1754, Walpole, George Selwyn, Chute, and others performed a version of the Catholic Mass in the chapel: "I carried down incense and mass-books, and we had most Catholic enjoyment of the chapel. In the evenings, indeed, we did *touch a card* a little to please George. . . . There is a vote of the Strawberry committee for great embellishments to the chapel, of which it will not be long before you hear something."[59] Walpole's quick movement from sacred (if mock) ritual to playing cards and interior design suggests something of the levity of the affair. Writing shortly afterward about the event to George Montagu, Walpole notes, "Mr Chute . . . was so pleased with the tenebrae in his own chapel, that he has fairly buried himself in it."[60] While we will never know the precise nature of this and other mock liturgies in Walpole's circle, they were based on a sophisticated understanding and appropriation of Catholicism: these men used Catholic/Gothic tropes to describe their homes as "monasteries" and "nunneries," and themselves as "abbots" and "brother monks." Sexuality accounts for at least one level of signification, since these comments trope Walpole and his circle as monosexual monastics, thereby alluding to Catholicism as an allegory of homoerotic brotherhood.

Chute and Walpole shared a lengthy friendship, much of which was expressed through a shared love of art, architecture, and collecting. Walpole's lament at the death of Chute in 1776 is one of the most beautiful and moving passages anywhere in his writings: "and now I have lost Mr Chute! It is a heavy blow; but such strokes reconcile one's self to parting with this pretty vision, life! What is it, when one has no longer those to whom one speaks as confidentially as to one's own soul? . . . Mr Chute and I agreed invariably in our principles; he was my counsel in my affairs, was my oracle in taste, the standard to whom I submitted my trifles, and the genius that presided over poor Strawberry!"[61] Although they regularly disagreed over specific issues and Chute's cautious nature rightly balanced Walpole's own impetuosity, the Vyne, Strawberry Hill, and Donnington Grove now stand as vital testaments to the friendship between two men.[62]

Lee Priory, Kent, and the Patronage of Thomas Barrett

Thomas Barrett's Lee Priory in Kent represents an important monument in the history of Gothic architecture and probably the most obvious homage to Strawberry Hill created within Walpole's milieu (fig. 124). It was designed by the leading architect of the late eighteenth century, James Wyatt, and decorated in part by John Carter (1748–1817). That it has not, until recently, enjoyed a more important place in the historiography of Gothic architecture can only be due to George Gilbert Scott's interior and exterior alterations, whereby brickwork replaced its original white stucco exterior, and, ultimately, the house's sad destruction in 1953. Fortunately, our understanding of the house and its interiors is facilitated by a wealth of documentary, antiquarian, and material evidence, much of which has recently come to light.[63]

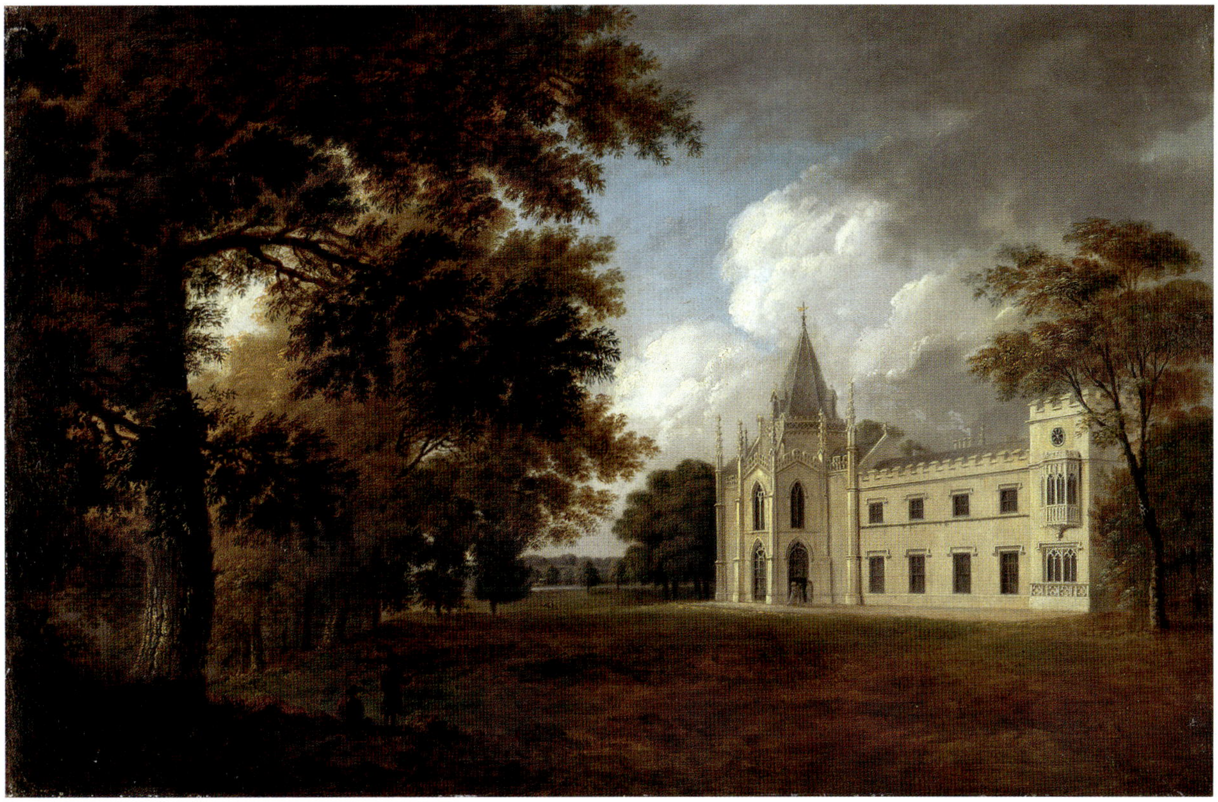

Fig. 124 John Dixon, *View of the South Façade of Lee Priory*, ca. 1800. Yale Centre for British Art, Paul Mellon Collection. Photo: Yale Centre for British Art.

Barrett's own place in the social and cultural world of English medievalism, architecture, and antiquarianism has also not been fully understood, and although he cut a less public figure than Horace Walpole, Hugh Honour's view of him as "one of the less notable members of Walpole's circle" now requires revision.[64] Barrett traveled to France and Italy on the Grand Tour, where he appears to have met George Chamberlayne (1739–1815), who would be a lifelong friend, and Lord Lincoln (Henry Fiennes Pelham-Clinton [1750–78], son of Walpole's much-loved cousin Henry Pelham Clinton [1720–94]). Via his familial connection to Lincoln, Walpole asked Horace Mann to receive them in Florence.[65] Chamberlayne's letters to Barrett recount aspects of their adventures that were conducted in the company of the sodomitical circle around Norton Nicholls (1742–1809, the friend and correspondent of Thomas Gray with whom Barrett lived in Florence) and the Scottish architect Lord Findlater (1750–1811), who had been exiled for homosexual offenses.[66] This youthful circle would remain constant for the rest of these men's lives.

Walpole, Gray, and Nicholls were senior men of taste, and their circle frequently overlapped with the younger circle around Barrett, almost thirty years junior to Walpole. Barrett and Walpole had what the latter called "a most sincere friendship."[67] Walpole mentored Barrett, providing him publications from the Strawberry Hill press and advising him on his architectural patronage and on the expansion of his art collection.[68] Barrett was also friendly with Thomas Gray, perhaps via Walpole or Norton Nicholls.[69] A significant collector, patron, and medievalist in his own right, Barrett shared many of the passions of the men in Walpole's circle, including an interest in Gothic art and its Catholic associations.[70] He would acquire William Cole's copy of Walpole's *Description* in the 1780s, after Cole's death.[71] Walpole, as it happens, had long known Lee and the Barrett family, having purchased parts of Thomas Barrett's father's art collection for Strawberry Hill in 1758, including the Limoges reliquary of Thomas Becket (fig. 15).[72] Also in the Barrett collection were the extraordinary Limoges candlesticks of circa 1180 (fig. 125) now in the Cloisters Museum, New York (although it is not clear whether Barrett Sr. or Barrett Jr. purchased them).[73] Thomas Barrett Jr.'s posthumous portrait appears in John Carter's "Occurrences in the Life, and Memorandums Relating to the Professional Persuits [*sic*] of J. C., F.A.S. Architect" (1817), showing the subject as a gentleman scholar and elite patron of the Gothic (fig. 126), alongside portraits of Horace Walpole, Richard Gough, Richard Bull (who commissioned Carter to draw the Strawberry Hill interiors), and others within Walpole's circle.[74] Carter's volume provides not only a visual and textual history of his patrons but also an account of the significant medievalists of the later eighteenth century, positing across his drawings and verbal portraits of these men a shared historical and aesthetic subjectivity. Barrett died unmarried in 1803, after converting to Catholicism the previous year.[75]

Lee Priory can now be studied in a dossier of photographs and antiquarian drawings, descriptions, and letters; the Strawberry Room (or Strawberry Closet) and its furniture, and furniture from the library, now at the Victoria and Albert Museum (figs. 127,

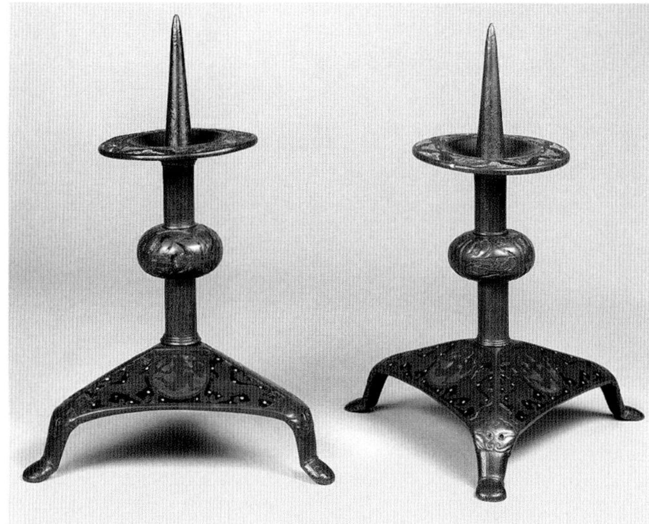

Fig. 125 Limoges champlevé enamel candlesticks from Lee Priory, ca. 1180. Formerly in Thomas Barrett's collection at Lee Priory. Now The Cloisters Collection, The Metropolitan Museum of Art, New York, 47.101.38. Photo: The Metropolitan Museum of Art, www.metmuseum.org.

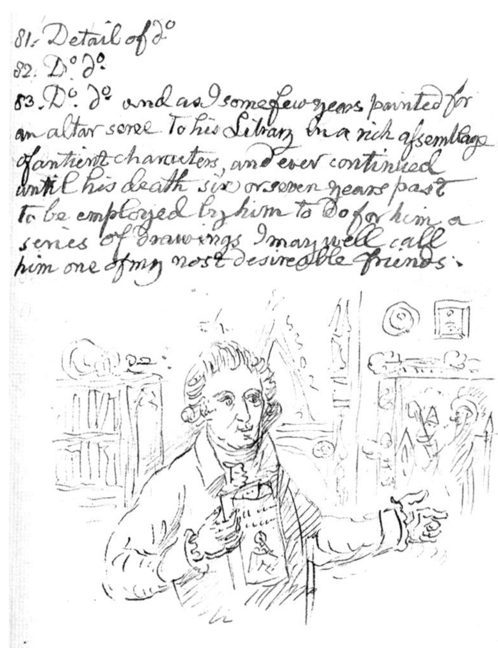

Fig. 126 John Carter, posthumous portrait of Thomas Barrett in his library, ca. 1817. King's College London, Leathes 7/4 17r. King's College London Archives.

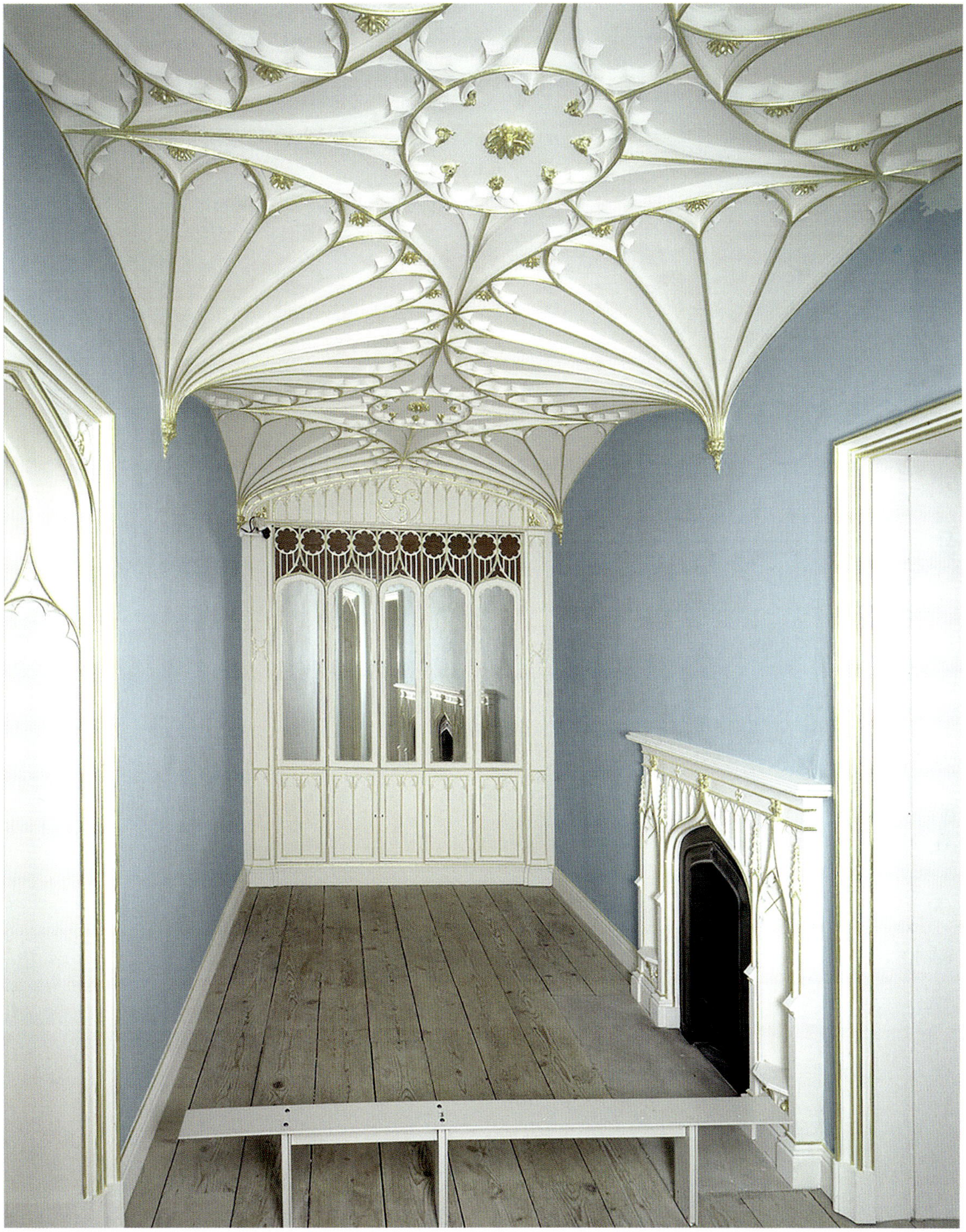

Fig. 127 James Wyatt, the Strawberry Room, Lee Priory, ca. 1785–90, built for Thomas Barrett. Victoria and Albert Museum, London, W.48.1–1953. Photo © Victoria and Albert Museum, London.

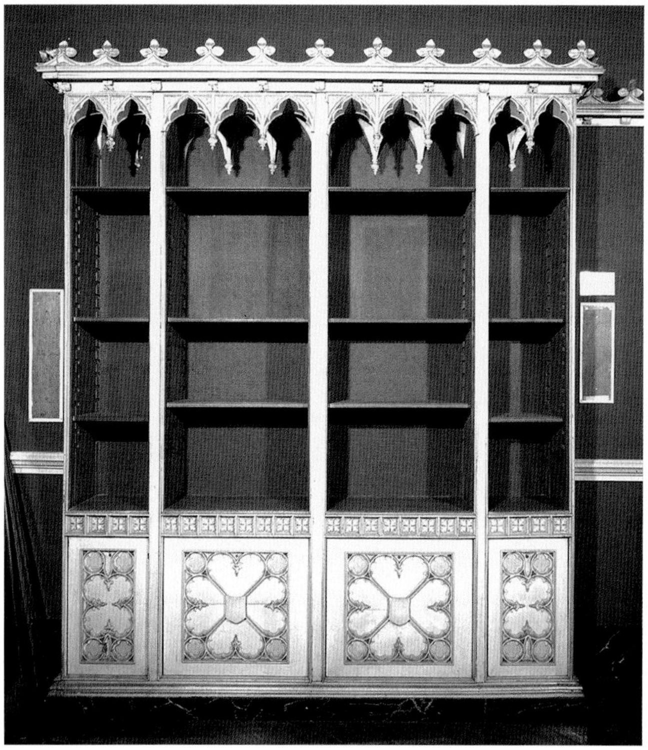

Fig. 128 James Wyatt, bookcase from Lee Priory library, ca. 1785–90. Victoria and Albert Museum, London, W.51–1953. Photo © Victoria and Albert Museum, London.

128); and the fragments of the library antechamber and its furniture currently in a private collection.[76] Like the majority of building projects undertaken by members of Walpole's circle, Barrett's was a comprehensive renovation of an existing structure, apparently seventeenth-century in date, rather than a new build. Unfortunately, nothing significant is known about the form of the seventeenth-century house.[77] Upon the death of his father in 1757, Thomas Barrett acquired Lee at the age of thirteen. The first evidence of work at the site comes from 1780, when Walpole visited the house and commented on recent work on its grounds.[78] In Walpole's next commentary, of August 1785, he claims to have seen James Wyatt's plans (multiple times) and "approve[d] them exceedingly."[79] Although 1785 has been taken to indicate that works at Lee were just about to begin, it is far more likely that Walpole's initial visit, of 1780, was the catalyst. By September 1781 Barratt appears to have engaged the services of James Wyatt to renovate the house, in the same year he began corresponding with John Carter over paintings for his home, and in 1782 unspecified works appear to have been in the planning stage, if not under way.[80] There is no reason to doubt that Walpole introduced and recommended Barrett to Wyatt (and no doubt to John Carter as well).[81] A 1785 drawing now in the British Library shows the tower and north frontage complete, which provides a likely *terminus ante quem* for the structure at Lee, but work on the interiors continued until circa 1790 (fig. 129). Wyatt sent his foreman, Mr. Matthews, to view Strawberry Hill in 1788, doubtless to inform aspects of his subsequent work.[82] It was not until 1794, only three years before his death, that Walpole commented upon Barrett's Strawberry Room, a room made self-consciously as an homage to Strawberry Hill. Given the dedicatory nature of the room, the plans for it were likely the ones presented to Walpole for his rapturous approval in 1785. "Great Works" were still imagined in 1802 (probably to the gardens) with the help of Norton Nicholls, but Barrett's failing health meant that they were never realized.[83]

Wyatt prepared both Gothic and neoclassical designs for Lee, but Barrett naturally chose the former, even if some of the final interiors had classical detailing, including the central staircase.[84] Part of the brief for Lee was, to be sure, to create a series of calculated allusions to Strawberry Hill. Scott's preparatory ground plan of the house, which survives, shows the *piano nobile* before its Victorian restoration (fig. 130). Based upon a central stair accessing three levels of the house built off all four sides, Lee is modeled most evidently after Strawberry

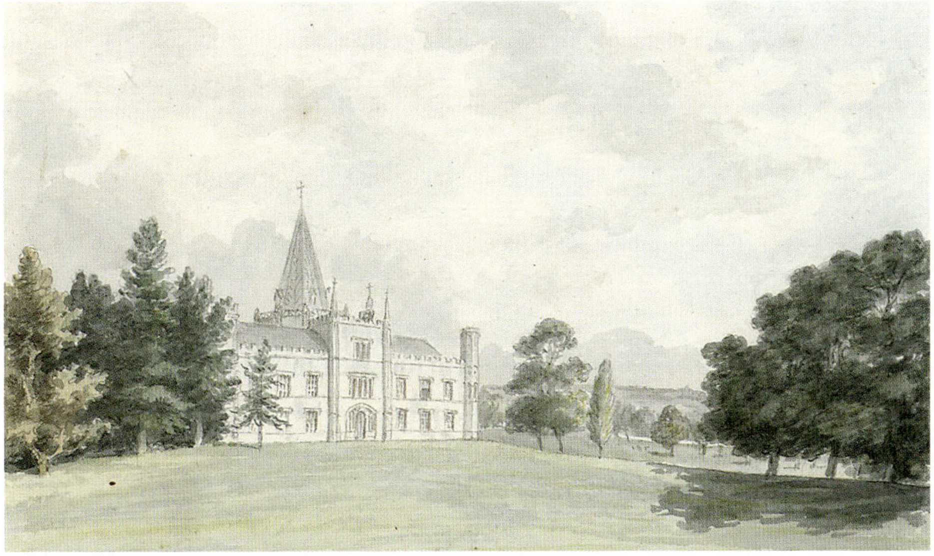

Fig. 129 John Carter (attrib.), "North view of Lee, the seat of Thos. Barrett Esq., near Canterbury, Taken 1785." British Library, London, Add MS 32366, fol. 40. Photo © The British Library Board.

Fig. 130 Lee Priory, ground plan. Created by Peter N. Lindfield.

Fig. 131 Dominican monastery of Batalha, Portugal, ca. 1386–1517. Photo: author.

Hill. As is well known, Wyatt's designs for the central octagon were based upon drawings of the crossing tower of Batalha, Portugal (fig. 131), a model that Wyatt would transform for his greatest Gothic building, William Beckford's Fonthill Abbey, a decade later.[85] It is less well known that interest in Batalha originated within Walpole's milieu. Batalha was an important source for eighteenth-century English Gothic designs via the 1760 account by Thomas Pitt that was circulated within antiquarian circles and eventually copied.[86] Describing the monastery as "the most elaborate & exquisite Gothic architecture I ever saw," Pitt believed that, due to its associations with English aristocracy, "it was executed by an Englishman."[87] Upon his return, Pitt became an adjunct to the Strawberry Committee—according to Walpole: "one of the very few that I reckon quite worthy of being at home at Strawberry."[88] Barrett's and Wyatt's knowledge of this important building was very likely mediated by Walpole.

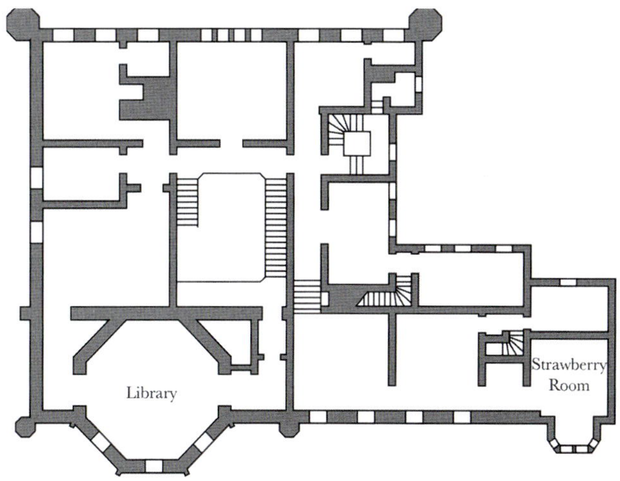

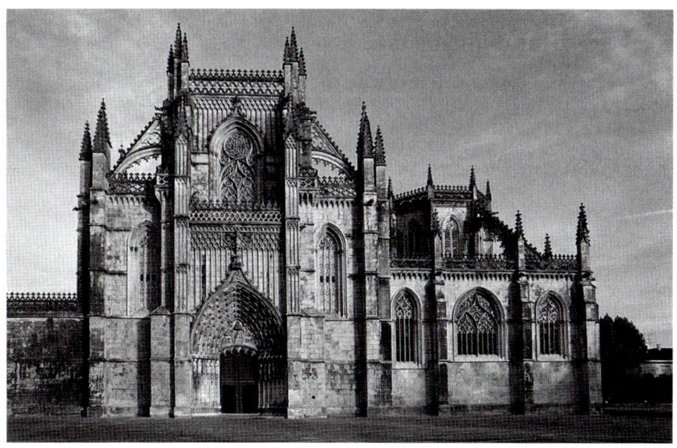

The remainder of the designs for Lee Priory appear to have been English in derivation. Its façades and many of its interior details were, for most viewers, intended to re-create a conventual setting based upon

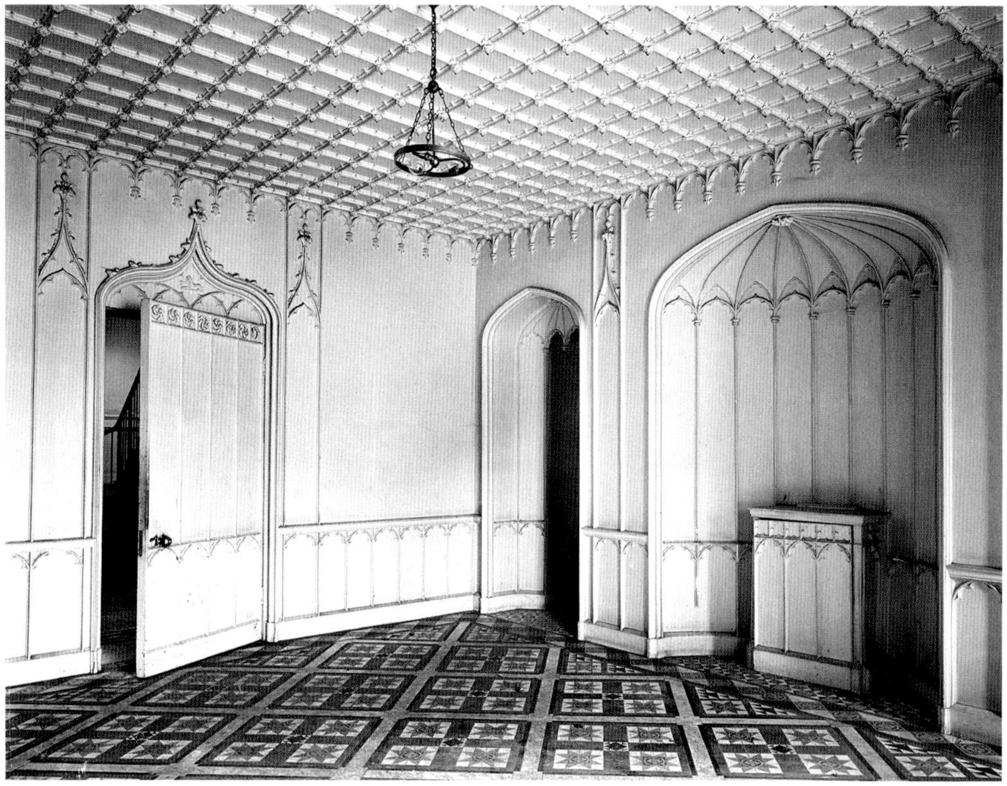

Fig. 132 Lee Priory entrance hall. By permission of Historic England Archive.

English precedents. The entrance hall was a stunning design of blind Decorated tracery patterns across its walls and doors, and a latticework ceiling of pointed quatrefoils terminating in a rich cornice (fig. 132). This ceiling may well have represented a creative, plastic response to the trompe l'oeil coffering on the entrance, or Paraclete, of Strawberry Hill. But the most straightforward allusion to Strawberry Hill was Barrett's Strawberry Room, a small room (221 × 572 cm) with a low fan-vaulted ceiling and a single fireplace, at the opposite end of the first floor from Barrett's library (fig. 127). The Strawberry Room was partially remodeled in Scott's restorations with a second doorway and a bay window in place of the original end window. A 1791 sketch by John Carter (fig. 133) entitled "View in the Walpole Closet" provides some idea of the original form and furnishings of the room as well as the original fenestration. Notable among the furnishings were the "ancient, of black ebony, curiously carved" stools.[89] These were what Walpole called "the true black blood" and were believed either to be medieval or to be appropriate to a medievalist interior (Walpole, Bateman, and eventually William Beckford employed them in their homes).[90] At the thematic center of the Strawberry Room, in the privileged space above the mantelpiece, was a single framed image: a copy of John Giles Eccardt's portrait of Horace Walpole from the Blue Bedchamber at Strawberry Hill (fig. 76) that Barrett commissioned (visible in fig. 133).[91] As noted above, Barrett's was one of at least two "Strawberry rooms" built in Walpole's circle, including that at the Vyne. But Barrett's room does not simply reference Walpole and his home, it also represents something like an embodiment of its dedicatee. Anchored by the

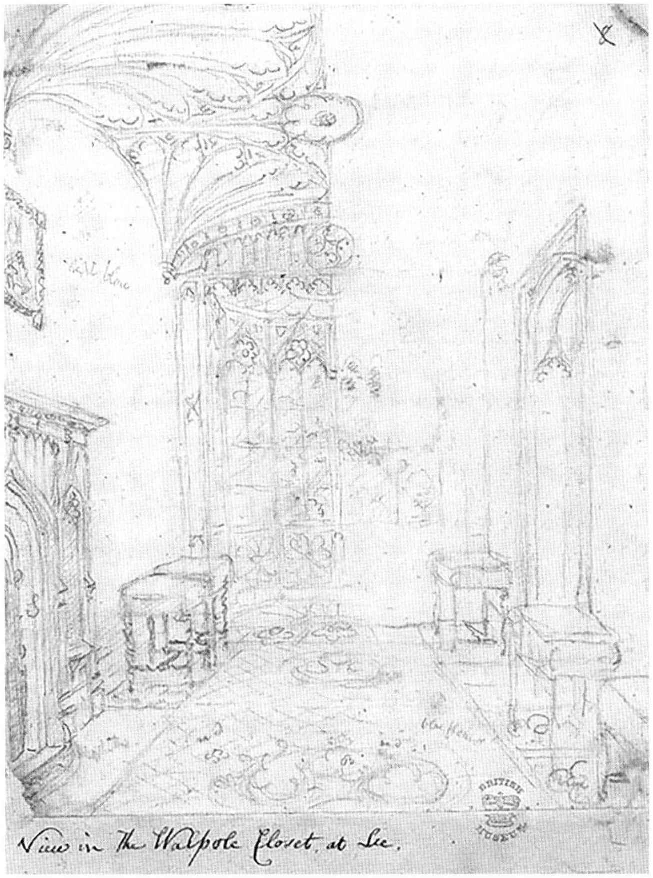

Fig. 133 John Carter, "View in the Walpole Closet at Lee," 1791. BL Add MS 29930, fol. 6. Photo © The British Library Board.

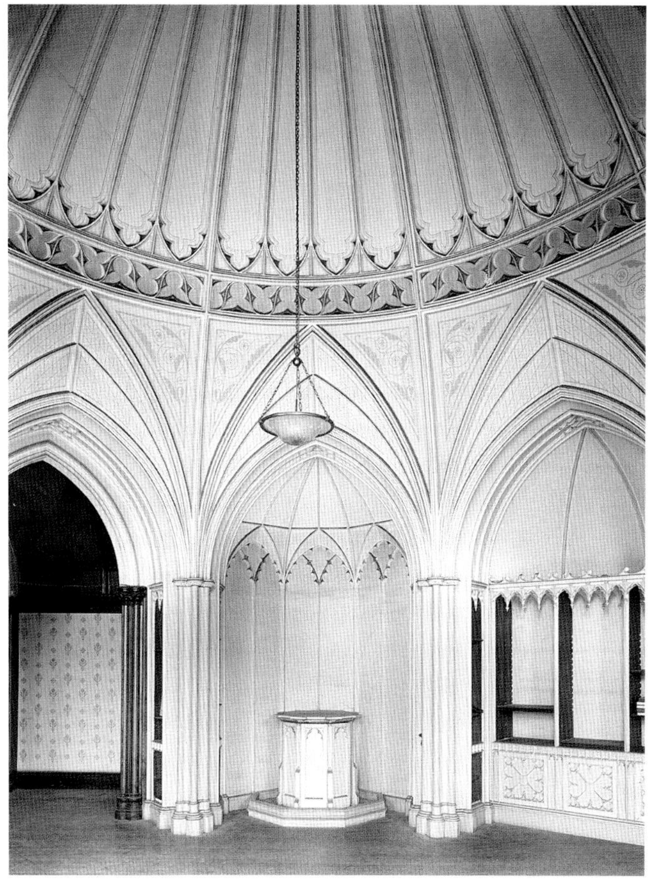

Fig. 134 Lee Priory library. By permission of Historic England Archive.

portrait, the style of the chamber—and of the house itself—becomes an homage to Horace Walpole and to Strawberry Hill.

We can nuance this allusion by exploring other spaces at Lee, namely the stunning octagonal library and its antechamber, which connected the library and the central staircase (figs. 134 and 135). A library became an important feature of the Gothic house during the eighteenth century, eliding Gothic architecture with traditions of scholarship originating in the monastery and its modern iterations in contemporary antiquarianism. But unlike the oblong libraries with bookcases located along its lateral walls, as at Arbury Hall, Donnington Grove, or Strawberry Hill, Barrett's library was a centrally planned structure with a dome and glazed louver. The design would seem to be a synthesis of two rooms at Strawberry Hill: the Round Room (figs. 29, 47), from which it derives its "rose-window" tracery on the vault, and the Tribune (fig. 36), which provides the model for the glazed light on the ceiling, which emitted light that was "mellowed by passing through a medium of stained and semi-transparent glass."[92] For Walpole, the interior simulated the place of a wealthy abbot who "avoided ostentation, but did not choose austere gloomth."[93] The Strawberry Hill Tribune's own "altarpiece" (Walpole's cabinet of miniatures) may also have inspired Lee's

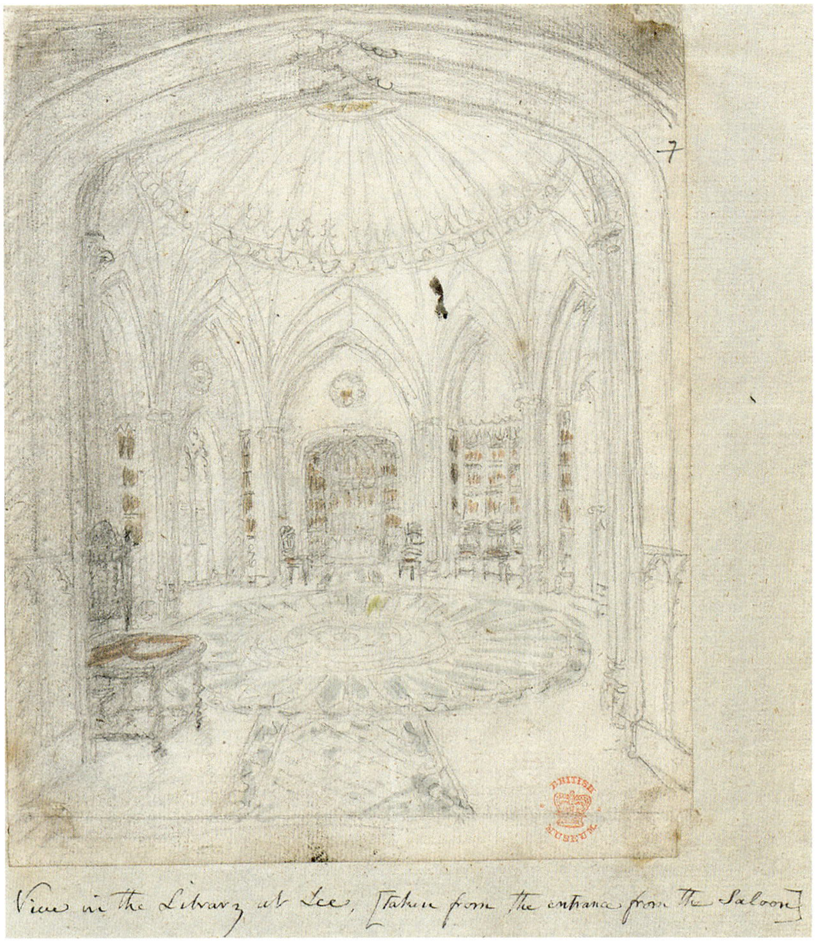

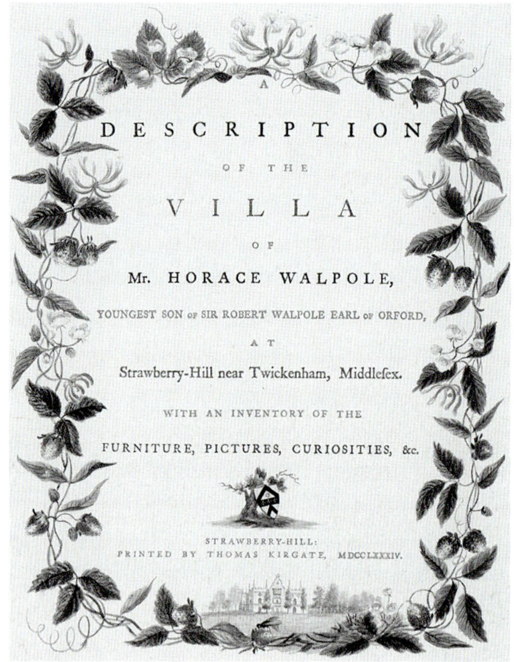

Fig. 135 John Carter, "View in the Library at Lee," 1791. British Library, London, Add MS 29930, fol. 5. Photo © The British Library Board.

Fig. 136 Frontispiece to Walpole's *Description* (1784). LWL 33 30 Copy 11 Folio. Courtesy of The Lewis Walpole Library, Yale University.

east altar niche and Gothic altarpiece, designed by John Carter in 1789–91 (still faintly visible in fig. 135). Although the altarpiece was still extant in 1958, nothing, regrettably, has come to light of this work.[94] Comprising eight full-length figures on panel of Saint George, a king, a queen, Saint Catherine, a monk, a nun, and two others (not recorded), together with a host of musical angels above, it was unique in Walpole's circle. Typical of Carter's increasingly replicative approach to the Gothic, the altarpiece was based on careful analysis of medieval styles of dress and armor. He borrowed from paintings at Westminster Abbey (especially the fourteenth-century portrait of Richard II) and Strawberry Hill—notably Walpole's portrait of Saint George that was hung on his own staircase—while the disposition of the figures was based on the sixteenth-century great window of St. Margaret's, Westminster (installed 1758).[95]

A more literal allusion to Strawberry Hill is evidenced in Wyatt's Gothic furniture for the library (fig. 128). Within the Library's diagonal niches were Gothic bookcases (now in the Victoria and Albert Museum) with finely rendered strawberry leaves that run across the cresting on top of them. As metonymic signs referring to the physical and cultural world of Strawberry Hill, strawberry leaves were employed in the graphic works of Walpole's circle, such as the 1784 frontispiece to

Walpole's *Description* (fig. 136). The recent discovery of the original fan vault and bookcases from the library antechamber has revealed that this motif was also employed in the bookcases in the adjoining room (fig. 137).[96] Barrett's use of the motif was a clever genuflection toward Strawberry Hill, an in-joke of sorts, which implied that Barrett and his home were the successors of Walpole's Gothic legacy. Notably, the same motif would occur at Ashridge Park in Hertfordshire after 1813, when Jeffry Wyatville took over the project from his uncle James Wyatt, thus suggesting the lengthy influence of Strawberry Hill on subsequent Gothic homes.

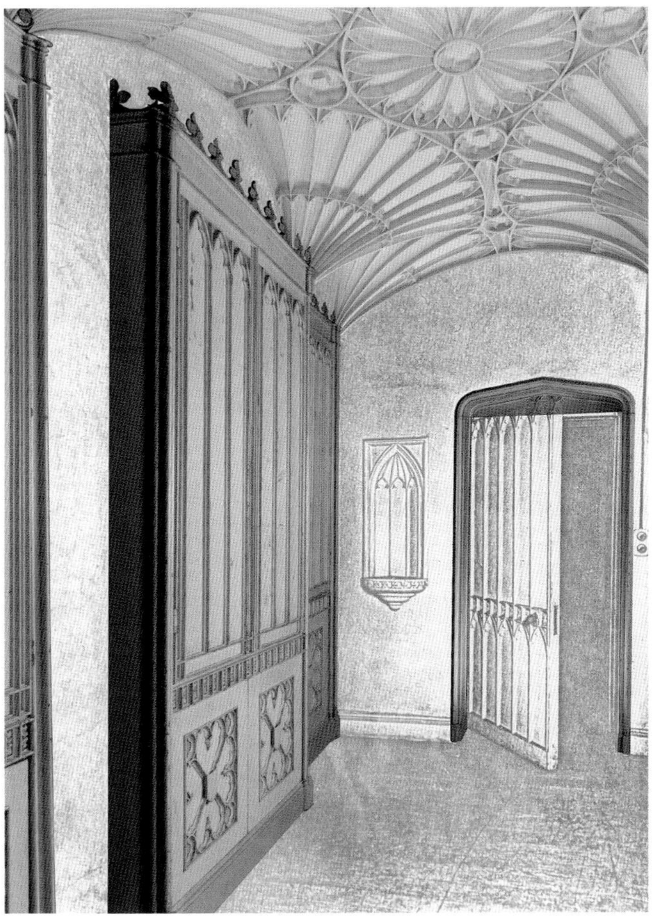

Fig. 137 Lee Priory, library antechamber reconstruction with newly discovered vault, door surround, and bookcases. Photo © Alex Puddy, Architectural Heritage Ltd., Taddington, England.

Walpole was extraordinarily impressed and flattered by Barrett's work at Lee, and he reserved for it what was perhaps his highest praise anywhere in his letters, calling the library "the most perfect thing I ever saw, and has the most the air it was intended to have, that of an abbot's library, supposing it could have been so exquisitely finished three hundred years ago." In another letter he writes, "I wish William of Wickam were alive to employ and reward Mr Wyatt—you would think the latter had designed the library for the former."[97] Describing it to Mary Berry, he states, "You will see a child of Strawberry prettier than the parent, and so executed and so finished! There is a delicious closet [the Strawberry Room] too, so flattering to me!"[98] Effervescent though it is, Walpole's response to Lee is complex. On one level, it expresses Walpole's flattery of his young friend for his emulation of, and allusion to, Walpole's famous home. But Barrett's assessment of Walpole and Strawberry Hill cannot simply be explained by the study and replication of architectural form. Barrett's contemporaries connected both his home's style and his personal "lifestyle" and affect with that of Walpole and of Thomas Gray.[99] Barrett's own emotional, intellectual, and erotic subjectivity was not only similar to Walpole's but in fact modeled upon it. The emulative building of Lee saw Barrett position himself within an architectural and sexual genealogy: a new generation of Gothic buildings modeled on Walpole's famous, if dated, exemplar.

Lee also posed a challenge to Walpole for this very reason. Emphasizing the continuity between the two homes, Walpole, in a 1788 letter to Barrett, denigrated

Strawberry Hill as an amateur attempt at the Gothic.[100] He was keenly aware that appreciation and replication of Gothic art had changed considerably from the 1740s, when he began Strawberry, to the 1780s and 1790s, when Lee was built. From Wyatt's careful renderings of Gothic form at Strawberry to John Carter's exact replication of medieval art and costume, Lee Priory was a more homogeneous Gothic structure, something Walpole captures in his description of its "Sober dignity without prelatic pomp."[101] Wyatt and Carter placed value on accurate simulation of medieval forms, thereby overturning the licentious play Walpole so valorized at Strawberry. Walpole's discussion of Lee closes with a glance over his shoulder at Strawberry as the "dawnings of an art."[102] Passages of this sort were both literal and rhetorical; emphasizing Strawberry Hill's place as the fountainhead of Georgian Gothic, they served to underscore that the child had outdone his father, thereby flattering the latter for the extraordinary example set for the former.

Donnington Grove, the Vyne, and Lee Priory provide important case studies with which to explore the significance of Strawberry Hill in connection with the architectural patronage of Walpole's circle. They also provide opportunities to reassess Walpole's own frequently self-congratulatory artistic judgments, none of which were ever objective or detached from his own emotional investment in the patron concerned. It is remarkable that Walpole wrote only one line about Donnington and in that line praised the labors of John Chute, not James Pettit Andrews. Whether a shared sexuality was a reason why Andrews emulated Strawberry Hill is unclear, but it is clear that he carefully replicated key aspects of the house as a site of antiquarian, literary, and historical endeavor. It may be significant that in 1764, shortly after acquiring the house and Chute's designs, Andrews published *The Savages of Europe*, his first significant literary enterprise. Andrews was an aspiring author, and his interests in the Strawberry Hill model are not difficult to understand. But neither is Walpole's complete lack of attention to the house and its patron in his writings: although they were surely acquainted, Walpole seems never to have embraced Andrews as a friend and may actually not have been flattered by the emulation he received. Walpole's praise of and frustration with John Chute—probably the closest person to him during the last decades of Chute's life—is easily read on the page. The love shared between the two men was, as I have said, principally mediated by aesthetic concerns, none more obvious than their complex negotiations at Strawberry and the Vyne. Barrett's work at Lee is interesting in this regard as well. Acquainted with Walpole via his Grand Tour companion—the son to Walpole's much-loved cousin Henry Seymour Conway—and via a house and collection Walpole knew and admired before the younger Barrett came of age, Barrett unsurprisingly attracted special attention from Walpole. Given that Barrett was a member of a queer circle junior to, but intertwined with, Walpole's, Barrett's own emulation of Walpole—both his own affect and mannerisms and his home at Strawberry—was clearly deeply meaningful to Walpole during the later years of his life. Barrett left no doubt that Walpole and his "paper house" would not, as Walpole feared, "soon vanish and be forgotten together!"[103]

And it would not. The template Walpole established at Strawberry Hill—eliding the persona of an antiquary, historian, collector, and man of taste with the modern Gothic house—was extraordinarily malleable, a fact that surely explains its long-standing resonance in the history of architecture.[104] It would take another study altogether to explore the influence of Strawberry

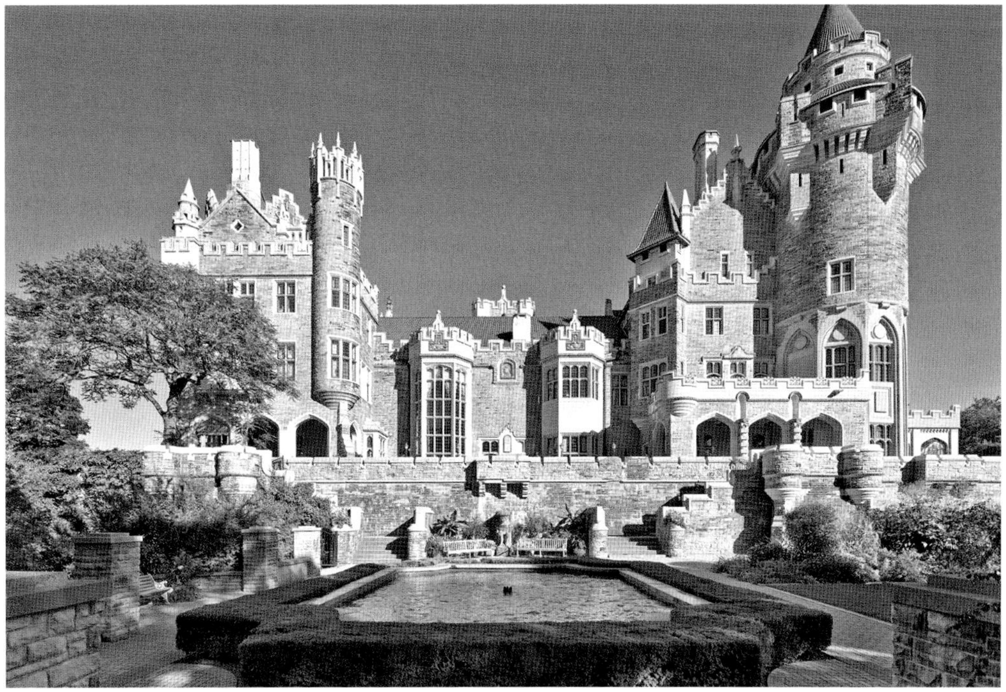

Fig. 138 Edward J. Lennox, Casa Loma, Toronto. Designed for Sir Henry Pellatt, 1911–14. Photo: author.

Hill on subsequent Gothic homes, although that study would surely show both the longevity of the Strawberry Hill model as much as its interpretability and versatility for later periods. A case in point is Casa Loma, the Gothic castle in Toronto built by Edward J. Lennox for the Canadian financier and industrialist Sir Henry Pellatt (1859–1939) in the early years of the twentieth century (fig. 138). Pellatt's spectacular Gothic home was conceived in a conscious genealogy of great Gothic houses that included both British and modern American examples. Emphasizing his own place in this genealogy, he purchased and hung "ancestral portraits" of Casa Loma within it: J. M. W. Turner's perspective view of William Beckford's Fonthill Abbey and a copy of Joshua Reynolds's 1756 *Portrait of Horace Walpole*, now in the Art Gallery of Ontario.[105] For Pellatt, the significations of Strawberry Hill (and, for that matter, Fonthill Abbey) were not sexual; rather, as an aspiring Canadian aristocrat (he would be knighted by Edward VII), he considered the Gothic houses of British history to be emblems of the chivalric and aristocratic worlds into which he sought entry.

6 From Strawberry Hill Gothic to the Gothic Revival

> The Gothic is singular in this;
> one seems easily at home in the Renaissance;
> one is not too strange in the Byzantine;
> as for the Roman, it is ourselves;
> and we could walk blindfolded through
> every chink and cranny of the Greek mind;
> all these styles seem modern, when we
> come close to them; but the Gothic gets away.
>
> —Henry Adams, *Mont-Saint-Michel and Chartres* (1904)

This book has explored the relationships between Gothic architecture and sexuality within the elite coterie centered around Horace Walpole. At its core has been the premise that the homoerotic bonds shared by Walpole and his associates provided a vital context in which the Gothic was adopted as a coterie taste among these men. As such, it has argued for a new understanding of the Strawberry Hill Gothic mode in eighteenth-century architecture. My goal here has been to explore these buildings and their collections using the terms in which they were imagined by their patrons, designers, and many of their visitors. I have tried, in other words, to understand why the particular Strawberry Hill Gothic mode came to be, why it looked the way it did, and what aesthetic criteria validated the distinctive approach to its Gothic sources and to the medieval past as a historical idiom. Although sexuality has not been central to previous considerations of the art and architecture of Walpole's circle (as it has been in Gothic literature, for example), it remains a facet of all human interaction and aesthetic formation, and its role in the creation of art and architecture should neither be overemphasized nor ignored by commentators. In writing this book, I am quite aware that it is not the last word on the subject; rather, it is a beginning.

When I began, I noted that all art-historical accounts of these men and their buildings inherit a lengthy and persistent historiographical tradition that has backhandedly appraised Walpole's oeuvre as either fanciful or charming "experiments" in or "parodies" of Gothic design (as in the case of Charles Eastlake) or more damningly as outright failures (following Kenneth Clark). As a result, these buildings and their furnishings have been subsumed into a biomorphic development in which early buildings in the style are naive, unstudied trifles that would become "corrected" or "disciplined" by the more accurate simulations of Gothic form after 1790–1800, leading inexorably to the "High Gothic Revival" architecture of the nineteenth century. Eastlake's aforementioned 1872 study, for example, concludes with George Frederick Bodley's St. John's in Tue Brook, Liverpool (1867–70), in which "the genuine grace of Medieval art seems at length to have been reached," thus positioning it at the end of a lengthy development of Gothic form.[1] With notable exceptions, the scholarly assumption persists that Georgian patrons and architects desired accurate simulations of medieval architecture but, due to a lack of understanding of that architecture, failed to achieve them.[2] Gazing upon Georgian architecture through a Victorian lens necessarily fails to provide an understanding that the aesthetic regime of the Georgian period was substantially different from that of the nineteenth century, which framed the very problem of "the Gothic Revival" in scholarship. In concluding this study, I want to locate its observations within some of the broader aesthetic changes of the eighteenth century in order to ask not only what forces allowed the Strawberry Hill Gothic style to come to be but also what factors may have endorsed its death as the Gothic idiom morphed into a more accurate simulation of medieval architecture at the end of the century.

Significantly, the very style label—Strawberry Hill Gothic—did not exist in Walpole's own lifetime but was itself imposed upon the style by its early nineteenth-century critics, such as Richard Griffin Braybrooke, for whom Strawberry Hill Gothic was "the style called after its patron [and] a mode of decoration sufficiently objectionable under any circumstances" (1836).[3] Others, such as the diarist Mrs. Arbuthnot, simply considered it to reflect "a good deal of bad taste" (1822).[4] Strawberry Hill Gothic, in other words, was given a name after the style had ceased to be current and could thus be compared and contrasted with later iterations of the style. A new, critical distance between critics and Walpole's oeuvre is evident in the long list of satires that appeared from circa 1800 onward, such as those by Thomas Rowlandson (fig. 16), which riff on Strawberry Hill's Catholic significations and poke fun at its foppish antiquarianism.[5] The 1842 sale of the contents of Strawberry Hill was a highly public event in which Walpole was the subject of much ridicule.[6] Thomas Crofton Croker's satiric account of the Strawberry Hill sale, *Specimen of the Catalogue of the Great Sale of Gooseberry Hall, with Puffatory Remarks* (1842), is a telling example of the raillery with which Walpole, his home, and his collection came to be viewed. Emblematically, the more sympathetic Lord Byron could claim, "It is the fashion to underrate Horace Walpole" (1821).[7]

Walpole, like any astute observer of the Georgian period, understood that he was living in a period of rapid stylistic and social change, and he was (painfully at times) aware that Strawberry Hill had become a period piece, an influential, if dated, example of the Gothic, by the last decades of his life. In a telling letter of 1788 to Thomas Barrett of Lee Priory, he recounts welcoming James Wyatt's foreman to inspect Strawberry Hill during Lee's building campaigns: "Mr Wyatt has made him [the foreman] too correct a Goth not to have seen all the imperfections and bad execution of my attempts; for neither Mr [Richard] Bentley nor my workmen had *studied* the science [of Gothic architecture], and I was always too desultory and impatient to consider that I should please myself more by allowing time, than by hurrying my plans into execution before they were ripe. My house therefore is but a sketch by beginners; yours is finished by a great master."[8]

As I suggested in the last chapter, this view of Lee was based on Walpole's understanding of it as a "child of Strawberry [Hill]." In this sense, its apparently superior handling of the Gothic backhandedly reflected praise on Strawberry Hill, its (now slightly tarnished) model or parent, considering it "the dawning of an art." Nonetheless, Walpole clearly understood that the current appraisal of the Gothic was substantially different from that he had imagined only decades before. He understood that Wyatt aimed for a more precise replication of medieval designs at Lee than his own architects had done at Strawberry and elsewhere, even if the building never attempted to replicate medieval stone construction. The use of the octagon at Batalha as the model for the first central tower at Lee and of scaled drawings of Gothic ornament and woodwork is, in this regard, striking. But it is also significant that, as in Walpole's circle, Wyatt had employed Batty Langley's and other pattern books in his earlier commissions to create decorative ensembles of Gothic motifs but had aimed to create closer simulations of Gothic form when he built Lee. As in Gothic architecture, so in Gothic literature: although *The Castle of Otranto* (1764/65) was one of Walpole's proudest achievements, by 1784 it too had become historicized as a product of its own midcentury past. As Walpole claimed to Hannah More, "It was fit for nothing but the age in which it was written, an age in which much was known; that required only to be amused, nor cared whether its amusements were conformable to truth and the models of good sense; that could not be spoiled; was in no danger of being too credulous; and rather wanted to be brought back to imagination, than to be led astray by it."[9] Walpole could look back on the long shadow his Gothic productions cast and understand that they were products of their time that sat uncomfortably with the changing aesthetics of the later years of the century.

During the last quarter of the century, architects and antiquaries—some within Walpole's own orbit of medievalists—were developing new methods of analyzing, recording, and replicating medieval architecture that significantly departed from the approaches employed by Walpole's circle in the 1740s through 1770s. A pivotal figure was the antiquary John Carter, official draughtsman of the Society of Antiquaries. Carter was Walpole's choice to record the interiors of Strawberry Hill in 1788 (fig. 36), and he would prepare imaginative responses to *The Castle of Otranto* in 1790 (fig. 20), and, probably via Walpole, he came into the employment of Thomas Barrett at Lee Priory. By 1801, however, a few years after Walpole's death, Carter could describe Georgian Gothic as "a half-begotten, misshapen, 'congestion' called 'Gothic architecture revived.'" He went on to describe its "villas, snug boxes, summer-houses, and theatres" as "glar[ing] with this mania of mock science."[10] Carter did not, of course, mention the buildings of Walpole's circle by name (and he could not, given that he worked on some of them), but there can be little doubt that he had them and related buildings in mind. The hybrid mode of Gothic/antique/Chinese design by William Hallett and Batty Langley that was so influential during the early and middle years of the eighteenth century was disdained by Carter as "a new architectural style . . . in appearance monstrous, and in deeds fantastic, powerful in patronage and ridiculous in effect." Understood as "a new way," Georgian Gothic was "puerile, odious, disquieting, and unintelligible . . . a grotesque meteor . . . [this] Fantastic

Order of Architecture now mounts the stage of novelty; thousands bare the head in servile adulation."[11] Carter would target his attacks at James Wyatt, whose Gothic style he understood to be analogous to, or at least an extension of, that of Batty Langley. But it was as much Wyatt's modern Gothic works (including William Beckford's Fonthill Abbey) as his bitterly contested "Improvements" to England's Gothic cathedral churches such as Salisbury, Hereford, and Lichfield between 1787 and 1797 that drew the ire of Carter and inspired a new approach to the preservation of ancient fabrics championed by the Society of Antiquaries.[12] A new desire to preserve medieval Gothic architecture resulted in a heightened interaction between medievalist research and architectural practice around 1800.

Underlying Carter's criticism of Wyatt was a fundamental difference of approach to Gothic design: despite his work at Lee, Wyatt, like Walpole and others, approached the Gothic as a stylistic vocabulary that could be recorded, manipulated, combined, and applied to the surfaces of buildings using modern materials with various degrees of fidelity to its original models and sources. Paradigmatically, Carter would consider Wyatt not to be "a scientific GOTHIC ARCHITECT," and, as he understood these words, he was right.[13] Carter approached the Gothic as a structural system based exclusively on medieval modes of design gleaned from careful archaeological study of standing medieval buildings. For Carter and others around 1800, the Gothic Revival reoriented itself from a style of decorative enrichment to something far closer to architectural simulation—a new and more intimate relationship between signifier and signified. The years around 1800 witnessed the compilation and publication of pivotal texts on Gothic architecture, notably Thomas Warton, James Bentham, Francis Grose, and John Milner's *Essays on Gothic Architecture* (1802) and Sir James Hall's "On the Origin and Principles of Gothic Architecture," published in the *Transactions of the Royal Society of Edinburgh* (1798). These changes have all been explored in depth elsewhere and have no further pertinence to this study, except insofar as they emphasize that the new approach to medieval Gothic art and architecture around 1800, focusing on careful archaeological study and structural analysis via scaled ground plans and elevations, witnessed the origins of medievalist art history as a "scientific" discipline, albeit one that had deep (if divergent) roots in the eighteenth century, as this book has shown. The attempts by Thomas Gray, Thomas Warton, and others in the eighteenth century to provide a chronological syntax of Gothic architecture were realized in the early years of the next century by Thomas Rickman, who would be considered "the founder of the modern science of Gothic Architecture" (notably, Gray's "Architectura Gothica" was published posthumously in 1814 by Thomas Mathias). Rickman's *Attempt to Discriminate the Styles of English Architecture* provided medievalist art history with many of the style labels (Early English, Decorated, Perpendicular, etc.) that it still employs. But it also gave the discipline its positivist vision of Gothic architecture as an art form that could be forensically dissected, analyzed, and arranged into genus and species consistent with contemporary studies in natural history.[14] It is beyond the scope of this study to explore the later history of these issues, but a fuller study could chart the development of taxonomic models in the scholarship on Gothic architecture, from Carter, Rickman, and others through to Paul Frankl, the "soldier of science" in mid-twentieth-century scholarship, and the persistence of this methodology well into the twentieth century, particularly in English scholarship.[15]

The question remains: how and why did this change in the approach to Gothic architecture occur, and what, if anything, does it have to do with sexuality? Having placed emphasis on "homosexual" coteries in the formation of Georgian Gothic, one could argue that the men who created the Strawberry Hill Gothic style simply passed on, and with them so did Strawberry Hill Gothic. There is some truth to that, since few left biological offspring, but they were of course only *primus inter pares* of great patrons of the Gothic in the period, and this argument gives them far more credit than they are due. Yet, as I have consistently argued, gender, sexuality, and architecture do not exist in vacuums but represent cognate manifestations of broader aesthetic structures. In exploring the change of representation in architecture between circa 1740 and 1800, I want to implicate sexuality, and to do so I borrow from Dror Wahrman's now-canonical study *The Making of the Modern Self*, in which Wahrman charts a fundamental break at the end of the eighteenth century from what he calls an *ancien régime* of identity circa 1700–1770 to a *modern régime* after circa 1770–80. Focusing on gender and sexuality and their manifestations in literature, fashion, and theater, Wahrman charts the fluid boundaries of human sexuality from the early and mid-eighteenth century, in which biological sex and gender were "occasionally mutable, potentially unfixed . . . even . . . a matter of choice," through to the closing years of the eighteenth century, with its sharp codification of the modern gender-sex configuration, which advocated, in Judith Butler's terms, "a mimetic relation of gender to sex whereby gender mirrors sex."[16] Wahrman describes this as a change from "gender play" between 1700 and 1770, characterized by a fluid boundary between an individual's biological gender and their own affect or performance of gender, to "gender panic" at the end of the century, in which deviations from accepted modes of "male" and female" comportment were unacceptable or shocking to contemporaries. Wahrman shows that English culture rapidly codified its conception of masculinity and femininity as fixed signifiers in which affect and performance (in their bodies as much as in other spheres, including fashion and art) mirrored a collective understanding of gender. His observations on gender are part of a wider account of aesthetic change and identity formation that he defines as "a rapid, swift, far-reaching rupture that spread like wildfire through the thickets of contemporary culture." These changes constitute part of a modern regime of identity that in many respects anticipated codifications of masculinity and femininity and the invention and employment of "heterosexuality" and "homosexuality" that defined nineteenth- and twentieth-century sexology.[17]

Wahrman, of course, is not concerned with architecture, although his study usefully informs our understanding of the built environment and the range of ethical and aesthetic concerns that it shares with the people that built and used it. I want to demonstrate the congruity of his arguments with the two interrelated narratives I have developed in the book. First, it will be clear that "gender play" usefully describes the affective nature of the various stereotypes developed to define and critique Walpole and his circle humorously as fops, finger-twirlers, and fribbles in the second and third quarters of the century and the Gothic buildings they built and inhabited. Each, in varying degrees, pokes fun at their effeminate deviations from contemporary "male" conduct and critiques (or occasionally celebrates) the hybrid genders of these men. While there were certainly moments of "gender panic" in the first three quarters of the eighteenth century, particularly when a man was "outed" in a legal or political context (as in William Guthrie's *Reply to the Counter-address*), "gender panic" best describes the virulent moralizing critiques of Walpole's circle that were penned after his death, in the early years of the nineteenth century (such as that by Thomas Babington Macaulay of 1833). As Abby Coykendall has noted, nineteenth-century critics of Walpole were particularly sensitive to the many "ambiguit[ies] of masculinity or heterosexuality" manifest in his writings and said as much with a vituperative force unknown in the previous century.[18] Second, a parallel transition from "play" to "panic" can be charted in the nature of the Gothic style. As noted above, the fribblishness and foppishness of Walpole's circle were read equally in their personal affect and in the style and decoration of their homes, which were understood by some to be an extension of their own gender hybridity, or "queerness." The fluid application of Gothic and occasionally antique or Chinese architectural motifs in the early phases of Strawberry Hill and particularly Old Windsor in the 1740s and 1750s—most based upon pattern books or antiquarian prints—is a form of architectural play, a conscious blending and contrasting of modes and styles without particular concern for the autonomy of their respective historical and geographical referents. The 1780s and 1790s saw what is often described as "a more studied approach to medieval sources" or "a more archaeological Gothic" in a range of monuments, including Lee Priory. For my purposes, the new approach to stylistic homogeneity and formal simulation, characterized by an attempt to carefully replicate medieval buildings, signified a parallel and related change. Both architecture and the human body came to be evaluated by fundamentally different criteria in the later eighteenth century: formal divergences from common modes cooled or calmed into a unified vision of representation.

The culture in which Walpole and his circle expressed themselves in the 1740s through 1770s by way of clothing, gesture, literature, epistolary correspondence, and art and architectural patronage was one in which particular aesthetic categories and ideals were fluid and unfixed. Walpole's famous 1750 account of the new villas along the Thames captures something of this: "The country wears a new face; everybody is improving their places. . . . The dispersed buildings, I mean, temples, bridges, etc. are generally Gothic or Chinese and give a whimsical air of novelty that is very pleasing." His contemporary commentary on the aesthetic fluidity of architecture in the present, on its variety and asymmetry, describes a "liberty of taste into which we are struck," indicating a lack of regulation policing aesthetic deviations from established norms and even a positive valuation of such deviations—whether in the built environment or the human body.[19] Here a wide range of texts offer analogues in contemporary culture, but a convenient one is the following comment by Joseph Addison: "At present therefore an unconstrained carriage, and a certain openness of behaviour, are the height of good-breeding. The fashionable world is grown free and easy; our manners sit more loose upon us; nothing is so modish as an agreeable negligence" (1711).[20]

Much could be said about this statement, but my point here is to suggest that the contraction and codification of human sexual semiotics (men as "male" and women as "female") parallel the increasingly intimate relationship of signifier to signified in architectural representation. As architecture needed to remain "true" to its forms and their points of origin (an ideal encapsulated in A. W. N. Pugin's *True Principles* [1841]), so too did the cultural and behavioral attributes of human sexuality necessarily adhere to their biological origins. Wahrman's account of epistemological change in the later eighteenth century agrees with other accounts of the period, from Christopher Breward's discussions of British fashion to Martin Myrone's account of masculinities in British painting and Stephen Bann's study of historical representation in France and Britain, in which he describes a new "critical preoccupation with [historical] authenticity, and the transgressive wish to simulate authenticity." Bann, again, is not dealing with architecture in this passage, but his account informs not only historical representation in texts and images but also the closing gap between signifier and signified in historicist forms prevalent in the built environment.[21]

Understanding the development of Gothic architecture within a broader arc of social, aesthetic, and sexual change in the eighteenth century may throw light on the checkered posthumous reception of Horace Walpole and Strawberry Hill. An important episode for such purposes is William Beckford's building of Fonthill Abbey, Wiltshire (by James Wyatt 1796–1813 and afterward by Beckford),[22] which I have alluded to elsewhere in this study (figs. 139 and 140). Beckford and Fonthill are regularly framed as successors to Walpole's Gothic, since, aside from his patronage of a Gothic home, Beckford also wrote the Gothic fantasy *Vathek* (1786), and his affair with his adolescent male cousin Kitty Courtenay amounts to one of the scandals of his age.[23] Beckford would explore many of the religious and political tropes of the Gothic that Walpole and his circle had developed, and aspects of his house were inspired by those of Walpole's circle (for example, St. Michael's Gallery at Fonthill appears to quote the Long Gallery at Strawberry Hill; the octagon at Fonthill followed the earlier model at Lee Priory; etc.).[24] As David Watkin suggests, Walpole represented a sort of "father figure" to Beckford because he established a cult of personality around the home of a famous literary man.[25] And yet, despite their apparent similarities, Beckford acknowledged little filial relationship with Walpole as a "queer" ancestor or Strawberry Hill as an originary essay in Gothic architecture and queer family romance. Indeed, Beckford's commentary on both is overtly dismissive and even "homophobic." He called Strawberry Hill "a miserable child's box," "a species of gothic mousetrap," and considered Walpole's home and collection to be an expression of its patron's "littleness"—a thinly veiled quip at Walpole's sexual affect. Beckford described Walpole's house as "Namby-Pamby" (or "Nimby-Pamby") and went on to adopt this as a personal nickname for Walpole.[26] "Namby Pamby" captures the element of infantile preciousness and affectation that Beckford found so offensive in Walpole. Describing the Strawberry Hill collection, Beckford apparently recounted to his biographer:

> Walpole hated me. I began Fonthill two or three years before his death. Mischief-making people annoyed him by saying I intended to buy up all his nic-nackery when he was dead. Some things I might have wished to possess—a good deal I would not have taken as a gift. . . . He built everything upon family honours and gossip—his writings are portraits of himself. He would have abused my heraldic emblazonments at Fonthill. He was full of spleen. He would have written and talked me and my buildings down to the ground—yet he affected the philosopher.[27]

Rather than connect himself with Walpole, Strawberry Hill, and Strawberry Hill Gothic in a genealogy—architectural, sexual, or both—as Walpole's friends had done in the 1750s through 1780s, Beckford decisively distances himself from him and his famous home. Beckford's comments are interesting on many levels, but it is striking that his understanding of Walpole as a rival in taste was seemingly one-sided: Walpole recorded little interest in Beckford, and he certainly did not live long enough to be either upset or delighted by his architecture, whatever Beckford might have said. Indeed, sharing features of Lee Priory, including its architect, James Wyatt, Fonthill could only have impressed Walpole. This competitive and acrimonious relationship with Walpole as a senior man of taste was Beckford's invention, although the assumption by others that he desired to acquire parts of the Strawberry Hill collection suggests that they understood an association between the men and their Gothic homes. If Beckford claims to have denied the Walpolean Gothic model and the Strawberry Hill Gothic mode, his heraldic displays did ally him with the former owner of Fonthill, Mervyn Touchet, Earl of Castlehaven (1593–1631), the subject of a famous sodomy trial in the Elizabethan period, a historical and site-specific queer family romance.[28] But in all of this, surely Beckford doth protest too much: while he actively dismissed Strawberry Hill and its collections as precious, effeminate, and old-fashioned (which by his time they surely were), he carefully followed Walpole's life, writings, and home and bought lots from the estate when they came up for sale in 1842.

Beckford's view of his relationship with Walpole and Strawberry Hill contrasts considerably with narratives of the Gothic that so frequently pair the two

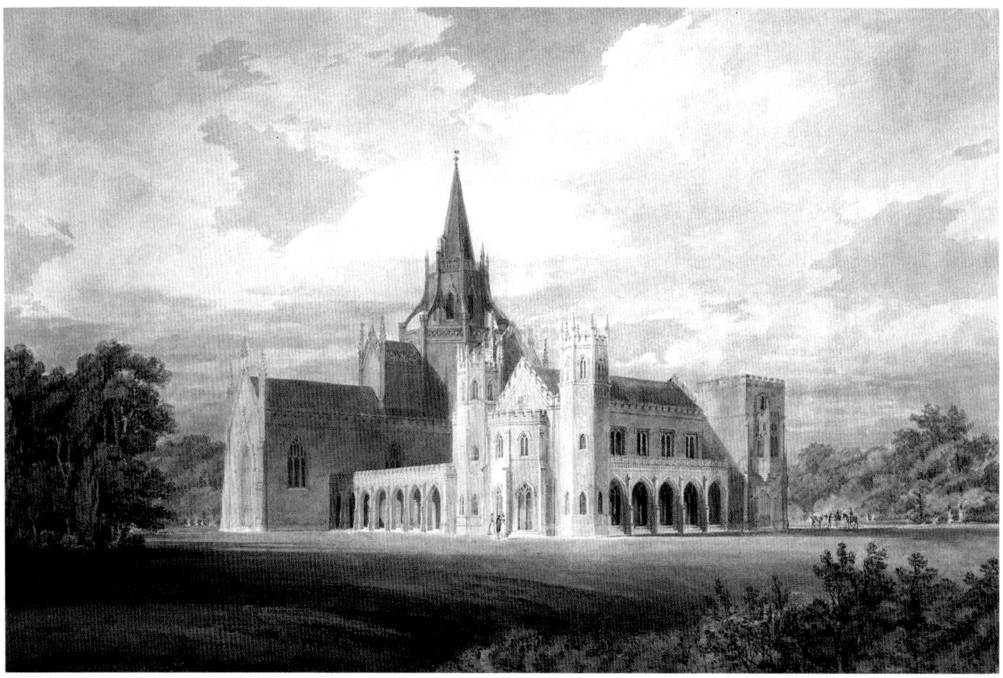

Fig. 139 Joseph M. W. Turner, *Perspective View of Fonthill Abbey from the South-West*, ca. 1799. Watercolor on paper. Wikimedia Commons.

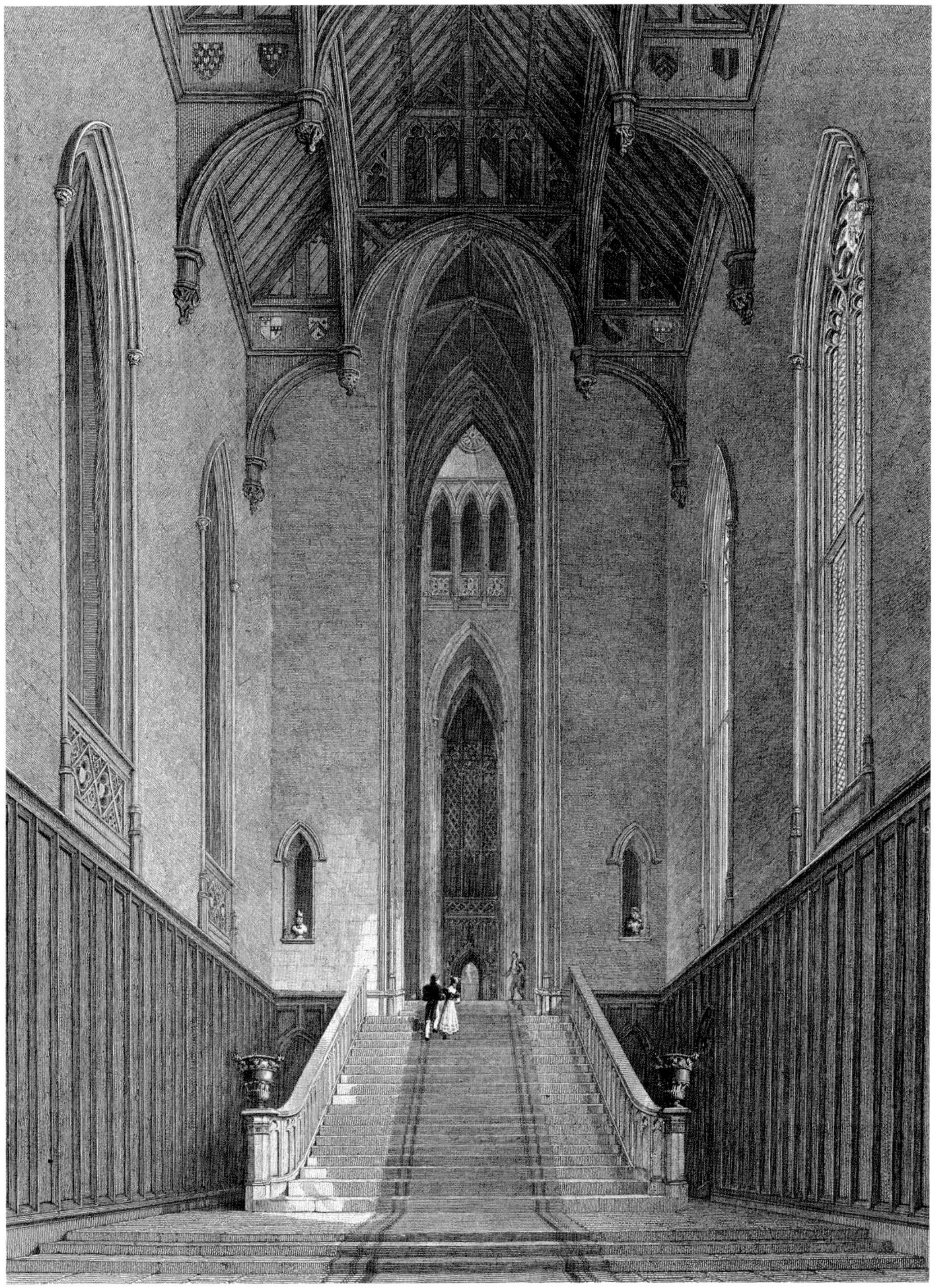

Fig. 140 "Fonthill Abbey: Interior of the Great Western Hall." From John Rutter, *Delineations of Fonthill and Its Abbey* (1823). Courtesy of W. D. Jordan Rare Books and Special Collections, Queen's University, Kingston, Ontario.

in a developmental sequence. While the similarity of Beckford's and Walpole's sexual orientations may be debatable (while both appear to have been principally homoerotic, there is no evidence that Walpole was a pederast, for example), what is clear is that, for Beckford, Walpole's model was aesthetically inconsistent with his own self-image. Typical of his period, Beckford broadly eschewed the fribbles and fops of Walpole's era and derided their licentious modes of display as an outdated and distasteful mode of masculinity. As Martin Myrone and others have shown, the 1770s saw the rise of a heightened critical discourse on the effeminization of English men, particularly in the light of intersecting discourses on luxury and commerce. Centered around the macaroni, critics claimed that the fears of the early eighteenth-century moralists had finally been realized and that "true nobility *now* consists in splendid titles, gay equipage, and princely palaces."[29] Characterized by Wahrman as "gender panic," the response of British men to this crisis was to reform themselves on the model of an idealized, long-lost masculinist aristocracy. This too affected queer fashioning: elsewhere Dominic Janes has charted a transition from a midcentury "art of elaboration that produced the macaroni to one of exquisite sartorial reserve that resulted in the Regency dandy."[30] While Beckford received his share of criticism for being a "coxcomb," his own masculine self-conception was in line with late-century reforms. This allows us to understand that, by the later eighteenth century, Strawberry Hill and the Strawberry Hill Gothic mode had become historicized; they belonged to a prehistory of the present and could be moralized as the product of a wayward age that had been reformed. While Beckford manifestly understood the apparent "queerness" of Walpole and Strawberry Hill, it may well be that, from Beckford's perspective, Walpole's own sexual orientations were less significant than the particular mode of effeminate masculinity that he cultivated.

The reputation of Horace Walpole, and of Strawberry Hill as a work of Gothic architecture, faced other difficulties. The formal change of the Gothic style noted above paralleled the transformation of the Gothic from its status as an other in relation to established cultural norms promoted by Walpole and his circle to its status as a style of nationalist and high Anglican (and then Catholic) hegemony at the height of the Victorian Gothic Revival. This radical shift took place in less than a generation and was punctuated by the publications, architecture, and furniture of A. C. Pugin (1762–1832) and his remarkable son A. W. N. Pugin (1812–1852), arguably the loudest voice in the shaping of Gothic architecture in the first half of the nineteenth century. A. W. N. Pugin's Gothic was in itself an exercise in moral and aesthetic reform, a radical denunciation of the British Industrial Revolution and an intentional return to the religious and aesthetic "purity" of the medieval past. Pugin's view of the Gothic as the singular style of Christian culture suggests something of the cordoning-off of the meanings of style in the period, even if Walpole would have his defenders in light of such sanctimoniousness.[31] In the universities, the Oxford Movement (Tractarianism) was begun around 1833 by John Henry Newman to renew the medieval liturgical practices of the Anglican Church, and the advocacy of the Cambridge Camden Society (founded 1839) positioned the study of Gothic architecture as an integral component in the new "Science of Ecclesiology." In 1843 the Cambridge Camden Society published what remains a classic text in medievalist art history, an annotated translation of William Durandus's

1296 *Rationale Divinorum* as *The Symbolism of Churches and Church Ornaments*, which offered Victorian architects and ecclesiologists a mystical encyclopedia of the meanings of all aspects of medieval churches and their liturgical functions.[32] In those precincts lay the origins of Gothic architecture as an academic discipline in England. I am necessarily painting in the broadest of brushstrokes in this discussion, but I do so to create a context in which to understand how and why Walpole and Strawberry Hill posed a significant problem to Victorian proponents of the Gothic. In general, they dealt with this problem either by denigrating Strawberry Hill Gothic (and occasionally Georgian Gothic in general) or by altogether ignoring it and whitewashing it out of histories of the Gothic style.[33] Aside from its being stylistically out-of-date and formally incongruous with current appraisals of Gothic architecture, a significant reason for this was that Walpolean Gothic carried the taint of sexual alterity, which posed a particular challenge to Victorian moralists. Dominic Janes has noted that nineteenth-century commentators on Walpolean Gothic "indicated a concern for strange and queer deviations from the moral norms of Victorian society, both in terms of visual appearances and personal behavior."[34] Following Wahrman's lead, architecture, the male body, and sexuality followed a common arc of development in the period. Gender play had become gender panic in bodies as much as buildings.

Although early Victorian Gothicists actively sought to distance themselves from the Gothic's potential connotation of alternative sexuality, this nexus was firmly established in English culture and would be revived and rethought by later generations. Many homoerotically-inclined writers, artists, and architects "looked to the past in the present to imagine the future"; for these men and women, modern social renewal was predicated upon an anachronic return to the medieval past, a reimagining of an imagined lost social structure.[35] A growing historiography of scholarship on homosexuality and modern medievalism can be cited. Artists in various media frequently returned to the Gothic for its ability to express a range of alternative subjectivities, including sexuality[36]: the Pre-Raphaelite artist Simeon Solomon (1840–1905) (friend to Oscar Wilde) and his friend William Burges (1827–1881) (also known to Wilde), who would be parodied as Georgius Oldhausen; the American Gothic Revival architect Ralph Adams Cram (1863–1942), who engaged with the ideal of radical anticapitalist social reform through a return to celibacy in queer monastic community in the (neo) Gothic monastery; Ninian Comper (1864–1960); the designers Charles Ricketts (1866–1931) and Charles Shannon (1863–1937); the German filmmaker Friedrich Wilhelm Murnau (1888–1931) (director of *Nosferatu: A Symphony of Horror*, 1922), who resided with his lovers in the Schloss Murnau in the Hollywood Hills; the Cambridge medievalist M. R. James (1862–1936), who is now known as much for his scholarship on medieval art as for his ghost stories; and the medievalist films of Derek Jarman (1942–1994). It would require another study altogether to trace the complex interrelationships of the Gothic and sexuality in England from, say, 1700, where this study began, to the end of the nineteenth or even twentieth century. But this study would surely indicate the extraordinarily morphological nature of the Gothic as Walpole initially imagined it, as an imaginative space for exploring alternative visions of English culture.

Notes

Preface

1. Fletcher, "Sins of the Fathers," 115. On the construction of the Middle Ages as modernity's "other" in American medievalist historiography, see Freedman and Spiegel, "Medievalisms Old and New"; Cantor, *Inventing the Middle Ages*, 47: "medieval civilization stands toward our postmodern culture as the conjunctive other, the intriguing shadow, the marginally distinctive double, the secret sharer of our dreams and anxieties"; and Holsinger, *Premodern Condition*.
2. Fothergill, *Strawberry Hill Set*.
3. See, for example, G. Worsley, "Origins of the Gothic Revival." For recent accounts of the postmedieval history of the Gothic in England, see Girouard, *Elizabethan Architecture*, esp. 41–54; Brooks, *Gothic Revival*; and Hall, *Gothic Architecture and Its Meanings*.
4. As, for example, in the field's dominant survey text, Luttikhuizen and Verkerk, *Snyder's Medieval Art*, 463–65; Frankl, *The Gothic*, esp. 392–94; and Rudolph, "Introduction: A Sense of Loss," esp. 12–13. On the history of collecting, see Boehm, "Pair of Limoges Candlesticks," and Caudron, "Connoisseurs of *Champlevé*." For manuscripts in particular, see Hindman, Rowe, and Camille, *Manuscript Illumination in the Modern Age*.
5. Biddick, *Shock of Medievalism*.
6. Aldrich, "Thomas Rickman's Handbook."
7. Valuable recent work includes Scala and Federico, *Post-historical Middle Ages*; Dinshaw, *How Soon Is Now?*; Matthews, *Medievalism: A Critical History*; and Utz, *Medievalism: A Manifesto*.
8. Reeve, "Gothic"; Reeve, "Teaching Medieval Art History." Significant studies include Brush, *Shaping of Art History*; Camille, *Gargoyles of Notre-Dame*; Diebold, "Medievalism"; Diebold, "'Living Source of Our Civilization'"; Mills, *Derek Jarman's Medieval Modern*; K. Murphy, *Memory and Modernity*; and Powell, *Depositions*. See also Männig, *Hans Sedlmayr's Kunstgeschichte*, and Amic and Le Men, *Cathédrales, 1789–1914*. See the valuable review essay by Grootenboer, "Every Period Gets the Medievalism It Deserves."
9. Some of its major episodes in the eighteenth and nineteenth centuries were created by the impending loss or chance discovery of works of medieval art, such as the thirteenth-century vault paintings at Salisbury Cathedral or the wall painting in the Painted Chamber at Westminster Palace. See Reeve, *Thirteenth-Century Wall Painting*, and Binski, *Painted Chamber at Westminster*.
10. For a recent overview, see Sankovitch, "Myth of the 'Myth.'"
11. Panofsky, "First Page of Giorgio Vasari's 'Libro.'" On the later employment of "medieval" and "medievalism" in English scholarship, see Matthews, "From Mediaeval to Mediaevalism."
12. Recent accounts of nonlinear temporalities in art history and literary studies have been of much use here. For example, Nagel, *Medieval Modern*, and Dinshaw, *How Soon Is Now?*
13. Workman as cited in Verduin, "The Founding and the Founder," 20. See also Diebold, "Medievalism." For a valuable critique of Workman, see Petersen, "Medieval Resurfacings, Old and New."
14. See most recently Utz, *Medievalism: A Manifesto*, esp. 81, citing Kathleen Verduin: "If 'medievalism' [. . .] denotes the whole range of postmedieval engagement with the Middle Ages, then 'medieval studies' themselves must be considered a facet of medievalism rather than the other way around."
15. Aldrich and Wotherspoon, *Who's Who in Gay and Lesbian History*, 557–58.
16. For example, Sedgwick, *Between Men*; Haggerty, *Men in Love*; Janes, *Picturing the Closet*; Janes, *Oscar Wilde Prefigured*.
17. Sontag, "Notes on 'Camp.'"
18. Fletcher, "Sins of the Fathers."

19. For example, Hurley, *Gothic Body*, 6; Massé, "Psychoanalysis and the Gothic"; Haggerty, *Queer Gothic*.

20. In addition to sources already mentioned, see Cameron, *Psychopathology of the Gothic Romance*, and Townsend, *Orders of the Gothic*.

21. Horner, "Gothic and Surrealism." I am grateful to the author for providing me a copy of the essay before going to press. See also Marwood, "Imaginary Dimensions," and Matheson, *Surrealism and the Gothic*.

22. Eco, "Return of the Middle Ages."

23. Myrone, *Gothic Nightmares*.

24. Reeve, "'Gothic Vatican'"; Reeve, "Gothic Architecture"; Reeve and Lindfield, "'Child of Strawberry'"; Reeve, "Dickie Bateman." Foyle, "Did Horace Walpole Build Strawberry Hill to Express His Sexuality?"

25. Kavaler, *Renaissance Gothic*.

Introduction

1. Alexander, *Medievalism*, 4.

2. For a recent assessment of Kent's Gothic designs, see White, "Kent and the Gothic Revival." A useful historiographical overview of these ideas is provided in Lindfield, *Georgian Gothic*.

3. Lindfield, *Georgian Gothic*, 3.

4. Braybrooke, *History of Audley End*, 127. For the chapel, see McCarthy, *Origins of the Gothic Revival*, plate 11.

5. As, for example, in T. Davis, *Gothick Taste*, and more recently in Crook, *Gothick Symposium*. See the useful account in G. Worsley, "What's in a 'K'?" The historiography has been usefully explored in Hall, introduction to *Gothic Architecture and Its Meanings*.

6. McCarthy, *Origins of the Gothic Revival*; Wainwright, *Romantic Interior*.

7. For example, the denigrating comments of Humphry Repton (1752–1818) in his *Memoirs*, 132: "The house is one of the earliest attempts at Modern Gothic, by which I mean that heterogeneous mixture of abbey, castle and manor house for which taste had been introduced by the experiments of Horace Walpole at Strawberry Hill. The public had pronounced this new style to be 'vastly pretty,' and the same mongrel breed of architecture has been propagated ever since." I borrow "not Gothic enough" from Bruzelius, "Rose by Any Other Name."

8. Mowl, *Horace Walpole*; Bentman, "Horace Walpole's Forbidden Passion"; J. Campbell, "'I Am No Giant'"; Coykendall, "Queer Counterhistory"; Elfenbein, *Romantic Genius*, 91–124; Haggerty, *Men in Love*; Haggerty, "Walpoliana"; Haggerty, "Queering Horace Walpole"; Haggerty, *Queer Gothic*; Haggerty, *Horace Walpole's Letters*; A. Williams, "Horace in Italy." George Haggerty is currently working on an extended biography of Horace Walpole.

9. Haggerty, *Queer Gothic*, esp. 71.

10. Lepine, "Queer Gothic," and Coykendall, "Queer Counterhistory."

11. K. Clark, *Gothic Revival*, 64. See also Lepine, "Persistence of Medievalism."

12. Betjeman, *Ghastly Good Taste*, 108.

13. K. Clark, *Gothic Revival*, 46–65; Brooks, *Gothic Revival*, 59; Hall, introduction to *Gothic Architecture and Its Meanings*, 11.

14. Mowl, *Horace Walpole*, 116; A. Moore, *Houghton Hall*.

15. Mowl, *Horace Walpole*, 7.

16. The artist Jan Hietala's *Inconclusive Evidence* is a creative response to art and sexuality at Strawberry Hill. I am grateful to the author for sending me a copy of his book.

17. Haggerty, "Strawberry Hill." The lack of attention to these issues has been noted in reviews. See Reeve, review of *Horace Walpole's Strawberry Hill*, and Mowl, review of *Horace Walpole's Strawberry Hill*: "Its editor . . . seems so embarrassed by Walpole's deviant sexual identity that, in his commissioning role, he has managed to airbrush out almost all accounts of Walpole's wildly romantic love life, even though they would have explained both the inspiration behind the house and his choice of its contents."

18. S. Clarke, *Strawberry Hill Press*; Harney, *Place-Making for the Imagination*; Lindfield, *Georgian Gothic*. The notable exception was the recent Horace Walpole and the Queer Eighteenth Century conference in February 2019. It is hoped that the papers from the conference will be published.

19. Craske, "From Burlington Gate to Billingsgate," 97.

20. Although not dealing with the eighteenth century, a notable exception is the recent catalogue Barlow, *Queer British Art*.

21. Still relevant on the disciplinary boundaries of eighteenth-century studies is Stafford, "Eighteenth Century."

22. See subsequently K. Harvey, *Reading Sex*.

23. Trumbach, *Heterosexuality and the Third Gender*. Trumbach expanded and clarified his thesis in two later essays, "Modern Sodomy" and "Transformation of Sodomy." See also Haggerty, *Men in Love*, and Barker-Benfield, *Culture of Sensibility*. Valuable overviews are Cocks, "Modernity and the Self," and Reay, "Writing the Modern Histories."

24. Cleland, *Memoirs of a Woman of Pleasure*, 196. Cited and discussed in McNeil, *Pretty Gentlemen*, esp. 439–40.

25. C. Piggott, *Female Jockey Club*, 202–3.

26. Guthrie, *Reply to the Counter-address*, 6–7.

27. "George Hardinge's Portrait of Walpole, June 1813," in Sabor, *Critical Heritage*, 290–91.

28. "Thomas Babington Macaulay, Unsigned Review of *Letters of Horace Walpole, Earl of Orford, to Sir Horace Mann, Edinburgh Review*, October 1833," in Sabor, *Critical Heritage*, 312–13. For further discussion of Walpole's sexuality in the historiography, see Frank, "Horace Walpole's Family Romances."

29. The role of female patronage of the modern styles has been emphasized in Porter, *Chinese Taste*; Sloboda, *Chinoiserie*; and Vickery, *Behind Closed Doors*. For female patronage of the Gothic in particular, see Lindfield, "Countess of Pomfret's Gothic Revival Furniture"; Mayer, "'Junketaceous Gothick'"; and P. Smith, "Lady Oxford's Alterations." See also Laurence, "Women Using Building."

30. Vickery, *Behind Closed Doors*, 258.

31. Ibid., and see, in general, 257–90.

32. Cited and discussed in J. Clark, *English Society*, 11.

33. J. Harris, *Palladian Revival*.

34. Jestin, "Richard Bentley the Younger," 94.

35. For Palladianism as "an icon or a house style for the aristocratic oligarchy of the Whigs, who ruled Britain for the better part of the eighteenth century," see Mowl and Earnshaw, *Insular Rococo*, 13. Of much use on these issues is Arciszewska and McKellar, *Articulating British Classicism*.

36. *HW Corr*, 20:127 (HW to Mann, 25 February 1750). See also Crown, "British Rococo"; Porter, *Chinese Taste*; and Sloboda, *Chinoiserie*.

37. Brown, *Estimate of the Manners*, 1:67.

38. B. Allen, *Tides in English Taste*, 2:94–99.

39. Barker-Benfield, *Culture of Sensibility*, chap. 3; Cryle and O'Connell, *Libertine Enlightenment*; Clery, *Feminization Debate*; Carter, *Men and the Emergence*; Nussbaum, "Effeminacy and Femininity."

40. *World*, no. 15 (12 April 1753): 73–78, quote on 78.

41. Janes, *Oscar Wilde Prefigured*.

42. *HW Corr*, 10:139 and n. 11 (HW to Montagu, 16 December 1764). Walpole continues, "*Maccaroni* was a name adopted by or given to the young men of fashion who returned from their travels in the present reign, and is supposed to have been derived from the Italian paste of that denomination." See also Mason, *Satirical Poems*, 69–70; West, "Darly Macaroni Prints"; and McNeil, *Pretty Gentlemen*.

43. *HW Corr*, 17:274 n. 31 (HW to Mann, 7 January 1742). See also Dubro, "Third Sex."

44. Weeks, "Horace Walpole's *Fairy Tale*," 173.

45. *HW Corr*, 35:109 (HW to Chute, 6 February 1759).

46. Lucy Moore, *Amphibious Thing*, 288–89.

47. Piozzi, *Thraliana*, 2:875. See also Fothergill, *Strawberry Hill Set*, 49–50, and Bentman, "Horace Walpole's Forbidden Passion."

48. For useful overviews, see Senelick, "Mollies or Men of Mode?"; King, *English Phallus*, esp. chap. 7; and Janes, *Oscar Wilde Prefigured*.

49. Heynen, "Modernity and Domesticity," and Craske, "Plan and Control."

50. For a famous example in Walpole's writings, see *HW Corr*, 20:127 (HW to Mann, 25 February 1750).

51. Walpole, *Anecdotes* (1876), 1:xvii. For Inigo Jones's take on this paradigm, see Anderson, "Masculine and Unaffected."

52. Wittkower, "Classical Theory," 204; Senelick, "Mollies or Men of Mode?"; McNeil, *Pretty Gentlemen*. As Christopher Breward has noted, "it is more than coincidental that self-identifying groups of sodomites, choosing to express their difference through dress and the body, should emerge at a historical moment of material progress, expansion and diversification." Breward, *Culture of Fashion*, 140.

53. Hatt, "Space, Surface, Self"; Potvin, *Bachelors of a Different Sort*; Cook, *Queer Domesticities*. See also Pilkey et al., *Sexuality and Gender at Home*, and Germann and Strobel, *Materializing Gender*.

54. *Correspondence of Thomas Gray*, 1:406–7; *HW Corr*, 35:173 (HW to Bentley, 18 May 1754), 35:157 (HW to Bentley, 19 December 1753). Gray describes "the annals of Strawberry" in a letter to Walpole dated 17 March 1754. *HW Corr*, 14:81.

55. W. Davis, "Queer Family Romance," and previously W. Davis, "Homoerotic Art Collection." For approaches to queer family romance outside the history of art, see Halperin, *How to Be Gay*, 223–41, and Heller, *Family Plots*, esp. 146–64.

56. W. Davis, "Queer Family Romance," 323.

57. As Dana Heller notes, "To come out by identifying oneself or someone else as 'family' is to trouble deeply the boundaries between culture and biology, the personal and the political." Heller, *Family Plots*, 149.

58. Pittock, "Treacherous Objects."

59. Vicinus, *Intimate Friends*, xxix. Discussed in context in Cocks, "Modernity and the Self," 1219–21; Tadmor, *Family and Friends*; and Tadmor, "Early Modern English Kinship."

60. Nick Groom, introduction to Walpole, *Castle of Otranto*, xxxvi.

61. *HW Corr*, 12:111.

62. A. Williams, "Reading Walpole Reading Shakespeare"; Fletcher, "Sins of the Fathers"; Haggerty, *Queer Gothic*; Heiland, *Gothic and Gender*; Frank, "Horace Walpole's Family Romances."

63. Baxandall, *Patterns of Intention*, 58–62, quote on 58–59. For a useful discussion, see Ambrose, "Influence."

64. Halperin, "Forgetting Foucault," 109. Halperin's advice guides the present study: "We need to find ways of asking how different historical cultures fashioned different sorts of links between sexual acts, on the one hand, and sexual tastes, styles, dispositions, characters, gender presentations, and forms of subjectivity, on the other." See the valuable account of teleology in gay and lesbian studies by Traub, "New Unhistoricism in Queer Studies."

65. See most recently Voloshkova, "'My Friend Mr. H. Walpole.'"

66. Hester Piozzi quoted in Gross, *Life of Anne Damer*, 146–47.

67. Roman, "Art of Lady Diana Beauclerk," 165.

68. *HW Corr*, 6:474 (HW to Madame de Deffand, 7 September 1777). See also Peltz, *Facing the Text*, 198–99.

69. Cocks, "Modernity and the Self," 1222.

70. Halperin, "How to Do the History."

71. Haggerty, "History of Homosexuality Reconsidered."

72. For the Judgment of Solomon, see Haggerty, "Walpoliana," and generally, see Bentman, "Horace Walpole's Forbidden Passion," 280–81.

73. O'Driscoll, "Molly and the Fop"; Norton, "Mother Clap's Molly House."

74. Reay, "Writing the Modern Histories," 217: "Arguably, the most useful sexual histories are those that provide depth of context without either assuming sexual identity or anticipating its complete absence; and without forcing taxonomies."

75. Richter and McGrath, "Representing Homosexuality"; Haggerty, *Men in Love*; Haggerty, "Male Love and Friendship"; Haggerty, "History of Homosexuality Reconsidered."

76. See, for example, Richter, "Winckelmann's Progeny," 35.

77. Halperin, *One Hundred Years of Homosexuality*, 41; and see Traub, "New Unhistoricism in Queer Studies."

78. See the useful commentary throughout W. Davis, *Queer Beauty*.

79. Halperin, *How to Be Gay*.

80. On "stylisticality," I am indebted to W. Davis, *General Theory of Visual Culture*.

Chapter 1

1. In a letter of 12 August 1769 to Rev. William Cole, Walpole outlined a plan for a history of Gothic architecture. *HW Corr*, 7:304.
2. Lipking, *Ordering of the Arts*, 141.
3. See William Mason's biography of Gray in *Monthly Review*, August 1775, 98.
4. Published in *Works of Thomas Gray*, 5:325–32.
5. Roberts, "Thomas Gray's Contribution." For the development of a stylistic succession of the Gothic in the eighteenth century, see Lindfield, *Georgian Gothic*, esp. 23–31. Gray's life has been sensitively treated in Mack, *Thomas Gray*. Grose's essay was initially published as a section (simply titled "Architecture") of his preface to *Antiquities of England and Wales*. The essay is reprinted in Warton et al., *Essays on Gothic Architecture*, 95–124. Walpole's circle was characteristically dismissive of Grose's work. *HW Corr*, 2:182 (Cole to HW, 30 December 1779).
6. Walpole, *Anecdotes* (1876), 1:116, cited and discussed in Roberts, "Thomas Gray's Contribution," 56.
7. *HW Corr*, 1:340–41 (HW to Cole, 15 August 1774).
8. *HW Corr*, 1:178–79 (HW to Cole, 15 July 1769).
9. Stokes, *Blecheley Diary of the Rev. William Cole*, page facing xxii; Palmer, *William Cole of Milton*, 32–43.
10. Rielly, "Thomas Warton's Gothic Sensibility."
11. Gray, *Poems and Letters*, 226, and Mack, *Thomas Gray*, 446.
12. Sankovitch, "Myth of the 'Myth.'" The scholarship on the English sources is extensive. See, for example, de Beer, "Gothic"; Germann, *Gothic Revival*; and Buchanan, "Interpretations of Medieval Architecture." For Wren, see Soo, *Wren's "Tracts" on Architecture*.
13. Hopkins, "'Mere Gothique Heaps of Stone'?"
14. Terry, *Poetry*, 186–323.
15. For recent reassessments of Langley, see Lindfield, "Serious Gothic," and Lindfield, "Georgian Gothic Fabrications." For Charles Over's text, which has received less treatment by scholars, see Over, *Ornamental Architecture*.
16. On the influence of Langley, see White, "Influence of Batty Langley," and White, "Wiston House Remodelled." For Thomas Gray's dislike of Halfpenny's designs and preference for Wenceslaus Hollar's, see Kalter, *Modern Antiques*, 114.
17. Some of the earliest pattern books on Gothic architecture, particularly those by Batty Langley, were manifestly influential on Walpole (who subscribed to Langley's *Ancient Architecture* of 1741 and whose copy, now at the Lewis Walpole Library, includes a drawing of the southeast elevation of Strawberry Hill by John Chute). The book is now LWL MS 49 630, marked on a rear flyleaf.
18. *HW Corr*, 35:233 (HW to Bentley, 5 July 1754).
19. *HW Corr*, 35:155 (HW to Bentley, September 1753).
20. Lipking, *Ordering of the Arts*, 145.
21. Ibid., 141–42. Warton's commentary on Gothic architecture, from his *Observations on the Fairy Queen of Spenser* of 1762, is reprinted in Warton et al., *Essays on Gothic Architecture*, 1–15. Alexander, *Medievalism*, 8–16.
22. Hadfield, "William Kent's Illustrations."
23. Darongsuwan, "Class and Gender Identity," 30–31.
24. *HW Corr*, 35:359 (HW to Strafford, 13 June 1781); 35:139 (HW to Bentley, 5 August 1752).
25. *HW Corr*, 31:342 (HW to Hannah More, 25 July 1790), 35:183 (HW to Bentley, 3 November 1754). See also S. Clarke, "Horace Walpole's Architectural Taste."
26. W. Davis, "Founding the Closet."
27. Jones, *Gender and the Formation of Taste*; Barrell, *Political Theory of Painting*; Barrell, "'Dangerous Goddess'"; J. Pococke, *Virtue, Commerce, and History*; Wittkower, "Classical Theory."
28. Bohls, "Disinterestedness and Denial," 16.
29. Ibid., 18.
30. For Walpole's circle as "men of feeling," see Janes, *Oscar Wilde Prefigured*, 55–86, and Haggerty, *Men in Love*. See, in general, Carter, *Men and the Emergence*.

31. Walpole, *Anecdotes* (1762), 1:107–8.

32. See *Spectator* 6, no. 415 (26 June 1712): 85: "Let any one reflect on the disposition of mind he finds in himself, at his first entrance into the Pantheon at Rome, and how the imagination is filled with something great and amazing; and, at the same time, consider how little, in proportion, he is effected with the inside of a Gothic cathedral, though it be five times larger than the other; which can arise from nothing else but the greatness of the manner in the one, and the meanness in the other." See also Harney, *Place-Making for the Imagination*, 47. Walpole was not alone; this passage may have inspired William Stukeley's 1740 comparisons between York Minster and St. Peters and between the York chapter house and the Parthenon. See S. Piggott, *William Stukeley*, 122.

33. Walpole, *Castle of Otranto*, 9.

34. Walpole, "Detached Thoughts," 368.

35. Styles and Vickery, introduction to *Gender, Taste, and Material Culture*, 14–15.

36. Gerard, *Essay on Taste*, 122–27.

37. Cited and discussed in Jones, *Gender and the Formation of Taste*, 9.

38. Battles, "Antiquarian Impulse."

39. Sha, *Perverse Romanticism*, chap. 3.

40. Walpole, *Anecdotes* (1762), 1:107–8.

41. As Barrett Kalter suggests, the Gothic promoted by Walpole and his circle "resisted the set schedule of modernity, with its logic of incremental change, prescriptive currency, and necessary superannuation." Kalter, *Modern Antiques*, 14.

42. Allan, "New Light on William Kent."

43. *HW Corr*, 33:42 (HW to Lady Ossory, 11 August 1778). On Walpole's associationism, see Harney, *Place-Making for the Imagination*.

44. *HW Corr*, 2:45–46 (HW to Cole, 22 May 1777). See also Musson, "King's College Chapel," 30.

45. Bohls, "Disinterestedness and Denial."

46. *HW Corr*, 35:161 (HW to Bentley, 2 March 1754). See also *HW Corr*, 35:184 (HW to Bentley, 3 November 1754).

47. Mowl, *Horace Walpole*, 7.

48. Bohls, "Disinterestedness and Denial," 18.

49. See Ruskin, *Seven Lamps of Architecture*, and, most influentially, his chapter "The Nature of Gothic" in *Stones of Venice*. See also Connelly, "Ruskin and the Savage Gothic"; Morris, "Origins of Ornamental Art"; and O'Neill, *Walter Crane*. These ideas entered into the historiography of academic medieval art history in Rudolph Berliner's classic essay "Freedom of Medieval Art."

50. On Walpole's sources, see McKinney, "History and Revivalism," 179–212, and for Gray's contribution, see esp. 194–96.

51. See Bradley, "Englishness of Gothic," and Frew, "Gothic Is English." The nature of the arch as a signifier of nationality—the pointed arched signifying Englishness, and the rounded arch, "Normanness"—was often explored in the middle of the eighteenth century, as, for example, in Ducarel, *Tour Through Normandy*. For Walpole's copy of the *Tour*, see Hazen, 668; see also Mateo, "In Search of the Origin."

52. Walpole, *Anecdotes* (1762), 1:107. Walpole was regularly consulted by subsequent scholars seeking to refine a chronology of medieval architecture. See, for example, the unpublished notes in the Arco Acuto MS, John Soane Museum, London.

53. *HW Corr*, 1:190–92 (HW to Cole, 11 August 1769), quotes on 190. Walpole's letter to Cole describing a history of Gothic Architecture was partially printed by Richard Gough in *Sepulchral Monuments in Great Britain*, pt. 1. For Walpole's response, see *HW Corr*, 42:168 (HW to Gough, 21 June 1786).

54. For example, the eastern arm of Canterbury Cathedral, the antique sources of which are explored in Binski, *Becket's Crown*, 3–27.

55. *HW Corr*, 1:191 (HW to Cole, 11 August 1769).

56. *HW Corr*, 11:22 (HW to Mary Berry, 30 June 1789).

57. Walpole, "State of Architecture to the End of the Reign of Henry VIII," in *Anecdotes* (1762), vol. 1, chap. 5. For a recent discussion, see Llewellyn, "*Anecdotes of Painting*," although this text naturally explores painting rather than architecture.

58. Rickman, *Attempt to Discriminate*.

59. See, for example, Quaintance, "Walpole's Whig Interpretation."

60. Walpole, *Anecdotes* (1876), 1:xii.

61. These aspects of Strawberry Hill have been emphasized in McKinney, "History and Revivalism"; McKinney, "Castle of My Ancestors"; G. Worsley, "Origins of the Gothic Revival"; and Groom, "Gothic Antiquity."

62. Kliger, *Goths in England*; R. J. Smith, *Gothic Bequest*; Price, *Reinventing Liberty*.

63. *HW Corr*, 9:197–98 (HW to Montagu, 14 October 1756). For Bateman, see chapter 4. For Beckford, see S. Clarke, "'Almost Innumerable Descents.'" The signatories of Magna Carta would also feature in James Barry's designs for the chamber of the House of Lords at Westminster (1848–53). See Droth, Edwards, and Hatt, *Sculpture Victorious*, 153–57.

64. *HW Corr*, 33:391 (HW to Ossory, 11 March 1783).

65. West cited in Kliger, *Goths in England*, 29–30.

66. McKinney, "History and Revivalism," 37–42.

67. Walpole not only purchased and read these letters but carefully annotated his copies, drawing attention to passages of particular significance. See Hazen, 3926, 3927. Walpole points to a pregnant passage in which Lyttelton compares the ancient Saxon constitution to architecture, creating an analogy between Gothic architecture and English liberty in letter 29:

> I have heard, said I, that the Laws of England are wisely framed and impartially administered. The old Gothick Pile we are now in, replied my Friend, will give you a just Idea of their Structure: The Foundations of it are deep and very lasting; it has stood many Ages, and with good Repairs may stand many more; but the Architecture is loaded with a Multiplicity of idle and useless Parts; when you examine it critically, many Faults and Imperfections will appear; yet upon the whole it has a mighty awful Air, and strickes [*sic*] you with Reverence and Respect.

Cited and discussed in McKinney, "History and Revivalism," 39.

68. Colton, "Merlin's Cave and Queen Caroline"; G. Clarke, "Grecian Taste and Gothic Virtue."

69. *HW Corr*, 35:76–77 (HW to Chute, 4 August 1753). In his copy of *Stowe: A Description* (1768), LWL 49 2387.4, p. 30, Walpole draws attention to Stowe's famous Gothic temple and includes a hitherto overlooked account of its imagery, with its manifestly political bent: "This was originally closed up on one side with paintings, in which was Fame drawing a veil over the reign of George II, but this was taken away on Lord Temple's coming into place."

70. Price, *Reinventing Liberty*, 31–32.

71. Walpole's upending of the values of the humanist tradition that privileged the antique over the medieval world had some precedent in English writing in which the Goths were understood to have introduced both political freedom and virtuous manners, both of which were corrupted by the Renaissance reintroduction of antiquity. Klein, "Liberty, Manners, and Politeness," esp. 593–94.

72. Walpole, *Anecdotes* (1762), 1:108.

73. Walpole, *Fugitive Pieces*, 2.

74. Walpole, *Anecdotes* (1762), 1:ix.

75. *HW Corr*, 17:495 (HW to Mann, 14 July 1742).

76. Walpole, *Anecdotes* (1762), 1:xvi–xvii.

77. I am grateful to Randolph Trumbach for discussing this with me.

78. Walpole's reference to Petronius here would appear to have genealogy in queer writing: it is mirrored in Oscar Wilde's *Picture of Dorian Gray* (chapter 11), in which the author's protagonist seeks not only to be London's *arbiter elegantiarum* but to "elaborate some new scheme of life . . . and find in the spiritualizing of the senses its highest realization." Wilde's role in the translation of the *Satyricon* has recently been disputed. See Boroughs, "Oscar Wilde's Translation of Petronius."

79. *HW Corr*, 37:406 (HW to Conway, 23 September 1755).

80. "Macaulay, Unsigned Review," in Sabor, *Critical Heritage*, 314. For Walpole's "more ambivalent attitude to the notion of ancient constitutional liberty," an attitude that expresses a "humorous exaggeration of the contemporary political concerns," see Price, *Reinventing Liberty*, 31.

81. Warton, *Joshua Reynolds's Painted Window*, 3–4.

82. Guest, "Wanton Muse."

83. W. Davis, "Winckelmann Divided," and Potts, *Flesh and the Ideal*.

84. W. Davis, "Winckelmann Divided," 141.

85. Sha, *Perverse Romanticism*.

86. *HW Corr*, 11:22 (HW to Mary Berry, 30 June 1789): "Your partiality to the pageantry of Popery I do approve, and I doubt whether the world will not be a loser (in its visionary enjoyments) by the extinction of that religion, as it was by the decay of chivalry and the proscription of the heathen deities."

87. *HW Corr*, 9:322 (HW to Montagu, 13 November 1760).

88. For the latten angel (or saint), see *HWSH*, cat. no. 30.

89. *HW Corr*, 20:372 (HW to Mann, 27 April 1753).

90. Baines, *Complete Critical Guide*, 79–81. See Carson, "'Exquisite Torture.'" Pope's *Eloisa to Abelard* inspired a number of eighteenth-century medievalist poems with the same name. As Maria Purves notes, Walpole's decision to create a Paraclete came immediately after James Cawthorn's popular version of *Abelard to Eloisa* (1746). Purves, *Gothic and Catholicism*, 76–77. Walpole owned and displayed at Strawberry Hill a picture by Richard Bentley "representing two lovers in a church looking at the tombs of Abelard and Eloisa." Walpole, *Description* (1798), 488. Alexander Pope was likewise a student of Gothic architecture, having studied the remains of Netley and Beaulieu and Sherborne Old Castle and having designed or aided in the design of early medievalizing garden follies, including his own grotto at Twickenham and Alfred's Hall in Cirencester in the 1720s through 1730s. For Pope's influence on Walpole, see Brownell, *Alexander Pope*, 99–100.

91. *HW Corr*, 10:43 (HW to Montagu, 24 September 1762).

92. Delany, *Autobiography and Correspondence* (1862), 1:177–78.

93. Haynes, *Pictures and Popery*; Haynes, "Culture of Judgement." For Walpole's youthful (1742) commentary on religious art, "Sermon on Painting," which vigorously defends the image as a religious tool but warns against improper use leading to idolatry, see Haynes, *Pictures and Popery*, 83–88.

94. Hill, "'Ivi'd Ruins,'" and Sweet, "Gothic Antiquarianism." The Catholic patron Bryant Barrett commissioned stunning Gothic additions to Milton Manor, Berkshire (from 1764), that have been understood as an expression of his Catholic faith. For Milton Manor, see M. Murphy, "King's Laceman." For John Carter, see Nurse and Crook, "John Carter," 238.

95. For Walpole's ownership of these texts, see Hazen, 424, 563, 2166; 611, 766; 862, 2065; 568, 590, 591, 729. For Walpole's assessment of Spelman, see recently Shell, *Oral Culture and Catholicism*, 33–37. Walpole also contributed to this historiography, publishing *Paul Hentzner's Travels* (1757), which provides accounts of significant buildings such as Westminster Abbey and Nonsuch Palace.

96. Parry, *Trophies of Time*. These paradigms would influence subsequent Gothicists, some of whom would be converts to Catholicism, particularly A. W. N. Pugin. See Hill, "Reformation to Millennium."

97. Evans, *History of the Society of Antiquaries*, 2.

98. See *HW Corr*, 35:146–47 (HW to Bentley, September 1753): "my love of abbeys shall not make me hate the Reformation till that makes me grow a Jacobite like the rest of my antiquarian predecessors." See also Walpole, *Anecdotes* (1762), 1:54: "There is no forgiving him [Henry VIII] that destruction of ancient monuments and gothic piles and painted glass by the suppression of monasteries; a reformation, as he called it, which we antiquaries most devoutly lament."

99. Rielly, "Thomas Warton's Gothic Sensibility," 152.

100. Stewart, "Notes on Distressed Genres," 11.

101. Tuite, "Cloistered Closets."

102. O'Malley, *Catholicism, Sexual Deviance*, 3; Roden, *Same-Sex Desire*; Gallagher, Roden, and Smith, *Catholic Figures, Queer Narratives*; Hanson, *Decadence and Catholicism*; Hilliard, "UnEnglish and Unmanly." See also Jordan, *Silence of Sodom*.

103. Hanson, *Decadence and Catholicism*, 7.

104. On the relationship between Catholicism and same-sex desire in eighteenth-century Gothic writing, see Haggerty, *Queer Gothic*, 63–83, and Townsend, "'Love in a Convent.'"

Although not centered on sexuality, Purves's *Gothic and Catholicism* argues for a more positive acceptance of Catholicism in England than traditionally understood.

105. See, for example, Monk of the Order of St. Francis, *Nocturnal Revels*, and for a recent discussion, Janes, "Unnatural Appetites."

106. "Reasons for the Growth of Sodomy" and E. Harris, *Handel as Orpheus*. The notion that homoerotic behavior was "imported" to England from Italy has a long history. See Crompton, *Byron and Greek Love*, 52. The formative influence of Walpole's Grand Tour has been discussed in A. Williams, "Monstrous Pleasures," and A. Williams, "Horace in Italy."

107. Sedgwick, *Epistemology of the Closet*, 140.

108. Haydon, *Anti-Catholicism*. Walpole's interests in and perceptions of Catholicism require further study. See Mowl, *Horace Walpole*, 235–36; Shell, *Oral Culture and Catholicism*, 33–36; O'Malley, *Catholicism, Sexual Deviance*, 14–15; and Purves, *Gothic and Catholicism*, esp. 15–16, 60–61.

109. *HW Corr*, 2:100 (HW to Cole, 12 July 1778).

110. Walpole, *Description* (1798), 397 n.; *HW Corr*, 10:168 (HW to Montagu, 23 August 1765). See also *HW Corr*, 35:421 (HW to Hamilton, 19 June 1774).

111. Walpole, *Description* (1798), 471, 473, 477, and, in general, Zajko, "'Listening with' Ovid." For Walpole's Becket reliquary, see *HWSH*, cat. no. 160. It was also recorded by William Cole in BL Add MS 5841, fol. 77, reproduced in Groom, "Gothic Antiquity," 56. Walpole acquired the reliquary from the collection of Thomas Barrett at Lee Priory. It is now in the Glasgow Museum.

112. *HW Corr*, 21:306 (HW to Mann, 8 July 1759).

113. On the duc de Nivernais's visit, see McEvoy, *Gothic Tourism*, 12–52.

114. *HW Corr*, 10:127 (HW to Montagu, 18 June 1764). Mowl, "William Beckford."

115. *HW Corr*, 35:185 (HW to Bentley, 3 November 1754).

116. *HW Corr*, 9:146–47 (HW to Montagu, 22 May 1753).

117. *HW Corr*, 9:102 (HW to Montagu, 28 September 1749). Elsewhere Walpole compares Strawberry Hill to the fabled house of the *Gerusalemme liberata*: *HW Corr*, 33:61 (HW to Ossory, 21 October 1778).

118. *HW Corr*, 9:50 (HW to Montagu, 2 July 1747).

119. Hanson, *Decadence and Catholicism*, 7, 24–25.

120. See recently Lord, *Hell-Fire Clubs*, 97–113, and Kelly, *Society of Dilettanti*, 77–89.

121. See Almon, *New Foundling Hospital for Wit*, 105. On Wilkes's association with the "Hellfire Club," see Cash, *John Wilkes*, 32–36.

122. Symes, "Flintwork, Freedom, and Fantasy"; Dashwood, *Dashwoods*, 45; Frith, "Sexuality and Politics."

123. See Simon, *Hogarth, France, and British Art*, 206–16, and Kelly, *Society of Dilettanti*, 80–82.

124. "Horace Walpole's Journals," 50; Lord, *Hell-Fire Clubs*, 101, 113; Dashwood, *Dashwoods*, 29.

125. Redford, "Grecian Taste and Neapolitan Spirit," 186.

126. Haggerty, *Queer Gothic*, 71.

127. McWhir, "Gothic Transgression of Disbelief," 37.

128. See, most recently, Reeve, "'Gothic Vatican'"; Lindfield, "Heraldry and the Architectural Imagination"; and Silver, "Visiting Strawberry Hill." For the visual tradition of images based upon the text, see Lindfield, "Imagining the Undefined Castle." The relationship between the spaces of Strawberry Hill and *The Castle of Otranto* were first explored in W. Lewis, "Genesis of Strawberry Hill," 88–90.

129. Walpole, *Castle of Otranto*, 17.

130. Ibid., 103.

131. Ibid., 5.

132. Ibid., 9.

133. The nexus of Gothic literature and architecture had been established by Alexander Pope, who had offered an analogy between Shakespeare's writing and "an ancient majestic piece of *Gothick* architecture." Pope, preface to *The Works of Shakespear* [*sic*]), 1:xxiii.

134. Walpole, *Castle of Otranto*, 9.

135. *HW Corr*, 1:88 (HW to Cole, 9 March 1765).

136. Lindfield, "Heraldry and the Architectural Imagination."

137. Burney, *Diary and Letters of Madam D'Arblay*, 2:483.

138. A. Williams, "Reading Walpole Reading Shakespeare," 17.

139. Haggerty, *Queer Gothic*; J. Campbell, "'I Am No Giant'"; Hughes and Smith, *Queering the Gothic*.

140. Mowl, *Horace Walpole*, 182–86, and Fincher, "Guessing the Mould." For revisions of this thesis, see J. Campbell, "'I Am No Giant.'"

141. Fincher, "Guessing the Mould," 233.

142. Haggerty, *Queer Gothic*, 2, 5.

143. The literature is extensive. In terms of imagery, one thinks of Pompeo Batoni's *Portrait of a Young Man* (ca. 1760–65, Metropolitan Museum of Art, New York), in which a Grand Tourist points to a marble relief of Antinous discovered at Hadrian's villa at Tivoli in 1737. As Whitney Davis notes, Batoni's painting did not position the young man as Hadrian, but rather as "a Winckelmann or an Albani to this Antinous." W. Davis, *Queer Beauty*, 27–30, quote on 29.

144. Ibid.; Potts, *Flesh and the Ideal*; Lubey, "Erotic Interiors."

Chapter 2

1. *HW Corr*, 9:350 (HW to Montagu, 25–30 March 1761), 23:166 (HW to Mann, 31 December 1769).

2. Saumarez Smith, *Eighteenth-Century Decoration*, 237; Crook, "Strawberry Hill Revisited, II," 1726.

3. Classically in McCarthy, *Origins of the Gothic Revival*.

4. The tourist trade at Strawberry Hill has been sensitively treated elsewhere: McEvoy, *Gothic Tourism*; S. Clarke, "'Lord God!'"; Snodin, "Going to Strawberry Hill."

5. See also the recent edition by Nicolas Barker, *Horace Walpole's Description*, a facsimile of the extra-illustrated copy for Charles Bedford.

6. For a recent discussion of estate portraiture, with further bibliography, see Bonehill, "View from the Gentleman's Seat."

7. Jestin, "Richard Bentley the Younger," 97–98.

8. Now LWL MS 49 2522.

9. *HW Corr*, 33:43 (HW to Ossory, 11 August 1778). The paired posterity of Walpole and Strawberry Hill was a common refrain in Walpole's writings. See also the preface to the 1784 *Description*, as well as *HW Corr*, 21:471 (HW to Mann, 27 January 1761) and 24:103 (HW to Mann, 17 May 1775).

10. "Unsigned, *Descriptions to the Plates of Thames Scenery*, 1818," in Sabor, *Critical Heritage*, 251. This relationship has been reinforced in recent scholarship: see Bann, "Historicizing Horace," 132, for Strawberry Hill as "a theatre for 'self-fashioning,'" and Harney, "Strawberry Hill," 72, for the estate as "a prime example of an associative, autobiographical site, where the man, the 'little Gothic castle' and the landscape are inextricably linked."

11. Homophobic tropes of physical and mental degeneracy were common in Walpole's posthumous critiques. See, for example, Watt, *Contesting the Gothic*, 22–23. For the connection of "weak" tastes with "weak" bodies of men of the third sex, see also Lancaster, *Pretty Gentleman*, 18.

12. "Macaulay, Unsigned Review," in Sabor, *Critical Heritage*, 312–13. See also Coykendall, "Queer Counterhistory."

13. "Macaulay, Unsigned Review," in Sabor, *Critical Heritage*, 324.

14. Haggerty, "Strawberry Hill," 77.

15. *HW Corr*, 24:209 (HW to Mann, 27 May 1776).

16. *HW Corr*, 14:184 (Gray to HW, April 1769).

17. *HW Corr*, 10:101 (HW to Montagu, 7 September 1763).

18. For example, George Hardinge states: "Some of [Walpole's] friends were as effeminate in appearance and in manner as himself and were as witty. Of these I remember two, Mr Chute and Mr George Montagu [an occasional member of the Strawberry Committee]. But others had effeminacy alone to recommend them." "Hardinge's Portrait of Walpole," in Sabor, *Critical Heritage*, 291.

19. Riely, "Horace Walpole.'"

20. Rousseau, *Perilous Enlightenment*, 181, cited and discussed in Mack, *Thomas Gray*, 238–39.

21. Gladwell, *Tipping Point*, chap. 2.

22. Rousseau, *Perilous Enlightenment*, 181. For the careers of these men on the Grand Tour, see ibid., 172–99. See also A. Williams, "Horace in Italy."

23. Also influential on Walpole was Dicky Bateman's Old Windsor, discussed in chapter 4.

24. Fothergill, *Strawberry Hill Set*, 42–73. Chute's bedroom was the Red Bedchamber, off the staircase. *HW Corr*, 20:381 (HW to Mann, 12 June 1753).

25. *Correspondence of Thomas Gray*, 1:406–7; *HW Corr*, 35:139 (HW to Bentley, 5 August 1752).

26. *HW Corr*, 35:157–58 (HW to Bentley, 19 December 1753):

> For the library, it cannot have the Strawberry imprimatur: the double arches and double pinnacles are most ungraceful; and the doors below the book-cases in Mr Chute's design had a conventual look, which yours totally wants. For this time, we shall put your genius in commission, and, like some other regents, execute our own plan without minding our sovereign. For the chimney, I do not wonder you missed our instructions: we could not contrive to understand them ourselves; and therefore, determining nothing but to have the old picture stuck in a thicket of pinnacles, we left it to you to find out *the how*. I believe it will be a little difficult; but as I suppose *facera quia impossibile est*, is full as easy as *credere*, why—you must do it.

27. McCarthy, *Origins of the Gothic Revival*, 68–69.

28. Ibid.; Lindfield, *Georgian Gothic*, 66–71.

29. *HW Corr*, 35:110–11 (HW to Chute, 4 November 1759). This letter is sensitively treated in Haggerty, *Horace Walpole's Letters*, 73–74, and McCarthy, *Origins of the Gothic Revival*, 74–76.

30. *HW Corr*, 35:115 (HW to Chute, 7 January 1766); 24:209–13 (HW to Mann, 27 May 1776).

31. For example, *HW Corr*, 9:79 (HW to Montagu, 20 October 1748).

32. Careful accounts of the phasing of the building are found in Rogers, "Walpole's Gothic," and Guillery and Snodin, "Strawberry Hill." Peter Lindfield's *Unbuilt Strawberry* (forthcoming) will shed much new light on the sequence of construction and on abandoned schemes for the house.

33. "The chimney-piece and windows are not truly Gothic, but were designed by Mr. W. Robinson of the Board of Works, before there was any design of farther improvements to the house." Walpole, *Description* (1798), 421.

34. Rogers, "Walpole's Gothic," 60.

35. *HW Corr*, 20:111 (HW to Mann, 10 January 1750).

36. *HW Corr*, 20:361–62 (HW to Mann, 4 March 1753).

37. *HW Corr*, 21:238 (HW to Mann, 9 September 1758): "A day may come that will produce a gallery, a round tower, a larger cloister, and a cabinet, in the manner of a little chapel—but I am too poor for these ambitious designs yet."

38. Guillery and Snodin, "Strawberry Hill," 119–20.

39. McCarthy, *Origins of the Gothic Revival*, 33–37.

40. *HW Corr*, 12:137 (HW to Mary Berry, 17 October 1794), my emphasis.

41. Walpole, *Description* (1798), 454.

42. Thurley, "The Reigns of Henry VII and Henry VIII," 151. J. H. Müntz's 1751 drawing of the Holbein Chamber ceiling is now LWL 49 3582 Folio.

43. Walpole, *Description* (1798), 454. For Thomas Gray's description of the room (which incorrectly attributes the chimneypiece to Rouen Cathedral as well), see *Correspondence of Thomas Gray*, 3:303.

44. Pommeraye, *S. Ouen de Rouen*, 192. Joseph Crook suggests—erroneously it seems—that the screen itself was based on a 1732 rococo-Gothic installation at Rouen by "Carré the elder," although he gives no source. Crook, "Strawberry Hill Revisited, II," 1727. His interpretation is followed in Mowl, *Horace Walpole*, 145. Walpole was in contact with the early Anglo-Norman antiquarian Andrew Coltée Ducarel from 1758 and owned copies of his *Anglo-Norman Antiquities Reconsidered* (London, 1767) (now Hazen, 3274) and *Tour Through Normandy* (London, 1754) (now Hazen, 668:6), suggesting that he could have been a conduit for drawings. See also Myers, "Dr Andrew Coltée Ducarel."

45. My thanks to Kai Hoshizaki for suggesting this to me.

46. For Wolsey's hat, see *HWSH*, cat. no. 129. The idea of a Holbein Room may have been based on the "Holbein room" at Cowdray House, which Walpole visited in 1749. *HW Corr*, 9:98–99 (HW to Montagu, 26 August 1749). The "Holbein room" at Cowdray requires further research. *A Catalogue of the Pictures at Cowdray-House* (Portsmouth, 1777) attributes a number of pictures in the house to Holbein, and the room might be that called the Grand Drawing Room, which had Holbeins and a number of other sixteenth-century paintings.

47. Walpole, *Description* (1798), 470.

48. Dart, *Westmonasterium*, vol. 2, plate 108. Tanner, "Tombs of Royal Babies," 34.

49. Hazen, 567.

50. Coldstream, "York Chapter House."

51. Phillips, "Tracery of the Great West Window."

52. Harvey, "Architectural History," 157. Walpole also had access to the window via images by Wenceslaus Hollar (1672) and Daniel King (1656). See Buttery, *York Minster Revealed*, 12.

53. *HW Corr*, 18:274 (Mann to HW, 27 July 1743). Elsewhere Mann jokes that he will send Walpole the Tribune as a gift: *HW Corr*, 17:324 (Mann to HW, 18 February 1742). Walpole often commented on the Tribune and critiqued Johann Zoffany's famous 1772–78 *Tribuna of the Uffizi* (now Royal Collection, Windsor Castle), with a representation of Mann. *HW Corr*, 24:526–27 (HW to Mann, 12 November 1779), 24:539–40 (Mann to HW, 10 December 1779).

54. Millikin, "Tribune in English Architecture."

55. "Horace Walpole's Journals," 37.

56. Crook, "Strawberry Hill Revisited, II," 1729.

57. *HW Corr*, 35:73 (HW to Chute, 4 August 1753).

58. *HWSH*, cat. no. 61.

59. Eastlake, *History of the Gothic Revival*, 47: "Ceilings, screens, niches, &c., are all copied, or rather parodied, from existing examples, but with utter disregard for the original purpose of the design. To Lord Orford [Horace Walpole], Gothic was Gothic, and that sufficed."

60. Jestin, "Richard Bentley the Younger," 126.

61. Coykendall, "Gothic Genealogies," and Frank, "Horace Walpole's Family Romances."

62. Walpole's replication of Henry VII's chapel was arguably the most influential model for subsequent Gothic Revival buildings, but it was preceded by the Countess of Oxford's Welbeck Abbey, which Walpole was familiar with. See McDonnell, "Stone, Stucco, and Papier Mâché."

63. Coope, "'Long Gallery.'"

64. Walpole, *Description* (1798), 442. The canopy on John of Eltham's tomb is now lost but was known to Horace Walpole via Dart's *Westmonasterium* (engraved in 1723).

65. See most recently Wilton-Ely, "Style and Serendipity."

66. Walpole, *Description* (1798), 469.

67. *HW Corr*, 41:39 (HW to Adam, 26 September 1766).

68. There were some precedents for round vaulted Gothic spaces in postmedieval architecture, as, for example, at Longford Castle, Wiltshire, ca. 1590. See Girouard, *Elizabethan Architecture*, 438–39. Whether Walpole knew Longford is unclear. See *HW Corr*, 38:25 (Hertford to HW, 1 September 1759).

69. Wainwright, *Romantic Interior*, 98–99.

70. *HW Corr*, 20:372 (HW to Mann, 27 April 1753), my emphasis.

71. Kalter, *Modern Antiques*, 109–48.

72. Guillery and Snodin, "Strawberry Hill," 122, figs. 24 and 25.

73. *HW Corr*, 35:150–51 (HW to Bentley, September 1753).

74. *HW Corr*, 35:420 (HW to Hamilton, 19 June 1774).

75. Mowl, *Horace Walpole*, 143.

76. J. Campbell, "'I Am No Giant,'" 256. On these issues, see also Morrissey, *From the Temple to the Castle*, 121–23; Calè, "Gray's Ode and Walpole's China Tub"; and Stewart, *On Longing*, 61–64.

77. *HW Corr*, 37:406 (HW to Conway, 23 September 1755), 42:285 (HW to Nichol, 6 July 1790), 42:99 (HW to Vesey, 18 June 1784).

78. *HW Corr*, 37:269 (HW to Conway, 8 June 1747). Elsewhere in Walpole's writings, Strawberry Hill becomes both dematerialized and scaleless: "it is really incredible how small

most of the rooms are. . . . For the rest of the house, I could send it to you in this letter as easily as the drawing [which accompanied it], only that I should have nowhere to live till the return of the post[!]." See the extended description in *HW Corr*, 20:379–84 (HW to Mann, 12 June 1753).

79. *HW Corr*, 40:255 (HW to Warton, 21 August 1762). Cited in Morrissey, *From the Temple to the Castle*, 122.

80. *HW Corr*, 35:182 (HW to Bentley, 27 July 1754).

81. Crown, "British Rococo," 281; Brownell, *Alexander Pope*, 271; A. Cooper, *Second Characters*, 131; Lancaster, *Pretty Gentleman*, 13.

82. Walpole, *Anecdotes* (1762), 1:107.

83. For example, in 1758 John Gwynn could divide medieval Gothic from "the wild, false, and fantastic modern architecture of that name." Gwynn (attributed), *English Architecture*, 1–2.

84. Walpole, *Anecdotes* (1762), 1:108.

85. Walpole argues for the supremacy of the licentiousness under Charles II over the austerities of the Presbyterians. Ibid., 1:xvii. In an unsigned letter by Walpole in the *World*, no. 160 (22 January 1756), he satirically puns on the reformation of license by Adam Fitz-Adam in the present in comparison to that in the medieval past.

86. On the Renaissance origins of this tradition, see Payne, *Architectural Treatise*, 15–21.

87. Horace Walpole's library held most of the canonical volumes on architecture available in the period. See Hazen. I have been able to examine many of these, but a complete study of Walpole's architectural books is now needed.

88. Evelyn, "Account of Architects and Architecture," 9–10. For Wren's critiques of Gothic churches, see Soo, *Wren's "Tracts" on Architecture*, 34–92. In general, see de Beer, "Gothic." The literary sources are usefully summarized in Lang, "Principles of the Gothic Revival."

89. C. Campbell, introduction to *Vitruvius Britannicus*.

90. In an unpaginated insertion in his own *Description*, Walpole recorded the following anecdote: "The year before the gallery was built, a stranger passed and asked an old farmer belonging to Mr Walpole, if Strawberry Hill was not an old house! He replied, 'yes, but my master designs to build one much older next year!'" LWL MS 49 2522. On postmedieval constructions and paradoxes of Gothic and modernism in architecture and theory, see Kaufmann, "'Gothico More Nondum Visa'"; Wamberg, "Ghiberti, Alberti"; and Kavaler, *Renaissance Gothic*.

91. Mitford, *Correspondence of Thomas Gray and William Mason*.

92. Symonds, "Eighteenth-Century Convert," 151.

93. Thomas, *View of the Town*, 18–20; Kuchta, *Three-Piece Suit*, 96; Barker-Benfield, *Culture of Sensibility*, 116. Also, for advice to young men countering effeminacy and licentiousness, see Fordyce, "Address XIII: On a Manly Spirit, as Opposed to Effeminacy," in *Addresses to Young Men*. To address the other side of the debate, Richard Payne Knight in his notorious *Discourse on the Worship of Priapus* could rail against "the prejudices of artificial decency" and argue in the guise of the relativist that "there is naturally no impurity or licentiousness in the moderate and regular gratification of any natural [i.e., sexual] appetite." Cited in Sha, *Perverse Romanticism*, 174.

94. King, *English Phallus*.

95. On these issues, see recently McEwen, *Vitruvius*, and Dodds and Tavernor, *Body and Building*.

96. Hart, "From Virgin to Courtesan," 315.

97. Anderson, "Masculine and Unaffected"; Hart, *Inigo Jones*, esp. chaps. 5 and 6. See also Ware, *Complete Body of Architecture*, 447, for the "plain manly noble orders" in comparison with the Gothic and Chinese styles, and N. Cooper, "Rank, Manners, and Display," 309–10, for Lord Chesterfield's 1749 advice to his son on the decorous use of classical ornament on a new façade—itself a mirror of the physicality of the youthful aristocrat.

98. Evelyn, "Account of Architects and Architecture," unpaginated, cited in part in Levine, *Between the Ancients and the Moderns*, 15.

99. See John Evelyn's dedicatory epistle to Sir John Denham in his translation of Roland de Fréart's *Parallèle de l'architecture*. Cited and discussed in Buchanan, "Interpretations of Medieval Architecture," 41.

100. Still of great value on these issues is Gombrich, *Sense of Order*, esp. 17–31.

101. Forrester, *Polite Philosopher*, 25:

> That true Politeness we can only call,
> Which looks like Jones's Fabrick at Whitehall:
> Where just Proportion we, with Pleasure, see,
> Tho built by Rule, yet from all Stiffness, free.
> Tho grand, yet plain, magnificent, not fine,
> The Ornaments adorning the Design,
> It fills our Minds with rational Delight,
> And pleases on Reflection, as at Sight.

102. Lipking, *Ordering of the Arts*, 146.

103. Vidler, *Architectural Uncanny*, 71–72. Karen Harvey has "recognize[d] qualities of spaces as material renditions of feminized and sexualized moral states" in eighteenth-century culture. See K. Harvey, "Gender, Space, and Modernity," 172.

104. Porter, *Chinese Taste*, 8. See subsequently Sloboda, *Chinoiserie*, 108–58.

105. On the eighteenth-century gendering of Gothic, see Guest, "Wanton Muse." On architecture, see Laurence, "Women Using Building," 301–2; P. Smith, "Lady Oxford's Alterations"; L. Worsley, "Female Architectural Patronage," 150–53; Brownell, *Alexander Pope*, 271; and Vickery, *Behind Closed Doors*, 257–90.

106. Walpole, *Anecdotes* (1876), 1:xvii.

107. *HW Corr*, 20:127 (HW to Mann, 25 February 1750).

108. J. Campbell, "'I Am No Giant,'" 245.

109. For example, Frank, "Horace Walpole's Family Romances," esp. 434.

110. For Strawberry Hill as a "notorious masterpiece of camp," see Myrone, *Gothic Nightmares*, 35.

111. Sontag, "Notes on 'Camp.'" The essay has been reprinted in Cleto, *Camp*, 53–65, with discussion in the editor's introduction at 1–43. The historiography on camp is considerable. See in particular M. Meyer, *Politics and Poetics of Camp*. For a recent discussion of Sontag's construction of camp in the context of eighteenth-century sexualities, see Gowrley, "Representing Camp."

112. Halperin, *How to Be Gay*.

113. Ross, "Uses of Camp," 66–67.

114. "Macaulay, Unsigned Review," in Sabor, *Critical Heritage*, 313, 323.

115. Here I paraphrase Wayne Dynes's perceptive entry in Dynes et al., *Encyclopedia of Homosexuality*, s.v. "camp": "The world of camp then serves to deconstruct the cult of seriousness and 'values' that sought to fill the gap produced by the fading of religion and traditional class society in the West."

116. Ross, "Uses of Camp," 55.

117. Halperin, *Saint Foucault*, 29.

Chapter 3

1. Nagel, *Medieval Modern*, 47.

2. Dukelskaya and Moore, *Capital Collection*.

3. A. Moore, "*Aedes Walpolianae*," 35, and Guilding, *Owning the Past*, 82: "The whole theatrical scheme, its materials, plasterwork and ancient and modern sculpture, was chosen to confirm his [Robert Walpole's] grasp of power, enumerate his virtues and confer upon him those that he lacked."

4. "Unsigned, *Descriptions*," in Sabor, *Critical Heritage*, 251, and "Macaulay, Unsigned Review," in ibid., 313.

5. Weisberg-Roberts, "Singular Objects and Multiple Meanings."

6. Lindfield, "Heraldry and the Architectural Imagination."

7. Aside from Reeve, "Gothic Architecture," the notable exceptions are Haggerty, *Horace Walpole's Letters*, and Hietala, *Inconclusive Evidence*. Following the essays and catalogue in *HWSH*, a number of studies have explored the collection and its interpretation, as well as Walpole's *Description*. See, for example, Silver, "Visiting Strawberry Hill"; Kalter, *Modern Antiques*; Lilley, "Studies in Uniquity"; Calè, "Gray's Ode and Walpole's China Tub"; and S. Clarke, "'Lord God!'"

8. J. Campbell, "Politics and Sexuality in Portraits," 283. See recently Einberg, "Lord Hervey's Choice." Notably, Hogarth's 1755 *Election* series was dedicated to a broadly homoerotic circle including Charles Hanbury Williams, Henry Fox, and others. See Krysmanski, *Hogarth's Hidden Parts*, 147.

9. Baker, Harrison, and Lang, "Bouchardon's British Sitters." For Walpole at Redlynch, which also held a copy of the Hervey Conversation Piece, see "Horace Walpole's Journals," 44.

10. Muensterberger, *Collecting*. For a critique of Muensterberger, see subsequently Camille and Rifkin, introduction to "Other Objects of Desire."

11. Camille and Rifkin, introduction to "Other Objects of Desire," 163–64.

12. In Weisberg-Roberts's terms, Walpole relied on "a profusion of contextualizing strategies—from framing, casing and 'restoring,' through annotation, extra-illustration and attribution, to romance, epistle, and history—that he applied to his possessions." Weisberg-Roberts, "Singular Objects and Multiple Meanings," 90.

13. W. Davis, "Queer Family Romance," 323–24, and W. Davis, "Site of Sexuality." On the Fonthill heraldry, see subsequently S. Clarke, "'Almost Innumerable Descents.'"

14. For Lee Priory, see chapter 5.

15. For the context of queer collections, I am indebted here to W. Davis, "Homoerotic Art Collection," and Vogtherr, "Absent Love in Pleasure Houses."

16. *HW Corr*, 21:160 (HW to Mann, 14 December 1757), 21:188–89 (HW to Mann, 14 April 1758).

17. The manuscript is now LWL 49 2599. See also Hazen, 2599.

18. Hazen, 421, 477, 2404, 3536, 3767. Walpole's copy of the Payne Knight work was given by the Society of Dilettanti "as an acknowledgement of the useful assistance received from him by the author in the prosecution of this work" (inscription by Sir Joseph Banks on the flyleaf of HW's copy), now Hazen, 2404, cited in *HW Corr*, 29:340 n. 12 (HW to Mason, 22 March 1796). Calling Payne Knight a "new Priapus," Walpole apparently disagreed with and was manifestly offended by this text, as well as, it seems, Knight's inclusion of an object from his collection. Arguably, the scandalous text necessarily put Walpole in an uncomfortably close relationship with the erotic libertinism of the Dilettanti—whether homoerotic or otherwise—something that ran counter to an image of the gentleman scholar that he cultivated. Joseph Farington recounts that Walpole laughed "at the systematizing plan of Knight, Townley etc. who attempt to prove the lascivious designs of antiquity to be *merely* emblematic of the creative power" (my emphasis). Cited in *HW Corr*, vol. 15, app. 3, 318–19. See also *HW Corr*, 29:340 (HW to Mason, 22 March 1796); 15:319 n. 20; 33:478–79 (HW to Ossory, 9 July 1785).

19. On the influence of the Grand Tour generally, see Arnold, "Illusion of Grandeur?"

20. Rousseau, *Perilous Enlightenment*, 86–87.

21. Walpole, *Description* (1798), 471, 467.

22. Lloyd, "Cabinet of Miniatures and Enamels"; Edwards, "Cabinets."

23. Saska, "Strawberry Hill."

24. Walpole, *Description* (1798), 479, 477. Walpole also owned a "bronze caste of the Hermaphrodite," bought from Dicky Bateman's sale, which was displayed in the Yellow Bedchamber. Ibid., 419.

25. Frith, "Sexuality and Politics," 309.

26. *HWSH*, cat. no. 191. Bowron, *Pompeo Batoni*, no. 76.

27. W. Davis, "Homoerotic Art Collection," 253–54.

28. Haggerty, *Horace Walpole's Letters*, 84–85; Stewart, *On Longing*, 61.

29. Edwards, "Cabinets," 128.

30. The erudite nature of Georgian erotica is emphasized in K. Harvey, *Reading Sex*, esp. 224.

31. Walpole, *Description* (1798), 450. Purchased by Walpole in 1758. See *HW Corr*, 21:189 (HW to Mann, 14 April 1758), 21:201–2 (Mann to HW, 13 May 1758).

32. See, for example, Worley, "Image of Ganymede in France," and Meyer, "'Nature Revers'd.'"

33. See Roman, "Portfolio of Satires."

34. Winckelmann's attraction to the Ganymede myth and its embodiment of a perceived antique ideal of intergenerational love was enough to dupe the connoisseur, who famously fell for a forgery, which he hastily published in his *Geschichte der Kunst* (1764). Pelzel, "Winckelmann, Mengs, and Casanova."

35. *HW Corr*, 17:112 (Mann to HW, 21 August 1741), 17:404 (Mann to HW, 7 May 1742), 17:164 n. 5 (HW to Mann, 5 October 1741).

36. For von Stosch, see now Hansson, "'Ma passion . . . ,'" and L. Lewis, "Philipp von Stosch." Ulf Hansson's forthcoming study of von Stosch is eagerly anticipated.

37. *HW Corr*, 18:369 (Mann to HW, 14 January 1744).

38. *HW Corr*, 17:263–64 (Mann to HW, 10 January 1742). Walpole may have seen these himself in Europe but would have known of them via von Stosch's *Pierres antiques gravées*, plates 21 and 67. For Walpole's copy of the text, see Hazen, 3762. For relations between Walpole and von Stosch, see Brownell, *Prime Minister of Taste*, 18–24.

39. For a discussion of the eagle, see *HWSH*, cat. no. 138.

40. *HWSH*, cat. no. 1. When asked by Mrs. Dickenson in 1788 for a print of Reynolds's portrait of him with his eagle, Walpole sent copies of prints of the eagle, which, in his words, were "a better memorandum of Strawberry Hill and of . . . Hor. Walpole." *HW Corr*, 31:263 (HW to Dickenson, 15 May 1788).

41. *HW Corr*, 3:405 (Deffand to HW, 26 December 1767). A creative response has, however, been offered by Hietala, *Inconclusive Evidence*, 116–21, 158–61.

42. *HW Corr*, 19:65–66 (Mann to HW, 13 July 1745).

43. I am grateful to Michael Koortbojian for discussing the meanings of the Boccapadugli Eagle with me. Jenkins and Sloan, *Vases and Volcanoes*, cat. no. 136. Notably, Walpole claims that Thomas Gray references the sculpture obliquely as Jove in his *Progress of Poesy: A Pindaric Ode*, in which "the magic lulls the feather'd king / With ruffled plumes and flagging wing." See Walpole's *Description* (1798), 463.

44. Pope-Hennessy, *Cellini*, 227–31; Barkan, *Transuming Passion*, 103–6; Saslow, *Ganymede in the Renaissance*, 142–74. I am grateful to Thomas Willette and James S. Saslow for discussing this with me.

45. W. Davis, *Queer Beauty*, 28–29.

46. Haggerty, *Horace Walpole's Letters*.

47. Lindfield, "'Hung Round with the Helmets.'" Walpole provided a detailed account of the heraldry in his extra-illustrated copy of the *Description* (now LWL MS 49 2523).

48. *Gentleman's Magazine* 9 (1739): 641.

49. The significance of dynasty for the early Gothic Revival has been emphasized by G. Worsley, "Origins of the Gothic Revival."

50. *HW Corr*, 35:270 (HW to Bentley, August 1756). For Welbeck, see P. Smith, "Lady Oxford's Alterations."

51. *HW Corr*, 9:186 (HW to Montagu, 20 April 1756).

52. *HW Corr*, 20:200 (HW to Mann, 18 October 1750); LWL MS 49 2523. For Asciotti at Strawberry Hill and Old Windsor, see *HW Corr*, 20:199 n. 26 (HW to Mann, 18 October 1750). On the heraldry, see now Snodin, "Signs and Signification."

53. *HW Corr*, 9:150 (HW to Montagu, 11 June 1753).

54. McKinney, "Castle of My Ancestors."

55. *HWSH*, cat. no. 34; *HW Corr*, 2:106; Wagner and D'Elboux, "Commemorative Brass."

56. For the stained glass, see Peover and Rogers, "New Light on Strawberry Hill."

57. *HW Corr*, 9:149–51 (HW to Montagu, 11 June 1753).

58. McKinney, "Castle of My Ancestors," 199.

59. Bann, "Historicizing Horace," 121–22.

60. *HW Corr*, 9:187–88 (HW to Montagu, 20 April 1756).

61. Walpole, *Castle of Otranto*, 17.

62. Frank, "Horace Walpole's Family Romances"; Fletcher, "Sins of the Fathers."

63. *HW Corr*, 37:289–90 (HW to Conway, 27 June 1748).

64. On "butterfly" and "butterfly men" as codes for the third sex, see, for example, the admonitory characterization in S. H., "Character of a Coxcomb," 174: "It is well known that one of these butterfly-men loves no created being so well as himself. . . . Though he extravagantly admires no lady, still he may be the friend and patron to many. Superficial women court his attention, because they are pleased with his finery: and sensible women have pleasantry enough to indulge his vanity and self-approbation. His forms of politeness and good humour are conspicuous, and he will grant a lady every thing they will ask of him, except his admiration and love."

65. Walpole, *Fugitive Pieces*, 40–42.

66. On the place of genealogical and familial imagery in the eighteenth-century library, including that at Strawberry Hill, see Hallett, *Reynolds*, 295–302.

67. Walpole, *Description* (1798), 442.

68. As though glossing the imagery of the library ceiling, Walpole quipped to the Countess of Ossory, "Thus you see, Madam, whichever way I turn myself, I have royal or Fitzroyal connections." *HW Corr*, 33:454 (HW to Ossory, 9 December 1784).

69. W. Lewis, "Genesis of Strawberry Hill," 67–69.

70. Lindfield, "Walpole's Panelled Heraldic Apartment."

71. Walpole, *Description* (1798), 442; *HWSH*, cat. no. 99.

72. Davoli, *Lost Treasures of Strawberry Hill*, 89.

73. Dukelskaya and Moore, *Capital Collection*, no. 212.

74. Clery, *Rise of Supernatural Fiction*, 75–76. Unsurprisingly, Walpole's appraisal of his father is complex and often conflicted. Aside from preparing the *Aedes Walpolianae*, he frequently defended his father's political record during his life and after his death. A. Moore, "*Aedes Walpolianae*." Walpole also owned images at Strawberry Hill that satirized Sir Robert's career, including "a most ridiculous vulgar brass medal struck by some Irish priest at Rome. On one side is a figure with a halter by which the Devil is leading it to Hell, with the words, 'Make room for Sir Robert,' and at the bottom, 'No excise.'" *HW Corr*, 21:202 (Mann to HW, 13 May 1758).

75. *HW Corr*, 23:549 (HW to Mann, 2 February 1774).

76. Clery, *Rise of Supernatural Fiction*, 75–76.

77. Frank, "Horace Walpole's Family Romances"; Coykendall, "Gothic Genealogies."

78. A. Williams, "Reading Walpole Reading Shakespeare." See also Lady Louisa Stuart's 1837 commentary on Walpole's paternity in Sabor, *Critical Heritage*, 327–31.

79. A. Williams, "Reading Walpole Reading Shakespeare," 24.

80. Snodin, "Going to Strawberry Hill," 41.

81. Eccardt was the subject of Walpole's poetic epistle "The Beauties" of 1746. See *HW Corr*, 30:324–29.

82. *HWSH*, cat. no. 39. On posthumous portraiture generally, see Retford, "Death in the Family."

83. A. Moore, "*Aedes Walpolianae*," 10.

84. *HW Corr*, 9:187 (HW to Montagu, 20 April 1756).

85. See Vickery, "Horace Walpole and Strawberry Hill." Walpole describes this hang in a letter to Richard Bentley: *HW Corr*, 35:174 (HW to Bentley, 18 May 1754).

86. Walpole's portrait of Charles Hanbury Williams, or a copy of it, sold at Christie's, South Kensington, 3 December 2013 (Lot 502), and now hangs at Fingask Castle, Perthshire. Williams's pose with "Isabella, or the Morning" is recorded in the 1842 sale catalogue. See Robins, *Catalogue*, 221. That the Fingask portrait may be Walpole's is also suggested by its dimensions, approximately 41 × 33 cm, which agree with the size of the other Eccardts in the series at Strawberry Hill. I am grateful to Andrew Threipland for providing me information on the portrait and permission to reproduce it. See Kerslake, *Early Georgian Portraits*, no. 383 n. 3. A nearly identical portrait of Hanbury Williams now in the National Portrait Gallery, London, and attributed to Eccardt (ca. 1746) features him holding a copy of "An Ode to the Honourable Henry Fox."

87. For the poem, see *Gray's English Poems*, 91–92.

88. See Walpole, *Description* (1798), 345–46. The images are catalogued in *HWSH*, cat. nos. 39–44, with additional bibliography.

89. See Cherry and Harris, "Eighteenth-Century Portraiture," and Retford, "Sensibility and Genealogy."

90. *HW Corr*, 35:419 (HW to Hamilton, 22 February 1774). Cited and discussed in Janes, *Oscar Wilde Prefigured*, 39.

91. Walpole, *Description* (1798), 436.

92. Robins, *Catalogue*, 207. See also Adams and Lewis, "Portraits of Horace Walpole," 10.

93. This volume is in a private collection but is referenced in S. Clarke, "'Lord God!,'" 377. I am grateful to the author for discussions of this passage.

94. The possible connection of these sketches to the later pastels has been noted by Russell, "Drawings by Rosalba," and by Cynthia Roman in *HWSH*, cat. no. 38. Only a single portrait sketch of John Chute at the Vyne, Hampshire, has come to light. For that sketch, see most recently Sani, *Rosalba*

Carriera, no. 388. Chute's sketch does appear to be a portrait, although this is difficult to square with the annotations in Kirgate's copy of the *Description*.

95. Redford, *Dilettanti*, 42; Redford, "Grecian Taste and Neapolitan Spirit."

96. Rousseau, *Perilous Enlightenment*, 174–75, 179. The sexual dimensions of Walpole's Grand Tour have also been explored in A. Williams, "Horace in Italy," and Mowl, *Horace Walpole*.

97. The picture hang has been described in Snodin, "Going to Strawberry Hill," 36–37.

98. Hallett, *Reynolds*, 300–301.

99. *HW Corr*, 35:200 (HW to Bentley, 24 December 1754).

100. The painting and its protagonists are discussed in Fothergill, *Strawberry Hill Set*, 74–105, quotations at 81, 105.

101. Bann, "Historicizing Horace," 126.

Chapter 4

1. For the quote from Mrs. Delany, see Vulliamy, *Aspasia*, 181.

2. As noted by J. Harris, "Pioneer in Gardening," 229, and Wainwright, *Romantic Interior*, 80–81.

3. Reeve, "Dickie Bateman."

4. For a brief account of the subsequent history of the house, see Tyack, Bradley, and Pevsner, *Berkshire*, 417. Aspects of both Chinese and Gothic ornament, including quantities of painted glass, were still present in 1922–34. This is noted in correspondence to Wilmarth Sheldon Lewis from Katherine Theodora Cater of 1947, now LWL WSL Correspondence folder cas-ce. These details are absent from the 1969 sale particulars in BRO D/EX 1051.15. For the sale catalogue following Bateman's death, see Christie, *Catalogue*.

5. *HW Corr*, 35:359 (HW to Strafford, 13 June 1781).

6. *HW Corr*, 40:52 (HW to Townsend, March 1745).

7. See most recently Friedman, *Eighteenth-Century Church in Britain*, 215–17; Colvin, "Henry Flitcroft"; and Whitehead, "Artisan Attitudes." An unqualified attribution of the church to Richard Bentley is offered in Jenkins, *England's Thousand Best Churches*, 277.

8. The furniture in particular is explored in Lindfield, *Georgian Gothic*, 72–78.

9. On the Shobdon Arches, see most recently Baxter, "Whose Heritage?"; Corpus of Romanesque Sculpture in Britain and Ireland at http://www.crsbi.ac.uk/site/3250; and Thurlby, *Herefordshire School*, 71–86. George Selwyn, however, did plan to take down and rebuild "a pretty old gateway" at Llanthony Priory, Wales, and to use it as a folly, but this was never executed. *HW Corr*, 35:154–55 (HW to Bentley, September 1753).

10. White, "Kent and the Gothic Revival," 260.

11. Lindfield, "Georgian Gothic Fabrications," 45–46.

12. Delany, *Autobiography and Correspondence* (1862), 1:176.

13. *HW Corr*, 20:166 (HW to Mann, 2 August 1750).

14. *HW Corr*, 35:359 (HW to Stafford, 13 June 1781).

15. Ibid. Storer constructed an early camera obscura that was employed to record views at Strawberry Hill. See Wilsher, "Horace Walpole."

16. *HW Corr*, 10:43 (HW to Montagu, 24 September 1762).

17. Dubro, "Third Sex," and Lucy Moore, *Amphibious Thing*. The Bateman brothers remained close all of their lives. HRO G39/111/E/488 is a touching account of Dicky's love for his sibling, who in exile had "been released from great pain and misery."

18. See, for example, BL Add MS 51348, fols. 43r–44v, for his role in commissions at contemporary Redlynch and elsewhere. Ibid., fol. 105r, provides some sense of the performance of his sexuality via his career as a man of taste and shopper: here he recounts his fears that Lady Ilchester will be dissatisfied with his work: "I am quite terrified lest she should not have had it [a letter] pray let her know I have had a dozen milliners with me, not all of them pretty, to enquire after Earthgrade ribbon—they all cough in my face and protest they don't know what I mean. They seem to think it only an excuse to see them[!]."

19. BL Add MS 51408, fol. 198r.

20. See the Charles Hanbury Williams Correspondence at Yale University, LWL CHW Corr, vol. 48, fols. 101v–102r.

21. C. Williams, *Works*, 1:72–73.

22. LWL CHW Corr, vol. 48, fol. 97r (6 August 1744). For Walpole's frustrated attempts to attract Charles Hanbury Williams to Houghton, see *HW Corr*, 30:60, 63–64, 65, 67–68.

23. See, for example, Walpole, *Description* (1798), 453, 455, 500, 506, 507, 508, 509, 510. For the ivory draughts pieces, see *HWSH*, cat. no. 155.

24. *Windsor and Its Environs*, 79.

25. *HW Corr*, 9:39 (HW to Montagu, 2 August 1746); Harwood, *Windsor Old and New*, 319–20.

26. *HW Corr*, 40:18 (Hervey to HW, 21 October 1735). See generally Calè, "Gray's Ode and Walpole's China Tub."

27. *HW Corr*, 35:177 (HW to Bentley, 9 July 1754); Walpole, *Description* (1798), 432. He also owned "a landscape in Indian ink, with Italian, Chinese and Gothic buildings; by Mr. Bentley, in his best style." Walpole, *Description* (1798), 428. This may well have been an image of Bateman's house and gardens before its Gothicization.

28. J. Harris, "Pioneer in Gardening"; J. Harris, *Gardens of Delight*, 1:12–15; R. Pococke, *Travels Through England*, 2:65. In 1749 Bateman's gardens were vandalized when he was away; fourteen large trees were cut down, and Bateman posted a reward for information about the culprits. See BL Add MS 51348, fols. 93r–94v.

29. These paintings were sold in the 2009 Old Masters sale at Christie's, London (sale 7744, lot 124), and are now in the possession of an anonymous owner.

30. J. Harris, "Pioneer in Gardening," 227. It appears that Bateman's redecoration of the interiors of Shobdon Court, Herefordshire, his late father's Palladian mansion, were similar in manner. The evidence is now found in HRO G39/III/E, a series of letters from Richard Bateman to Mr. Fallowes, the estate manager at Shobdon between 1739 and 1763. For his acquisition of Chinese porcelain for Shobdon in 1740, see HRO G39/III/E/37 (1740), and for the Chinese bedroom, see HRO G/39/III/E/242 (10 January 1749).

31. Painted in gouache on vellum, these paintings had deteriorated somewhat by the time they were photographed, making some details indiscernible. J. Harris, *Gardens of Delight*, 1:12–13.

32. R. Pococke, *Travels Through England*, 2:64. Fortunately, the veracity of Robins's view can be tested against a slightly later view by Thomas Sandby, which proves that he was accurate in most details. See Harwood, *Windsor Old and New*, page facing 320.

33. R. Pococke, *Travels Through England*, 2:64; Hazeltine, "Study of William Shenstone," 77, citing Wellesley College Library, Shenstone MS, 1753–54. This page also includes an overlooked Latin "Inscription on a small Mausoleum supported by Four Ionic Pillars" in Bateman's garden.

34. Some of the original windows were put to new uses at the property and are still extant.

35. A Chinese porch is mentioned in letters regarding Bateman's portrait by Robert Levrac-Tournières (fig. 78). Undoubtedly to celebrate his role as "founder of the Sharawadgi taste," Dicky asked that the panel, presumably from Old Windsor, be included in the background, thus suggesting that the work on the front may predate 1741. J. Harris, "Pioneer in Gardening," 230; Cannon-Brookes, "Robert Tournières." In 1985 the original manuscript containing these letters was lost and was, even then, only known from a typescript. It has not been possible for the present author to consult the typescript. Cannon-Brookes, "Robert Tournières," 145 n. 1.

36. *HW Corr*, 20:199–200 (HW to Mann, 18 October 1750).

37. R. Pococke, *Travels Through England*, 2:64.

38. As Roger White has recently argued, Kent may have designed the Gothic church at Houghton. See White, "Kent and the Gothic Revival," 250–51.

39. For a list of projects within Bateman's circle between ca. 1730 and 1750, see Lane, "Shobdon Church," 24. For the use of Flitcroft's designs at Redlynch in the mid 1740s, see BL Add MS 51348, fol. 52r.

40. Baxter, "Whose Heritage?," 164.

41. BL RP 2377 (i), letter 2 (11 August 1759). This passage is often cited out of context from the partial transcription in Climenson, *Elizabeth Montagu*, 2:192.

42. Delany, *Autobiography and Correspondence* (1861), 3:618.

43. Ibid. (1862), 1:176, 177–78.

44. It has not been possible to reproduce all of the images now available of Old Windsor. Some views not reproduced here are in McCarthy, *Origins of the Gothic Revival*; J. Harris, "Pioneer in Gardening"; and J. Harris, *Gardens of Delight*.

45. J. Cooper, *Letters Concerning Taste*, 60. A similar critique was advanced in the *World*, no. 12 (22 March 1753): 68–69: "A few years ago every thing was Gothic; our houses, our beds, our book-cases, and our couches were all copied from some parts or other of our old cathedrals." Walpole advocated the use of prints such as Dugdale's for Gothic designs: "The general disuse of Gothic architecture, and the decay and alterations so frequently made in churches, give prints a chance of being the sole preservatives of that style." Walpole, *Description* (1798), 395.

46. Bateman to Lord Ilchester (Stephen Fox), BL Add MS 51349, fol. 95r. Christie, *Catalogue*, 7, mentions "a bell dated 1366," which may be the object alluded to in this letter.

47. BL Add MS 51349, fols. 95r–96v.

48. "The Hon. Rich. Bateman at Old Windsor has altered his offices in 1758 according to a plan given by Mr Bentley." *HW Corr*, 35:644.

49. "His cloister of founders, which by the way is Mr Bentley's, is delightful." *HW Corr*, 10:43 (HW to Montagu, 24 September 1762).

50. Watts, "Life and Work," 21–25, 49–53.

51. McCarthy, *Origins of the Gothic Revival*, 104.

52. Pote, *Delices de Windsore*, 93.

53. *Windsor and Its Environs*, 82–83. These may have been the "twenty-two [framed paintings of] English worthies, poets &c" mentioned in the details of the 3 May sale account. Christie, *Catalogue*, 3.

54. McCarthy, *Origins of the Gothic Revival*, 192 n. 36: inscription on the verso of Caducanus drawing, "Funeral monument of Caducanus, once Bishop of Hereford. J. H. Muntz Hereford 1759. The same erected at Old Windsor for the Honble [*sic*] R.: Bateman."

55. Walpole wrote covetously about them to William Cole on 9 March 1765. *HW Corr*, 1:90. See also Wainwright, *Romantic Interior*, 58–59, 106, and Cornforth, *Early Georgian Interiors*, 234–35.

56. Walpole writes to George Montagu, "I envy him his old chairs and his tomb of Caducanus" (both of which were in the cloister). *HW Corr*, 10:43 (24 September 1762).

57. Keating, *Foras Feasa ar Éirinn*. The text was translated into English in 1723. See O'Halloran, "Triumph of 'Virtuous Liberty.'"

58. See, however, Baxter, "Whose Heritage?,"164.

59. Delany, *Autobiography and Correspondence* (1862), 1:176.

60. *Windsor and Its Environs*, 79–70.

61. HRO G39/111/E 467 (22 November 1757).

62. Delany, *Autobiography and Correspondence* (1862), 1:177–78.

63. Walpole, *Description* (1798), 508; *HW Corr*, 1:325 (HW to Cole, 4 May 1774). For the Malmesbury Châsse, see Wainwright, *Romantic Interior*, 134; Caudron, "Connoisseurs of *Champlève*," 16–18; and Lowden and Cherry, *Medieval Ivories and Works of Art*, 28–29.

64. BL Add MS 51408, fol. 212v.

65. *HW Corr*, 10:168 (HW to Montagu, 23 August 1765).

66. Despite the fact that Mrs. Delany had lengthy homoerotic relationships with women, she remained traditional in her views and appears to have felt no solidarity with men of the third sex or their tastes. Lisa Moore, "Queer Gardens."

67. *HW Corr*, 9:197–98 (HW to Montagu, 14 October 1756).

68. This was noted in contemporary descriptions. For example, *Windsor and Its Environs*, 81, and Pote, *Delices de Windsore*, 80. Richard Pococke also draws attention to this and recounts the results of recent excavations near Bateman's residence to unearth medieval foundations. R. Pococke, *Travels Through England*, 2:64.

69. *Windsor and Its Environs*, 82. The stained glass was still extant in 1934 and was described in a letter to Wilmarth Sheldon Lewis by its former resident Katherine Theodora Cater. See note 4 above.

70. *Windsor and Its Environs*, 82.

71. Pote, *Delices de Windsore*, 93.

72. *Windsor and Its Environs*, 82.

73. BL Add MS 51348, fol. 94r.

74. As noted in a letter by Mrs. Delany of 29 January 1747 (Newport Public Library, 2, fol. 105), recently published in E. Harris, *Handel as Orpheus*, 19.

75. *HW Corr*, 30:307–10, at 309.

76. Christie, *Catalogue*, 6, 8.

77. Cannon-Brookes, "Robert Tournières," 143. Bateman was also responsible for transporting statuary for Lord Foley and storing it at his family estate at Shobdon Court. HRO G39/E/71 (1740). Lord Foley is often mentioned in Bateman's correspondence. On 31 July 1762, for example, he was staying at Old Windsor en route to his own home. BL Add MS 51350, fol. 147v.

78. Walpole and Bateman planned a visit to Redlynch to visit Stephen Fox in 1762. See *HW Corr*, 40:249 (HW to Ilchester, 10 June 1762).

79. See most recently Lucy Moore, *Amphibious Thing*, 76, 93. Alexander Pope describes Hervey in his *Epistle to Dr. Arbuthnot*: "Now high, now low, now Master up, now Miss, / And he himself one vile Antithesis. . . . / Fop at the Toilet, Flatt'rer at the Board, / Now trips a Lady, and now struts a Lord." For Walpole's paraphrase of Lady Montagu's observation, see *HW Corr*, 17:274 n. 31 (HW to Mann, 7 January 1742).

80. *HW Corr*, 32:241 (HW to Ossory, 23 July 1775) 1: 325 (HW to Cole, 4 May 1774). The portrait hung in his flower-garden cottage at Strawberry Hill. See Walpole, *Description* (1798), 509.

81. See, for example, Walpole's 1745 wishes for Mistley Hall, Essex, which blended antique, Gothic, and Chinese features. *HW Corr*, 30:87 (HW to Hanbury Williams, 25 June 1745).

82. Porter, *Chinese Taste*, 115–30.

83. *HW Corr*, 35:241 (HW to Bentley, 4 August 1755). See also *HW Corr*, 35:233–34 (HW to Bentley, 5 July 1755). For Walpole's later distrust of hybridity, see S. Clarke, "Horace Walpole's Architectural Taste," esp. 235–37.

84. Porter, *Chinese Taste*, 121–26. See in general Llewellyn, "*Anecdotes of Painting*."

85. See note 41 above.

86. Delany, *Autobiography and Correspondence* (1862), 1:176–78, and Vulliamy, *Aspasia*, 180–81.

87. *Dictionary of Love*.

88. On the fribble in general, see King, *English Phallus*, esp. 239–48; King, *Queer Articulations*, 64–69, 128–34, 261–62, 267; Senelick, "Mollies or Men of Mode?"; and Trumbach, "Transformation of Sodomy," 841–42.

89. Garrick, *Private Correspondence*, 1:138–39. Wilmarth Sheldon Lewis was of the opinion that Warburton referred to Thomas Gray, but it is as likely to have been Bateman for the reasons given here. See *HW Corr*, 13:39 n. 265. Walpole's "fribblishness" was also noted in Thomas Babington Macaulay's famous 1833 critique. See Stephen, *Hours in a Library*, 1:348.

90. From 1747 to 1776 the play was performed at least 125 times at the Drury Lane Theatre alone. See Pedicord, *Theatrical Public*, 199, and Burling and Franken, "Garrick's Alterations."

91. Garrick, *Miss in Her Teens*, 23.

92. Ibid., 20.

93. Goldsmid, *Pretty Gentleman*, 26, 30.

94. Fribble, *Tittle Tattle*.

95. Brown, *Estimate of the Manners*, 1:60–61.

96. Churchill, *Poems*, 1:15. See generally Kavanagh, "'Of Neuter Gender.'"

97. Delany, *Autobiography and Correspondence* (1861), 2:453.

98. Harwood, *Windsor Old and New*, 320.

99. See "Edmond Malone's Portrait of Walpole, 1783," in Sabor, *Critical Heritage*, 260. Others may have been the intended target of Garrick's fribble. See Ritchie, "Garrick's *Male-Coquette*."

100. Stylistic hybridity was a current concern of Lord Lyttelton. Writing to Elizabeth Montagu in the same year (1759), he expressed concern that his own building project at Hagley Hall, Worcestershire, would be similarly critiqued as "little better than *a gothick house modernised*. The Goths will think it too Græcian and the Græcians too Gothic." Lyttelton

as cited in Climenson, *Elizabeth Montagu*, 2:148–49. See also Combe, *Letters of the Late Lord Lyttelton*, letter 20, on hybridity in architecture.

101. *World*, no. 15 (12 April 1753). See also J. Cooper, *Letters Concerning Taste*, letter 9, and Vickery, *Behind Closed Doors*, 102.

102. J. Cooper, *Letters Concerning Taste*, 57–58. Cited and discussed in Jones, *Gender and the Formation of Taste*, 9.

103. *World*, no. 26 (28 June 1753).

104. Churchill, *Poems*, 1:15–16; Garrick, *Fribbleriad*, frontispiece.

105. I cite here the English translation: Lavater, *Essays on Physiognomy*, 3:213. On the reception of the text in England, see Graham, "Lavater's Physiognamy in England."

106. My reference to the "*gaudy gout*" is a paraphrase of Elizabeth Montagu's 1749 description of Chinoiserie, cited in Oswald, "Mrs. Montagu and the Chinese Taste," 1328.

107. Delany, *Autobiography and Correspondence* (1861), 2:273, 415. Mrs. Delany also commemorated Bateman in her list of flower donors. See Ford, "Progress in Plants," 220.

108. Melchior-Bonnet, *Mirror*, 177.

109. Dittelbach, "Die Illusio verspottet sich selbst"; Laroque, "Miroirs de la Villa Palagonia"; Chaimovich, "Mirrors of Society"; Ezell, "Looking Glass Histories." For an overview of costs and production in London, see Child, *World Mirrors*, 17–23, and Parker, "Rococo and Formal Order."

110. The use of mirrors as aids to vision in the early eighteenth-century English interior has not been carefully studied. For Mrs. Pritchard's Chinese pavilion at her Twickenham villa, see, for example, *Short Account of the Principal Seats*, 7: "In several parts there are looking glasses so artfully placed in the Chinese Houses, that the prospect is seen by every person, from every different part of the room, which in the afternoon, when the barges are coming up, presents the most beautiful moving picture imaginable."

111. The use of books in the antiquarian home as a foppish conceit was not uncommon. See Carter, *Men and the Emergence*, 149.

112. *Windsor and Its Environs*, 80.

113. "Insignificancy" stood at the center of the characterization of Fribble in *Miss in Her Teens* (32): Captain Loveit chides him: "Thou art of a species too despicable for correction; therefore be gone; and if I see you here again, your insignificancy shan't protect you."

114. Porter, *Chinese Taste*, and Sloboda, *Chinoiserie*.

115. King, *English Phallus*, 229, and Carter, *Men and the Emergence*, 148–50. For the "fop" as a category of fastidious, narcissistic masculinity, see also *Dictionary of Love*: "He passes most of his time in ogling himself in a glass, primming his figure, and caressing his curls and toupee."

116. Delany, *Autobiography and Correspondence* (1862), 2:25.

117. For these ideas, see Sha, *Perverse Romanticism*, chap. 3.

118. W. Davis, *Queer Beauty*, 187–242. On the subsequent nineteenth-century history of these ideas in architectural description, see Hatt, "Space, Surface, Self."

119. *HW Corr*, 1:325 (HW to Cole, 4 May 1774). Walpole's friends also expressed interest in the sale and in Bateman's artifacts. In a letter to Walpole, Cole writes, "I never wished for money more than at this instant, to enable me to have purchased St Anthony or St Francis over the door at Mr Bateman's, with some other of his relics, and particularly Caducanus the Welsh bishop." *HW Corr*, 1:327 (19 May 1774).

120. *HW Corr*, 32:241 (HW to Ossory, 23 July 1775).

Chapter 5

1. Gray to Warton, 18 September 1754, in *Works of Thomas Gray*, 3:121. See also Kalter, *Modern Antiques*, 109–48.

2. Latour and Lowe, "Migration of the Aura," quote on 278.

3. *HW Corr*, 12:111 (HW to Mary Berry, 27 September 1794), 11:59 (HW to Mary Berry, 27 August 1789), 11:98 (HW to Mary Berry, 23 July 1790).

4. Another image is LWL 49 3490, fol. 46, with the inscription "Chaucer's Grove, John Chute Archit."

5. Walpole, *Description* (1798), 504, 428, 427, 452, 504.

6. Related biological structures inform emulations of Walpole's Gothic fiction. In its preface, Clara Reeve's *Old English Baron: A Gothic Story* (1777/78) declares itself to be "the literary offspring of the Castle of Otranto." See Coykendall, "Gothic Genealogies," 443.

7. Brideoake, *Ladies of Llangollen*, 108. See also Wainwright, *Romantic Interior*, 274–75. A careful account of the architecture and furnishings of Plas Newydd is now needed.

8. Brideoake, *Ladies of Llangollen*, 111.

9. The interiors of Abbotsford and their indebtedness to Strawberry Hill are discussed in Wainwright, *Romantic Interior*, 147–208.

10. Allen, *Tides in English Taste*, 2:93.

11. Elfenbein, *Romantic Genius*.

12. For a portrait of Andrews (now at the Society of Antiquaries, London), see Franklin, Nurse, and Tudor-Craig, *Catalogue of Paintings*, no. 68.

13. See the entry on Andrews in the online Oxford Dictionary of National Biography. For his contribution to the history of children's literature, see Immel, "James Pettit Andrews's 'Books.'" The fullest account Andrews's work at Donnington to date is Hussey, "Donnington Grove, Berkshire—I," and Hussey, "Donnington Grove, Berkshire—II." See also McCarthy, *Origins of the Gothic Revival*, 92–97.

14. However, only one late (1789) visit is recorded. *HW Corr*, 12:234.

15. The essay was reprinted in Warton et al., *Essays on Gothic Architecture*, 95–124.

16. Most of the significant designs are illustrated in McCarthy, *Origins of the Gothic Revival*, 92–97.

17. Andrews's scrapbooks were originally brought to light by Christopher Hussey in "Georgian Scrapbook." They were sold again at Sotheby's, New York, 25 June 2001, as "Dessins Grotesques MS," 3 vols. See *A Private Collection of Illustrated Books and Fine Bindings* (New York: Sotheby's, 25 June 2001), 16–17. The manuscript is now in the collection of the Antiquariat Bibermühle, Ramsen, Switzerland. I am most grateful to Heribert Tenschert for granting me access to the manuscripts and the right to reproduce images from them here. It has only been possible to refer to a few images in what follows. Andrews's scrapbooks deserve a study of their own. I am also grateful to Peter Lindfield for his help with attributing the drawings.

18. McCarthy, *Origins of the Gothic Revival*, 92.

19. "Donnington Grove."

20. See James Pettit Andrews's contribution to *Collections Towards a Parochial History*, 76.

21. The auction is noted in BRO D/EX2275/1, p. 58: "In the beginning of the year 1783 was Mr Pettit Andrews auction at Donnington Grove sold by Mr Knight—this Pettit Andrews was a very troublesome man to the County was a Justice of Peace [*sic*]."

22. *Collections Towards a Parochial History*, 83. The 1822 inventory is now BRO D/ENM.1/E23.

23. *HW Corr*, 35:642.

24. Penrose, *Flights of Fancy*, 1–10.

25. Walpole, *Castle of Otranto*, 7.

26. Antiquariat Bibermühle, Ramsen, "Dessins Grotesques MS," vol. 3, n.p. Andrews's papers contain seven sketches from Walpole's manuscript. The first in the sequence notes, "The original drawing was given to Horace Walpole, and is in the Library at Strawberry Hill." For Walpole's copy of Giovanni Battista Braccelli, *Bizzarie di varie figure* (1624), see Hazen, 2344. The manuscript is now Pierpont Morgan Library, New York, PML77163. Added to the back of the manuscript are drawings by Penrose dated 1778 that are copies of those in "Dessins Grotesques," which must have been a gift from the author to Walpole. I am grateful to John McQuillen at the Morgan Library for his help with the manuscript. Walpole's *Description* (1798), 448, recounts, "Bizarie di varie figure di Giovan Batista Bracelli, pittore Fiorentino al Illmo. S. Don Pietro Medici: 1624. This most rare and singular book contains prints of human figures formed by the strangest materials, as diamonds, hoops, bladders, pieces of carpentry, battledoors, kitchen-stuff, &c. &c. It seems to be the composition of a madman, but the drawings are masterly."

27. Hussey, "Georgian Scrapbook," 1292.

28. *HW Corr*, 20:381 (HW to Mann, 12 June 1753).

29. McCarthy, *Origins of the Gothic Revival*, 93–94.

30. Fothergill, *Strawberry Hill Set*, 50.

31. *HW Corr*, 20:449 (HW to Mann, 6 October 1754), 35:186 (HW to Bentley, 3 November 1754).

32. Walpole's 1755 Inventionary is now *HW Corr*, 35:639–40. The Inventionary and other vital letters pertaining to Chute's ownership of the Vyne are abridged and assembled in Chute, *History of the Vyne*.

33. *HW Corr*, 35:639. For this picture hang as "a true Strawberry Circle," see Howard, *Vyne*, 55.

34. HantsRO 31 M57/642/14, fol. 39v.

35. Chute, *History of the Vyne*, 1.

36. HantsRO 31 M57/646 (1776 inventory of the Vyne) maintains the title "Strawberry Parlour."

37. McCarthy, *Origins of the Gothic Revival*, 99–102.

38. This room is explored in depth in Lindfield, *Unbuilt Strawberry*.

39. *HW Corr*, 9:216 (HW to Montagu, 25 August 1757).

40. McCarthy, *Origins of the Gothic Revival*, 98.

41. Noted in his "Description of the Vyne" in *HW Corr*, 35:641.

42. *HW Corr*, 20:485 (HW to Mann, 16 July 1755).

43. By 1757 Walpole could claim, "The very altar-piece that I sent for to Italy is not placed yet. But when he could refrain from making the little Gothic columbarium for his family which I proposed and Mr Bentley had drawn so divinely, it is not probable he should do anything else." *HW Corr*, 9:216 (HW to Montagu, 25 August 1757).

44. For an excellent overview, see Howard, *Vyne*.

45. McCarthy, *Origins of the Gothic Revival*, 173.

46. *HW Corr*, 35:185–86 (HW to Bentley, 3 November 1754).

47. "Spiridone Roma, a poor painter from one of the Greek Islands came to England some time about the year 1700, and was employed by John Chute, esq., in painting his chapel at the Vyne for about two years; but being very idle, he was dismissed and set up in London as a painter of Portraits." Walpole, *Anecdotes* (1937), 72–78; Moore and Sitwell, "Spiridione Roma at the Vyne."

48. Moore and Sitwell, "Spiridione Roma at the Vyne," 27.

49. *HW Corr*, 35:154 (HW to Bentley, September 1753). For an account of the "forest theory" of the Gothic in the eighteenth century, see Reeve, "Of Druids."

50. Moore and Sitwell, "Spiridione Roma at the Vyne." Chute's screen was an expansion of an original Tudor screen in this position. Howard and Wilson, *Vyne*, 87. Thanks to Maurice Howard for discussing this with me.

51. Eberlein, "Curtain in Raphael's Sistine *Madonna*."

52. Bowdler, "Speaker's Sepulchre."

53. Ibid., 47.

54. Bricks stamped 1771 were discovered in recent conservation work. A later date prompts a reassessment of the sequence of Chute's designs for the tomb chamber, which are often dated to ca. 1756, but many are clearly ca. 1770. See Rowell, "Stained Glass," 448 nn. 41, 42.

55. Lindfield, *Unbuilt Strawberry*; McCarthy, *Origins of the Gothic Revival*, figs. 220, 221.

56. Wayment, "Stained Glass"; McCarthy, *Origins of the Gothic Revival*, 175.

57. Recent accounts of the eighteenth-century stained glass suggest that Chute bought these windows when he was planning the chapel in the 1750s and laid them aside. Rowell, "Stained Glass," 447–48.

58. *HW Corr*, 20:489 (Mann to HW, 16 August 1755), 20:485 (HW to Mann, 6 July 1755).

59. *HW Corr*, 35:185 (HW to Bentley, 3 November 1754).

60. *HW Corr*, 9:166 (HW to Montagu, 16 November 1754).

61. *HW Corr*, 24:209 (HW to Mann, 27 May 1776).

62. Recent art installations at the Vyne have explored the bonds between John Chute and Horace Walpole. See M. Smith, "Queering the Historic House."

63. Reeve and Lindfield, "'Child of Strawberry.'"

64. Honour, "House of the Gothic Revival," 1665.

65. "I shall wait for your *recommandés* with impatience, and shall with joy exert all my little abilities to convince Lord Lincoln and Mr Chamberlayne and you how ambitious I am of showing attentions to those for whom you interest yourself." *HW*

Corr, 23:228 (Mann to HW, 21 August 1770). At this point Walpole had not met Chamberlayne and does not mention Barrett. See *HW Corr*, 23:224 (HW to Mann, 26 July 1770).

66. LWL MSS File 18, 25 January 1772:

> James, you know [James Bucknell Grunston, 1747–1809] favours himself one of the most lovely youths man or woman can set eyes on, and that posterity may not be deprived of the pleasure of looking on his charms, he has been sitting for his picture, in full dress with one hand leaning on his sword and the other playing with Cobler [his dog]. The painter, not so much satisfied with his beauty as he himself is, has taken a great deal of pains to flatter him, but in this I think he has not succeeded. Lord Findlater's John told him to hang it up in the bog house, for then, says he, whoever comes there if he is disappointed of his sh——g will be sure at least to spew.

The less racy correspondence is printed in Symonds, "Eighteenth-Century Convert." On Findlater, see Tait, "Lord Findlater." Nicholls's 1772 letters to Barrett at Lee recall their Grand Tour and Findlater's friendship. See *Works of Thomas Gray*, 5:167–71. Nicholls would introduce Gray to the last love of his life, the Swiss aristocrat Charles Victor de Bonstetten (1745–1832). Further letters between Nicholls, Gray, and Barrett are in the Norton Nicholls Papers, now Yale University, Beinecke OSB MSS c 467.

67. *HW Corr*, 12:136 (HW to Mary Berry, 17 October 1794).

68. Dibdin, *Bibliographical Decameron*, 3:461, records that Walpole gave Barrett a complete run of the materials from the Strawberry Hill press. See Brydges Barrett, *List of Pictures*, 45. Barrett bought an image by J. Mabeuse (Jan Gossaert, 1478–1532) upon Walpole's advice after the French Revolution. It is described in Britton and Brayley, *Beauties of England and Wales*, 8:1093–94. Walpole would subsequently differ with Wyatt and Barrett on its placement in the Library. *HW Corr*, 43:362 (HW to Barrett, 14 May 1792), 12:136–37 (HW to Mary Berry, 17 October 1794). New York, Pierpont Morgan MA 3078 is a letter from Carter to Barrett dated 13 December 1791:

> I received the favour of your answer to my letter about the painting of the Virgin and Child, but before I made a final agreement with the owner of the picture I thought it proper to wait on Mr Walpole for his opinion of it, which if favourable, would give you Sir, the greater satisfaction in the purchase of it, as you could not have the opportunity to see it yourself. Mr Walpole was pleased to like the picture itself, but when he came to hear of the price, 25 guineas, he was surprised beyond every thing and said he thought 5 guineas would be a great price for it, indeed. From this, sir, I carried back the picture to the owner, not on any account willing to go on my opinion over Mr Walpole's. I am very sorry, Sir, that I have given you all this trouble, but I trust your kindness will excuse it. You may Sir when you come to town have an opportunity to see it if agreeable if it should remain unsold.

69. Dibdin, *Bibliographical Decameron*, 3:458.

70. Barrett received numerous letters from George Chamberlayne, a recent Catholic convert in exile in Douai, urging Barrett to convert to Catholicism. Lee Priory and Gothic architecture in general featured in their correspondence: "trial by jury, Magna Charta, laws defining treason, all the fundamental principles of British nobility, are due to those ancient worthies who built your churches, founded your colleges, and whose Gothic magnificence you frequently respect in the ruins which have stood the attacks of wild fanaticism," etc. Symonds, "Eighteenth-Century Convert," 150. See also Dibdin, *Bibliographical Decameron*, 3:460.

71. *HW Corr*, 33:575–76 n. 16 (HW to Ossory, 15 September 1787).

72. See note 111 to chapter 1.

73. Boehm, "Pair of Limoges Candlesticks."

74. King's College, London, Leathes 7/4, II. Nurse and Crook, "John Carter," 222–23.

75. For the subsequent history of the house and the Brydges family, see Goodsall, "Lee Priory and the Brydges Circle."

76. Aside from others cited below, the most significant sources have been the 1952 photographic survey National Monuments Record 2451/14–31; the survey of the house's proportions, English Heritage MD94/06067–6101; and the 1918 and 1859 sale catalogues, National Monuments Record SC 00556 and 00582. Fragments of the library antechamber and its furnishings are, as of this writing, for sale at Architectural Heritage, Gloucestershire. Stephen Calloway, formerly of the Victoria and Albert Museum, has kindly shared images of the bookcases in his collection that originated in the Lee Priory library.

77. Brydges Barrett, *List of Pictures*, 7, records that "the size [i.e., the envelope of the building] was scarcely increased. The old dining-room was pulled down; and on its scite [*sic*] was erected the present drawing-room, and library over it, surmounted by a beautiful spire."

78. In "Horace Walpole's Journals," Walpole provides an account of the collection of the house in 1780, before its Gothicization. See also *HW Corr*, 29:78 (HW to Mason, 31 August 1780).

79. *HW Corr*, 35:635 (HW to Hardinge, August 1785).

80. Symonds, "Eighteenth-Century Convert," 145. From 11 September: "It will be very entertaining to hear how the exquisite taste of a Wyatt arranged your house." Ibid., 146. Dibdin's *Bibliographical Decameron* confirms that "about 1782 he called in the aid of the celebrated architect James Wyatt to alter the family mansion at Lee . . . Wyatt designed several plans, some Grecian and some Gothic. The latter style was adopted; and took several years to carry to execution; during all which Mr. Barrett gave himself up to it with so much enthusiasm, that it almost engrossed his attention" (3:458).

81. Robinson, *James Wyatt*, 221, and Dale, *James Wyatt*, 132–33.

82. Matthews is recorded in Walpole's list of visitors for 1788 as "Mr Matthew, Mr Wyat's foreman and one." *HW Corr*, 12:229. Wyatt had seen the house the previous year. *HW Corr*, 12:227.

83. Yale, Beinecke OSB MSS c 467, fol. 87r (Barrett to Nicholls, 16 October 1802). Walpole would give a copy of the duc de Nivernais's translation of his own *Essay on Modern Gardening* to Barrett. *HW Corr*, 12:259.

84. Brydges Barrett, *List of Pictures*, 6–7. What are likely some of Wyatt's presentation drawings are in the Victoria and Albert Museum, E 1896–1948/92.D.59. Another presentation drawing, showing Wyatt's classicizing ceiling for "Mr Barrett's Dining Room," is in New York's Metropolitan Museum, 58.511, fol. 65r.

85. Robinson, *James Wyatt*, 220–21.

86. Frew and Wallace, "Thomas Pitt"; Mateo, "In Search of the Origin."

87. Frew and Wallace, "Thomas Pitt," 585.

88. *HW Corr*, 10:101 (HW to Montagu, 7 September 1763).

89. Britton and Brayley, *Beauties of England and Wales*, 8:1093.

90. This was based upon Walpole's belief that the stools he admired at Esher Place, Surrey, hailed from Cardinal Wolsey's time rather than from the remodeling by William Kent.

91. The copy of Eccardt's portrait was first recorded in 1808 in the Strawberry Room, but there is every reason to believe it was intended for that space from 1787. Britton and Brayley, *Beauties of England and Wales*, 8:1095.

92. Ibid., 1093.

93. *HW Corr*, 12:137 (HW to Mary Berry, 17 October 1794).

94. See the 1958 survey National Monuments Record EH SC 00582 (unpaginated). "In the recess at the NW end is a kind of altar table, over which are paintings of Eight small whole length figures of St George, Richard the Second, Anne his Queen, a monk, a nun, etc. Then, in niches above are several beautiful figures of Angels, playing upon musical instruments." This is largely confirmed by Britton and Brayley, *Beauties of England and Wales*, 8:1093: "In a recess at the east end, is a kind of altar-table, over which are paintings of eight small whole-lengths, by Mr. John Carter, of St. George, Richard the Second, Anne his Queen, a Monk, a Nun, &c. in niches, with various beautiful minute figures above, of angels playing on different musical instruments: the great taste, and exquisite execution, displayed in these paintings, evince the very superior knowledge of the artist, whose critical acquaintance with the costume of past ages, is exemplified by them in the most powerful manner."

95. The documentation for the paintings is now Bretherton Collection, Leeds, Misc. Letters 2 Carter 2–8. Carter made careful sketches of the figure of Saint George in the staircase

at Strawberry Hill in 1788, now Huntington Library MS 130368, fol. 52r. For St. Margaret's, see Wayment, "East Window of St. Margaret's."

96. For discussion, see Lindfield, "Further Allusion to Strawberry Hill."

97. *HW Corr*, 12:136 (HW to Mary Berry, 17 October 1794), 31:342 (HW to More, 25 July 1790).

98. *HW Corr*, 12:111 (HW to Mary Berry, 27 September 1794).

99. Brydges, *Autobiography*, 2:88: "Mr. Barrett lived very handsomely, and prided himself on his regard to etiquette and outward appearance. His manners were polished, perhaps a little finical; and he had something of the fastidiousness of Lord Orford and Gray, with both of whom he was intimate. One of his most intimate friends through life was the Rev. Norton Nicolls, Gray's correspondent—a very clever man, with a great deal of erudition; but, it must be confessed, a supreme coxcomb."

100. *HW Corr*, 42:221 (HW to Barrett, 5 June 1788).

101. *HW Corr*, 31:342 (HW to More, 25 July 1790).

102. *HW Corr*, 42:221 (HW to Barrett, 5 June 1788).

103. *HW Corr*, 33:42 (HW to Ossory, 11 August 1778).

104. On the influence of Walpole, Strawberry Hill, and its collection on two significant nineteenth-century houses in London, see S. Clarke, "Rosamond's Bower."

105. Coffman, "Casa Loma." For Walpole's portrait, which once belonged to Charles Churchill and Lady Mary Churchill (Walpole's sister), see Adams and Lewis, "Portraits of Horace Walpole," 16.

Chapter 6

1. Eastlake, *History of the Gothic Revival*, 371.
2. Hall, "Georgian Gothic."
3. Braybrooke, *History of Audley End*, 126.
4. *Journal of Mrs. Arbuthnot*, 1:176.
5. Saska, "Strawberry Hill."
6. S. Clarke, "Strawberry Hill Sale of 1842."
7. Cited and discussed in Reynolds, "Gothic and the Architectural Imagination," 89.
8. *HW Corr*, 42:220–21 (HW to [Barrett], 5 June 1788).
9. *HW Corr*, 31:221 (HW to More, 13 November 1784). Cited and discussed in Wright, "Gothic."
10. Crook, *John Carter*, 45.
11. Ibid., 46.
12. See most recently Reeve, "Hereford Screen"; Lindfield, *Georgian Gothic*, 182–94; and Robinson, *James Wyatt*.
13. Crook, *John Carter*, 51.
14. Aldrich, "Thomas Rickman's Handbook." See also Biddick, *Shock of Medievalism*, 19–57. In 1826 the antiquary John Britton could list more than sixty studies of medieval architecture published in as many years. Britton, *Chronological History*.
15. See Crossley, introduction to Frankl, *Gothic Architecture*.
16. Wahrman, *Making of the Modern Self*, 40, 44. See previously Binhammer, "Sex Panic of the 1790s."
17. Wahrman, *Making of the Modern Self*, 47.
18. Coykendall, "Queer Counterhistory," 121.
19. *HW Corr*, 20:166 (HW to Mann, 2 August 1750), 20:127 (HW to Mann, 25 February 1750).
20. Addison, no. 119, in *The Spectator*, 58, cited and discussed in Breward, *Culture of Fashion*, 118.
21. Breward, *Culture of Fashion*, 109–44; Myrone, *Bodybuilding*, esp. 12; Bann, *Clothing of Clio*, 2. See subsequently Bann, "Historicizing Horace."
22. See most recently Gemmett, *William Beckford's Fonthill*, and Dakers, *Fonthill Recovered*.
23. Walpole and Beckford are paired equally in accounts of Gothic literature and architecture. See, for example, Wainwright, *Romantic Interior*. One of the most illuminating accounts of Beckford's sexuality is Benyon, "'Mr Beckford's Favourite Propensity.'" On *Vathek*, see Lindfield and Townshend, "Reading *Vathek* and Fonthill Abbey."
24. Aldrich, "William Beckford's Abbey at Fonthill."
25. Watkin, "Beckford, Soane, and Hope," 34.

26. McLeod, "Collector's Obsession"; S. Clarke, "'All Ardour, All Intrepidity'"; S. Clarke, "Beckford and Nimby Pamby." "Nimby Pamby" as a slur derived from Henry Carey's 1725 text entitled *Namby Pamby*.

27. Redding, "Recollections," 308. Claiming that he would not have Chinoiserie furniture at Fonthill, Beckford cites Walpole, however denigratingly, as an exemplar: "Horace Walpole would not have suffered it in his toyshop at Strawberry Hill." Melville, *Life and Letters of William Beckford*, 320.

28. W. Davis, "Queer Family Romance."

29. Myrone, *Bodybuilding*, 112.

30. Janes, *Oscar Wilde Prefigured*, 57.

31. "Let no one say Walpole's fantastic residence monopolizes all the frivolities of architecture, or all its improprieties. Yet, from his various expressions, it is plain he was neither so presumptuous nor so ignorant as to deem his Castle critically impregnable, albeit our architects conceit every little fritter and filigree chapel they stick up, a combination of infinite wisdom and knowledge, like Solomon's Temple." "Strawberry Hill—Horace Walpole."

32. Durandus, *Symbolism of Churches*. For the current version of the text, see Thibodeau, *Rationale Divinorum Officiorum*. For the use of Durandus in medieval art history, see Reeve, *Thirteenth-Century Wall Painting*, 104–8.

33. See, for example, Webster, "'Absolutely Wretched.'"

34. Janes, "Early Victorian Moral Anxiety," 138.

35. Stein, "American Literary History," 863.

36. Barlow, *Queer British Art*; McGregor, "Queer Orthodoxy"; Shand-Tucci, *Boston Bohemia*; Lepine, "Queer Gothic"; Potvin, *Bachelors of a Different Sort*, esp. 81–130. On Robert Kerr's literary satire of Burges, see Crook, *William Burges*, 36–38. For Burges's sexuality, see Roquet, "Life in Costume," 176–78, 239; Welter, "*Schloss* Murnau"; P. Murphy, *Medieval Studies*; and Mills, *Derek Jarman's Medieval Modern*.

Bibliography

Adams, Charles Kingsley, and Wilmarth S. Lewis. "The Portraits of Horace Walpole." *Walpole Society* 42 (1968–70): 1–34.

Adams, Henry. *Mont-Saint-Michel and Chartres*. Boston: Houghton Mifflin, 1913. Originally published in 1904.

Addison, James. *The Spectator*. Vol. 3. Philadelphia: James Crissy, 1824.

Aldrich, Megan. "Creating an Authentic Style: John Soane's Gothic Library at Stowe." In *Art and Authenticity*, edited by Megan Aldrich and Jos Hackforth-Jones, 122–37. Farnham, Surrey: Lund Humphries, 2012.

———. "Thomas Rickman's Handbook of Gothic Architecture and the Taxonomic Classification of the Past." In *Antiquaries and Archaists: The Past in the Past, the Past in the Present*, edited by Megan Aldrich and Robert J. Wallis, 62–74. Reading, U.K.: Spire Books, 2009.

———. "William Beckford's Abbey at Fonthill: From the Picturesque to the Sublime." In *William Beckford, 1760–1844: An Eye for the Magnificent*, edited by Derek E. Ostergard, 117–38. New Haven: Yale University Press, 2001.

Aldrich, Robert, and Garry Wotherspoon, eds. *Who's Who in Gay and Lesbian History: From Antiquity to World War II*. London: Routledge, 2002.

Alexander, Michael. *Medievalism: The Middle Ages in Modern England*. New Haven: Yale University Press, 2007.

Allan, Juliet. "New Light on William Kent at Hampton Court Palace." *Architectural History* 27 (1984): 50–58.

Allen, Beverley Sprague. *Tides in English Taste (1619–1800): A Background for the Study of Literature*. 2 vols. 1937. New York: Pageant Books, 1958.

Almon, John. *The New Foundling Hospital for Wit*. London: J. Debrett, 1786.

Ambrose, Kirk. "Influence." In "Medieval Art History Today—Critical Terms," special issue, *Studies in Iconography* 33 (2012): 197–206.

Amic, Sylvain, and Ségolène Le Men, eds. *Cathédrales, 1789–1914: Un myth moderne*. Rouen: Somogy éditions d'art, 2014. Exhibition catalogue.

Anderson, Christy. "Masculine and Unaffected: Inigo Jones and the Classical Ideal." *Art Journal* 56, no. 2 (1997): 48–54.

Arbuthnot, Harriet Fane. *The Journal of Mrs. Arbuthnot, 1820–1832*. Edited by Francis Bamford and the Duke of Wellington. 2 vols. London: Macmillan, 1950.

Arciszewska, Barbara, and Elizabeth McKellar, eds. *Articulating British Classicism: New Approaches to Eighteenth-Century Architecture*. Aldershot, U.K.: Ashgate, 2004.

Arnold, Dana. "The Illusion of Grandeur? Antiquity, Grand Tourism, and the Country House." In *The Georgian Country House: Architecture, Landscape, and Society*, 100–116. Stroud: Sutton, 1998.

Baines, Paul. *The Complete Critical Guide to Alexander Pope*. London: Routledge, 2000.

Baker, Malcolm, Colin Harrison, and Alastair Lang. "Bouchardon's British Sitters: Sculptural Portraiture in Rome and the Classicizing Bust Around 1730." *Burlington Magazine* 142, no. 1173 (2000): 752–62.

Bann, Stephen. *The Clothing of Clio: A Study of the Representation of History in Nineteenth-Century Britain and France*. 1984. Reprint, Cambridge: Cambridge University Press, 2010.

———. "Historicizing Horace." In *HWSH*, 117–33.

Barkan, Leonard. *Transuming Passion: Ganymede and the Erotics of Humanism*. Stanford: Stanford University Press, 1991.

Barker-Benfield, Graham J. *The Culture of Sensibility: Sex and Society in Eighteenth-Century Britain*. Chicago: University of Chicago Press, 1992.

Barlow, Clare, ed. *Queer British Art, 1861–1967*. London: Tate, 2017. Exhibition catalogue.

Barrell, John. "'The Dangerous Goddess': Masculinity, Prestige, and the Aesthetic in Early Eighteenth-Century Britain." *Cultural Critique* 12 (1989): 101–31.

———. *The Political Theory of Painting from Reynolds to Hazlitt: "The Body of the Politic."* Rev. ed. New Haven: Yale University Press, 1995.

Battles, Kelly Eileen. "The Antiquarian Impulse: History, Affect, and Material Culture in Eighteenth- and Nineteenth-Century British Literature." Ph.D. diss., Michigan State University, 2008.

Baxandall, Michael. *Patterns of Intention: On the Historical Explanation of Pictures*. New Haven: Yale University Press, 1985.

Baxter, Ron. "Whose Heritage? The Problem of the Shobdon Arches." *JBAA* 163 (2010): 154–76.

Beer, E. S. de. "Gothic: Origin and Diffusion of the Term; The Idea of Style in Architecture." *Journal of the Warburg and Courtauld Institutes* 11 (1948): 143–62.

Bentman, Raymond. "Horace Walpole's Forbidden Passion." In *Queer Representations: Reading Lives, Reading Cultures*, edited by Martin Duberman, 276–89. New York: New York University Press, 1997.

Benyon, John. "'Mr Beckford's Favourite Propensity': The Erotics of Boyhood and the Emergence of a Sexual Self in Late-Eighteenth-Century England." In *William Beckford and the New Millennium*, edited by Kenneth W. Graham and Kevin Berland, 7–36. New York: AMS, 2004.

Berliner, Rudolph. "The Freedom of Medieval Art." *Gazette des beaux arts* 6, no. 28 (1945): 263–88.

Bernstein, Susan. *Housing Problems: Writing and Architecture in Goethe, Walpole, Freud, and Heidegger*. Stanford: Stanford University Press, 2008.

Betjeman, John. *Ghastly Good Taste, or A Depressing Story of the Rise and Fall of English Architecture*. London: Chapman & Hall, 1933.

Biddick, Kathleen. *The Shock of Medievalism*. Durham: Duke University Press, 1998.

Binhammer, Katherine. "The Sex Panic of the 1790s." *Journal of the History of Sexuality* 6, no. 3 (1996): 409–34.

Binski, Paul. *Becket's Crown: Art and Imagination in Gothic England, 1170–1300*. New Haven: Yale University Press, 2004.

———. *The Painted Chamber at Westminster*. London: Society of Antiquaries of London, 1986.

Boehm, Barbara Drake. "A Pair of Limoges Candlesticks in the Cloisters Collection." In *The Cloisters: Studies in Honor of the Fiftieth Anniversary*, edited by Elizabeth C. Parker and Mary B. Shepard, 147–66. New York: Metropolitan Museum of Art, 1992.

Bohls, Elizabeth A. "Disinterestedness and Denial of the Particular: Locke, Adam Smith, and the Subject of Aesthetics." In *Eighteenth-Century Aesthetics and the Reconstruction of Art*, edited by Paul Mattick, 16–51. Cambridge: Cambridge University Press, 2008.

Bonehill, John. "The View from the Gentleman's Seat." In *Court, Country, City: British Art and Architecture, 1660–1735*, edited by Mark Hallett, Nigel Llewellyn, and Martin Myrone, 383–410. New Haven: Yale Center for British Art, Paul Mellon Centre for Studies in British Art, 2016.

Boroughs, Rod. "Oscar Wilde's Translation of Petronius: The Story of a Literary Hoax." *English Literature in Transition, 1880–1920* 38, no. 1 (1995): 9–49.

Bowdler, Roger. "The Speaker's Sepulchre: Chaloner Chute's Tomb at The Vyne." *Apollo* 155, no. 482 (2002): 46–50.

Bowron, Edgar Peters. *Pompeo Batoni: A Complete Catalogue of His Paintings*. New Haven: Yale University Press, 2016.

Braccelli, Giovanni Battista. *Bizzarie di varie figure*. Livorno, 1624.

Bradley, Simon. "The Englishness of Gothic: Theories and Interpretations from William Gilpin to J. H. Parker." *Architectural History* 45 (2002): 325–46.

Braybrooke, Richard Griffin. *The History of Audley End*. London: Samuel Bentley, 1836.

Breward, Christopher. *The Culture of Fashion: A New History of Fashionable Dress*. Manchester: Manchester University Press, 1995.

Brideoake, Fiona. *The Ladies of Llangollen: Desire, Indeterminacy, and the Legacies of Criticism*. Lewisburg: Bucknell University Press, 2017.

Brindle, Steven. *Windsor Castle: A Thousand Years of a Royal Palace* (London: Royal Collection Trust, 2018).

Britton, John. *Chronological History and Graphic Illustrations of Christian Architecture in England*. London: Longman, 1826.

Britton, John, and Edward Wedlake Brayley. *Beauties of England and Wales*. 18 vols. London: Vernor & Hood, 1801–15.

Brooks, Chris. *Gothic Revival*. London: Phaidon, 1999.

Brown, John. *An Estimate of the Manners and Principles of the Times*. 2 vols. London: L. Davis & C. Reymers, 1757.

Brownell, Morris R. *Alexander Pope and the Arts of Georgian England*. Oxford: Clarendon Press, 1978.

———. *The Prime Minister of Taste: A Portrait of Horace Walpole*. New Haven: Yale University Press, 2001.

Brush, Kathryn. *The Shaping of Art History: Wilhelm Vöge, Adolph Goldschmidt, and the Study of Medieval Art*. Cambridge: Cambridge University Press, 1996.

Bruzelius, Caroline. "A Rose by Any Other Name: The 'Not Gothic Enough' Architecture of Italy (Again)." In Reeve, *Reading Gothic Architecture*, 93–109.

Brydges, Egerton. *The Autobiography, Times, Opinions, and Contemporaries of Sir Egerton Brydges*. 2 vols. London: Cochrane & M'Crone, 1834.

Brydges Barrett, Thomas B. *List of Pictures at the Seat of T. B. Brydges Barrett, Esq., at Lee Priory in the County of Kent*. Lee Priory: J. Warwick, 1817.

Buchanan, Alexandrina. "Interpretations of Medieval Architecture, c. 1550–1750." In *Gothic Architecture and Its Meanings, 1550–1830*, edited by Michael Hall, 27–52. Reading: Spire Books, 2002.

Burling, William J., and William Franken. "Garrick's Alterations of 'Miss in Her Teens.'" *Huntington Library Quarterly* 62 (1999): 145–52.

Burney, Fanny. *Diary and Letters of Madam D'Arblay*. Edited by Charlotte Barrett. 7 vols. New York: Macmillan, 1904.

Buttery, Darrell. *York Minster Revealed: Pictures of York Minster from the Seventeenth Century to the Present*. York: York Civic Trust, 2007.

Calè, Luisa. "Gray's Ode and Walpole's China Tub: The Order of the Book and the Paper Lives of an Object." *Eighteenth-Century Studies* 45, no. 1 (2011): 105–25.

Cameron, Ed. *The Psychopathology of the Gothic Romance: Perversion, Neuroses, and Psychosis in Early Works of the Genre*. Jefferson, N.C.: McFarland, 2010.

Camille, Michael. *The Gargoyles of Notre-Dame: Medievalism and the Monsters of Modernity*. Chicago: University of Chicago Press, 2009.

Camille, Michael, and Adrian Rifkin. Introduction to "Other Objects of Desire: Collectors and Collecting Queerly," special issue, *Art History* 24, no. 2 (2001): 163–68.

Campbell, Colen. *Vitruvius Britannicus, or The British Architect*. 3 vols. London, 1715–25.

Campbell, Jill. "'I Am No Giant': Horace Walpole, Heterosexual Incest, and Love Among Men." *Eighteenth Century* 39, no. 3 (1998): 238–60.

———. "Politics and Sexuality in Portraits of John, Lord Hervey." *Word and Image* 6, no. 4 (1990): 281–97.

Cannon-Brookes, Peter. "Robert Tournières, Lord Bateman, and Two Picture Frames." *International Journal of Museum Management and Curatorship* 4 (1985): 141–45.

Cantor, Norman F. *Inventing the Middle Ages: The Lives, Works, and Ideas of the Great Medievalists of the Twentieth Century*. New York: Harper Perennial, 1991.

Carson, Anne Elizabeth. "'Exquisite Torture': The Autoeroticism of Pope's Eloisa." *Eighteenth-Century Studies* 40, no. 4 (2007): 615–29.

Carter, Philip. *Men and the Emergence of Polite Society, Britain, 1660–1800*. Harlow, U.K.: Pearson Education, 2001.

Cash, Arthur H. *John Wilkes: The Scandalous Father of Civil Liberty*. New Haven: Yale University Press, 2006.

A Catalogue of the Pictures at Cowdray-House, the Seat of the Right Honourable Lord Viscount Montague, near Midhurst, Sussex. Portsmouth: R. Carr, 1777.

A Catalogue of the Genuine and Exceedingly Fine Collection of Miniature and Other Paintings of Thomas Barrett Esq. (Deceas'd) Brought from His Seat at Lee, near Canterbury in Kent. London, 1758.

Caudron, Simone. "Connoisseurs of *Champlevé* Limoges Enamels in Eighteenth-Century England." In *Collectors and Collections*, British Museum Yearbook 2, edited by Richard Camber, 9–23. London: British Museum Publications, 1977.

Chaimovich, Felipe. "Mirrors of Society: Versailles and the Use of Flat Reflected Images." *Visual Resources* 24, no. 4 (2008): 353–67.

Cherry, Deborah, and Jennifer Harris. "Eighteenth-Century Portraiture and the Seventeenth-Century Past: Gainsborough and Van Dyck." *Art History* 5, no. 3 (1982): 287–309.

Child, Graham. *World Mirrors, 1650–1900*. London: Sotheby's, 1990.

Christie, James. *Catalogue of That Much Esteemed and Truly Valuable Museum of the Hon. Richard Bateman* [. . .]. London, 1774.

Churchill, Charles. *Poems, by Charles Churchill*. 3 vols. London: J. Wilkes, 1776.

Chute, Chaloner William. *A History of the Vyne in Hampshire*. Winchester: Jacob & Johnson, 1888.

Clark, J. C. D. *English Society, 1660–1832: Religion, Ideology, and Politics During the Ancien Régime*. Cambridge: Cambridge University Press, 2000.

Clark, Kenneth. *The Gothic Revival: An Essay in the History of Taste*. 3rd ed. London: John Murray, 1962.

Clarke, George. "Grecian Taste and Gothic Virtue: Lord Cobham's Gardening Programme and Its Iconography." *Apollo* 97, no. 136 (1973): 566–71.

Clarke, Stephen. "'All Ardour, All Intrepidity': William Beckford at the Strawberry Hill Sale." *1650–1850: Ideas, Aesthetics, and Inquiries in the Early Modern Era* 18 (2011): 57–108.

———. "'The Almost Innumerable Descents of the Owner and His Late Wife': William Beckford's Use of Heraldry at Fonthill Abbey." *Beckford Journal* 20 (2014): 42–61.

———. "Beckford and Nimby Pamby: William Beckford's Notes in Horace Walpole's *Works*." *Book Collector* 63 (2014): 47–81.

———. "Horace Walpole's Architectural Taste." *1650–1850: Ideas, Aesthetics, and Enquiries in the Early Modern Era* 16 (2009): 223–44.

———. "'Lord God! Jesus! What a House!': Describing and Visiting Strawberry Hill." *Journal for Eighteenth-Century Studies* 33, no. 3 (2010): 357–80.

———. "Rosamond's Bower, The Pryor's Bank, and the Long Shadow of Strawberry Hill." *Journal of the History of Collections* 26, no. 2 (2014): 287–306.

———. *The Strawberry Hill Press and Its Printing House: An Account and an Iconography*. New Haven: Lewis Walpole Library, Yale University, 2011.

———. "The Strawberry Hill Sale of 1842: 'The Most Distinguished Gem That Has Ever Adorned the Annals of Auctions.'" In *HWSH*, 261–74.

Cleland, John. *Memoirs of a Woman of Pleasure*. London: Thomas Parker for Ralph Griffiths, 1748–49.

Clery, Emma J. *The Feminization Debate in Eighteenth-Century England: Literature, Commerce, and Luxury*. Basingstoke, U.K.: Palgrave Macmillan, 2004.

———. *The Rise of Supernatural Fiction, 1762–1800*. Cambridge: Cambridge University Press, 1995.

Cleto, Fabio, ed. *Camp: Queer Aesthetics and the Performing Subject*. Michigan: University of Michigan Press, 1999.

Climenson, Emily T. *Elizabeth Montagu: The Queen of the Bluestockings; Her Correspondence from 1720 to 1761*. 2 vols. London: John Murray, 1906.

Cocks, Harry G. "Modernity and the Self in the History of Sexuality." *Historical Journal* 49, no. 4 (2006): 1211–27.

Coffman, Peter. "Casa Loma and the Gothic Imagination." *Journal of the Society for the Study of Architecture in Canada* 28, nos. 3–4 (2003): 3–12.

Coldstream, Nicola. "York Chapter House." *JBAA* 35 (1972): 15–23.

Collections Towards a Parochial History of Berkshire. London: J. Nichols, 1783.

Colton, Judith. "Merlin's Cave and Queen Caroline: Garden Art as Political Propaganda." *Eighteenth-Century Studies* 10, no. 1 (1976): 1–20.

Colvin, Howard. "Henry Flitcroft, William Kent, and Shobdon Church, Herefordshire." In *Essays in Scots and English Architectural History: A Festschrift in Honour of John Frew*, edited by David Jones and Sam McKinstry, 1–8. Donnington, Lincolnshire: Shaun Tyas, 2009.

Combe, William. *Letters of the Late Lord Lyttelton*. Dublin, 1785.

Connelly, Frances S. "John Ruskin and the Savage Gothic." *Journal of Art Historiography* 12 (2015): 1–16.

Cook, Matt. *Queer Domesticities: Homosexuality and Home Life in Twentieth-Century London*. Basingstoke, U.K.: Palgrave Macmillan, 2014.

Coope, Rosalys. "The 'Long Gallery': Its Origins, Development, Use, and Decoration." *Architectural History* 29 (1986): 43–84.

Cooper, Anthony Ashley, Earl of Shaftesbury. *Second Characters, or The Language of Forms*. Edited by Benjamin Rand. Cambridge: Cambridge University Press, 1914.

Cooper, John Gilbert. *Letters Concerning Taste*. 3rd ed. London: R. & J. Dodsley, 1757.

Cooper, Nicholas. "Rank, Manners, and Display: The Gentlemanly House, 1500–1700." *Transactions of the Royal Historical Society* 12 (2002): 291–310.

Cornforth, John. *Early Georgian Interiors*. New Haven: Yale University Press, 2004.

Coykendall, Abby. "Gothic Genealogies, the Family Romance, and Clara Reeve's *The Old English Baron*." *Eighteenth-Century Fiction* 17, no. 3 (2005): 443–80.

———. "Queer Counterhistory and the Specter of Effeminacy." In *Heteronormativity in Eighteenth-Century Literature and Culture*, edited by Ana de Freitas Boe and Abby Coykendall, 111–30. Aldershot, U.K.: Ashgate, 2015.

Craske, Matthew. "From Burlington Gate to Billingsgate: James Ralph's Attempt to Impose Burlingtonian Classicism as a Canon of Public Taste." In Arciszewska and McKellar, *Articulating British Classicism*, 97–117.

———. "Plan and Control: Design and the Competitive Spirit in Early and Mid-Eighteenth-Century England." *Journal of Design History* 12, no. 3 (1999): 187–216.

Croker, Thomas Crofton. *Specimen of the Catalogue of the Great Sale of Gooseberry Hall, with Puffatory Remarks*. London: T. & W. Boone, 1842.

Crompton, Louis. *Byron and Greek Love: Homophobia in Nineteenth-Century England*. Berkeley: University of California Press, 1985.

Crook, Joseph Mordaunt, ed. *A Gothick Symposium at the Victoria and Albert Museum*. London, 1983.

———. *John Carter and the Mind of the Gothic Revival*. London: Society of Antiquaries of London, 1995.

———. "Strawberry Hill Revisited, II." *Country Life* 154 (1973): 1726–30.

———. *William Burges and the High Victorian Dream*. London: John Murray, 1981.

Crossley, Paul. Introduction to Frankl, *Gothic Architecture*, 41–50.

Crown, Patricia. "British Rococo as Social and Political Style." *Eighteenth-Century Studies* 23, no. 3 (1990): 269–82.

Cryle, Peter, and Lisa O'Connell, eds. *Libertine Enlightenment: Sex, Liberty, and License in the Eighteenth Century*. Basingstoke, U.K.: Palgrave Macmillan, 2004.

Dakers, Caroline. *Fonthill Recovered: A Cultural History*. London: University College London Press, 2018.

Dale, Anthony. *James Wyatt, Architect, 1746–1813*. Oxford: Blackwell, 1956.

Darongsuwan, Nida. "Class and Gender Identity in 'Male Gothic' from Walpole to Byron." Ph.D. diss., University of York, 2008.

Dart, John. *Westmonasterium, or The History and Antiquities of the Abbey Church of St. Peters Westminster*. 2 vols. London: T. Bowles & J. Bowles, 1742.

Dashwood, Sir Francis. *The Dashwoods of West Wycombe*. London: Aurum, 1987.

Davis, Terence. *The Gothick Taste*. Newton Abbot, Devon: David & Charles, 1974.

Davis, Whitney. "Founding the Closet: Sexuality and the Creation of Art History." *Art Documentation* 11, no. 4 (1992): 171–75.

———. *A General Theory of Visual Culture*. Princeton: Princeton University Press, 2011.

———. "Homoerotic Art Collection from 1750–1920." *Art History* 24, no. 2 (2001): 247–77.

———. *Queer Beauty: Sexuality and Aesthetics from Winckelmann to Freud and Beyond*. New York: Columbia University Press, 2010.

———. "Queer Family Romance in Collecting Visual Culture." *GLQ* 17, nos. 2–3 (2011): 309–29.

———. "The Site of Sexuality: William Beckford's Fonthill Abbey, 1780–1824." In *Archaeologies of Sexuality*, edited by Robert A. Schmidt and Barbara L. Voss, 104–13. London: Routledge, 2000.

———. "Winckelmann Divided: Mourning the Death of Art History." In *Gay and Lesbian Studies in Art History*, edited by Whitney Davis, 141–60. New York: Haworth, 1994.

Davoli, Silvia. *Lost Treasures of Strawberry Hill: Masterpieces from Horace Walpole's Collection*. London: Scala, 2018.

Delany, Mrs. [Mary]. *The Autobiography and Correspondence of Mary Granville, Mrs. Delany*. Edited by Lady Llanover. 3 vols. London: R. Bentley, 1861.

———. *The Autobiography and Correspondence of Mary Granville, Mrs. Delany*. Edited by Lady Llanover. 2nd ser. 3 vols. London: R. Bentley, 1862.

De Wolfe, Elsie. *The House in Good Taste*. New York: Century, 1913.

Dibdin, Thomas F. *The Bibliographical Decameron; or, Ten Days Pleasant Discourse upon Illuminated Manuscripts*. 3 vols. London: Shakespeare Press, 1817.

The Dictionary of Love. London: R. Griffiths, 1753.

Diebold, William J. "'A Living Source of Our Civilization': The Exhibition *Deutsche Groesse / Grandeur de l'Allemagne / Duitsche Grootheid* in Brussels, 1942." In *Arts of Display*, edited by H. Perry Chapman, Frits Scholten, and Joanna Woodall, 292–319. Leiden: Brill, 2015.

———. "Medievalism." In "Medieval Art History Today—Critical Terms," special issue, *Studies in Iconography* 33 (2012): 247–56.

Dinshaw, Carolyn. *How Soon Is Now? Medieval Texts, Amateur Readers, and the Queerness of Time*. Durham: Duke University Press, 2012.

Dittelbach, Thomas. "Die Illusio verspottet sich selbst: Goethes Spiegeltheorem und die Villa dei Mostri des Fürsten von Palagonia." *Zeitschrift für Kunstgeschichte* 68 (2005): 501–20.

Dodds, George, and Robert Tavernor, eds. *Body and Building: Essays on the Changing Relation of Body and Architecture*. Cambridge: MIT Press, 2005.

"Donnington Grove." *Gentleman's Magazine* 42 (1772): 561–62.

Droth, Martina, Jason Edwards, and Michael Hatt, eds. *Sculpture Victorious: Art in an Age of Invention, 1837–1901*. New Haven: Yale University Press, 2014.

Dubro, James R. "The Third Sex: Lord Hervey and His Coterie." *Eighteenth-Century Life* 2, no. 4 (1976): 89–95.

Ducarel, Andrew Coltée. *Anglo-Norman Antiquities Reconsidered*. London: T. Spilsbury, 1767.

———. *A Tour Through Normandy*. London: John Woodyer, 1754.

Dukelskaya, Larissa, and Andrew Moore, eds. *A Capital Collection: Houghton Hall and the Hermitage*. New Haven: Yale University Press, 2002.

Durandus, William. *The Symbolism of Churches and Church Ornaments: A Translation of the First Book of the "Rationale Divinorum Officiorum."* Translated and edited by John M. Neale and Benjamin Webb. Leeds: T. W. Green, 1843.

Dynes, Wayne R., Warren Johansson, William A. Percy, and Stephen Donaldson, eds. *Encyclopedia of Homosexuality*. 2 vols. New York: Garland, 1990.

Eastlake, Charles L. *A History of the Gothic Revival*. London: Longmans, Green, 1872.

Eberlein, Johann Konrad. "The Curtain in Raphael's Sistine *Madonna*." *Art Bulletin* 65, no. 1 (1983): 61–77.

Eco, Umberto. "The Return of the Middle Ages." In *Travels in Hyperreality*, translated by William Weaver, 59–86. New York: Harcourt, 1986.

Edwards, Ralph. "Cabinets Made for Horace Walpole and Thomas Brand." *Burlington Magazine* 74, no. 432 (1939): 128–31.

Einberg, Elizabeth. "Lord Hervey's Choice: Reconsidering the *Hervey Conversation Piece* by William Hogarth (1697–1764)." *British Art Journal* 17, no. 1 (2016): 8–15.

Elfenbein, Andrew. *Romantic Genius: The Prehistory of a Homosexual Role*. New York: Columbia University Press, 1999.

Evans, Joan. *A History of the Society of Antiquaries*. Oxford: Oxford University Press, 1956.

Evelyn, John. "An Account of Architects and Architecture." In *A Parallel of the Ancient Architecture with the Modern*, by Roland de Fréart, translated by John Evelyn, paginated separately. 2nd ed. London: D. Brown, 1707.

Ezell, Margaret J. M. "Looking Glass Histories." *Journal of British Studies* 43, no. 3 (2004): 317–38.

Fay, Elizabeth A. *Fashioning Faces: The Portraitive Mode in British Romanticism*. Durham: University of New Hampshire Press, 2010.

Fincher, Max. "Guessing the Mould: Homosocial Sins and Identity in Horace Walpole's *The Castle of Otranto*." *Gothic Studies* 3, no. 3 (2001): 229–45.

Fletcher, John. "The Sins of the Fathers: The Persistence of Gothic." In *Romanticism and Postmodernism*, edited by Edward Larrissy, 113–40. Cambridge: Cambridge University Press, 1999.

Ford, Lisa. "A Progress in Plants: Mrs. Delany's Botanical Sources." In *Mrs. Delany and Her Circle*, edited by Mark Laird and Alicia Weisberg-Roberts, 204–23. New Haven: Yale University Press, 2009.

Fordyce, James. *Addresses to Young Men*. London: T. Cadell, 1777.

Forrester, James. *The Polite Philosopher; or, An Essay in That Art Which Makes a Man Happy in Himself, and Agreeable to Others*. Dublin, 1734.

Fothergill, Brian. *The Strawberry Hill Set: Horace Walpole and His Circle*. London: Faber & Faber, 1983.

Foyle, Jonathan. "Did Horace Walpole Build Strawberry Hill to Express His Sexuality?" *Financial Times*, 3 June 2016.

Frank, Marcie. "Horace Walpole's Family Romances." *Modern Philology* 100, no. 3 (2003): 417–35.

Frankl, Paul. *The Gothic: Literary Sources and Interpretations Through Eight Centuries*. Princeton: Princeton University Press, 1960.

———. *Gothic Architecture*. Edited and revised by Paul Crossley. New Haven: Yale University Press, 2000.

Franklin, Jill A., Bernard Nurse, and Pamela Tudor-Craig, eds. *Catalogue of Paintings in the Collection of the Society of Antiquaries of London*. London: Harvey Miller, 2015.

Fréart, Roland de. *A Parallel of the Antient Architecture with the Modern*. Translated by John Evelyn. London: Thomas Roycroft for John Place, 1664. (Originally published in French as *Parallèle de l'architecture antique avec la moderne* [1650].)

Freedman, Paul, and Gabrielle M. Spiegel. "Medievalisms Old and New: The Rediscovery of Alterity in North American Medieval Studies." *American Historical Review* 103 (1998): 667–704.

Frew, John M. "Gothic Is English: John Carter and the Revival of the Gothic as England's National Style." *Art Bulletin* 64, no. 2 (1982): 315–19.

Frew, John M., and Carey Wallace. "Thomas Pitt, Portugal, and the Gothic Cult of Batalha." *Burlington Magazine* 128, no. 1001 (1986): 582–85.

Fribble, Timothy [Jonathan Swift]. *Tittle Tattle; or, Taste A-la-Mode: A New Farce*. London: R. Griffiths, 1749.

"The Fribbleriad." *Critical Review, or The Annals of Literature,* January–June 1761, 494.

Friedman, Terry. *The Eighteenth-Century Church in Britain*. New Haven: Yale University Press, 2011.

Frith, Wendy. "Sexuality and Politics in the Gardens at West Wycombe and Medmenham Abbey." In *Bourgeois and Aristocratic Cultural Encounters in Garden Art, 1550–1850*, edited by Michel Conan, 285–309. Washington, D.C.: Dumbarton Oaks, 2002.

Gallagher, Lowell, Frederick S. Roden, and Patricia J. Smith. *Catholic Figures, Queer Narratives*. Basingstoke, U.K.: Palgrave Macmillan, 2006.

Garrick, David. *The Fribbleriad*. London: J. Coote, 1761.

———. *Miss in Her Teens: Or, The Medley of Lovers; A Farce in Two Acts*. London: J. & R. Tonson & S. Draper, 1747.

———. *The Private Correspondence of David Garrick*. 2 vols. London: Henry Colburn & Richard Bentley, 1831–32.

Gemmett, Robert. J. *William Beckford's Fonthill: Architecture, Landscape, and the Arts*. Croyden: Fonthill Media, 2016.

Gerard, Alexander. *An Essay on Taste*. London: A. Millar, A. Kincaid, and J. Bell, 1759.

Germann, Georg. *Gothic Revival in Europe and Britain: Sources, Influences, and Ideas*. Translated by Gerald Onn. Cambridge: MIT Press, 1973.

Germann, Jennifer G., and Heidi A. Strobel, eds. *Materializing Gender in Eighteenth-Century Europe*. London: Routledge, 2017.

Girouard, Mark. *Elizabethan Architecture: Its Rise and Fall, 1540–1640*. New Haven: Yale University Press, 2009.

Gladwell, Malcolm. *The Tipping Point: How Little Things Can Make a Big Difference*. Boston: Back Bay Books, 2002.

Goldsmid, Edmund, ed. *The Pretty Gentleman; or, Softness of Manners Vindicated from the False Ridicule Exhibited Under the Character of William Fribble, Esq*. Edinburgh: privately printed, 1885.

Gombrich, Ernst H. *The Sense of Order: A Study in the Psychology of Decorative Art*. Oxford: Phaidon, 1979.

Goodsall, Robert H. "Lee Priory and the Brydges Circle." *Archaeologia Cantiana* 77 (1962): 1–26.

Gough, Richard. *Sepulchral Monuments in Great Britain Applied to Illustrate the History of Families, Manners, Habits, and Arts, at the Different Periods from the Norman Conquest to the Seventeenth Century*. 2 pts. in 5 vols. London: J. Nichols for the author, 1786–96.

Gowrley, Freya. "Representing Camp: Constructing Macaroni Masculinity in Eighteenth-Century Visual Satire." *ABO: Interactive Journal for Women and the Arts, 1640–1830*, vol. 9, no. 1 (2019), article 4.

Graham, John. "Lavater's Physiognomy in England." *Journal of the History of Ideas* 22, no. 4 (1961): 561–72.

Gray, Thomas. *Correspondence of Thomas Gray*. Edited by Paget Toynbee and Leonard Whibley. 3 vols. Oxford: Clarendon Press, 1935.

———. *Gray's English Poems*. Edited by Duncan C. Tovey. 1922. Reprint, Cambridge: Cambridge University Press, 2014.

———. *The Poems and Letters of Thomas Gray*. Edited by William Mason. London: R. Priestley, 1820.

———. *The Works of Thomas Gray*. Edited by John Mitford. 5 vols. London: W. Pickering, 1835–47.

Groom, Nick. "Gothic Antiquity: From the Sack of Rome to *The Castle of Otranto*." In Townsend, *Terror and Wonder*, 38–67.

Grootenboer, Hanneke. "Every Period Gets the Medievalism It Deserves." *Oxford Art Journal* 36, no. 1 (2013): 137–42.

Grose, Francis. *The Antiquities of England and Wales*. 4 vols. London: S. Hooper, 1772–76.

Gross, Jonathan D. *The Life of Anne Damer: Portrait of a Regency Artist*. Lanham, Md.: Lexington Books, 2014.

Guest, Harriet. "The Wanton Muse: Politics and Gender in Gothic Theory After 1760." In *Beyond Romanticism: New Approaches to Texts and Contexts, 1780–1832*, edited by Stephen Copley and John Whale, 118–39. London: Routledge, 1992.

Guilding, Ruth. *Owning the Past: Why the English Collected Antique Sculpture, 1640–1840*. New Haven: Yale University Press, 2014.

Guillery, Peter, and Michael Snodin. "Strawberry Hill: Building and Site." *Architectural History* 38 (1995): 102–28.

Guthrie, William. *A Reply to the Counter-address; Being a Vindication of the Pamphlet Entitled, An Address to the Public, on the Late Dismission of a General Officer*. London: W. Nicoll, 1764.

Gwynn, John (attributed). *English Architecture, or The Publick Buildings of London and Westminster*. London: T. Osborne, 1758.

Hadfield, Andrew. "William Kent's Illustrations of *The Faerie Queene*." *Spenser Studies* 14, no. 1 (1999): 1–15.

Haggerty, George E. "Epistolary Relations: Walpole and Cole." *Studies in Eighteenth-Century Culture* 33 (2004): 175–92.

———. "The History of Homosexuality Reconsidered." In *Developments in the Histories of Sexualities: In Search of the Normal, 1600–1800*, edited by Chris Mounsey, 1–15. Lewisburg: Bucknell University Press, 2013.

———. *Horace Walpole's Letters: Masculinity and Friendship in the Eighteenth Century*. Lewisburg: Bucknell University Press, 2011.

———. "Male Love and Friendship in the Eighteenth Century." In *Love, Sex, Intimacy, and Friendship Between Men, 1550–1800*, edited by Katherine O'Donnell and Michael O'Rourke, 70–81. London: Palgrave Macmillan, 2003.

———. *Men in Love: Masculinity and Sexuality in the Eighteenth Century*. New York: Columbia University Press, 1999.

———. *Queer Gothic*. Urbana: University of Illinois Press, 2006.

———. "Queering Horace Walpole." *Studies in English Literature* 46, no. 3 (2006): 543–62.

———. "Strawberry Hill: Friendship and Taste." In *HWSH*, 76–85.

———. "Walpoliana." *Eighteenth-Century Studies* 34, no. 2 (2001): 227–49.

Hall, Michael. "Georgian Gothic Is No Longer the Eccentric Style It Used to Be." *Apollo*, 28 October 2016. https://www.apollo-magazine.com/georgian-gothic-is-no-longer-the-eccentric-style-it-used-to-be.

———, ed. *Gothic Architecture and Its Meanings, 1550–1830*. Reading: Spire Books, 2002.

———. Introduction to *Gothic Architecture and Its Meanings*, 7–26.

Hallett, Mark. *Reynolds: Portraiture in Action*. New Haven: Yale University Press, 2014.

Halperin, David M. "Forgetting Foucault: Acts, Identities, and the History of Sexuality." *Representations* 63 (1998): 93–120.

———. *How to Be Gay*. Cambridge: Belknap Press, 2014.

———. "How to Do the History of Male Homosexuality." *GLQ* 6, no. 1 (2000): 87–124.

———. *One Hundred Years of Homosexuality: And Other Essays on Greek Love*. New York: Routledge, 1990.

———. *Saint Foucault: Towards a Gay Hagiography*. Oxford: Oxford University Press, 1995.

Hanson, Ellis. *Decadence and Catholicism*. Cambridge: Harvard University Press, 1997.

Hansson, Ulf. R. "'Ma passion . . . ma folie dominante': Stosch, Winckelmann, and the Allure of the Engraved Gems of the Ancients." *MDCCC 1800* 3 (2014): 13–33.

Harney, Marion. *Place-Making for the Imagination: Horace Walpole and Strawberry Hill*. Farnham, Surrey: Ashgate, 2013.

———. "Strawberry Hill." *Architectural Review* 224, no. 1341 (2008): 72–76.

Harris, Ellen T. *Handel as Orpheus: Voice and Desire in the Chamber Cantatas*. Cambridge: Harvard University Press, 2001.

Harris, John. *Gardens of Delight: The Rococo English Landscape of Thomas Robins the Elder*. 2 vols. London: Basilisk Press, 1978.

———. *The Palladian Revival: Lord Burlington, His Villa and Garden at Chiswick*. New Haven: Yale University Press, 1994.

———. "A Pioneer in Gardening: Dickie Bateman Re-assessed." *Apollo* 138, no. 380 (1993): 227–33.

Hart, Vaughan. "From Virgin to Courtesan in Early English Vitruvian Books." In *Paper Palaces: The Rise of the Renaissance Architectural Treatise*, edited by Vaughan Hart and Peter Hicks, 297–320. New Haven: Yale University Press, 1998.

———. *Inigo Jones: The Architect of Kings*. New Haven: Yale University Press, 2011.

Harvey, John. "Architectural History from 1291–1558." In *A History of York Minster*, edited by George E. Aylmer and Reginald Cant, 149–92. Oxford: Clarendon Press, 1977.

Harvey, Karen. "Gender, Space, and Modernity in Eighteenth-Century England: A Place Called Sex." *History Workshop Journal* 51 (2001): 158–79.

———. *Reading Sex in the Eighteenth Century: Bodies and Gender in English Erotic Culture*. Cambridge: Cambridge University Press, 2004.

Harwood, Thomas Eustace. *Windsor Old and New*. London: printed for the author, 1929.

Hatt, Michael. "Space, Surface, Self: Homosexuality and the Aesthetic Interior." *Visual Culture in Britain* 8, no. 1 (2007): 105–28.

Haydon, Colin. *Anti-Catholicism in Eighteenth-Century England, c. 1714–80: A Political and Social Study*. Manchester: Manchester University Press, 1993.

Haynes, Clare. "The Culture of Judgement: Art and Anti-Catholicism in England, c. 1660–1760." *Historical Research* 78 (2005): 483–505.

———. *Pictures and Popery: Art and Religion in England, 1660–1760*. Aldershot, U.K.: Ashgate, 2006.

Hazeltine, Alice I. "A Study of William Shenstone and His Critics, with Fifteen Unpublished Poems and Three of His Unpublished Latin Inscriptions." M.A. thesis, Wellesley College, 1913.

Hazen, Allen T. *A Catalogue of Horace Walpole's Library*. 3 vols. New Haven: Yale University Press, 1969.

Heiland, Donna. *Gothic and Gender: An Introduction*. Malden, Mass.: Blackwell, 2004.

Heller, Dana. *Family Plots: The De-Oedipalization of Popular Culture*. Philadelphia: University of Pennsylvania Press, 1995.

Heynen, Hilde. "Modernity and Domesticity: Tensions and Contradictions." In *Negotiating Domesticity: Spatial Productions of Gender in Modern Architecture*, edited by Hilde Heynen and Gülsüm Baydar, 1–29. New York: Routledge, 2005.

Hietala, Jan. *Inconclusive Evidence: Spatial Gender Politics at Strawberry Hill, 1747–58*. Baunach, Germany: AADR, 2013.

Hill, Rosemary. "'The Ivi'd Ruins of Forlorn Grace Dieu': Catholics, Romantics, and Late Georgian Gothic." In *Gothic Architecture and Its Meanings, 1550–1830*, edited by Michael Hall, 159–84. Reading: Spire Books, 2002.

———. "Reformation to Millennium: Pugin's Contrasts in the History of English Thought." *JSAH* 58, no. 1 (1999): 26–41.

Hilliard, David. "UnEnglish and Unmanly: Anglo-Catholicism and Homosexuality." *Victorian Studies* 25, no. 2 (1982): 181–210.

Hindman, Sandra, Nina Rowe, and Michael Camille. *Manuscript Illumination in the Modern Age: Recovery and Reconstruction*. Evanston, Ill.: Mary & Leigh Block Museum of Art, 2001. Exhibition catalogue.

Holly, Michael Ann. *The Melancholy Art*. Princeton: Princeton University Press, 2013.

Holsinger, Bruce. *The Premodern Condition: Medievalism and the Making of Theory*. Chicago: University of Chicago Press, 2005.

Honour, Hugh. "A House of the Gothic Revival." *Country Life* 111 (1952): 1665–66.

Hopkins, Owen. "'Mere Gothique Heaps of Stone'? Uses and Abuses of the 'Gothic' in James Ralph's *Critical Review* (1734)." *Immediations* 2, no. 3 (2010): 7–29.

Horner, Avril. "Gothic and Surrealism: Subculture, Counterculture, and Cultural Assimilation." In *The Edinburgh Companion to Gothic and the Arts*, edited by David Punter, 148–58. Edinburgh: Edinburgh University Press, 2019.

Howard, Maurice. *The Vyne, Hampshire*. London: National Trust, 2015.

Howard, Maurice, and Edward Wilson. *The Vyne: A Tudor House Revealed*. London: National Trust, 2003.

Hughes, William, and Andrew Smith, eds. *Queering the Gothic*. Manchester: Manchester University Press, 2009.

Hurley, Kelly. *The Gothic Body: Sexuality, Materialism, and Degeneration at the Fin de Siècle*. Cambridge: Cambridge University Press, 1997.

Hussey, Christopher. "Donnington Grove, Berkshire—I." *Country Life* 124 (1958): 588–91.

———. "Donnington Grove, Berkshire—II." *Country Life* 124 (1958): 654–57.

———. "A Georgian Scrapbook at Donnington Grove." *Country Life* 126 (1959): 1292–93.

Immel, Andrea. "James Pettit Andrews's 'Books' (1790): The First Critical Survey of English Children's Literature." *Children's Literature* 28 (2000): 147–63.

Janes, Dominic. "Early Victorian Moral Anxiety and the Queer Legacy of the Eighteenth-Century Gothic Revival." In *Material Religion in Modern Britain: The Spirit of Things*, edited by Timothy W. Jones and Lucinda Matthews-Jones, 125–43. London: Palgrave Macmillan, 2015.

———. *Oscar Wilde Prefigured: Queer Fashioning* and *British Caricature, 1750–1900*. Chicago: University of Chicago Press, 2016.

———. *Picturing the Closet: Male Secrecy and Homosexual Visibility in Britain*. Oxford: Oxford University Press, 2015.

———. "Unnatural Appetites: Sodomitical Panic in Hogarth's *The Gate of Calais*, or, *O the Roast Beef of Old England* (1748)." *Oxford Art Journal* 35, no. 1 (2012): 19–31.

Jenkins, Ian, and Kim Sloan. *Vases and Volcanoes: Sir William Hamilton and His Collection*. London: British Museum Press, 1996.

Jenkins, Simon. *England's Thousand Best Churches*. London: Penguin, 2000.

Jestin, Loftus. "Richard Bentley the Younger (1708–1782): A Critical Biography." Ph.D. diss., Yale University, 1985.

Jones, Robert W. *Gender and the Formation of Taste in Eighteenth-Century Britain: An Analysis of Beauty*. Cambridge: Cambridge University Press, 1998.

Jordan, Mark D. *The Silence of Sodom: Homosexuality in Modern Catholicism*. Chicago: University of Chicago Press, 2000.

Kalter, Barrett. *Modern Antiques: The Material Past in England, 1660–1780*. Lewisburg: Bucknell University Press, 2012.

Kaufmann, Thomas DaCosta. "'Gothico More Nondum Visa': The 'Modern Gothic' Architecture of Jan Blažej Santini Aichl." In *The Eloquent Artist: Essays on Art, Art Theory, and Architecture, Sixteenth to Nineteenth Century*, edited by Thomas DaCosta Kaufmann, 371–91. London: Pindar, 2004.

Kavaler, Ethan M. *Renaissance Gothic: Architecture and the Arts in Northern Europe, 1470–1540*. New Haven: Yale University Press, 2012.

Kavanagh, Declan William. "'Of Neuter Gender, Tho' of Irish Growth': Charles Churchill's Fribble." *Irish University Review* 43, no. 1 (2013): 119–30.

Keating, Geoffrey. *Foras Feasa ar Éirinn: The History of Ireland*, edited and translated by David Comyn and Patrick S. Dinneen. 4 vols. London: Irish Texts Society, 1902–14.

Kelly, Jason M. *The Society of Dilettanti: Archaeology and Identity in the British Enlightenment*. New Haven: Yale University Press, 2009.

Kerslake, John F. *Early Georgian Portraits*. London: H. M. Stationery Office, 1977.

King, Thomas A. *The English Phallus*. Vol. 1 of *The Gendering of Men, 1600–1750*. Madison: University of Wisconsin Press, 2004.

———. "The Fop, the Canting Queen, and the Deferral of Gender." In *Presenting Gender: Changing Sex in Early-Modern Culture*, edited by Chris Mounsey, 94–135. Lewisburg: Bucknell University Press, 2001.

———. *Queer Articulations*. Vol. 2 of *The Gendering of Men, 1600–1750*. Madison: University of Wisconsin Press, 2008.

Klein, Lawrence E. "Liberty, Manners, and Politeness in Early Eighteenth-Century England." *Historical Journal* 32, no. 3 (1989): 583–605.

Kliger, Samuel. *The Goths in England: A Study in Seventeenth and Eighteenth Century Thought*. Cambridge: Harvard University Press, 1952.

Krysmanski, Bernd W. *Hogarth's Hidden Parts: Satiric Allusion, Erotic Wit, Blasphemous Bawdiness, and Dark Humour in Eighteenth-Century English Art*. Hildesheim: Georg Olms, 2010.

Kuchta, David. *The Three-Piece Suit and Modern Masculinity: England, 1550–1850*. Berkeley: University of California Press, 2002.

Lancaster, Nathaniel. *The Pretty Gentleman, or Softness of Manners Vindicated from the False Ridicule Exhibited Under the Character of William Fribble, Esq*. London: M. Cooper, 1747.

Lane, Joan. "Shobdon Church, Herefordshire: A Rococo-Gothic Masterpiece." *Apollo* 141, no. 395 (1995): 23–27.

Lang, S. "The Principles of the Gothic Revival in England." *JSAH* 25, no. 4 (1966): 240–67.

Laqueur, Thomas. *Making Sex: Body and Gender from the Greeks to Freud*. Cambridge: Harvard University Press, 1990.

Laroque, Didier. "Les miroirs de la Villa Palagonia." In *Miroirs: XV*[es] *entretiens de la Garenne Lemot*, edited by Jackie Pigeaud, 263–71. Rennes: Presses universitaires de Rennes, 2011.

Latour, Bruno, and Adam Lowe. "The Migration of the Aura, or How to Explore the Original Through Its Facsimiles." In *Switching Codes: Thinking Through Digital Technology in the Humanities and the Arts*, edited by Thomas Bartscherer and Roderick Coover, 275–97. Chicago: University of Chicago Press, 2011.

Laurence, Anne. "Women Using Building in Seventeenth-Century England: A Question of Sources?" *Transactions of the Royal Historical Society* 13 (2003): 293–303.

Lavater, Johann Kaspar. *Essays on Physiognomy*. Translated by Thomas Holcroft. 3 vols. London: G. G. J. & J. Robinson, 1783.

Lepine, Ayla. "The Persistence of Medievalism: Kenneth Clark and the Gothic Revival." *Architectural History* 57 (2014): 323–56.

———. "Queer Gothic." *Architectural Review* 237, no. 1415 (2015): 110–11.

Levine, Joseph M. *Between the Ancients and the Moderns: Baroque Culture in Restoration England*. New Haven: Yale University Press, 1999.

Lewis, Lesley. "Philipp von Stosch." *Apollo* 85, no. 63 (1967): 320–27.

Lewis, Wilmarth Sheldon. "The Genesis of Strawberry Hill." *Metropolitan Museum Studies* 5, no. 1 (1934): 57–92.

Lilley, James D. "Studies in Uniquity: Horace Walpole's Singular Collection." *ELH* 80, no. 1 (2013): 93–124.

Lindfield, Peter N. "The Countess of Pomfret's Gothic Revival Furniture." *Georgian Group Journal* 22 (2014): 77–94.

———. "A Further Allusion to Strawberry Hill at Lee Priory, Kent." *Burlington Magazine* 158, no. 1365 (2016): 979.

———. "Georgian Gothic Fabrications in the Antiquarian Style: William Kent, Batty Langley, and Horace Walpole." In *Gothic Legacies: Four Centuries of Tradition and Innovation in Art and Architecture*, edited by Laura Cleaver and Ayla Lepine, 38–59. Newcastle upon Tyne: Cambridge Scholars, 2012.

———. *Georgian Gothic: Medievalist Architecture, Furniture, and Interiors, 1730–1840*. Woodbridge: Boydell Press, 2016.

———. "Heraldry and the Architectural Imagination: John Carter's Visualisation of *The Castle of Otranto*." *Antiquaries Journal* 96 (2016): 291–313.

———. "'Hung Round with the Helmets, Breast-Plates, and Swords of Our Ancestors': Allusions to Chivalry in Eighteenth-Century Gothicism." In *Chivalry and the Medieval Past*, edited by Katie Stevenson and Barbara Gribling, 61–98. Woodbridge: Boydell Press, 2016.

———. "Imagining the Undefined Castle in *The Castle of Otranto*: Engravings and Interpretations." *Image and Narrative* 18, no. 3 (2017): 46–63.

———. "Serious Gothic and 'Doing the Ancient Buildings': Batty Langley's *Ancient Architecture* and 'Principal Geometric Elevations.'" *Architectural History* 57 (2014): 141–73.

———. *Unbuilt Strawberry*. Donington, U.K.: Shaun Tyas, 2019 (forthcoming).

———. "Walpole's Panelled Heraldic Apartment at Strawberry Hill." *British Art Journal* 18, no. 3 (2018): 92–98.

Lindfield, Peter N., and Dale Townshend. "Reading *Vathek* and Fonthill Abbey: William Beckford's Architectural Imagination." In Dakers, *Fonthill Recovered*, 284–301.

Lipking, Lawrence. *The Ordering of the Arts in Eighteenth-Century England*. Princeton: Princeton University Press, 1970.

Llewellyn, Nigel. "The *Anecdotes of Painting* and Continental European Art History." In *HWSH*, 137–49.

Lloyd, Stephen. "The Cabinet of Miniatures and Enamels." In *HWSH*, 98–99.

———. "The Digby Miniatures." In *HWSH*, 188–89.

Lord, Evelyn. *The Hell-Fire Clubs: Sex, Satanism, and Secret Societies*. New Haven: Yale University Press, 2008.

Lowden, John, and John Cherry. *Medieval Ivories and Works of Art: The Thomson Collection at the Art Gallery of Ontario*. Toronto: Art Gallery of Ontario, 2008.

Lubey, Kathleen. "Erotic Interiors in Joseph Addison's Imagination." *Eighteenth-Century Fiction* 20, no. 3 (2008): 415–44.

Luttikhuizen, Henry, and Dorothy Verkerk, eds. *Snyder's Medieval Art*. 2nd ed. Upper Saddle River, N.J.: Pearson, 2009.

Mack, Robert L. *Thomas Gray: A Life*. New Haven: Yale University Press, 2000.

Männig, Maria. *Hans Sedlmayr's Kunstgeschichte: Eine kritische Studie*. Cologne: Böhlau, 2016.

Marwood, Kimberley. "Imaginary Dimensions: Women, Surrealism, and the Gothic." In *Women and Gothic*, edited by Maria Purves, 39–62. Cambridge: Cambridge Scholars, 2014.

Mason, William. *Satirical Poems Published Anonymously by William Mason, with Notes by Horace Walpole*. Edited by Paget Toynbee. Oxford: Clarendon Press, 1926.

Massé, Michelle A. "Psychoanalysis and the Gothic." In *A New Companion to the Gothic*, edited by David Punter, 307–20. Malden, Mass.: Wiley-Blackwell, 2012.

Mateo, Matilde. "In Search of the Origin of the Gothic: Thomas Pitt's Travel in Spain in 1760." *Journal of Art Historiography* 15 (2016): 1–22.

Matheson, Neil. *Surrealism and the Gothic: Castles of the Interior*. Abingdon, Oxon: Routledge, 2018.

Matthews, David. "From Mediaeval to Mediaevalism: A New Semantic History." *Review of English Studies* 62, no. 257 (2011): 695–715.

———. *Medievalism: A Critical History*. Cambridge: D. S. Brewer, 2015.

Mayer, Laura. "'Junketaceous Gothick': Elizabeth Percy's Patronage of Alnwick Castle, Northumberland." In *Women and Gothic*, edited by Maria Purves, 25–38. Newcastle upon Tyne: Cambridge Scholars, 2014.

McCarthy, Michael. *The Origins of the Gothic Revival*. New Haven: Yale University Press, 1987.

McDonnell, Joseph. "Stone, Stucco, and Papier Mâché: Fan Vaulting from Henry VII's Chapel, Westminster Abbey, to Monkstown Parish Church." In *Studies in the Gothic Revival*, edited by Michael McCarthy and Karina O'Neill, 3–20. Dublin: Four Courts Press, 2008.

McEvoy, Emma. *Gothic Tourism*. Basingstoke, U.K.: Palgrave Macmillan, 2015.

McEwen, Indra Kagis. *Vitruvius: Writing the Body of Architecture*. Cambridge: MIT Press, 2003.

McGregor, Jonathan. "A Queer Orthodoxy: Monastic Socialism and Celibate Sexuality in Vida Dutton Scudder and Ralph Adams Cram." *Journal of American Studies* 52 (2018): 65–90.

McKinney, David Duane. "The Castle of My Ancestors: Horace Walpole and Strawberry Hill." *Journal for Eighteenth-Century Studies* 13, no. 2 (1990): 199–214.

———. "History and Revivalism: Horace Walpole's Promotion of the Gothic Style of Architecture." Ph.D. diss., University of Virginia, 1992.

McLeod, Bet. "A Collector's Obsession." *Apollo* 171, no. 576 (2010): 60–65.

McNeil, Peter. *Pretty Gentlemen: Macaroni Men and the Eighteenth-Century Fashion World*. New Haven: Yale University Press, 2018.

———. "'That Doubtful Gender': Macaroni Dress and Male Sexualities." *Fashion Theory* 3, no. 4 (1999): 411–47.

McWhir, Ann. "The Gothic Transgression of Disbelief: Walpole, Radcliffe, and Lewis." In *Gothic Fictions: Prohibition/Transgression*, edited by Kenneth W. Graham, 29–48. New York: AMS, 1989.

Melchior-Bonnet, Sabine. *The Mirror: A History*. Translated by Katharine H. Jewett. London: Routledge, 2002.

Melville, Lewis. *The Life and Letters of William Beckford of Fonthill*. New York: Duffield, 1910.

Meyer, Moe, ed. *The Politics and Poetics of Camp*. London: Routledge, 1994.

Meyer, Richard. "'Nature Revers'd': Satire and Homosexual Difference in Hogarth's London." In *The Other Hogarth: Aesthetics of Difference*, edited by Bernadette Fort and Angela Rosenthal, 162–75. Princeton: Princeton University Press, 2001.

Millikin, Sandra. "The Tribune in English Architecture." *Burlington Magazine* 112, no. 808 (1970): 442–46.

Mills, Robert. *Derek Jarman's Medieval Modern*. Woodbridge: Boydell & Brewer, 2018.

Mitford, John, ed. *The Correspondence of Thomas Gray and William Mason, to Which Are Added Some Letters Addressed by Gray to the Rev. James Brown*. London: Richard Bentley, 1853.

Monk of the Order of St. Francis. *Nocturnal Revels; or, The History of the King's Place, and Other Modern Nunneries* [. . .] *with the Portraits of the Most Celebrated Demireps and Courtezans of This Period*. 2 vols. London: M. Goadby, 1779.

Moore, Andrew. "*Aedes Walpolianae*: The Collection as Edifice." In Dukelskaya and Moore, *Capital Collection*, 1–54.

———, ed. *Houghton Hall: The Prime Minister, the Empress, and the Heritage*. London: Philip Wilson, 1996.

Moore, Cathal, and Christine Sitwell. "Spiridione Roma at the Vyne: Reconstructing the Work of a 'Very Idle' Painter." *Apollo* 147, no. 434 (1998): 25–29.

Moore, Lisa L. "Queer Gardens: Mary Delany's Flowers and Friendships." *Eighteenth-Century Studies* 39, no. 1 (2005): 49–70.

Moore, Lucy. *Amphibious Thing: The Life of Lord Hervey*. London: Viking, 2000.

Morris, William. "The Origins of Ornamental Art." In *William Morris on Art and Socialism*, edited by Norman Kelvin, 159–73. Mineola, N.Y.: Dover, 1999.

Morrissey, Lee. *From the Temple to the Castle: An Architectural History of British Literature, 1660–1760*. Charlottesville: University of Virginia Press, 1999.

Mowl, Timothy. *Horace Walpole: The Great Outsider*. London: John Murray, 1996.

———. Review of *Horace Walpole's Strawberry Hill*, edited by Michael Snodin. *Times Higher Education*, 18 March 2010.

———. "William Beckford: A Biographical Perspective." In *William Beckford, 1760–1844: An Eye for the Magnificent*, edited by Derek E. Ostergard, 17–32. New Haven: Yale University Press, 2001.

Mowl, Timothy, and Brian Earnshaw. *An Insular Rococo: Architecture, Politics, and Society in Ireland and England, 1710–1770*. London: Reaktion, 1999.

Muensterberger, Werner. *Collecting: An Unruly Passion; Psychological Perspectives*. New York: Harcourt, Brace, 1994.

Murphy, Kevin D. *Memory and Modernity: Viollet-le-Duc at Vézelay*. University Park: Pennsylvania State University Press, 2000.

Murphy, Martin. "The King's Laceman and the Bishop's Friend: Bryant Barrett (c. 1715–1790), Merchant and Squire." *Recusant History* 30, no. 1 (2010): 107–19.

Murphy, Patrick J. *Medieval Studies and the Ghost Stories of M. R. James*. University Park: Pennsylvania State University Press, 2017.

Musgrave, William. *A Brief and True History of Sir Robert Walpole, and His Family, from Their Original, to the Present Time*. London: E. Curll, 1738.

Musson, Jeremy. "King's College Chapel: Aesthetic and Architectural Responses." In *King's College Chapel, 1515–2015: Art, Music, and Religion in Cambridge*, edited by Jean Michel Massing and Nicolette Zeeman, 25–62. London: Harvey Miller, 2014.

Myers, Robin. "Dr Andrew Coltée Ducarel (1713–1785), Pioneer of Anglo-Norman Studies." In *Antiquaries, Book Collectors, and the Circles of Learning*, edited by Robin Myers and Michael Harris, 45–70. Winchester: St. Paul's Bibliographies, 1996.

Myrone, Martin. *Bodybuilding: Reforming Masculinities in British Art, 1750–1810*. New Haven: Yale University Press, 2005.

———. *Gothic Nightmares: Fuseli, Blake, and the Romantic Imagination*. London: Tate, 2006. Exhibition catalogue.

Nagel, Alexander. *Medieval Modern: Art out of Time*. London: Thames & Hudson, 2012.

Norton, Rictor. "The Raid on Mother Clap's Molly House." *Gay Subculture in Georgian England*, 5 February 2005. http://rictornorton.co.uk/eighteen/mother.htm.

Nurse, Bernard, and Joseph Mordaunt Crook. "John Carter, FSA (1748–1817): 'The Ingenious, and Very Accurate Draughtsman.'" *Antiquaries Journal* 91 (2011): 211–52.

Nussbaum, Felicity. "Effeminacy and Femininity: Domestic Prose Satire and *David Simple*." *Eighteenth-Century Fiction* 11, no. 4 (1999): 421–44.

O'Driscoll, Sally. "The Molly and the Fop: Untangling Effeminacy in the Eighteenth Century." In *Developments in the History of Sexualities: In Search of the Normal, 1600–1800*, edited by Chris Mounsey, 145–72. Lewisburg: Bucknell University Press, 2013.

O'Halloran, Clare. "The Triumph of 'Virtuous Liberty': Representations of the Vikings and Brian Boru in Eighteenth-Century Histories." *Eighteenth-Century Ireland* 22 (2007): 151–63.

O'Malley, Patrick R. *Catholicism, Sexual Deviance, and Victorian Gothic Culture*. Cambridge: Cambridge University Press, 2006.

———. "Epistemology of the Cloister: Victorian England's Queer Catholicism." *GLQ* 15, no. 4 (2009): 535–64.

O'Neill, M. *Walter Crane: The Arts and Crafts, Painting, and Politics, 1875–1890*. New Haven: Yale University Press, 2011.

Oswald, Arthur. "Mrs. Montagu and the Chinese Taste." *Country Life* 114 (1953): 1328.

Over, Charles. *Ornamental Architecture in the Gothic, Chinese, and Modern Taste*. London: R. Sayer, 1758.

Palmer, William M. *William Cole of Milton*. Cambridge: Galloway & Porter, 1935.

Panofsky, Erwin. "The First Page of Giorgio Vasari's 'Libro': A Study on the Gothic Style in the Judgment of the Italian Renaissance." In *Meaning in the Visual Arts*, 169–235. New York: Doubleday, 1955.

Parker, James. "Rococo and Formal Order in English Furniture." *Metropolitan Museum of Art Bulletin*, n.s., 15, no. 5 (1957): 129–40.

Parry, Graham. *The Trophies of Time: English Antiquaries of the Seventeenth Century*. Oxford: Oxford University Press, 1995.

Payne, Alina A. *The Architectural Treatise in the Italian Renaissance: Architectural Invention, Ornament, and Literary Culture*. Cambridge: Cambridge University Press, 1999.

Pedicord, Harry William. *The Theatrical Public in the Time of Garrick*. Carbondale: Southern Illinois University Press, 1954.

Peltz, Lucy. *Facing the Text: Extra-Illustration, Print Culture, and Society in Britain, 1769–1840*. San Marino, Calif.: Huntington Library, Art Collections, and Botanical Gardens, 2017.

Pelzel, Thomas. "Winckelmann, Mengs, and Casanova: A Reappraisal of a Famous Eighteenth-Century Forgery." *Art Bulletin* 54, no. 3 (1972): 300–315.

Penrose, Thomas. *Flights of Fancy*. London: J. Walter, 1775.

Peover, Michael, and Kevin Rogers. "New Light on Strawberry Hill: Walpole's Display of Glass and the Representation of the Ancient Abbey." *Journal of Stained Glass* 34 (2010): 8–51.

Petersen, Nils Holger. "Medieval Resurfacings, Old and New." *Studies in Medievalism* 20 (2011): 35–42.

Phillips, Derek. "The Tracery of the Great West Window at York Minster." *JBAA* 152 (1999): 24–48.

Piggott, Charles. *The Female Jockey Club*. London: D. I. Eaton, 1794.

Piggott, Stuart. *William Stukeley: An Eighteenth-Century Antiquary*. Rev. and enl. ed. London: Thames & Hudson, 1985.

Pilkey, Brent, Rachael M. Scicluna, Ben Campkin, and Barbara Penner, eds. *Sexuality and Gender at Home: Experience, Politics, Transgression*. London: Bloomsbury Academic, 2017.

Piozzi, Hester Lynch. *Thraliana: The Diary of Hester Lynch Thrale (Later Mrs. Piozzi), 1776–1809*. Edited by Katherine E. Balderston. 2 vols. 2nd ed. Oxford: Clarendon Press, 1951.

Pittock, Murray. "Treacherous Objects: Towards a Theory of Jacobite Material Culture." *Journal for Eighteenth-Century Studies* 34, no. 1 (2011): 39–63.

Pococke, John G. A. *Virtue, Commerce, and History: Essays on Political Thought and History, Chiefly in the Eighteenth Century*. Cambridge: Cambridge University Press, 1986.

Pococke, Richard. *The Travels Through England of Dr. Richard Pococke*. Edited by James Joel Cartwright. 2 vols. Cambridge: Camden Society, 1888–89.

Pointon, Marcia. *Hanging the Head: Portraiture and Social Formation in Eighteenth-Century England*. New Haven: Yale University Press, 1993.

Pommeraye, Jean-François. *Histoire de l'abbaye royale de S. Ouen de Rouen*. Rouen: Richard Lallemant & Louys du Menil, 1662.

Pope, Alexander. *An Epistle from Mr. Pope to Dr. Arbuthnot*. London: George Faulkner, 1735.

———. Preface to *The Works of Shakespear* [*sic*], 1:i–xxiv. London: Jacob Tonson, 1725.

Pope-Hennessy, John. *Cellini*. London: Macmillan, 1985.

Porter, David. *The Chinese Taste in Eighteenth-Century England*. Cambridge: Cambridge University Press, 2010.

Pote, Joseph. *Les delices de Windsore*. 3rd ed. Eton: Joseph & Thomas Pote, 1771.

Potts, Alex. *Flesh and the Ideal: Winckelmann and the Origins of Art History*. New Haven: Yale University Press, 1994.

Potvin, John. *Bachelors of a Different Sort: Queer Aesthetics, Material Culture, and the Modern Interior in Britain*. Manchester: Manchester University Press, 2014.

Powell, Amy Knight. *Depositions: Scenes from the Late Medieval Church and the Modern Museum*. New York: Zone Books, 2012.

Price, Fiona. *Reinventing Liberty: Nation, Commerce, and the Historical Novel from Walpole to Scott*. Edinburgh: Edinburgh University Press, 2016.

Purves, Maria. *The Gothic and Catholicism: Religion, Cultural Exchange, and the Popular Novel, 1785–1829*. Cardiff: University of Wales Press, 2009.

Quaintance, Richard E. "Walpole's Whig Interpretation of Landscaping History." *Studies in Eighteenth-Century Culture* 9 (1979): 285–300.

Reay, Barry. "Writing the Modern Histories of Homosexual England." *Historical Journal* 52, no. 1 (2009): 213–33.

"Reasons for the Growth of Sodomy (1749)." In *Secret Sexualities: A Sourcebook of 17th and 18th Century Writing*, edited by Ian McCormick, 138–39. London: Routledge, 1997.

Redding, Cyrus. "Recollections of the Author of 'Vathek.'" *New Monthly Magazine* 71 (1844): 302–19.

Redford, Bruce. *Dilettanti: The Antic and the Antique in Eighteenth-Century England*. Los Angeles: Getty Museum, 2008.

———. "Grecian Taste and Neapolitan Spirit: Grand Tour Portraits of the Society of Dilettanti." In *Rediscovering the Ancient World on the Bay of Naples, 1710–1890*, edited by Carol C. Mattusch, 177–88. New Haven: Yale University Press, 2013.

Reeve, Matthew M. "Dickie Bateman and the Gothicization of Old Windsor: Gothic Architecture and Sexuality in the Circle of Horace Walpole." *Architectural History* 56 (2013): 97–131.

———. "Gothic." In "Medieval Art History Today—Critical Terms," special issue, *Studies in Iconography* 33 (2012): 233–46.

———. "Gothic Architecture, Sexuality, and License at Horace Walpole's Strawberry Hill." *Art Bulletin* 95, no. 3 (2013): 411–39.

———. "'A Gothic Vatican of Greece and Rome': Horace Walpole, Strawberry Hill, and the Narratives of Gothic." In *Tributes to Pierre du Prey: Architecture and the Classical Tradition, from Pliny to Posterity*, edited by Matthew M. Reeve, 185–209. New York: Harvey Miller, 2014.

———. "The Hereford Screen: A Pre-History." *British Art Studies*, no. 5 (2017). https://doi.org/10.17658/issn.2058-5462/issue-05/mreeve.

———. "Of Druids, the Gothic, and the Origins of Architecture: The Garden Designs of William Stukeley (1687–1765)." *British Art Journal* 13, no. 3 (2012): 9–18.

———, ed. *Reading Gothic Architecture*. Turnhout: Brepols, 2008.

———. Review of *Horace Walpole's Strawberry Hill*, edited by Michael Snodin. *Antiquaries Journal* 91 (2011): 390–92.

———. "Teaching Medieval Art History: Medievalism." *ICMA News* 3 (December 2015): 8–12.

———. *Thirteenth-Century Wall Painting of Salisbury Cathedral: Art, Liturgy, and Reform*. Woodbridge, U.K.: Boydell & Brewer, 2008.

Reeve, Matthew M., and Peter N. Lindfield. "'A Child of Strawberry': Thomas Barrett and Lee Priory, Kent." *Burlington Magazine* 157 (2015): 836–42.

Repton, Humphry. *Humphry Repton's Memoirs*. Edited by Ann Gore and George Carter. Norwich, U.K.: Michael Russell, 2005.

Retford, Kate. "A Death in the Family: Posthumous Portraiture in Eighteenth-Century England." *Art History* 33, no. 1 (2010): 74–97.

———. "Gender and the Marital Portrait in Eighteenth-Century England: 'A Sort of Sex in Souls.'" *Journal for Eighteenth-Century Studies* 27, no. 1 (2004): 99–120.

———. "Sensibility and Genealogy in the Eighteenth-Century Family Portrait: The Collection at Kedleston Hall." *Historical Journal* 46, no. 3 (2003): 533–60.

Reynolds, Nicole. "Gothic and the Architectural Imagination, 1740–1840." In *The Gothic World*, edited by Glennis Byron and Dale Townsend, 85–97. London: Routledge, 2014.

Richter, Simon. "Winckelmann's Progeny: Homosocial Networking in the Eighteenth Century." In *Outing Goethe and His Age*, edited by Alice A. Kuzniar, 33–46. Stanford: Stanford University Press, 1996.

Richter, Simon, and Patrick McGrath. "Representing Homosexuality: Winckelmann and the Aesthetics of Friendship." *Monatshefte* 86, no. 1 (1994): 45–58.

Rickman, Thomas. *An Attempt to Discriminate the Styles of English Architecture from the Conquest to the Reformation*. London: Longman, Hurst, Rees, Orme, and Brown, 1817.

Rielly, Edward J. "Thomas Warton's Gothic Sensibility." *Man and Nature* 10 (1991): 147–58.

Riely, John. "Horace Walpole, the 'Strawberry Committee' and the 'Committee of Taste.'" App. 4 in *HWSH*.

Ritchie, Leslie. "Garrick's *Male-Coquette* and Theatrical Masculinities." In *Refiguring the Coquette: Essays on Culture and Coquetry*, edited by Shelley King and Yaël Schlick, 164–98. Lewisburg: Bucknell University Press, 2008.

Roberts, Marion. "Thomas Gray's Contribution to the Study of Medieval Architecture." *Architectural History* 36 (1993): 49–68.

Robins, George. *A Catalogue of the Classic Contents of Strawberry Hill Collected by Horace Walpole*. London: Smith & Robins, 1842.

Robinson, John Martin. *James Wyatt, 1747–1813: Architect to George III*. New Haven: Yale University Press, 2012.

Roden, Frederick S. *Same-Sex Desire in Victorian Religious Culture*. Basingstoke, U.K.: Palgrave Macmillan, 2002.

Rogers, Kevin. "Walpole's Gothic: Creating a Fictive History." In *HWSH*, 59–73.

Roman, Cynthia. "The Art of Lady Diana Beauclerk: Horace Walpole and Female Genius." In *HWSH*, 155–69.

———. "A Portfolio of Satires from Horace Walpole's Collection." *Print Quarterly* 25, no. 2 (2008): 166–71.

Roquet, Nicholas. "Life in Costume: The Architectural Fictions and Anachronisms of William Burges." Ph.D. diss., McGill University, 2011.

Ross, Andrew. "Uses of Camp." In *Camp Grounds: Style and Homosexuality*, edited by David Bergman, 54–77. Amherst: University of Massachusetts Press, 1993.

Rousseau, George S. *Perilous Enlightenment: Pre- and Post-modern Discourses: Sexual, Historical*. Manchester: Manchester University Press, 1991.

Rowell, Christopher. "Stained Glass by John Rowell and William Price the Younger at The Vyne." *Burlington Magazine* 145, no. 1203 (2003): 443–51.

Rudolph, Conrad. "Introduction: A Sense of Loss; An Overview of the Historiography of Romanesque and Gothic Art." In *A Companion to Medieval Art: Romanesque and Gothic in Northern Europe*, edited by Conrad Rudolph, 1–43. Malden, Mass.: Blackwell, 2006.

Ruskin, John. *The Seven Lamps of Architecture*. London: Smith, Elder, 1849.

———. *The Stones of Venice*. 3 vols. London: Smith, Elder, 1851–53.

Russell, Francis. "Drawings by Rosalba." *Burlington Magazine* 139, no. 1128 (1997): 196–98.

Sabor, Peter, ed. *Horace Walpole: The Critical Heritage*. London: Routledge & Kegan Paul, 1988.

Sani, Bernardina. *Rosalba Carriera, 1673–1757: Maestra del pastello dell'Europa ancien régime*. Turin: Allemandi, 2007.

Sankovitch, Anne-Marie. "The Myth of the 'Myth of the Medieval': Gothic Architecture in Vasari's *Rinascita* and Panofsky's Renaissance." *RES* 40 (2001): 29–50.

Saska, Hope. "Strawberry Hill: The Laughing View." In *HWSH*, 249–60.

Saslow, James M. *Ganymede in the Renaissance: Homosexuality in Art and Society*. New Haven: Yale University Press, 1986.

Saumarez Smith, Charles. *Eighteenth-Century Decoration: Design and the Domestic Interior in England*. New York: Harry N. Abrams, 1993.

Scala, Elizabeth, and Sylvia Federico, eds. *The Post-historical Middle Ages*. New York: Palgrave Macmillan, 2009.

Sedgwick, Eve Kosofsky. *Between Men: English Literature and Male Homosocial Desire*. New York: Columbia University Press, 1985.

———. *Epistemology of the Closet*. Berkeley: University of California Press, 1990.

Senelick, Laurence. "Mollies or Men of Mode? Sodomy and the Eighteenth-Century London Stage." *Journal of the History of Sexuality* 1, no. 1 (1990): 33–67.

S. H. "Character of a Coxcomb." *Lady's Magazine* 24 (1793): 173–75.

Sha, Richard C. *Perverse Romanticism: Aesthetics and Sexuality in Britain, 1750–1832*. Baltimore: Johns Hopkins University Press, 2008.

Shand-Tucci, Douglass. *Boston Bohemia, 1881–1900*. Vol. 1 of *Ralph Adams Cram: Life and Architecture*. Amherst: University of Massachusetts Press, 1996.

Shell, Alison. *Oral Culture and Catholicism in Early Modern England*. Cambridge: Cambridge University Press, 2007.

A Short Account of the Principal Seats and Gardens In and About Richmond and Kew. Brentford: P. Norbury, 1763.

Silver, Sean R. "Visiting Strawberry Hill: Horace Walpole's Gothic Historiography." *Eighteenth-Century Fiction* 21, no. 4 (2009): 535–64.

Simon, Robin. *Hogarth, France, and British Art: The Rise of the Arts in 18th-Century Britain*. London: Hogarth Arts, 2007.

Sloboda, Stacey. *Chinoiserie: Commerce and Critical Ornament in Eighteenth-Century Britain*. Manchester: Manchester University Press, 2014.

Smith, Matt. "Queering the Historic House: Destabilizing Heteronormativity in the National Trust." In Pilkey et al., *Sexuality and Gender at Home*, 105–20.

Smith, Peter. "Lady Oxford's Alterations at Welbeck Abbey, 1741–55." *Georgian Group Journal* 11 (2001): 133–68.

Smith, R. J. *The Gothic Bequest: Medieval Institutions in British Thought, 1688–1863*. Cambridge: Cambridge University Press, 1987.

Snodin, Michael. "Going to Strawberry Hill." In *HWSH*, 15–37.

———, ed. *Horace Walpole's Strawberry Hill*. New Haven: Yale University Press, 2007.

———. "Signs and Signification: Heraldry at Strawberry Hill." In *The Display of Heraldry*, edited by Fiona Robertson and Peter N. Lindfield. London: Heraldry Society, forthcoming.

Sontag, Susan. "Notes on 'Camp.'" In *Against Interpretation and Other Essays*, 275–92. New York: Farrar, Straus & Giroux, 1966.

Soo, Lydia M. *Wren's "Tracts" on Architecture and Other Writings*. Cambridge: Cambridge University Press, 1998.

Stafford, Barbara Maria. "The Eighteenth Century: Towards an Interdisciplinary Model." *Art Bulletin* 70, no. 1 (1988): 6–24.

Stein, Jordan Alexander. "American Literary History and Queer Temporalities." *American Literary History* 25, no. 4 (2013): 855–69.

Stephen, Leslie. *Hours in a Library*. New ed. 3 vols. London: Smith, Elder, 1892.

Stewart, Susan. "Notes on Distressed Genres." *Journal of American Folklore* 104, no. 411 (1991): 5–31.

———. *On Longing: Narratives of the Miniature, the Gigantic, the Souvenir, the Collection*. Durham: Duke University Press, 2003.

Stokes, Francis G. *The Blecheley Diary of the Rev. William Cole, M.A., F.S.A., 1765–67*. London: Constable, 1931.

Stosch, Philipp von. *Pierres antiques gravées, sur lesquelles les graveurs ont mis leurs noms, dessinées et gravées en cuivre sur les originaux ou d'après les empreintes, par Barnard Picart*. Amsterdam, 1725.

"Strawberry Hill—Horace Walpole." *Athenaeum* 753 (2 April 1842): 293–94.

Street, George Edmund. "On the Future of Art in England." *Ecclesiologist* 19 (1858): 232–40.

Styles, John, and Amanda Vickery, eds. *Gender, Taste, and Material Culture in Britain and North America, 1700–1830*. New Haven: Yale Center for British Art, Paul Mellon Centre for Studies in British Art, 2007.

Sweet, Rosemary. "Gothic Antiquarianism in the Eighteenth Century." In *The Gothic World*, edited by Glennis Byron and Dale Townsend, 15–26. London: Routledge, 2014.

Symes, Michael. "Flintwork, Freedom, and Fantasy: The Landscape at West Wycombe Park, Buckinghamshire." *Garden History* 33, no. 1 (2005): 1–30.

Symonds, E. M. "An Eighteenth-Century Convert." *Month* 97 (1901): 139–52, 247–57.

Tadmor, Naomi. "Early Modern English Kinship in the Long Run: Reflections on Continuity and Change." *Continuity and Change* 25, no. 1 (2010): 15–48.

———. *Family and Friends in Eighteenth-Century England: Household, Kinship, and Patronage*. Cambridge: Cambridge University Press, 2001.

Tait, A. A. "Lord Findlater, Architect." *Burlington Magazine* 128, no. 1003 (1986): 737–41.

Tanner, Joan D. "Tombs of Royal Babies in Westminster Abbey." *JBAA* 16 (1953): 25–40.

Terry, Richard. *Poetry and the Making of the English Literary Past, 1660–1781*. Oxford: Oxford University Press, 2001.

Thibodeau, Timothy M., trans. *The Rationale Divinorum Officiorum of William Durand of Mende: A New Translation of the Prologue and Book One*. New York: Columbia University Press, 2007.

Thomas, Gilbert. *A View of the Town: In an Epistle to a Friend in the Country; A Satire*. London: R. Penny, 1735.

Thomassin, Simon. *Recueil des figures, groupes, thermes, fontaines, vases, statues, et autres ornemens de Versailles*. Amsterdam: Pierre Mortier, 1695.

Thurlby, Malcolm. *The Herefordshire School of Romanesque Sculpture*. Little Logaston, U.K.: Logaston Press, 1999.

Thurley, Simon. "The Reigns of Henry VII and Henry VIII." In Brindle, *Windsor Castle*, 146–57.

Townsend, Dale. "'Love in a Convent': Or, Gothic and the Perverse Father of Queer Enjoyment." In Hughes and Smith, *Queering the Gothic*, 11–35.

———. *The Orders of the Gothic: Foucault, Lacan, and the Subject of Gothic Writing, 1764–1820*. New York: AMS, 2007.

———, ed. *Terror and Wonder: The Gothic Imagination*. London: British Library, 2014.

Traub, Valerie. "The New Unhistoricism in Queer Studies." *PMLA* 128, no. 1 (2013): 21–39.

Trumbach, Randolph. "Modern Sodomy: The Origins of Homosexuality, 1700–1800." In *A Gay History of Britain: Love and Sex Between Men Since the Middle Ages*, edited by Matt Cook, 77–106. Oxford: Greenwood World, 2007.

———. *Heterosexuality and the Third Gender in Enlightenment London*. Vol. 1 of *Sex and the Gender Revolution*. Chicago: University of Chicago Press, 1998.

———. "The Transformation of Sodomy from the Renaissance to the Modern World and Its General Sexual Consequences." *Signs* 37, no. 4 (2012): 832–48.

Tuite, Clara. "Cloistered Closets: Enlightenment Pornography, the Confessional State, Homosexual Persecution, and *The Monk*." *Romanticism on the Net* 8 (1997). https://doi.org/10.7202/005766ar.

Tyack, Geoffrey, Simon Bradley, and Nikolaus Pevsner. *Berkshire*. New Haven: Yale University Press, 2010.

Utz, Richard. *Medievalism: A Manifesto*. Bradford, U.K.: ARC Humanities Press, 2017.

Verduin, Kathleen. "The Founding and the Founder: Medievalism and the Legacy of Leslie J. Workman." *Studies in Medievalism* 17 (2009): 1–27.

Vicinus, Martha. *Intimate Friends: Women Who Loved Women, 1778–1928*. Chicago: University of Chicago Press, 2004.

Vickery, Amanda. *Behind Closed Doors: At Home in Georgian England*. New Haven: Yale University Press, 2009.

———. "Horace Walpole and Strawberry Hill." *Guardian*, 19 February 2010.

Vidler, Anthony. *The Architectural Uncanny: Essays in the Modern Unhomely*. Cambridge: MIT Press, 1992.

Vogtherr, Christophe Martin. "Absent Love in Pleasure Houses: Frederick II of Prussia as Art Collector and Patron." *Art History* 24, no. 2 (2001): 231–46.

Voloshkova, Natalia. "'My Friend Mr. H. Walpole': Mary Hamilton, Horace Walpole, and the Art of Conversation." *Image and Narrative* 18, no. 3 (2017): 94–106.

Vulliamy, Colwyn E. *Aspasia: The Life and Letters of Mary Granville, Mrs Delany (1700–1788)*. London: Geoffrey Bles, 1935.

Wagner, Anthony R., and R. H. D'Elboux. "A Commemorative Brass to Bishop Ralph Walpole from the Cloister at Strawberry Hill." *Transactions of the Monumental Brass Society* 8, no. 3 (1945): 99–102.

Wahrman, Dror. *The Making of the Modern Self: Identity and Culture in Eighteenth-Century England*. New Haven: Yale University Press, 2006.

Wainwright, Clive. *The Romantic Interior: The British Collector at Home, 1750–1850*. New Haven: Yale University Press, 1989.

Walpole, Horace. *Aedes Walpolianae; or, A Description of the Collection of Pictures at Houghton-Hall in Norfolk, the Seat of the Right Honourable Sir Robert Walpole, Earl of Orford*. London, 1747.

———. *Anecdotes of Painting in England*. 4 vols. Twickenham: Thomas Farmer, 1762–71.

———. *Anecdotes of Painting in England*. 3rd ed. 4 vols. London: J. Dodsley, 1782.

———. *Anecdotes of Painting in England*. New ed. Revised by Ralph N. Wornum. 3 vols. London: Chatto & Windus, 1876.

———. *Anecdotes of Painting in England*. Edited by F. W. Hilles and P. B. Daghlan. New Haven: Yale University Press, 1937.

———. *The Castle of Otranto*. Edited by Nick Groom. Oxford: Oxford University Press, 2014.

———. *A Description of the Villa of Mr. Horace Walpole* [. . .] *at Strawberry-Hill near Twickenham, Middlesex*. Strawberry Hill: Thomas Kirgate, 1784. Reprinted in *Works of Horatio Walpole*, 2:393–516.

———. "Detached Thoughts." In *Works of Horatio Walpole*, 4:368–72.

———. *Essay on Modern Gardening*. Strawberry Hill, Twickenham: T. Kirgate, 1785.

———. *Fugitive Pieces in Verse and Prose*. Strawberry Hill, Twickenham, 1758.

———. *Horace Walpole's Description of the Villa at Strawberry-Hill: A Facsimile of the Copy Extra-Illustrated for Charles Bedford in the Collection of Lord Waldegrave of North Hill*. Edited by Nicolas Barker. London: Roxburghe Club, 2010.

———. "Horace Walpole's Journals of Visits to Country Seats &c." Transcribed and edited by Paget Toynbee. Special issue, *Walpole Society* 16 (1927–28).

———, ed. and trans. *Paul Hentzner's Travels in England, During the Reign of Queen Elizabeth*. London: Edward Jeffery, 1797. (Originally *A Journey into England*. Strawberry Hill, Twickenham, 1757.)

———. *The Works of Horatio Walpole, Earl of Orford*. 5 vols. London: G. G. & J. Robinson & J. Edwards, 1798.

———. *The Yale Edition of Horace Walpole's Correspondence*. Edited by Wilmarth S. Lewis. 48 vols. New Haven: Yale University Press, 1937–83.

Wamberg, Jacob. "Ghiberti, Alberti, and the Modernity of Gothic." *Analecta Romana Instituti Danici* 21 (1993): 173–211.

Ware, Isaac. *A Complete Body of Architecture*. 1756. Reprint, London: J. Rivington, L. Davis & C. Reymers, R. Baldwin, W. Owen, H. Woodfall, W. Strahan, and B. Collins, 1768.

Warton, Thomas. *Verses on Sir Joshua Reynolds's Painted Window at New-College Oxford*. London: J. Dodsley, 1782.

Warton, Thomas, James Bentham, Francis Grose, and John Milner. 2nd ed. *Essays on Gothic Architecture*. London: Architectural Library, 1802.

Watkin, David. "Beckford, Soane, and Hope: The Psychology of the Collector." In *William Beckford, 1760–1844: An Eye for the Magnificent*, edited by Derek E. Ostergard, 33–48. New Haven: Yale University Press, 2001.

Watt, James. *Contesting the Gothic: Fiction, Genre, and Cultural Conflict, 1764–1832*. Cambridge: Cambridge University Press, 1999.

Watts, Teresa S. "The Life and Work of Johann Heinrich Müntz (1727–1798)." Ph.D. diss., University of Toronto, 1986.

Wayment, Hilary G. "The East Window of St. Margaret's, Westminster." *Antiquaries Journal* 61, no. 2 (1981): 292–301.

———. "The Stained Glass of the Chapel of the Vyne and the Chapel of the Holy Ghost, Basingstoke." *Archaeologia* 107 (1982): 141–52.

Webster, Christopher. "'Absolutely Wretched': Camdenian Attitudes to the Late Georgian Church." In *"A Church as It Should Be": The Cambridge Camden Society and Its Influence*, edited by Christopher Webster and John Elliott, 1–21. Stamford: Shaun Tyas, 2000.

Weeks, Jacquilyn. "Horace Walpole's *Fairy Tale*." *Marvels and Tales* 28, no. 1 (2014): 167–79.

Weisberg-Roberts, Alicia. "Singular Objects and Multiple Meanings." In *HWSH*, 87–106.

Welter, Volker M. "*Schloss* Murnau, Hollywoodland, CA 90068." *Cabinet* 63 (2017): 41–49.

West, Shearer. "The Darly Macaroni Prints and the Politics of 'Private Man.'" *Eighteenth-Century Life* 25, no. 2 (2001): 170–82.

White, Roger. "The Influence of Batty Langley." In Crook, *Gothick Symposium*, n.p.

———. "Kent and the Gothic Revival." In *William Kent: Designing Georgian Britain*, edited by Susan Weber, 247–70. New Haven: Yale University Press, 2013.

———. "Wiston House Remodelled." *Architectural History* 27 (1984): 241–54.

Whitehead, David. "Artisan Attitudes to Gothic in Georgian Herefordshire." *Georgian Group Journal* 17 (2009): 61–76.

Williams, Anne. "Horace in Italy: Discovering a Gothic Imagination." *Gothic Studies* 8, no. 1 (2006): 22–34.

———. "Monstrous Pleasures: Horace Walpole, Opera, and the Conception of Gothic." *Gothic Studies* 2, no. 1 (2000): 104–18.

———. "Reading Walpole Reading Shakespeare." In *Shakespearean Gothic*, edited by Christy Desmet and Anne Williams, 13–36. Cardiff: University of Wales Press, 2009.

Williams, Charles Hanbury. *The Works of the Right Honourable Sir Chas. Hanbury Williams*. Edited by Horace Walpole. 3 vols. London: E. Jeffery & Son, 1822.

Wilsher, Ann. "Horace Walpole, William Storer, and the Accurate Delineator." *History of Photography* 4, no. 3 (1980): 247–49.

Wilton-Ely, John. "Style and Serendipity: Adam, Walpole, and Strawberry Hill." *British Art Journal* 11, no. 3 (2011): 3–14.

Windsor and Its Environs. London: Newbery & Carnan & J. Blakeney, 1768.

Wittkower, Rudolph. "Classical Theory and Eighteenth-Century Sensibility." In *Palladio and English Palladianism*, 193–204. London: Thames & Hudson, 1983.

Worley, Michael Preston. "The Image of Ganymede in France, 1730–1820: The Survival of a Homoerotic Myth." *Art Bulletin* 76, no. 4 (1994): 630–43.

Worsley, Giles. "The Origins of the Gothic Revival: A Reappraisal." *Transactions of the Royal Historical Society* 3 (1993): 105–50.

———. "What's in a 'K'?" *Country Life* 188 (1994): 74–77.

Worsley, Lucy. "Female Architectural Patronage in the Eighteenth Century and the Case of Henrietta Cavendish Holles Harley." *Architectural History* 48 (2005): 139–62.

Wright, Angela. "Gothic, 1764–1820." In Townsend, *Terror and Wonder*, 68–93.

Zajko, Vanda. "'Listening with' Ovid: Intersexuality, Queer Theory, and the Myth of Hermaphroditus and Salmacis." *Helios* 36, no. 2 (2009): 175–202.

Index

Italicized page numbers indicate illustrations.
Endnotes are referenced with "n" followed by the endnote number.